The Baltic Transformed

New International Relations of Europe
Series Editor: Ronald H. Linden

The Baltic Transformed

Complexity Theory and European Security

WALTER C. CLEMENS JR.

ROWMAN & LITTLEFIELD PUBLISHERS, INC.
Lanham • Boulder • New York • Oxford

For Stu and family
Friend, counselor, and critic for half a century

ROWMAN & LITTLEFIELD PUBLISHERS, INC.

Published in the United States of America
by Rowman & Littlefield Publishers, Inc.
4720 Boston Way, Lanham, Maryland 20706
http://www.rowmanlittlefield.com

12 Hid's Copse Road
Cumnor Hill, Oxford OX2 9JJ, England

British Library Cataloguing in Publication Information Available

Library of Congress Cataloging-in-Publication Data

Clemens, Walter C.
   The Baltic transformed : complexity theory and European security / Walter C. Clemens.
      p. cm. — (New international relations of Europe)
   Includes bibliographical references and index.
   ISBN 0-8476-9858-0 (alk. paper) — ISBN 0-8476-9859-9 (pbk. : alk. paper)
   1. Baltic States—Politics and government—1991– . 2. Baltic States—Foreign relations.
3. Security, International. 4. Conflict management. 5. Baltic States—Ethnic relations. 6.
Baltic States—History—Autonomy and independence movements. I. Title. II. Series.

DK502.75.C49 2001
947.908′6—dc21   00–062733

Printed in the United States of America

♾The paper used in this publication meets the minimum requirements of American National Standard for Information Sciences—Permanence of Paper for Printed Library Materials, ANSI/NISO Z39.48–1992.

Contents

List of Abbreviations

BALTBAT	Baltic Peacekeeping Battalion
BALTDEFCOL	Baltic Defense College
BALTNET	Baltic Airspace Surveillance Network
BALTRON	joint minesweeper squadron
BALTSEA	Baltic Security Assistance Group
CIS	Commonwealth of Independent States
CNN	Cable News Network
CPSU	Communist Party of the Soviet Union
EU	European Union
FFF	For Fatherland and Freedom
GDI	Gender Development Index
GDP	gross domestic product
GEM	Gender Empowerment Index
HDI	Human Development Index
ICBM	intercontinental ballistic missile
IGO	international governmental organization
IMF	International Monetary Fund
IR	international relations
IT	information technology
LDLP	Lithuanian Democratic Labor Party
NATO	North Atlantic Treaty Organization
NGO	Nongovernmental Organization
OSCE	Organization for Security and Cooperation in Europe
PfP	Partnership for Peace
PM	prime minister
PPP	purchasing power parity
RF	Russian Federation
RSFSR	Russian Soviet Federative Socialist Republic
SDA	Social Democratic Alliance
UNDP	United Nations Development Programme
VIC	vertically integrated company
WEU	Western European Union

List of Tables

Empire, Self-Rule, and Interdependence in the Baltic Region: A Chronology

BEFORE EMPIRES AND NATION-STATES

B.C. 10,000–8000: Ice age glaciers retreat.

B.C. 7500–4000: Stone age Kunda culture settlements leave traces in the Pärnu River valley of what today is Estonia.

B.C. 4000–1500: Finnic and Baltic tribes settle on the eastern Baltic coast, absorbing earlier occupants.

B.C. 1500–1 A.D.: Nomadic hunters and fisher folk take up agriculture.

1–500 A.D.: Finnic tribes have increasing contact with the ancestors of Latvians and Lithuanians.

6th century A.D.: Great migrations generate chaos and economic downturn. Slavic tribes expand against existing Baltic settlements.

800–1000: Finnic and Baltic tribes interact with Slavs to their east and with Viking/Varangian raiders/traders.

KYIVAN RUS'

855: Varangians reach Kyiv and form the Kyivan Rus' state.

882: Kyiv subjects Novgorod.

1000: The Kyivan state reaches its peak extent, including a claim to Tartu (Iuriev in Russian, Dorpat in German).

1054–1150: The Kyivan state fragments and declines.

1240: Kyiv is overrun by Mongols.

MEDIEVAL LIVONIA AND THE HANSA

1143–1159: Lübeck is founded.

Late 12th century: Germanic merchants, missionaries, and crusaders arrive in medieval Livonia (today's Latvia and Estonia).

1198: Berthold, bishop of Livonia, is killed by Livonians.

1201: Bishop Albert of Livonia founds Riga.

1202: The Livonian Order of Sword Brothers is established.

1219: Danes conquer northern Estonian tribes and establish Tallinn.

1237: Defeated in battle by Lithuanians, the Livonian Order merges with the Teutonic Order to the west, but remains a separate branch.

1242 and 1260: The Livonian Order is defeated by Alexander Nevsky and then by Lithuanians.

1262–1300: Riga becomes a Hanseatic city-state, as do Tallinn, Narva, and many other Baltic ports and urban centers.

1370: Hanseatic partners impose the Treaty of Stralsund on Denmark.

1422: The Livonian Diet (Landtag) of Germanic landlords holds its first meeting.

1517: Martin Luther posts his 95 Theses in Wittenberg.

1525: The Teutonic Order's grand master accepts the Reformation and is invested as Duke of Prussia by Sigismund, sovereign of Poland and Lithuania. First books are published in Estonian and Latvian.

1536: Denmark and Sweden crush the Hanseatic fleet.

1561: The Livonian Order ends as the grand master receives the hereditary duchy of Courland under Polish-Lithuanian suzerainty.

1561: Tallinn places itself under Swedish protection.

1629–1645: All Livonia becomes Sweden's Baltic Provinces.

1669: The Hanseatic diet meets for the last time.

LITHUANIA AND POLAND

1008: First mention of Lithuania (in a German chronicle).

1251–1253: Mindaugas adopts Christianity and is named king of Lithuania by the pope.

14th century: Led by Grand Duke Gediminas (d. 1342), Lithuania expands into Belarus and Ukraine and becomes a major actor in European politics.

1322–1323 and 1362–1363: Kyiv falls to Lithuanians.

1385: A grandson of Gediminas, Lithuanian grand duke Jogaila, becomes Wladyslaw II Jagiello, King of Poland.

1387: Most Lithuanians, Europe's last pagans, accept Christianity by way of Catholic Poland.

1410 and 1466: Lithuanians defeat German knightly orders.

1547: The first book in Lithuanian is published.

1569: The Union of Lublin establishes a Polish-Lithuanian confederation.

1582: Polish-Lithuanian forces take Riga and southern Livonia.

1611: Polish-Lithuanian forces occupy Muscovy and pull back.

1735: Bible is published in Lithuanian.

MUSCOVY EXPANDS

1300: Muscovy begins to expand.

1478: Ivan III conquers Novgorod and brings Muscovy to the Gulf of Finland and a common frontier with Lithuania.

1505: Muscovy dominates all Russian lands.

1552–1584: Muscovy conquers Kazan, Tatar, and Finno-Ugric lands on the Volga River.

1558: Ivan IV seizes Narva, but Russian forces fail to take Livonia and it falls to Sweden and Poland-Lithuania in 1581–1582.

1598–1613: The "Time of Troubles" power struggle in Moscow encourages Sweden and Poland to vie for influence in Russian affairs.

1648–1654: Cossacks on the lower Dnepr rebel against Polish-Lithuanian rule and transfer their allegiance to Muscovy.

1649: Russian explorers reach the Pacific coast.

1686: "Eternal Peace" agreed between Poland and Russia.

1689: Muscovy signs the Treaty of Nerchinsk with China.

SWEDEN'S BALTIC PROVINCES

1397: Denmark organizes the Union of Kalmar with Norway and Sweden to resist Hanseatic expansion in the Baltic Sea.

1523: Sweden-Finland breaks from union with Denmark and Norway.

1561: Sweden acquires Tallinn and the adjoining region.

1563–1570: The Seven Years War of the North: Denmark, Lübeck, and Poland against Sweden.

1581: Sweden retakes Narva and dominates the trade routes to Novgorod and Pskov for a century.

1618–1648: During the Thirty Years War Sweden replaces Denmark as the paramount power in the Baltic region.

1600–1629: Sweden wins Livonia after fighting Poland-Lithuania and then Russia. Sweden takes Riga in 1621.

1630–1632: Sweden initiates judicial reforms in Livonia.

1654–1661: Russians attack Polish and Swedish lands in the Baltic.

1660–1661: Sweden makes peace with Poland and with Russia.

1688: Sweden decrees an "Estate reduction" in its Baltic provinces.

1688–1694: The Old and New Testaments are published in Latvian.

1700–1721: Great Northern War: Sweden defeats Russia at Narva in 1700, but Russia crushes Sweden at Poltava in 1709. The 1721 Treaty of Nystad transfers Sweden's Baltic provinces and parts of Finland to Russia.

IMPERIAL RUSSIA

1700–1721: The Russian Empire takes much of the Baltic coast and part of Kavelia.

1739: The Bible is published in Estonian.

1772–1795: Partitions put much of Poland and Lithuania under Russian rule. Russia also takes the Crimea, Kamchatka, and Chukchi.

1809–1815: Russia takes Finland and then most of Poland. Russia also expands into the Transcaucasus and establishes Fort Ross in California.

1816–1819: Serfs are emancipated in Estonia, Courland, and Livonia (well before the 1861 emancipation in Lithuania, Latgale, and Russia proper).

1830–1831 and 1861–1864: Russian forces crush uprisings by Poles and Lithuanians.

1845–1848: Many Baltic Lutheran peasants convert to Russian Orthodoxy.

1864–1904: Russia bans Lithuanian publications in the Latin alphabet.

1880s–1890s: Russification measures are imposed in the Baltic provinces.

1895: The Russian Empire attains its peak size after conquests in Central Asia and the Far East.

1904–1905: Imperial Russia is expelled from Manchuria, loses southern Sakhalin to Japan, and faces revolution at home. Worker strikes, peasant uprisings, and demands for political autonomy shake the Baltic and other parts of tsarist Russia. The tsar permits a parliament (Duma) but imperial and Baltic German forces punish dissident Balts.

March 1917: The democratic "Provisional Government" replaces tsarist rule.

SOVIET RUSSIA/USSR AND THE BALTICS

November 1917: The Bolshevik Revolution overthrows Russia's Provisional Government.

1918–1920: Independent states emerge in Poland, Finland, Estonia, Latvia, and Lithuania and are recognized by Soviet Russia in 1920, following defeats of the Red Army. But Soviet Russia retakes Ukraine, Belarus, the Transcaucasus, and Central Asia.

1919–1943: The Communist International in Moscow instructs Communist Parties abroad.

1922–1924: The USSR is formed.

1926–1927: Antanas Smetona establishes an authoritarian presidency in Lithuania.

1934: Authoritarian rule is established in Latvia and Estonia.

1934: The three Baltic states form the Baltic Entente, but without a military alliance.

1936: A revised "Stalin" Constitution of the USSR provides the right of secession to union-republics.

August 23, 1939: Secret protocols of the Soviet-German Nonaggression Pact partition the Baltic and Eastern Europe.

1939–1940: Having invaded and seized parts of Poland and Finland, the Soviets occupy and annex the Baltic states.

1940–1941: The Soviets arrest and deport tens of thousands of Baltic civilians.

June 1941 to 1944: The Germans occupy the Baltic states and extend the Holocaust to the large Jewish populations of Latvia and Lithuania.

1944–1945: The Soviets reoccupy the Baltic countries. They arrest and deport tens of thousands. The USSR retakes parts of Poland and southern Sakhalin. Anti-Soviet guerrilla units in the Baltic hold out until the early 1950s.

1945–1948: Satellitization of Eastern Europe except Yugoslavia.

1953–1964: Following Stalin's death, Nikita Khrushchev gradually becomes head of the "collective leadership" in the Kremlin.

1964–1982: Leonid Brezhnev is the top Soviet leader.

THE MOVEMENT TO REGAIN INDEPENDENCE
(TO BE READ WITH CHAPTER 3)

1975: The Conference on Security and Cooperation in Europe signs the Helsinki accords, obligating all thirty-five signatories (including the USSR) to respect human rights and permit local and international monitoring thereof.

1976: Soviet authorities try to repress nongovernmental monitoring groups established in the Baltic and other parts of the USSR to monitor the Helsinki accords.

1977: Eighteen scientists in Estonia protest Soviet oil-shale and phosphate mining.

1979: The Baltic Charter, signed by Lithuanian, Latvian, and Estonian dissidents, demands nullification of the Nazi-Soviet pact secret protocols.

1980: Letter to Soviet newspapers by forty Estonian intellectuals asserts that native Estonians should have "the final word on the destiny of their land and people."

1982–1985: Yuri Andropov succeeds Brezhnev; Konstantin Chernenko succeeds Andropov; Mikhail Gorbachev succeeds Chernenko.

March 11, 1985: Gorbachev is elected general secretary, Central Committee, Communist Party of the Soviet Union (CPSU).

May 23, 1986: Soviet foreign minister Eduard Shevardnadze commends "new thinking."

July 31, 1986: Gorbachev commends perestroika (economic reconstruction) and later endorses glasnost (openness) and "socialist legality."

September 15–16, 1986: U.S. officials restate Washington's nonrecognition policy at a public meeting in Jurmala, Latvia.

December 16–18, 1986: Demonstrations on ethnic issues take place in Kazakstan.

Spring 1987: Estonians protest proposed phosphate mining.

July 6, 1987: Crimean Tatars demonstrate in Red Square, asking for permission to return to the Crimea from Central Asia.

August 23, 1987: Balts demonstrate on the anniversary of Hitler-Stalin Pact.

September 10, 1987: KGB (secret police) chairman Viktor Chebrikov charges that Western agents stir up the national minorities.

September 26, 1987: Four Estonian intellectuals propose economic autonomy.

October 1, 1987: Belarusians commemorate Stalin-era executions at Kuropaty.

January 22, 1988: The Estonian National Independence Party is founded.

February 13, 1988: Riots by Armenians in Nagorno-Karabakh, officially part of Azerbaijan.

February 18, 1988: Boris Yeltsin is removed from the CPSU Politburo.

February 24, 1988: Four thousand demonstrators in Tallinn commemorate the seventieth anniversary of Estonian independence.

February 28, 1988: Pogroms are carried out against Armenians in Sumgait, Azerbaijan.

June 14, 1988: Balts commemorate 1941 deportations.

July 23, 1988: Balts protest the anniversary of 1940 annexations.

September 30–October 1, 1988: Aleksandr Yakovlev takes charge of the CPSU Central Committee International Department and Gorbachev becomes chairman of USSR Presidium (President).

October 1988: Inaugural congresses are held by the popular fronts in Estonia and Latvia and by Sajudis in Lithuania.

November 16, 1988: The Estonian Supreme Soviet declares sovereignty and assumes control of state property—actions called null and void by the USSR Supreme Soviet on November 26.

1989: The Soviet hold on Eastern Europe and East Germany collapses.

January 18–February 24, 1989: The Estonian Supreme Soviet declares Estonian the state language; Latvia follows suit; Estonia's pre-1940 flag is raised in Tallinn.

March 26, 1989: Yeltsin and the Baltic popular front members do well in elections to the USSR Congress of People's Deputies; most Balts align with the Interregional Group, led by Yeltsin, Andrei Sakharov, and other reformists.

March 18, 1989: The Lithuanian Supreme Soviet declares sovereignty; Latvia follows suit on July 28.

August 23, 1989: One to two million Balts form a human chain from Tallinn to Riga to Vilnius.

August 26, 1989: The CPSU Central Committee issues a stern warning to Balts.

September 8–October 1989: The Ukrainian Rukh (similar to a Baltic popular front) holds a constituent congress in Kyiv and displays the flag of independent Ukraine.

November 9, 1989: The Berlin Wall falls.

November 12, 1989: The Estonian Supreme Soviet annuls Estonia's 1940 incorporation into the USSR.

December 20, 1989: The Lithuanian Communist Party withdraws from the CPSU, an act rejected by the CPSU Central Committee on December 25–26.

December 24, 1989: The USSR Congress of People's Deputies declares invalid from inception the secret protocols of the Nazi-Soviet pact but does not rescind annexation of the Baltic states.

January 11–13, 1990: Gorbachev visits Vilnius but fails to persuade the Lithuanian Communist Party to remain in the CPSU.

March 11, 1990: The Lithuanian Supreme Council declares the restoration of Lithuania's independence and elects Landsbergis chief of state.

March 11–12, 1990: The Congress of Estonia, elected by citizens of Estonia, meets, aiming to supplant the Estonian Supreme Soviet.

March 14, 1990: Gorbachev is elected USSR president by the Congress of People's Deputies.

April 18, 1990: Russia cuts deliveries of oil to Lithuania following a Gorbachev ultimatum; it resumes deliveries on June 30, after the Lithuanian parliament votes a temporary suspension of its independence declaration.

May 8, 1990: Republic of Estonia interwar symbols are restored.

May 29, 1990: Yeltsin is elected chairman of the Russian Soviet Federative Socialist Republic (RSFSR) Supreme Soviet.

June 18, 1990: The RSFSR Supreme Soviet declares sovereignty and declares that its laws take precedence over those of the USSR.

July 16, 1990: Ukraine declares its sovereignty, followed by Belarus on July 27 and by many other union-republics in succeeding months.

January 10, 1991: Gorbachev orders Lithuania to restore the "constitutional order" or suffer the consequences.

January 13, 1991: Soviet troops take the television tower in Vilnius but do not attack the Supreme Council (parliament) building. Fifteen people are killed in the repression.

January 14, 1991: Russian leader Yeltsin in Tallinn signs mutual recognition of sovereignty with all three Baltic states; Yeltsin urges Soviet troops not to fire on Baltic civilians.

January 20, 1991: Demonstrators in Moscow and Leningrad protest repression in Lithuania.

January 24, 1991: U.S. ambassador Jack Matlock delivers a letter from President George Bush to Gorbachev threatening to cut ties if violence continues in Lithuania; Gorbachev insists he is acting to avoid civil war.

February 9, 1991: More than 90 percent of Lithuanian voters support independence.

February 12, 1991: Iceland declares that its 1922 recognition of Lithuania is still valid and states its intention to restore diplomatic relations.

March 3, 1991: Referendums on independence are held in Estonia and Latvia: some three-fourths of participants support independence.

March 14–16, 1991: Secretary of State James Baker meets Baltic leaders in Moscow.

March 17, 1991: A majority of participants in a union-wide referendum favor a voluntary union.

March 31, 1991: The Warsaw Pact (the Soviet alliance system) is officially dissolved.

April 23, 1991: Nine republic leaders reach an agreement with Gorbachev on a revised Union Treaty.

June 12, 1991: Yeltsin is elected president of the RSFSR with 57.3 percent of the vote in a general election.

July 12, 1991: The USSR Supreme Soviet approves the Union Treaty in principle but suggests changes.

July 28, 1991: Gorbachev informs Yeltsin and Kazakstan president Nursultan Nazarbayev that he will remove KGB leader Vladimir Kriuchkov and USSR prime minister Valentin Pavlov after the Union Treaty is signed on August 20.

August 2, 1991: Gorbachev announces the Union Treaty is "open for signing."

August 17–21, 1991: A hard-line coup to oust Gorbachev aborts; Yeltsin emerges as the dominant Russian leader.

August 20–21, 1991: Estonia and Latvia declare their independence, which is soon recognized by Russia, Iceland, and dozens of other countries.

August 24, 1991: Gorbachev suspends CPSU activities and resigns as general secretary; Ukraine declares its independence, subject to a referendum on December 1, 1991.

August 25–31, 1991: Declarations of independence are issued by Belarus, Moldova, Azerbaijan, Uzbekistan, and Kyrgyzstan.

September 2, 1991: The United States recognizes the independent governments of Estonia, Latvia, and Lithuania.

September 6, 1991: The USSR State Council recognizes the independence of Estonia, Latvia, and Lithuania; Georgia severs ties with the USSR.

December 1–5, 1991: Ukrainian citizens vote for independence; the Ukrainian parliament revokes Ukraine's accession to the USSR treaty.

December 7–8, 1991: The presidents of Russia, Ukraine, and Belarus decide to end the USSR and create a Commonwealth of Independent States; they are joined by eight other republics at Alma Ata on December 22—but not by Estonia, Latvia, Lithuania, or Georgia.

December 25, 1991: The Russian flag replaces the Soviet over the Kremlin.

DEVELOPMENTS AFTER INDEPENDENCE REGAINED

September 10–16, 1991: Estonia, Latvia, and Lithuania apply for membership in the World Bank and the European Bank for Reconstruction and Development.

September 17, 1991: The three Baltic states are admitted to the UN.

September 19, 1991: The U.S. Overseas Private Investment Corporation, which supports U.S. investors, begins to operate in the Baltic countries. The USSR begins to pay for using Latvia's oil terminal.

October 21–24, 1991: Latvia and then Estonia become associate members of the North Atlantic Assembly, a consultative body of NATO.

November 22, 1991: France transfers to Latvia one thousand kilos of gold deposited in the 1930s.

November–December, 1991: The U.S. accords most-favored-nations status to the three Baltic countries.

December 11, 1991: Latvia adopts a law on registering citizens of pre-1940 Latvia and their descendants. The law is criticized by Russian speakers in Latvia, by the Kremlin, and by some human rights groups in Europe.

1992: Referendums in Estonia and Lithuania approve new constitutions; Latvia reinstitutes its 1922 constitution.

1992: In Estonia Edgar Savisaar's left-leaning government resigns early in the year and moderate Tiit Vähi forms a new government. Later in the year, a nationalist, market-oriented coalition wins parliamentary elections. Lennart Meri is elected president. He designates Mart Laar as prime minister (PM).

1992: All three Baltic states join the World Bank and International Monetary Fund.

1992: Each Baltic country presses for withdrawal of Russian troops.

1992: Estonia and then Latvia leave the ruble zone. Estonia ties its new currency, the *kroon,* to the German Mark.

1992: Competing in the Olympics as independent countries for the first time since the 1930s, athletes from each Baltic state win medals at the Barcelona Olympics.

1992: Russian president Yeltsin begins to censure Latvia and Estonia for not observing the rights of Russian-speaking citizens.

1992: Sweden will compensate Estonia and Lithuania for the loss of gold deposited in the 1930s.

1992: The Lithuanian Democratic Labor Party (former Communists) wins control of parliament from Sajudis.

1993: Former Communist leader Algirdas Brazauskas is elected president of Lithuania.

1993: The *litas* is reintroduced as Lithuania's currency.

1993: The last Russian troops depart Lithuania.

1993: The *lats* becomes legal tender in Latvia.

1993: Latvia's Way, an offshoot of the Popular Front, wins a plurality of seats in parliament. It joins with the Agrarian Union to form a coalition government with Valdis Birkavs as prime minister (PM). Parliament elects Guntis Ulmanis president of Latvia.

1994: The Baltic states join NATO's Partnership for Peace. Russian troops withdraw from Estonia and Latvia but Russians may use the radar at Skrunda, Latvia, until 1998.

1994: Latvia's Way forms a new coalition with Maris Gailis as prime minister.

1995: When Latvia's parliamentary elections produce no clear winner, President Ulmanis names businessman Andris Skele PM.

1995: In Estonia a center-left coalition wins control of parliament.

1995: In Lithuania two large banks collapse amid charges of wrong-doing.

1996: The Homeland Union, an offshoot of Sajudis, wins control of Lithuania's parliament and Gediminas Vagnorius is PM.

1996: Ulmanis is elected Latvia's president for a second three-year term.

1996: Meri wins a second term as Estonia's president.

1996: Baltic athletes win medals at the Atlanta Olympics.

1997: Estonia is first Baltic state accepted as a candidate for admission to the European Union.

1998: Russia intensifies pressures on Latvia over its treatment of noncitizens. Later in the year, the Russian currency and economy crash, pulling down Baltic economies—especially Lithuania's.

1998: Valdas Adamkus is elected Lithuania's president.

1999: In Latvia Vaira Vike-Freiberga is elected president and Skele returns as PM.

1999: In Estonia a center-right coalition headed by Laar returns to power.

2000: In Russia Boris Yeltsin steps down and Vladimir Putin becomes president after intensifying attacks on Chechnya.

2000: In Latvia Skele resigns and Andris Berzins becomes PM.

2000: Leftists win the most votes in Lithuania's parliamentary elections, but a moderate coalition wins control of parliament. Coalition leader Rolandas Paksas is named PM (a job he held briefly in 1999).

2000: Baltic athletes excel at the Sydney Olympics.

EUROPEAN AND NORTH ATLANTIC COOPERATION

1947–1951: The European Recovery Program helps rebuild and unify Europe but Stalin does not permit the USSR or its allies to take part.

1949: The North Atlantic Treaty Organization (NATO) is founded to contain Soviet advances.

1955: The Western European Union (WEU) is founded to facilitate West Germany's admission to NATO; the WEU is disbanded in 2000.

1957: Six countries sign the Treaty of Rome, establishing the European Economic Community.

1975: The Helsinki accords initiate a process leading to formation of the Organization for Security and Cooperation in Europe.

1987: Twelve European Community members pledge to form a European market without internal barriers.

1995: The Schengen Convention to transfer internal controls of persons and goods and to their external borders comes into force for many but not all EU members.

1996: Estonia takes a six-month term chairing the Council of Europe.

1997: Russia and Ukraine acquire consultative voices in NATO.

1998–1999: Baltic and other non-EU members are invited to discuss accession to the Schengen Convention.

1998: The United States and the three Baltic states sign a Charter of Partnership pledging to consult if a partner perceives a security threat.

1999: NATO admits Poland, Hungary, and the Czech Republic and later attacks Serbia; the Baltic Defense College holds its first classes in Tartu; the Russian parliament passes a law on compatriots abroad.

2000: The Baltic republics and other states intensify their efforts to join NATO and the European Union.

Foreword

Since the end of the Cold War and the breakup of the Soviet Union, regional and local conflicts have taken center stage in world attention. Each conflict, whether in the Balkans, Africa, Asia, or elsewhere, is unique, but there are some common elements, most notably an attempt to resolve political or social problems by violent means. Scholars and government officials have devoted increasing attention to the roots of these conflicts and have, in a fumbling and not always consistent manner, sought ways to prevent or assuage the humanitarian disasters resulting from such conflicts.

While specialists in international relations have produced many studies of failed states and local conflicts, they have paid less attention to successful new (or renewed) states and to examples of revolutionary change without widespread conflict. Nevertheless, if we are to understand what went wrong in some areas, it is important to grasp why things went right in others. Such a comparison would not provide all the answers the world community needs to deal with local and regional conflict, but the factors that facilitate success are bound to be relevant to an analysis of failure.

Walter Clemens's study of the Baltic transformation will do much to restore a balance between studies of failure and studies of success. There can be no question that Estonia, Latvia, and Lithuania have succeeded where others have failed. Their success is not because their goal of restoring their independence was easier to reach than were the goals of other newly independent countries. Few observers in 1985 would have considered it possible that the three Baltic states would be independent within six years. Few observers in the 1970s and 1980s imagined that the Soviet Union would collapse peacefully well before the end of the century. Andrei Amalrik predicted the end of the USSR in his *Will the Soviet Union Survive until 1984?* but predicated his forecast on a war with China.

If, in 1985 and perhaps even as late as 1990, anyone had asked a gathering of specialists on the Soviet Union and eastern Europe whether Yugoslavia or the Soviet Union was more in danger of breaking up, the overwhelming majority probably would have chosen Yugoslavia. (In fact, the Soviet Union collapsed first, though not by much.) If the same group had been asked to select which of the two countries was most likely to experience violence if central authority collapsed, at least as many would have picked the Soviet Union as those who would have picked Yugoslavia—probably more. The Soviet Union had been a closed society longer than Yugoslavia, and totalitarian controls had been more severe during most of its history.

What, precisely, made the disintegration of the Soviet Union different from the breakup of Yugoslavia? And what made the Baltic states different from Tajikistan, Georgia, Armenia, and Azerbaijan, where the collapse of Soviet authority brought civil war or internecine struggle?

Clemens's careful study provides much of the detail needed for an answer to the latter question. As an observer of the process of liberation, what strikes me as the most fundamental difference was the determination of the leaders of the Baltic liberation movements to use only peaceful means to press their case. They refrained not only from any resort to force, but also from any violent response when force was used against them, such as on January 13, 1991, when Soviet special forces attacked the television tower in Vilnius.

Baltic restraint was crucially important. Elements in the Communist Party, the KGB, and the Soviet armed forces would have used any violent acts by the Balts as a pretext to subdue the three republics with overwhelming force. Baltic restraint made it difficult for the Soviet hard-liners to justify a crackdown. When they finally attempted one in August 1991, it was too late. The country refused to go along.

Baltic restraint was fundamental, but it was assisted by other factors. Mikhail Gorbachev, the Soviet president, was personally opposed to the use of force and refused to authorize the massive repression that would have been required to control the independence movements in the three Baltic countries. Furthermore, many Russians, both those resident in the Baltic states and those in Soviet Russia favored Baltic independence. They understood that Russia itself (or even the Soviet Union as a whole) could not be free if the Baltic states were not free. Thus, the Baltic states had significant political allies in the imperial metropole.

The fact that the United States and most Western European countries had never recognized the annexation of the Baltic states was important to Baltic morale and facilitated U.S. and other Western political support for Baltic independence. It was not, however, the most decisive factor in the Baltic success. All other union-republics obtained independence from the Soviet Union in 1991, even though the United States and its allies considered them legally part of the Soviet Union. I would therefore argue that the Baltic success in achieving independence peacefully owed more to Baltic tactics and the policies of the Soviet and Russian presidents than to legal principles. While President Gorbachev did not favor Baltic independence, he opposed using force to suppress independence movements. Boris Yeltsin, elected president of Russia in June 1991, favored Baltic independence consistently, at least from 1990, and the Russian parliament voted to accept the independence of Estonia, Latvia, and Lithuania before the USSR Supreme Soviet did.

Those Soviet republics whose leaders resorted to violence did not fare well, even when the collapse of the Soviet Union liberated them in a constitutional sense. One faction in Tajikistan moved against its political opposition with violence, precipitating a civil war that has disrupted the country ever since and has foreclosed the possibility of economic development. In Georgia, force was used against Georgia's minorities, which also precipitated a civil war, from which the country is only gradually recovering. Armenia and Azerbaijan have been locked in competition for sovereignty over the enclave called Nagorno-Karabakh in Russian and have as yet been unable to convert a tenuous cease-fire into a lasting peace. The contrast with Estonia, Latvia, and Lithuania is striking, and here again we see that the contrast is between nations that resorted to violence and those that refrained from it.

Clemens's description of the way the Baltic states won their independence and what they have done with it since should be essential reading for everyone concerned with the prevalence of violence in many parts of the world today. It shows how an approach that relies entirely on political pressure and is patient, playing for the breaks, can succeed. Armed rebellion, however heroic, is likely to bring misery to all sides. Ultimately, human rights can only be protected by the societies in which people live. Outsiders can never do it in a world that rejects imperialism.

The second theme Clemens treats is the relevance of the Baltic experience to theories of international relations. He rightly notes that classical "realism" proved inadequate to explain the end of the Cold War. The "complexity theory" he elucidates and defends adds useful dimensions to our understanding of the success and failure of states and of the manner in which nations interact with one another. The experience of the three Baltic states is crucial to any political theory precisely because it provides an example of what works in an international environment littered with failure.

Important as their experience is for current foreign policy and for theory, the Baltic states also justify close study because of the inherent values of their unique cultures—in some respects quite different one from another, while in others remarkably similar. Their geographic position and common fate as part of the Russian empire and of the Soviet Union has caused many outside observers to think of them only as a group, assuming a uniformity of culture which in fact does not exist.

One of the virtues of *The Baltic Transformed* is its emphasis on the individual character of the three countries. Culturally, each is a jewel, with literature, art, and music that can take their place with the best European products of the century. But each jewel is distinctive, with individual shape and coloration. Though all have to surmount the ravages the forty-odd years of communism inflicted on their societies, economies, and environment, differing circumstances have required different approaches. Lithuania has pursued more inclusive policies toward citizenship than have either Latvia or Estonia, but ethnic minorities make up barely a fifth of Lithuania's total population. Latvia, with close to half of its population non-Latvian, felt obliged to follow more restrictive policies, as did Estonia.

All three countries moved rapidly to reorient their foreign ties to the north and west. Estonia had a particular affinity to Finland because of language and culture, not to speak of geographic proximity. Lithuania has settled its earlier differences with Poland and seems to be resurrecting many of the historic ties binding the two countries. Latvia has looked to the Nordic group as a whole, but particularly Sweden, refuge to a substantial émigré community during the Soviet decades. All aspire to membership in the European Union and the North Atlantic Treaty Organization.

By virtue of their history, their location, the quality of their leadership, and their culture, Estonia, Latvia, and Lithuania have an importance for the world community far out of proportion to their size. This volume helps us understand how the Baltic transformation occurred and the lessons it offers all of us.

Jack F. Matlock Jr.
Former U.S. Ambassador to the Soviet Union

Jack F. Matlock Jr. is George F. Kennan Professor at the Institute for Advanced Study, Princeton, New Jersey. He was U.S. Ambassador to the Soviet Union from 1987 to 1991 and is the author of *Autopsy on an Empire: The American Ambassador's Account of the Collapse of the Soviet Union.*

Preface: Why the Baltic?

Why should outsiders pay attention to "Balts"—Estonians, Latvians, and Lithuanians? If we seek to understand Europe, why read about small peoples ruled by others for much of the second millennium? Why not focus instead on the mightiest movers and shakers—the Germans, Swedes, and Russians who dominated the Baltic coast for centuries?

The transformation of Estonia, Latvia, and Lithuania at the cusp of the third millennium is interesting, important, and a positive story—with possible lessons for other societies. In the late 1980s and early 1990s the three Davids helped demolish Goliath—the Soviet empire. In the 1990s the Baltic republics developed what complexity theorists call "fitness"—the ability to cope effectively with complex challenges at home and abroad.

Balts' security needs—military, political, economic, environmental—interact with those of other Europeans. The well-being of Europe depends on its outer reaches as well as its "Euro-European" core. No border area is more critical to European security than the shatterbelt where the three Baltic countries face both West and East. In the twenty-first century the Baltic region is probably more important to Europe than the Balkans, a thousand miles to the south. Ethnic strife roils the Balkans, but NATO directly meets Russia in the Baltic. The Baltic region—*pribaltika* in Russian—is also vital to Russia, though Moscow after 1991 believed its most pressing security problems were in the south.

To think clearly about Baltic issues, we must nuance our vocabulary. For starters, the three Baltic republics did not *gain* independence from the USSR in 1991: they *regained* the independent statehoods acquired after World War I and suffocated by Stalin and Hitler in 1940. The Baltic states were never "former Soviet republics" in a legal sense: they were *occupied* states. Their annexation by the USSR in 1940 was coerced—never recognized de jure by most Western governments.

This is not arcane word-splitting. The Baltic republics insisted in the 1990s that they were the successor states to the interwar Baltic states. The Russian Federation (RF), however, claimed a sphere of influence in what it termed the "near abroad"— all former Soviet border republics. RF authorities held that the Baltic republics had been integral parts of the USSR, no different from the Ukrainian, Kyrgyz, or other "Soviet Socialist Republics." Claiming the RF to be the successor state to the tsarist empire as well as the USSR, the Russian parliament in 1999 adopted a law asserting that the RF has the right and duty to protect all "compatriots." The law defined "compatriots" to include all former Russian or Soviet citizens, plus their descendants, even those who had accepted citizenship in other states or were now stateless in the former Soviet borderlands. By this definition, most adults in the Baltic countries were "compatriots"—even the titular Estonians, Latvians, and Lithuanians. So were many persons in Poland, Finland, and Alaska who descended from subjects of Imperial Russia! President Boris Yeltsin warned the RF parliament that the "compatriot" doctrine had no legal foundation and could be seen as an intrusion in the internal affairs of other states. But the State Duma and Federation Council enshrined it in law anyway—another neoimperialist act Balts dared not ignore.

Half a century of de facto Soviet rule left multiple wounds. Long subjected to top-down commands and plans, Balts were unschooled in democratic politics or market economics. Many Balts expected in the 1990s that independence regained would simply bring them "the Soviet system plus freedom." When the old welfare networks withered, many Balts felt cheated.[1]

Nonetheless Balts transformed their lives in the 1990s and pressed for admission to the European Union (EU) and NATO. The Baltic republics were not being *integrated* but *reintegrated* with Europe. No other European peoples have inhabited the same territory longer than Estonians, Latvians, and Lithuanians. None speaks an older language. Latvian and Lithuanian are the closest exemplars of the supposed matrix of most European languages.

It can be misleading to speak of the Baltic states as "small" because their territories and populations are larger than many states in the EU, NATO, and the United Nations. Lithuania was once one the largest states in Europe. In 1683 Lithuanian-Polish armies broke the Turkish siege of Vienna. The Duchy of Courland on the Latvian coast had imperial holdings in Africa and the Caribbean.

Neither size nor income determines excellence. Estonians in 2000 earned only one-third the average per capita income for the EU. Still, Estonia was among the most literate and electronically "wired" countries in Europe. One-tenth of Estonians used the Internet. Recognizing the Baltic region's intellectual and economic dynamism, nearly as many nonresidents filed patent applications in each Baltic state as in Singapore.

Baltic armies were minuscule in the late 1990s but sent troops to NATO and UN peacekeeping missions in Bosnia, Kosovo, and Lebanon. Striving for interoperability with NATO, Baltic forces joined many Partnership for Peace exercises.

A growing Baltic confidence was manifest in the 2000 Sydney Olympics. If counted as one unit, the three Baltic republics garnered eleven medals—ranking them eighth in medals per capita—just behind another "small" country, the Netherlands.[2] Estonian Erki Nool won the Sydney decathlon, ranking him as the world's top all-round athlete. Estonia's three medals gave it more awards per capita than any other country save Australia, Cuba, and Norway.[3] In the months after the Olympics, Latvian cyclist Romans Vainsteins triumphed in the World Cycling Championship in France. Lithuanian Jurgis Kairys won the World Cup for Acrobatic Flying in Japan with his "cobra" move—flying vertically on the plane's tail before striking in any direction, all to music by Mozart.[4]

COMPARATIVE PERSPECTIVES

To study European politics we analyze how each country elects its government, how each society deals with the EU, how majorities interact with ethnic minorities. But we must also know how each society got to where it is today. When we compare political development and transitions to democracy and market economics, we should also consider historical backgrounds: How long was a people subject to authoritarian rule? Was the authoritarian regime home-grown or foreign? What costs—human, cultural, material—did it impose? How did it end?

Some Europeans lived under their own dictators for several decades before, during, and after World War II; some suffered Nazi or Fascist occupation during the war; Poles and other Eastern Europeans endured local Communist dictatorships from the mid-1940s until the late 1980s.

But few if any Europeans were subject to harsh alien rule for so long as Balts. Europeans and then Russians enserfed or collectivized Estonians and Latvians for nearly eight hundred years; Polonized gentry and Soviet Communists ruled Lithuanians for many centuries. Each Baltic people experienced just three decades of independent self-rule in the twentieth century—the 1920s–1930s and the 1990s. When Balts regained independence in 1991, very few people still alive had participated in a free election or a free economic enterprise.

In short, the Baltic transformation can be viewed not only through the prism of comparative politics but also in terms of comparative imperialism and comparative liberation struggle. As we shall see, however, Balts were not path dependent. Their lives were shaped but not paralyzed by history—not straitjacketed by the *longue durée*.

I could see in 1958 when I attended Moscow University that the Baltic region might be an Achilles' heel for the USSR. Latvian students joined our American basketball team and played so rough against Russians that we were soon called "Canadian hockey players." When the Khrushchev regime opened the Baltic capitals for visits by foreigners, I got permission to visit Riga. But the KGB took no chances. Two tails, a dark-haired man and a blonde woman, joined me on the overnight train from Leningrad to Riga. When I looked out my hotel window in Riga, a man peered at me with binoculars from across the street. Four or five of his comrades trailed me as I toured the city's museums and medieval churches. If the KGB wished to discourage contact between an American visitor and Latvians, they succeeded. I talked to no Latvians except hotel staff during my stay. There was no point in endangering Latvian lives.

Seventeen years later, controls had eased. Soviet leader Mikhail S. Gorbachev had unleashed a campaign for *glasnost*—openness. In 1986 the Soviet authorities permitted Jack F. Matlock Jr., a U.S. State Department officer, to address a conference in Latvia. Matlock reminded the audience that the U.S. government had never recognized the annexation of Latvia, Estonia, and Lithuania by the USSR.

Visiting Tallinn in 1988, I discovered that the official Soviet press was applying glasnost to ethnic strife between Estonians and the Russian speakers in their midst. One could now learn a great deal from Communist newspapers without reading between the lines. Later that year intellectuals and public figures in each Baltic republic formed "popular fronts" to promote Gorbachev's call for "reconstruction." Soon, however, the fronts challenged Communist Party rule. Their demands escalated from autonomy to sovereignty to independence. Balts used a nonviolent "Singing Revolution" to undermine and break from Soviet rule.

In 1991 the Baltic republics regained their independence and took their seats in the United Nations. But winning a liberation struggle was different from rebuilding an independent way of life. After half a century of Communist rule, could Balts establish a democratic polity with a free market and play a constructive role in Europe and the world stage?

A decade later, the answer was "yes." By 2000 the Baltic republics were the only former units of the USSR to be ranked "free" by Freedom House, the only units to have regained their 1990 levels of economic activity, and the only former Soviet republics actively considered for membership in the EU and in NATO. What is more, the Baltic transformation remained nonviolent. No one died in ethnic or political struggles in the decade after independence.

Baltic achievements in the 1990s were as remarkable as the transformation of West Germany in the 1950s–1960s and East Asia in the 1970s–1980s. The present book chronicles these achievements and seeks to explain them. To describe them is not easy; to explain them is even more difficult; to anticipate their future contours, more difficult still.

To describe the transformation is difficult because it took place in many distinct but interrelated domains—politics and business, education and the Internet, science and the environment. Each country—indeed, each region and sector—moved at its own pace. Nothing moved in a straight line. There were shortfalls as well as advances. And many puzzles.

HOW?

How to explain the transformation? Why did Balts not suffer from the same malaise that beset Belarus, Ukraine, and Russia? Why did Balts and Russian-speaking settlers not fight one another like Bosnian Serbs and Muslims?

The work of my late friend and colleague David McClelland could be relevant. His book, *The Achieving Society,* confirmed Max Weber's thesis that culture can be crucial to achievement. Northern European culture had shaped Baltic life for many centuries, Soviet Communist culture for the last fifty years. What remained of each influence? Could liberal Germanic influences be stronger in Estonia than in the former East Germany, a land little changed more than a decade after reunification with the West?

Michael Doyle's book *Empires* might help explain the strengths and failings of the Soviet and other empires along the Baltic cost. Doyle's equally interesting studies of Immanuel Kant's work on representative government, trade, and peace might shed light on the Baltic transformation.

Articles and books by Robert O. Keohane and Joseph S. Nye shaped our understanding of interdependence for decades. Their models helped me analyze the USSR and global interdependence. Might interdependence also be a useful way to study the Baltic between Russia and Europe?

Another friend, Stuart Kauffman, left his laboratories at the University of Pennsylvania to develop complexity theory at the Santa Fe Institute in New Mexico. Complexity theorists hoped that their insights could apply in many domains of life and knowledge. If so, might not the Baltic case offer a way to test the utility of complexity theory in social sciences? This book tries to answer both questions.

At the onset of the twenty-first century the transformation of Estonia, Latvia, and Lithuania in the new Europe is a work in progress. So too is complexity theory. This theory, along with Kantian liberalism and the Keohane-Nye model of complex interdependence, is being refined. The Baltic region is coevolving with the rest of Europe, Russia, and the world. Security becomes indivisible. So too are the ways to understand and enhance it. A key to both security and knowledge, this book argues, is cooperation for mutual gain.

A NOTE ON DOCUMENTATION AND STYLE

Footnotes are minimized to conserve space. Most works used in the research are listed only in the selected references. More detailed citations are available from the author at <wclemens@bu.edu>.

Most diacritical markings are omitted. Russian transliterations usually follow the Library of Congress.

NOTES

Information about the author and his books is available at www.WalterClemens.net

1. Vytautas Landsbergis at the Center for European Studies, Harvard University, November 14, 2000.

2. This analysis excludes the Bahamas and other countries that won fewer than ten medals but did very well on a per capita basis.

3. The Baltic republics did much better than the United States, Russia, China, and most other countries competing in the 2000 Olympics. U.S. athletes brought home more medals than those from any other country, but the United States placed twenty-fourth in medals per capita—well behind Belarus, Russia, and Ukraine. The Lithuanian men's basketball squad nearly upset the U.S. champions. With Daina Gudzineviciute taking the gold in women's trap shooting, Lithuania won five medals—eighth in medals per capita; Latvia placed tenth in medals per capita.

4. Latvian pilot Gunars Dukste won the 2000 World Cities Cup air balloon contest, while Lithuanian pilots won the top three places in the Eurocentras 2000 championship for air balloons. Two Latvian hockey players got multimillion dollar contracts from the Carolina Hurricanes. The first Estonian yacht circling the globe departed Australia for home. In October Estonian Carmen Kass was named *Vogue* model of the year in New York.

Acknowledgments

The book owes a great deal to friends and colleagues: Karen Dawisha, Monica Florescu, Heinz Gärtner, Mirga Girnius, Paul Goble, Matt Hammon, Priit Järve, Stuart Kauffman, Mari-Ann Kelam, Tunne Kelam, Violetta Kelertas, Olav F. Knudsen, Arvo Kuddo, Vytautas Landsbergis, Miriam Lanskoy, Ronald H. Linden, Kate Martin, Jack F. Matlock Jr., Susan McEachern, Alexander Motyl, Bruce Parrott, Uri Ra'anan, Toivo U. Raun, Julia Reznick, Milda B. Richardson, Guntis Smidchens, Richard F. Staar, Daina Stankevics, S. Frederick Starr, Rein Taagepera, and William Urban. Other intellectual debts are noted in the selected references section and the endnotes. Ali Ho Clemens prepared the graphics and helped me to think through many issues in this book.

Helpful comments on the work were made by participants in conferences held by the Harriman Institute, Columbia University; the Irving B. Harris School of Public Policy, University of Chicago; the National Foreign Affairs Training Center, U.S. State Department; the International Studies Association; the Association for the Advancement of Baltic Studies; the Pan-European Conference on International Relations; the Conference on Baltic Studies in Europe; the Baltic Sea Foundation Summer Course; and the Baltic Research Program at Södertörns University College, Sweden.

The book benefits from the helpful staff and resources of the Institute for the Study of Ideology, Conflict, and Policy, Boston University; the Davis Center for Russian Studies and Belfer Center for Science and International Affairs, Harvard University; the Russian Littoral Project of the University of Maryland and the School for Advanced International Studies; Columbia University; Copenhagen University; Södertörns University College, Stockholm University, and the Royal Library in Sweden; and from documentation released by David Johnson and the CDI Russia Weekly, Radio Free Europe/Radio Liberty, and Balt-L.

Parts of the book are adapted from articles published in *Demokratizatsiya, Lituanus, Nationalities Papers, Nationalism and Ethnic Politics, SAIS Review*, and in several books, cited in the notes.

SWEDEN

Åland
(Ahvenanmaa)

Turku

Helsinki

Gulf of Finland

St. Petersburg

Stockholm

Tallinn

Narva

Narvskoye
Reservoir

Hiiumaa
(Dagö)

Vormsi

Rapla

Tapa

Kohtla
Järve

RUSSIAN
FEDERATION

Kärdla

Haapsalu

ESTONIA

Mustvee

Saaremaa
(Ösel)

Muhu

Virtsu

Pöltsamaa

L. Peipsi
(Chudskoye Ozero)

Kihelkonna

Kuressaare

Pärnu

Viljandi

Tartu

B
A
L
T
I
C

S
E
A

Manilaid
Kihnu

Võrtsjärv

L. Pihkva
(Pskovskoye Ozero)

Ruhnu

Ainaži

Valga

Võru

Irveš Šaurums

Gulf of
Riga

Valmiera

Pskov

Gotland
(SWEDEN)

Ventspils

LATVIA

Gulbene

U
t
r
o
y
a

V
e
l
i
k
a
y
a

Kuldīga

Jūrmala

Riga

Saldus

Liepāja

Jelgava

Daugava

Jēkabpils

Rezekne

Biržai

Daugavpils

Siauliai

Panevėžys

Polatsk

Klaipėda

LITHUANIA

Utena

Zapadnaya Dvina

Kėdainiai

Taurage

Nemunas

Ukmergė

Kaunas

Neman

Vilnius

Kuršskiy
Zaliv

Kaliningrad

RUSSIAN
FEDERATION

Marijampole

Gdynia

Gulf of
Gdansk

Gusev

Alytus

Barysaw

Gdansk

Elbląg

POLAND

Minsk

Olsztyn

Hrodna

BELARUS

Nyoman

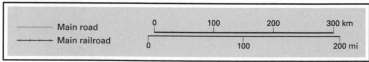

Main road

Main railroad

0   100   200   300 km

0   100   200 mi

The Baltic region before and after World War II. Reprinted by permission of Romuald J. Misiunas and Rein Taagepera, *The Baltic States: Years of Dependence, 1940–1990* (Berkeley, Calif.: University of California Press, 1983), xxi.

1

Coping with Complexity: Alternative Explanations

Tunne Kelam

A MANY-SIDED TRANSFORMATION

A bright light appeared in the new Europe forming at the cusp of the third millennium. Having regained their independence in 1991 from the Soviet Union, the Baltic republics of Estonia, Latvia, and Lithuania were making strong headway in the difficult transitions to political democracy, a market economy, and constructive participation in world affairs.

The transformation of Baltic life began in the 1980s, the last decade of Soviet imperium. Indeed, the three Baltic Davids played major roles in toppling the Soviet Goliath. As Soviet power declined, Estonians, Latvians, and Lithuanians regained and strengthened values they held dear. Seldom if ever did Balts cope so well with complex challenges at home and abroad.

The Baltic transformation was/is a many-sided process—a work in progress as a new millennium began. Each Baltic country had its own features, and each proceeded at its own pace. But the rates of change across the region belied any claim that the "transition to a fuller market and more comprehensive democracy is always evolutionary and managed and takes decades."[1] The Baltic transformations did not require decades and none was "managed" from above or from outside—not from Brussels, not from Washington. Each arose more from the bottom up than from the top down or the outside in. Indeed, Estonia's decision to peg its currency to the German mark ran against advice from the International Monetary Fund.

Balts transformed their political and economic life far more successfully than their neighbors in Russia, Belarus, or other regions of the former Soviet Union. To be sure, former Soviet client-states such as Poland, Hungary, the Czech Republic, and Slovakia also made rapid economic and political progress in the 1990s. But unlike the Baltic states, none of these countries had been annexed and absorbed into the Soviet Union; each had richer natural resources than the Baltic republics; each had experimented with economic and political reforms for decades before the Soviet breakup; and each attracted much attention from Western governments and investors.

Box 1.1. Who Are the "Balts"?

The "Balts" on whom this book focuses are Estonians, Latvians, and Lithuanians. But many other peoples live and have lived on Baltic shores, including Finns, Russians, Poles, Germans, Danes, and Swedes. Strictly speaking, only Latvian and Lithuanian are "Baltic" languages of the Indo-European family. Danes, Swedes, and Germans use Indo-European Germanic tongues; Poles and Russians, Indo-European Slavic tongues. Estonian and Finnish are not Indo-European but Finno-Ugric languages. The Finno-Ugric ancestors of Estonians and Finns inhabited many parts of what is now Russia, including Siberia. Finnic-speaking settlers came to the Baltic shores around 3500 B.C.; the progenitors of Lithuanians and Latvians, around 2000 B.C.; the eastern Slavs around A.D. 500.

Peoples such as Rugians and Old Prussians who lived on the Baltic shores are no more. Most of the Germans who for centuries dominated both town and agricultural life in today's Estonia and Latvia departed after World War I or just before World War II. The Jewish communities that thrived in Riga, Vilnius, and elsewhere in the Baltic countries were nearly exterminated in the 1940s. Most of the Jews still living in Poland after the Holocaust departed in the 1960s. Linguistic and cultural minorities such as the Ingrians and the Kashubians nearly disappeared.[1]

---

[1]See however Kaarina Ylonen, *Religion and Ethnicity: The Renaissance of the Ingrian Church after the End of Communist Rule* (Tampere: Research Institute of the Evangelical Lutheran Church of Finland, 1998). One of the oldest Kashub texts is *Der kleine Catechissmus D. Martini Lutheri. Deutsch und Wendisch gegen einander gesetzt* (Cologne: Bohlau, 1958), which includes appendices from the Old and New Testament as published in Danzig in 1643.

Baltic achievements were more remarkable than Germany's "economic miracle" of the 1950s, because Balts proceeded from much less favorable conditions. Germany merely resumed after World War II an economic ascent launched in the previous century from very strong foundations. Germany's previous experience with self-rule was also far stronger than that of the Baltic peoples, who had been repressed by foreigners for centuries except for the 1920s and 1930s.

Baltic developments resembled more what the World Bank called the "East Asian miracle." Like Taiwan, Balts had to work with limited natural resources and amid the threats of a powerful neighbor.

But the Baltic was not the Balkans. Balts avoided the anarchy, bloodshed, and strongman rule that supplanted Communist domination in much of the former Yugoslavia. Not only did Balts manage to pull away from Soviet domination using nonviolent means, but—after independence was achieved—they avoided serious communal violence. Fewer than fifty Balts and no Soviet troops or Slavic settlers died from political violence in the 1980s as the Baltic republics broke from Soviet rule. In the 1990s no deaths or violent conflicts due to ethnic differences were reported in the Baltic republics, even though native and Slavic-speaking communities expressed many grievances toward each other. There were many gang fights, extortionist murders, and suicides in the Baltic; anti-Semites desecrated Jewish synagogues and (in April 1999) the Holocaust memorial in Riga; some Balts violated Soviet Army cemeteries; still, there was little ethnic violence. The near absence of communal fighting in the Baltic countries at the end of the twentieth century contrasted not only with the former Yugoslavia and with many other parts of the USSR (for example, Tajikistan), but also with racial strife in the United States, the United Kingdom, Germany, and France. Despite the potential for ethnic discord, Balts developed a comity of relative social harmony.

The transition of the reborn Baltic republics into functioning members of the "First World" was not perfect. Human development lagged behind political and economic achievements. The new politics did not elicit strong participation by young people; the new societies devoted few resources to integrating ethnic minorities; and the new economics did little to cushion the transitional costs for the poor and the elderly. These and other failures are detailed in chapters 4–7. But was the glass half empty or half full? Did Baltic performance after 1991 warrant a vote of thumbs down or thumbs up?

This book contends that Baltic performance in the decade after 1991 was deeply flawed but quite good relative to resources and tasks at hand. Not only did Balts score many near-term achievements, but they also laid the foundations for gradual amelioration of underlying problems. Shortfalls had to be expected, and many problems would take time to ameliorate. Integration of minorities might take decades. More could and should have been done to strengthen the social welfare net in the 1990s. If the new economics succeeded, however, the next generations of elderly could retire with greater confidence in their material assets. Their own savings and pensions would rest on stronger foundations than in the 1990s.

Many problems remained as a new century began. Still, the progress achieved in the previous fifteen years was remarkable. How could it be explained?

CONTENDING CONCEPTS AND EXPLANATIONS

Geography

Balts have long lived on the "amber coast," the southeastern littoral of the Baltic Sea — the major source of the world's amber.[2] Russians called this region *pribaltika* — the area adjoining the Baltic Sea.[3] For Germans, the Baltic was the *Ostsee* (East Sea).[4]

The Baltic is a vast sea covering more than 166,000 square miles, but it is nearly landlocked and often icebound. For centuries Baltic ports and their hinterlands provided the grain needed to protect Europeans from bad harvests, the copper for their coins, and much of the timber, tar, pitch, hemp, and flax for their ships. Denmark became rich by taxing the commerce passing between the Baltic and the North Sea. But Denmark was just one of many powers striving to dominate the Baltic. Danes, Germans, Swedes, Poles, Russians, and others vied for power in the region. Their struggles interacted with the rivalries of England, France, and the Netherlands; with contests between the Hapsburg and Bourbon dynasties; and with conflicts between Catholics and Protestants.

The Baltic region has long been rich in amber, furs, grain, and (in Estonia) oil shale and hydropower. But the region is resource-poor relative to Russia, Poland, or Germany. Baltic geography presents many challenges — long winters, much rain and fog, seas often frozen or rough, and much rocky soil.

To live at the crossroads of Europe and Eurasia presents major opportunities but even greater dangers. The Baltic region attracted not just traders but invaders. For one thousand years and more traders and would-be conquerors came from all directions seeking to make Baltic ports, amber, and other resources their own. The harbors of St. Petersburg and Tallinn are often ice-bound in winter, but not Riga or Klaipeda.

The Baltic lands and populations are small relative to their neighbors. Estonia occupies 17,666 square miles (45,226 square kilometers)—about the size of New Hampshire and Vermont combined. It borders on Latvia and Russia, and its sea coasts look toward Finland and Sweden. Its population of 1,408,523 in 2000 gave it a density of seventy-seven persons per square mile.

Latvia covers 25,400 square mile (64,100 square kilometers)—about the size of West Virginia. With 2,353,874 people in 2000, there were 93 per square mile. It borders Lithuania, Estonia, Belarus, and Russia. Lithuania is slightly larger than Latvia: 25,212 square miles (65,200 square kilometer.). But in 2000 it had a much larger population: 3,584,966, a density of 142 per square mile. It borders Belarus, Latvia, Poland, and Russia at Kaliningrad.

Our visions of geographical regions, margins and cores, centers and peripheries result not just from the raw facts but how we look at them. "Baltic" is a construct more often used by outsiders than by the peoples to whom it is applied. Estonians, Latvians, and Lithuanians have long identified first of all each with their own tribe or state. When they looked toward a broader association, it was rarely toward other "Balts." Instead, each of these peoples looked north, west, or south for affiliations—and almost never east.

The end of the Cold War and the prospects of expanding the European Union eastward made it possible to reformulate our images of Europe and the Baltic region. We no longer thought of Estonia, Latvia, and Lithuania as tiny appendages to the Soviet empire. Instead they could be viewed as parts of Central Europe, Northern Europe, or simply Europe.

In 2000 Balts were divided about whether to go it alone or together. Estonia would not object to being the first Baltic republic admitted into the European Union while Latvia and Lithuania waited for the next round, but both Estonia and Latvia took umbrage when a U.S. senator proposed that, of Baltic countries, only Lithuania be admitted in the next wave of NATO expansion. For his part, Estonia's foreign minister Toomas Ilves portrayed his country as a Scandinavian rather than a Baltic country. In November 2000 he noted that nearly half of Estonia's trade went to Finland and Sweden while less than one-tenth went to Latvia and Lithuania, and he asserted "there's nothing more to say." Trying to underline Estonia's Scandinavian identity, Ilves's ministry sent out holiday greeting cards explaining that Estonia, Finland, Sweden, and Norway were the only countries in Europe where "jul" (yule) means "Christmas." Merchants and politicians in Estonia as well as Latvia and Lithuania urged Ilves to hold his tongue on such matters.

History

The Baltic transformation at the end of the twentieth century departed sharply from a long history in which Balts lived more as objects—passive victims—than as agents of their own destiny. The record of the second millennium offered Balts more ground for despair than for pride or confidence. If great civilizations are creative responses to challenges, Balts usually failed the test. A long record showed that Baltic feuding and disunity often helped foreigners to divide and rule.

Armed monks and knights imposed Christianity on Estonians and Latvians in the thirteenth century. Western imperialists ruled the Baltic lands even longer than Russians. Westerners brought Christianity, literacy, and nationalism. The last pagans in Europe, Lithuanians eventually accepted Catholicism as part of a strategic alliance with Poland in the fourteenth century.

For more than five hundred years, as we shall see in the next chapter, German-speaking merchants and artisans dominated political, economic, and cultural life in Tallinn (known by Germans as Reval) and Riga. German lords (seigneurs—"Baltic barons") ruled the manors, where they held Estonians and Latvians as serfs—sometimes breaking up families and selling them like cattle. Germans wrote off Estonians, Latvians, and other subjected peoples as *undeutsche*—"not-German," and perhaps not fully human. Lithuanian and Polish nobles also viewed their peasants with disdain.

When Baltic barons chose Protestantism in the sixteenth century, their serfs followed. With Protestantism came literacy. The first book published in Estonian was a Lutheran catechism printed in 1535. By the end of the century most Estonians and Latvians, even peasants, were literate. Literacy rates in the Baltic provinces were higher than in any part of the tsarist empire. The empire's oldest universities were in Vilnius (1579) and Tartu (1632). Balts became avid readers in the nineteenth century and continued, even under Soviet rule, to place great trust in education.

Tsar Peter the Great opened a window on Europe for Russia. In little more than a century the Russian Empire expanded along the shores of the Baltic Sea, seizing Estonia, Latvia, Lithuania, much of Poland, and Finland. Peter took Estonia and Latvia from Sweden in a long war in which half to three-fourths of the local population died from fighting, hunger, and pestilence. In the late eighteenth century Catherine the Great took Lithuania and parts of Poland. In 1808–1809 Tsar Alexander took Finland from Sweden.

In the second half of the nineteenth century all these peoples—Finns, Estonians, Latvians, Lithuanians, and Poles—experienced a cultural awakening, as did many other peoples living under the Russian, Austro-Hungarian, Prussian, and Ottoman empires. Balts and other minorities joined in the 1905 Revolution against tsarist rule in Russia. But the tsarist realm endured until World War I, when it collapsed along with the Austro-Hungarian, Prussian, and Ottoman regimes.

In March 1917 the tsarist regime gave way to a democratic Provisional Government, which the Bolsheviks overthrew in November. Two years before, Imperial German troops had advanced into Vilnius, ancient capital of Lithuania, and in early 1918 the Germans occupied much of Estonia and Latvia. Amid this chaos each Baltic people asserted its autonomy and then, in 1918, its independence. When Germany entered an armistice with the Entente and the United States in November 1918, the Kaiser's armies began to withdraw from the Baltic. Estonian and Latvian nationalists then faced military dangers from Baltic Germans and from Soviet Russia. Baltic Germans mobilized troops to regain control of land they had dominated for centuries. And though civil war engulfed Russia, the Soviet government in 1919 sent Red Army units to win back what Lenin called "Estland." Attack and counterattack raged throughout 1919 and early 1920. In May 1919 Estonian forces joined anti-Communist "White" Russians and drove back the Red Army into Russian territory. Estonian troops also helped destroy Red forces in northern Latvia and to dislodge Baltic German troops from Riga. Baltic armies benefited from the efforts of British, French, Finnish, and other foreign forces to destroy the young Soviet regime and, in 1920, from Poland's war with the Soviets.

In 1920 Soviet Russia signed peace treaties with Estonia, Lithuania, Latvia, Poland, and Finland, and recognized their independent statehoods. Independence did not come cheaply for any of them. Thirteen months of fighting cost Estonia 3,588 dead and 13,775 wounded and left it with heavy debts to Finland, Britain, France, and the United States.

Each Baltic state soon joined the League of Nations. But their independence lasted only twenty years. The 1920s and 1930s demonstrated again how difficult it could be for Balts and other Eastern Europeans to stand together or collaborate against external threats.

Estonia and Latvia were content with their 1920 boundaries, but Lithuania was revisionist. Vilnius was the country's ancient capital but most of its inhabitants now spoke Polish, Belarusian, or Yiddish. When the Red Army occupied Vilnius in January 1919, the Lithuanian Council retreated to Kaunas. The Paris Peace Conference assigned Vilnius to Lithuania, but Poland took it from Lithuanian control. Following a plebiscite of uncertain legitimacy, Vilnius became part of Poland in 1922—a source of great tension between Lithuania and Poland. Kaunas served as Lithuania's capital between the world wars.

Lithuania also had claims on its western border. It seized the Baltic port of Klaipeda—Memel to its German inhabitants—from League of Nations administrators in 1923. Germany took back Klaipeda/Memel in March 1939 and offered Lithuania a military alliance against Poland. Lithuania declined the deal, even though it included Vilnius as a prize.

In August 1939 Hitler and Stalin agreed to partition the lands between Germany and the USSR. Berlin recognized eastern Poland, Latvia, Estonia, and Finland as within the Soviet sphere, to which Lithuania (excepting the Memel district) was added in September. Vilnius, the Germans and Soviets agreed, should go to Lithuania.

German and Soviet forces invaded Poland in September 1939. The Red Army occupied eastern Poland and the Kremlin transferred Vilnius and some adjoining lands to Lithuania.

Finland's turn came in November. Their lands invaded by the Red Army, Finns put up stiff resistance. They lost some land by a treaty signed in March 1940 but retained their independence, and later joined German forces fighting the USSR.

Estonia, Latvia, and Lithuania, however, capitulated to Soviet threats in 1939–1940. In September-October 1939 the Kremlin demanded and got mutual assistance treaties with each Baltic state permitting Soviet military bases on their territories. In June 1940 the USSR accused the Baltic states of not abiding by their 1939 obligations. More Soviet troops poured into each Baltic state and Soviet commissars appointed new cabinets. New "elections" approved a single slate of candidates for parliament; the new parliaments asked that their countries become republics within the USSR—requests that were then rubber-stamped by the USSR Supreme Soviet in August.

When Hitler invaded the USSR in the summer of 1941, German troops quickly occupied the Baltic states. Some Balts volunteered and others were forced to fight with the German *Wehrmacht* against the Soviets. The Red Army retook the *pribaltika* for the USSR in 1944. But many Balts fled to the woods and mounted anti-Soviet guerrilla campaigns that continued into the 1950s.

Large numbers of the Baltic populations, including many of the best educated and most prominent, were killed, deported, or forced into exile in the 1940s. Private farms and enterprises were collectivized.

Led by the United States, no Western European state except Hitler's Germany and Sweden ever recognized Soviet annexation of the three Baltic states. For all practical purposes, however, Estonia, Latvia, and Lithuania remained under Soviet rule for half a century. The Communists in Moscow and their local satraps sought to Russify and Sovietize the Baltic countries. For better or worse, the Soviets did much to industrialize the region—especially Estonia and Latvia—and to promote Soviet-style education. But Balts retained a lead: their middle schools ran one to three years longer than Soviet Russian schools. Baltic living standards were among the highest in the USSR. Infant mortality was far lower than in Russia.

In Estonia and Latvia, and less so in Lithuania, native populations had to accommodate waves of settlers from Russia and other parts of the USSR. By the 1980s Russian or another Slavic tongue was the first language of more than half the populations in the larger cities and in certain regions of the Baltic republics.

For the Soviet leaders as for the tsars, the Baltic provided a buffer against Western invaders and a launch pad for a potential Russian attack on Europe. By the 1980s the three Baltic republics were among the most militarized regions of the USSR. Secret police agents were vigilant against dissidents. Nonetheless, as we shall see in chapter 3, Balts began to act as though they were free. The Kremlin formally recognized their independence once again in September 1991.

Breaking with the longue durée

Do social institutions depend upon inheritance? The French *annales* school of history and many modern social scientists (see box 1.2) believe so. Baltic experience suggests, however, that the weight of history sometimes shapes and limits social change for generation after generation . . . but sometimes not. Balts incorporated some influences from Western and Northern Europe and discarded others. Balts sucessfully broke from their heritage of repression in the 1920s and again in the 1990s. They sloughed off any habits or preconceptions of servitude.

Perhaps history played a heavier role in Aalborg, Denmark (see box 1.2), than in the three Baltic states. Traditional social distinctions and privileges had stronger foundations in long-stable Denmark than in the Baltic lands, convulsed by revolutionary change in the 1920s, 1940s, and 1990s. To be sure, Communist rule generated a privileged class in the Baltic, but this stratum dissolved after 1991.

Balts were not path-dependent. History was not the future for Balts. The *longue durée* provided the matrix for their lives but was not decisive. Balts did not act like people enslaved for centuries. Where they went when independent was not where they started. After 1991 Balts created market economies and real democracies like

Box 1.2. Continuity and Change in Denmark, Italy, and the USA

Seeking to explain the failure in the 1970s of urban reforms in Aalborg, Denmark, Bent Flyvbjerg pointed to collusion between the town government and its business elite stretching back over five hundred years. Recognizing that Aalborg was a trading town, a royal decree in the fifteenth century stipulated that its mayors and aldermen had to come from the merchant and burgher class. In succeeding centuries, Aalborg's magistrates made up the government both for the city and the merchant's guild, upholding the merchants' interests against other classes. This pattern persisted in the late twentieth century, when the Aalborg Chamber of Industry and Commerce collaborated with the government's Technical Department to thwart urban reforms meant to regulate vehicular traffic. Merchants in the town center feared that rerouting cars and buses would cut into their sales. The Technical Department and the Chamber had an implicit contract to negotiate on all issues of joint concern.[1]

Similarly, Robert D. Putnam traced the political culture of Italy—strong communal ties in the north and what Edward Banfield called "amoral familialism" in the south—back one thousand years. Putnam explained that voluntary cooperation may be easier in a community that has "inherited a substantial stock of social capital"—norms of reciprocity and networks of civic engagement. "Citizens of civic communities find examples of successful horizontal relationships in their history, whereas those in less civic regions find, at best, examples of vertical supplication."[2] Putnam is probably correct about some countries.[3] Sugar planters in the Caribbean and merchant imperialists in India used divide-and-conquer tactics to break communal ties among their subjects. But Putnam's subsequent study of social capital in the United States did not bow to the *longue durée*. Putnam found sharp differences in Americans' tolerance and engagement tied to the experiences of particular generations.[4]

---

[1] Bent Flyvbjerg, *Rationality and Power: Democracy in Practice* (Chicago: University of Chicago Press, 1998).

[2] Robert D. Putnam, *Making Democracy Work: Civic Traditions in Modern Italy* (Princeton, N.J.: Princeton University Press, 1993), pp. 167, 174.

[3] His portrait of Italian history, however, seems oversimplified. In medieval times, life in northern Italy was often rent by feuds within and between city-states, manipulated by the Vatican and by outside invaders. In the 1920s, the northern Italians first embraced Mussolini and Fascism. In the 1990s it appeared that Christian Democrats of Rome and the north had long cooperated with *mafiosi* in the south.

[4] Thus, Americans born in the years 1940–1945 tended to be much more tolerant than those born earlier. But Americans born after 1945 tended to be less civically engaged than previous generations. See Robert D. Putnam, *Bowling Alone: The Collapse and Revival of American Community* (New York: Simon & Schuster, 2000), p. 357.

those some had read about but that few had ever experienced. Balts rapidly transformed their institutions to qualify for admission to the Council of Europe and, they hoped, NATO and the European Union. Alien rule did not destroy Balts' capacity for self-organization. This was probably the greatest miracle on the amber coast.

Elites make what they will of history. Leaders in post-Soviet Novgorod emphasized the city's historic role as a model of self-rule by a merchant oligarchy associated with the Hanseatic trading states along the Baltic Sea.[5] Leaders in Pskov could also have stressed its Hanseatic ties, but some chose to emphasize its role as a bulwark against Germanic expansion.

Civilization

The "clash of civilizations" added to conflicts of interest dividing West and East. Most Balts felt they belonged to Europe's Catholic- and Protestant-based civilization—not to Russia and Eastern Orthodoxy. Western Christianity was more individualistic, more rationalist, and less mystical than Eastern Orthodoxy.

The post-1991 Baltic transformation probably benefited from the work ethic and other Protestant traditions that helped the rise of capitalism. Protestant virtues of industry and thrift supplanted the Catholic virtues of faith, hope, and charity. Lutheranism fostered both literacy and individualism by its insistence that each person should be able to read the Bible and interpret it for him/herself.[6] Calvinists did so by their belief in predestination, which led some to hope that material prosperity in this life augured God's blessing.[7] Also, unlike Catholics, many Protestants approved lending money for interest.

In time Protestantism encouraged not only economic enterprise but democracy; it fostered not only industry and thrift but also literacy and an ideology of equality and tolerance. These consequences did not evolve overnight or in a linear fashion. But the

---

Box 1.3. The Politics of Western and Eastern Christianity

Christianity displaced paganism in the Baltic lands in the thirteenth and fourteenth centuries. Catholicism prevailed in what became Estonia and Latvia, while Russian Orthodoxy penetrated Lithuania. As Lithuanians came to fear Russia and edged closer to Poland, Catholicism got the upper hand in Lithuania. In the sixteenth century Lutheranism replaced Catholicism in Estonia and most of Latvia and made some inroads in Lithuania. When tsarist Russia absorbed the Baltic lands in the eighteenth century, Orthodox influences expanded. Golden-domed Orthodox cathedrals appeared in Tallinn, Riga, and Vilnius. Tsarist Russia used Orthodoxy to promote Russification and Russian interests. So, later on, did Communist and post-Communist Russians. But Russia's gains were minimal. Balts knew that many Russian Orthodox priests collaborated with the Soviet KGB. In Lithuania, Catholic churches spearheaded resistance to Soviet rule.

After 1991, many Balts continued to see Russian Orthodox churches as tools of Kremlin policy. Entering a dispute between rival seats of Orthodox power, Estonia's courts in the 1990s ruled that Orthodox properties in Estonia belonged to those faithful (about fifty thousand) who looked to the patriarch in Istanbul for guidance rather than to those (some one hundred thousand) who followed the metropolitan in Moscow. Estonian authorities did not evict the pro-Moscow side, but Russian Orthodox priests fumed when they lost the legal right to churches they had used during decades of Soviet rule. In 2000, the Estonian government honored Patriarch Bartholomew from Istanbul when he visited Tallinn, while Russian Orthodox churchmen there refused to meet him. They venerated instead Metropolitan Aleksei in Moscow, a man whom others saw as a longtime Soviet KGB/Kremlin agent.

Jewish influences had also been strong for centuries in some Baltic towns. Vilnius before World War II was called the "Jerusalem of the north." But most Baltic Jews were killed by Nazi occupiers aided by some Baltic collaborators. In 2000, as we shall see in chapter 7, anti-Semitism still flared in the Baltic, resisted by others who struggled for mutual respect.

Reformation gradually contributed to the growth of political as well as economic liberty in the West. Protestant beliefs passed from German states and Sweden into the Baltic lands, especially Estonia and Latvia. They were transmitted by Protestant ministers, teachers, and university lecturers. Proximity to Europe meant that Balts could be shaped more by the Renaissance, the Reformation, and the Enlightenment than were most Russians.[8]

The religious wars were fought with ideas as well as soldiers. Lutheran and Calvinist ideas also reached Poland and Lithuania. Starting in the 1520s, the newly formed Duchy of Prussia promoted both Lutheranism and literacy among Poles and Lithuanians. Twelve years after the first book printed in Estonian, the first in Lithuanian was also a Lutheran catechism—published in 1547. Sunday gospels were published in Lithuanian in 1579 and the entire Bible was published in the language in 1735. The Prussian duke established a university at Königsberg that trained Lithuanians for pastoral work. Most Poles and Lithuanians remained Catholic, however, thanks in part to a strong Counter Reformation mounted by Jesuits who, among other activities, established a university in Vilnius in the 1570s.[9]

Some Russian tsars and tsarinas sought to learn from Europe, only to revert to more authoritarian ways. The weight of tradition could not be overthrown by the occasional tutoring of some *philosophe*. Russians were taught to accept fatalistically the whims of authority. Their children were not schooled in Horatio Alger myths but in folk tales advising that wealth and happiness come by magic or by deceit. Hard work in these stories is seldom rewarded. Indeed, a brother and sister who go into the forest to gather wood for their aging parents' hearth are as likely to be zapped by Father Frost as to get home safely.

Magic and deceit against the rulers are extolled in the fairy tales of other cultures. But "life itself" confirmed for Russians that hard work may not be rewarded. In Stalin's time, state terror seemed random. In Brezhnev's era, riches went to those with "connections." In the 1990s, Kremlin cronies became overnight millionaires, while small businesses and savings were wiped out by government fiat or rouble devaluations, as in August 1998.

How much of a Protestant work ethic remained in the Baltic region after half a century of Soviet rule was unclear. But the economic conditions in the 1990s showed Balts that hard work could earn wealth. The economic as well as the political outlooks of most Balts, including Lithuanians, was closer to views in Frankfurt or Geneva than to those prevailing in Moscow or Kyiv.

Nationalism

In the Baltic, as elsewhere, nationalism stoked cultural creativity and a politics of independence, but it also led to myopic failures to cooperate for mutual gain.

What is a "nation"? Joseph Stalin tried to define "nation" in objective terms. In his essay, "Marxism and the National Question" (1913), Stalin asserted: "A nation is a historically constituted, stable community of people, formed on the basis of a common language, territory, economic life, and psychological make-up manifested in a common culture." But few nations fit Stalin's criteria. Each Baltic people mixed with others for centuries. Until the nineteenth century, most humans identified with the village or land where they lived, hunted, or farmed—not with some abstract "nation."

Contrary to Stalin, many scholars now see nationhood as a subjective reality. A nation is a group of people who believe or feel that they constitute a nation. It is an imagined community, because most members can never know one another personally and because they choose to emphasize what unites them rather than what separates them.[10]

Nationalists feel that "we as a nation, have had a great past and, working together, will build a great future." Nationalists usually look back as well as forward. If necessary, they invent a new past. Nationalism is sometimes a secular religion—a belief that each person should feel a deep, perhaps supreme, loyalty to the nation. For extreme nationalists, the nation is the tree, the individual a branch. The tree nourishes the branch but can live without it; the branch can be sacrificed for the tree. Few Balts, however, have become so fanatic as to embrace this kind of nationalism.

What makes individuals feel bonded in one nation? Why do they emphasize what unites them rather than what divides them? A sense of nationhood can be nurtured by many factors—a shared mythology, shared religious texts printed in the vernacular, a communications infrastructure, or shared experiences coping with shared threats and opportunities. Baltic nationalism had these and other well-springs, including

- Territory: Having lived on the amber coast for millennia, Estonians, Latvians, and Lithuanians became deeply attached to their territories as well as to their languages and cultures.
- Alien rule and external threats: Foreign rule spurred Baltic nationalisms in the nineteenth and twentieth centuries. For Balts, nationalism offered a way to counter political repression. In Soviet times some Baltic women gave their places at universities to males so the men would not be conscripted into the Soviet Army.
- Fear of extinction: Balts in the 1980s feared that their genes and cultures could disappear unless they cast off alien controls.
- Environmentalism: Fear that their environment would be destroyed by aliens buoyed nationalists throughout the former USSR, from Lake Baikal to Estonia's phosphate mines to Chernobyl.

Many peoples believe they are "chosen" by God or Fate to do great things; some feel entitled to exploit the nonelect. But this source of nationalism has been nearly absent in the Baltic. Except for some Lithuanians many centuries ago, no Balts have felt entitled to conquer other peoples.

Blinded by ethnocentrism and later by nationalism, however, Baltic peoples seldom acted in concert to protect their shared interests. Allegiances were usually to family, tribe, or faction—not to some larger community. Divided Latvian and Estonian tribes succumbed to German-led "Sword Brothers" in the thirteenth century and remained under alien rule for nearly eight hundred years. Lithuanian forces, however, routed the Sword Brothers in 1236 and joined with Polish troops to defeat the Teutonic Knights in 1410 and again in 1435.

In the Baltic, as in most of Europe, nationalism emerged only in the nineteenth century. Most Balts then were still peasants, but modernization buttressed nationalism. The introduction of railroads permitted church choirs from scattered parishes to come together for festivals of traditional music. People met, recalled, celebrated, and strengthened their common heritage. Tsarist Russian and later Soviet officials tried to throttle Baltic nationalisms, but Balts persisted with music festivals that affirmed their national identities. Their drive for independence in the 1980s became a "Singing Revolution." As one participant put it, "Somehow we sang ourselves free from Soviet repression, both personally and politically."[11] Music sustained Balts, as it did repressed Irish and Jews.

Throttled by Russian tsars but encouraged by Woodrow Wilson, local nationalisms fueled the creation of the three Baltic republics in the 1920s. Put down again by Soviet commissars but given some leeway by Gorbachev's Kremlin, Baltic nationalisms reemerged in the 1980s.

Is nationalism a primordial force or a construct? National consciousness is not inherent in genes, territory, or even language. How Balts live in the twenty-first century derives from an ancient peasant ethos heavily influenced by outside cultures. Even Christianity was an alien import. History makes and constantly remakes what we call "race," "nation," "culture," and "language."

Some nationalisms are comparatively liberal, open, and tolerant; others are authoritarian, closed, and aggressive. One of the greatest challenges facing the Baltic republics as the twenty-first century began was how to strengthen their own cultures and languages while integrating the Slavic-speakers who overnight became ethnic minorities in 1991. Forced population transfers were not an ethical or practical option. New modes of coexistence had to be forged.

Looking into the twenty-first century, how could the nationalisms of Estonians, Latvians, and Lithuanians—again housed in independent states—coexist with the sentiments of Slavic-speakers in their midst? Would Baltic natives and Slavic settlers feel as one in a unified country or remain distant from one another—perhaps like Walloons and Flemings in Belgium or Jews and Arabs in Israel? How all parties sought to cope with ethnic diversity is examined in chapter 7.

Baltic cultures were also at risk from the steamroller of globalization. Thus, an Estonian friend sent a Christmas card in 1996 saying, "Come back to Tallinn before McDonald's takes over." If Tiananmen Square had the largest U.S. hamburger assembly line in the world, how could tiny Baltic republics resist the trend? By 1999 there was a McDonald's even in Narva, not far from the Crusader fort across the river from Russia.

How would local ties in the Baltic mesh with the outside world? How would Baltic natives and Slavic settlers interact with the transnational forces arising from a uniting Europe and a "McWorld" global culture? Would their offspring utilize one, two, three, or more languages? Would it be a Baltic or Slavic tongue in one context and English, German, or Chinese in others?

Interdependence

Interdependence is mutual vulnerability—a condition in which the well-being of two or more actors is vulnerable, or at least sensitive, to changes in the condition or policies of the other.[12] For more than one thousand years Balts have shared vulnerabilities with one another, with other Europeans, and with Russians. But Balts have usually depended more on others than the reverse.

Interdependence is neither good nor bad. How humans deal with this condition is up to them. Actors may seek one-sided or mutual gain. Many societies, large and small, decline when their members fail to pool their strengths for the common good. Though interdependence may foster mutual gain, it can also lead to pain—mutual or one-sided.

As the third millennium began, the security and material well-being of all Europe, the Baltic region, and Russia were interdependent. Recognition of shared vulnerability should discourage self-righteousness and encourage empathy. But the fact of interdependence does not suffice to make one from many. Often it does not even inspire cooperation.

Complexity Theory

Complexity theory offers another way to look at interdependence and its policy implications in the Baltic region. This book argues that, despite some weighty limitations, complexity theory can enlarge our vision and complement other approaches to the study of international relations.

Complexity theory modifies Darwin's emphasis on natural selection as the key to evolution. Survival is determined not just by luck (the correspondence between genetic mutations and environmental conditions), but by a capacity for self-organization and mutual aid. Applied to politics, complexity theory suggests that Social Darwinists and ultrarealists are wrong: outcomes are not determined by raw power plus cunning.

Developed by scholars from various disciplines, complexity theory integrates concepts from many fields to produce a new slant on evolution.[13] Its exponents seek a general theory able to explain many different types of phenomena—social as well as biological and physical. If complexity theory fulfills this goal, it should also help us to understand development and security issues, as in the Baltic region.

Complexity theory is anchored in seven basic concepts: fitness, coevolution, emergence and self-organization, agent-based systems, self-organized criticality, punctuated equilibrium, and fitness landscapes.

Fitness

Complexity theory defines fitness as the ability to cope with complexity; to process information about and deal with many variables; and to survive challenges and make the most of opportunity. The theory posits that all life forms exist on a spectrum ranging from instability (chaos) to ultrastability (ordered hierarchy). Fitness is found between rigid order and chaos—not in a crystal where every atom resides in an ordered hierarchy, nor in gases whose molecules move at random. Some analysts like to say that fitness is found at the "edge of chaos." It is more accurate to think of fitness as located at the top of a bell-shaped curve leading downward toward chaos and rigid order. Move too far toward either pole, and you lose fitness.

Coevolution

No organism evolves alone. Every individual, species, and society coevolves with others and with their shared environment. A change in any one actor or environment can alter the fitness of multiple actors. This is the "butterfly effect" of chaos theory. The more variables shape a system, the harder to anticipate how change in one element will affect others.

Nonlinearity and complexity are hallmarks of human social networks. Complexity theory endeavors to explain the process of complex adaptation within complex systems—whether they be ecosystems, the Internet, or political systems.

Emergence

Coevolution often gives rise to "emergent properties"—holistic phenomena richer than the sum of their parts, even their genes and chemical ingredients. Thus, an infant's brain can learn more rules than are contained in its genes. Evolution manifests "order for free." This could but need not imply a Creator or grand Watchmaker.

Agent-Based Systems

An agent-based system is one in which independent actors self-organize to form an emergent phenomenon without central direction from above. Thus, many species interlock in a coral reef and provide one another protection from predators, temperature extremes, and strong currents. Without planning, they cooperate for mutual gain. Like a coral reef, every durable ecosystem is an emergent phenomenon.

Self-Organized Criticality

Balanced between order and chaos, a fit being is like a sand pile which, if one more grain of sand is added, may collapse in an avalanche. This fragile equilibrium is called self-organized criticality. The sand pile metaphor, however, is not universally accepted. Also, scientists in many fields noticed in the late 1990s that critical events occur more often—both earlier and later—than forecast in a bell-shaped curve.

Punctuated Equilibrium

The concept of punctuated equilibrium underscores that evolution is often marked by surges of speciation and avalanches of extinction rather than by gradual change.[14] Species often develop quickly, endure with little change for a long time, and then die out suddenly. Thanks to mutation and self-organization, members of the species find their niche and hang on to it. When their environment changes, they must adapt or disappear. The rise, long ascendancy, and decline of the Hanseatic city-states on the Baltic coast, discussed in chapter 2, fits the pattern of punctuated equilibrium.

Fitness Landscapes

Complexity theory suggests that coevolution can be mapped as a rugged landscape in which the relative fitness of each organism exhibits peaks and valleys as a consequence of coevolution. As in an arms race, a predator and its prey may peak or decline according to changes in their offensive and defensive capabilities. If attackers acquire more lethal weapons, the fitness peak of the prey will drop. If individuals among the prey population acquire characteristics that reduce their vulnerability, their peaks will rise.

Indicators of Societal Fitness

For a human society, fitness is the ability to cope with complex challenges and opportunities at home and abroad; to defend society and its values against internal and external threats; and to provide conditions in which its members can choose how to fulfill their human potential.

Fitness is a key ingredient in conversion power—the ability to convert tangible and intangible assets into fitness and influence. Other forms of capital are also important to fitness. Human capital—trained, industrious, and healthy human beings—is both a means to and a measure of fitness. Intellectual capital is the stock of knowledge and infrastructure for using and perpetuating education, science, and technology.

How does fitness differ from power? Like power, fitness has many dimensions. It is a deeper condition from which material, intangible, and other kinds of power and influence can emerge.

Societal fitness must be evaluated relative to conditions at home and across borders. There is no one measure of fitness, such as population growth or energy consumption per capita. Still, a society's infant mortality rate provides a first approximation, for it reflects many dimensions of fitness. As we shall see in chapter 6, the UN Development Programme's Human Development Index (HDI) provides additional standards. The HDI assesses each country's attainments in physical health, education, purchasing power, gender equality, and other indicators of justice. A society with a low infant mortality rate and a high HDI is fitter than a society with high infant mortality and a low HDI.

Human fitness is jeopardized by authoritarian rule. Communist systems led the twentieth century in demicide (killing one's own people), genocide (killing another people), and politicide (killing political foes). Among the peoples who suffered from Soviet mass murders were Balts, Ukrainians, Kazaks, and Chechens.[15]

A society may be internally fit but weak in the international arena. Overall fitness requires a capacity to defend against external threats and, in a world where peace is indivisible, to contribute to collective security.

The fitness of regional and global systems can be judged by their ability to foster peace, economic well-being, justice, liberty, cultural and spiritual development, and environmental health. A world system in which many people die needlessly lacks fitness. Humanity in the twentieth century suffered more than a hundred million deaths from war and even more from demicide. Even these losses pale next to the damage to public health resulting from underdevelopment, racial and ethnic discrimination, and gender bias.[16]

A system in which millions—indeed, billions—of people are at risk from violent death also lacks fitness. If even a fraction of the U.S. or Russian nuclear arsenals were fired, millions would die. Even more millions would become ill from the effects of radiation and pollution. Nuclear winter might set in.

Fitness requires some order and some freedom, but a fit society avoids the Scylla of rigid hierarchy and Charybdis of social chaos.

Liberal Peace Theory: Self-Organization, Trade, Law, Hospitality

Development requires peace. Both thrive on self-organization. The logic of liberal peace theory was set forth in 1795–1796 by Immanuel Kant, who lived in the former Hanseatic port town of Königsberg. The key to peace, Kant argued, was "republican" or representative government—not monarchy or direct democracy (then convulsing France).

Representative government can be an oligarchy (government of the few) or democratic (government of the many).[17] Either way, republicanism is synergistic: it contributes to and gains from international organization and law, the spirit of trade, and an enlightened culture of mutual respect. Peoples that *perceive* one another as sharing republican values have seldom if ever fought each other. Indeed, in the twentieth century they often banded together and usually prevailed against dictatorships. As we shall see in chapter 2, many of Kant's postulates were approximated by the Hanseatic city-states that dominated Baltic life for many centuries. Kant's views on these matters illuminate Balts' efforts since 1991 to build a civil society and join the united democracies of the North Atlantic.[18]

Whereas Kant expected peace to arise from below, his neighbor and peer, Vasilii F. Malinovskii called in 1803 for an authoritarian peace imposed from the top down. A retired Russian diplomat, Malinovskii wrote and taught in another Baltic port city, St. Petersburg. He advocated a league of Europe's states (including Russia) to enforce collective security. His ideas adumbrated the Holy Alliance proposed by Tsar Alexander I in 1815.[19]

Kant endorsed self-organization, Malinovskii top-down organization. Experience backs Kant. Societies based on self-rule are geared to mutual gain. Democratic societies have created for their members the highest living standards in history. The top twenty-five countries on the Human Development Index (HDI) in the late 1990s were all democracies. Authoritarian regimes tend to be exploitative. They seek power and/or wealth for the rulers and the state rather than for their subjects. The authoritarian USSR was more fit for war than for peace. Still suffering from extremes of authoritarianism and anarchy, Russia placed sixty-second in world HDI rankings in 1998—below many "developing" countries.

POLICY IMPLICATIONS: MUTUAL GAIN THEORY

Complexity theory converges with liberal peace theory and a normative theory of mutual gain grounded in interdependence. The synthesis of these theories suggests that a fit society is likely to be *self-organized* for the mutual gain of its members and, as international conditions permit, with other societies. In principle a society or an international system could also be organized for the common good from the top down by an enlightened despot, but this is unlikely. An enlightened despot's vision will probably be myopic due to vested interests and ignorance of local strengths and problems.

Humans can choose whether to go it alone or cooperate with neighbors. They may seek to create values with others for mutual gain or to claim and seize values for private gain.[20] "Value-claiming" signifies an effort to treat other actors as though life were a zero-sum game in which one side's gains must equal the other's losses. By contrast, "value-creating" assumes that the pie can be expanded, permitting each side to gain ever more.

Mutual gain theory suggests that political actors are more likely to enhance their objectives if they can frame and implement value-creating strategies aimed at mutual gain than if they pursue one-sided gain. Policies oriented to conditional cooperation are more likely to enhance an actor's interests than are those exploiting others' vulnerabilities. But cooperation depends upon reciprocity—promoted by self-interest, sanctions, and safeguards.

The time frame in which exploitation can pay becomes ever shorter. Thus, the Hanseatic traders monopolized Baltic trade and lived as a privileged class in city-states such as Tallinn and Riga for centuries. The Soviet regime managed to exploit its subjects for several generations. In a world of escalating interdependence, profitable exploitation is difficult to sustain longer than, say, a decade.

To assess the theories outlined in this chapter, let us review "who did what to whom" or "with whom" on the amber coast across the second millennium.

Caption for Chapter 1 Photo: Balts used nonviolent resistance to transform their lives and cultivate what complexity theorists call "self-organization." This girl took part in the Song of Estonia Festival in September 1988 along with more than 250,000 other persons—a quarter of the native Estonian population.

The first Estonian national song festival was organized in Tartu in 1869; the first Latvian in Riga in 1873; the first Lithuanian in 1924—delayed by an Imperial Russian ban on publishing materials in the Lithuanian language and then by World War I. "Songs of the nation, sounds of the nation!—Come out of the darkness of forgetfulness into the light. You seize the patriot's heart. . . . You are the living history of the Latvian nation." These words by Latvian commentator Varaidosu Sanders applied to Estonian and Lithuanian music as well.

NOTES

1. Jerry F. Hough, *Democratization and Revolution in the USSR, 1985–1991* (Washington, D.C.: Brookings, 1997), p. 490.

2. Amber is a hard, translucent fossil resin valued for jewelry. The region's connection with the wider world is illustrated by the fact that the word "amber" comes from the Arabic *'ambar*. Baltic amber was sought by Romans at the time of Christ.

3. Russians call the major lake separating today's Estonia and Russia *Chudskoe* from *chud'* [a collective name for Finnic peoples] and *chudo* [miracle]. For Russians, the Estonians and other Finns were *chudskie*—strange and terrifying.

4. *Ostsee* also echoed the German *osti* for the peoples of the eastern Baltic region, the Estonian *eesti*, and Latin *aesti*, which Romans applied to several Baltic peoples.

5. Nicolai Petro, "The Novgorod Region: A Russian Success Story," *Post-Soviet Affairs* 15, no. 3 (1999), pp. 235–61 at 254–56.

6. Sweden's state church decreed in 1686 that everyone—including children, farmhands, and maidservants—should "learn to read and see with their own eyes what God bids and commands in His Holy Word." Most Swedes learned to read within their own families, for there were few schools. By 1740 nearly all Swedes, male and female, could read (but not write)—almost 160 years before general literacy was achieved in England. Egil Johansson, "The History of Literacy in Sweden," in *Literacy and Social Development in the West: A Reader,* ed. Harvey J. Graff (Cambridge: Cambridge University Press, 1981), pp. 151–82 at 157, 180. In the 1990s the UN Development Programme found gender equality in Sweden to be highest in the world.

7. Other worldviews can also foster a "Protestant work ethic," even if they are not Christian. Thus, many Japanese and Chinese find in their own cultures reasons to strive, save, invest, and plan for material success. Every "achieving society" socializes its children to believe that they should work and that work will be rewarded. David C. McClelland, *The Achieving Society* (Princeton: D. Van Nostrand, 1961). For a listing of works by Max Weber and others on these topics, see Lawrence E. Harrison, *Underdevelopment As a State of Mind* (Lanham, Md.: Madison, 1985).

8. How all this happened—indeed, *whether* it happened—is debated. Did—could—provincial clergy and teachers make European intellectual and spiritual movements resonate for Baltic peasants and workers? If ideas determine political action, how is it that the epicenter of the Renaissance later gave birth to Mussolini? Of the Reformation, Hitler? Of the Enlightenment, Robespierre? See Jack F. Matlock Jr., "The Poor Neighbor," review of Martin Malia's *Russia under Western Eyes* in the *New York Times Book Review,* April 11, 1999, p. 11.

9. Still, for the next three centuries the formerly anti-Lithuanian, Germanic Prussia became the main source of native Lithuanian literature and, in the nineteenth century, a haven for Lithuanians from Russification. See V. Stanley Vardys and Judith B. Sedaitis, *Lithuania: The Rebel Nation* (Boulder, Co.: Westview, 1997), pp. 15–16.

10. Benedict Anderson, *Imagined Communities: Reflections on the Spread of Nationalism,* rev. ed. (London: Verso, 1991).

11. Steven J. Pierson, "We Sang Ourselves Free: Musical Experience and Development among Christian Estonians from Repression to Independence," paper presented at the Conference on Baltic Studies in Europe held at Södertörns University College, Sweden, in July 1999.

12. Interdependent actors are linked so closely that a change in the conditions or policies of one actor will impact the other in ways that it cannot easily change. Sensitivity means liability to costly effects imposed from outside before any policies are devised to cope with the new situation. Vulnerability means continued liability to costly effects imposed from outside despite efforts to alter or escape the situation. See Robert O. Keohane and Joseph S. Nye, *Power and Interdependence,* 2d ed. (New York: HarperCollins, 1989), chap. 1. Kenneth Waltz, however, argues that to accept interdependence as sensitivity guts the term of any political meaning.

13. The following interpretation of complexity theory is based on the work of Stuart Kauffman and other scholars—from Nobel physics laureate Murray Gell-Mann to Nobel economics laureate Kenneth Arrow—who have interacted at the Santa Fe Institute. For references, see section XII in the selected references at the end of this book.

14. See Stephen Jay Gould, *Wonderful Life: The Burgess Shale and the Nature of History* (New York: Norton, 1989).

15. Rudolph J. Rummel, *Lethal Politics: Soviet Genocide and Mass Murder since 1917* (New Brunswick, N.J.: Transaction, 1996).

16. The death toll from the twentieth century's wars amounted to 1.2 million lives per year, a little more than 2 percent of the total average death rate of 55 million per year. This cut less than 1.5 years from the present world life expectancy of 65 years.

U.S. life expectancy grew by more than twenty years in the twentieth century. But poor people in the United States lived ten years less than middle- and upper-income groups, and blacks lived a few years less than whites. Philip Morrison and Kosta Tsipis, *Reason Enough to Hope: America and the World of the Twenty-first Century* (Cambridge, Mass.: MIT Press, 1998), p. 26.

17. This distinction is made by Spencer R. Waert, who uses it to sift history from ancient Greece to the twentieth century. See his *Never at War: Democracies Will Not Fight One Another* (New York: Yale University Press, 1998). The subtitle should read "why neither oligarchies nor democracies will fight other oligarchies or other democracies." The seminal articles on liberal peace by Michael W. Doyle are amplified in his *Ways of War and Peace: Realism, Liberalism, and Socialism* (New York: Norton, 1997).

18. Text in Immanuel Kant, *Perpetual Peace and Other Essays* (Indianapolis: Hackett, 1983), pp. 107–143.

19. V. F. Malinovskii, *Rassuzhdenie o mire i voine,* completed in 1798. Two of the three parts were published in 1803 and republished in *Traktaty o vechnom mire,* I. S. Andreeva and A. V. Gulyga, eds. (Moscow: Izdatel'stvo sotsial'no-ekonomicheskoi literatury, 1963), pp. 213–54. The third part was later published in Poland and Italy. See Paola Ferretti, *A Russian Advocate of Peace: Vasilii Malinovskii (1765–1814)* (Dordrecht: Kluwer Academic, 1998).

20. The terms *value-claiming* and *value-creating* were developed at the Harvard University Negotiation Roundtable. See David A. Lax and James K. Sebenius, *The Manager as Negotiator: Bargaining for Cooperation and Competitive Gain* (New York: Free Press, 1986).

2

Self-Organization versus Autocracy: Crusaders to Commissars

Complexity theory contends that order emerges spontaneously—"for free"—among all the constituents of life, from quarks to fruit flies to human societies. Adding to this optimistic view, others contend that biology imprints in all humans a quest for order—in family life and in society at large. The proclivity to cooperate is encoded in our genes.[1]

But the human record belies these cheerful assurances. Surely genes do not dictate either cooperation or aggression. Humans behave in diverse ways. They are malleable. They can build and cooperate with or exploit and even destroy one another. Humans can be mobilized from the top down or by self-organization or not at all.

No government or society is perfect, but some are fitter than others. Good government and fitness are relative—not absolutes. They are points on a spectrum. World history—including many centuries of Baltic experience—shows that governments often fail to make even moderately good use of their resources. To be sure, some societies master complex challenges, and gain from doing so, but many others do not. Some societies meet certain kinds of challenges but not others.

NONSTATE ACTORS AND STATES IN BALTIC LIFE

Many forms of social life appeared and disappeared on the amber coast in the second millennium. Their diversity and varying longevity illustrate the many ways that humans can organize their lives. Not until the twentieth century was the nation-state an ideal pursued by many actors.

Previewing this chapter, table 2.1 lists the main actors on the Baltic stage from the Viking era until the breakdown of the Soviet empire. It ranks their fitness—high, medium, or low—relative to the resources available to them, and the extent to which they practiced self-organization. Explanations of the rankings are in the text that follows.

Table 2.1
Fitness on the Amber Coast: Correlations with Self-Organization

Actors	Self-Organization	Fitness
Vikings/Varangians	M	M
Estonian and Latvian tribes	L	L
Teutonic Knights	M	M
Hanseatic towns	H	H
Lithuania before 1569	M	M
Swedish absolutism in 17th century	L	H
Polish Republic in 18th century	L	L
Tsarist Empire	L	L–M
Baltic republics in 1920s–1930s	M	L–M
Soviet Empire	L-M	M

H = high, M = medium, L = low

FITNESS ON THE AMBER COAST: CORRELATIONS WITH SELF-ORGANIZATION

With several important exceptions, the fittest actors relied heavily on self-organization, the least fit on commands and coercion. The least fit resided in a rigid order that sometimes turned into chaos. The fittest actors operated near the apex of a bell curve between order and chaos. But the table highlights a paradox: only two actors received high fitness rankings, yet they followed opposite routes. The Hansas enhanced their fitness by self-organization, seventeenth century Sweden by top-down but enlightened absolutism.

THEORY MEETS REALITY: BACKGROUND

Vikings/Varangians

Scandinavians interacted with Baltic peoples long before the Vikings emerged in the eighth and ninth centuries. But Vikings were driven by energies and ambitions greater than their ancestors. Vikings/Varangians passed through the eastern Baltic in search of booty and trade in Kazaria, Byzantium, Baghdad, and beyond. They imposed tributary regimes on Balts late in the first millennium. On several occasions Balts threw off these regimes, but the Scandinavians returned with greater force. Seeking bigger game to the south, however, Varangians did little to disturb life on the amber coast. Some Varangians halted in northern Russia—with Slavic and Estonian cooperation or acquiescence—and turned Novgorod into a vital commercial center linking Europe with Eurasia.

By many measures the Vikings/Varangians were immensely fit. Their ability to cope with complexity is underscored if we consider the harsh habitat from which they emerged, the rough waters and passages they traveled, and the limited numbers with which they confronted and often mastered more settled societies. But the Viking way of life lasted only a few centuries. Wherever Vikings traveled, except Iceland, they assimilated—losing their religion as well as their language.

How Vikings decided to embark on long journeys, when to fight, and when to trade is not clear. Exploring alien and often hostile lands, Vikings probably depended even more on top-down leadership than those Scandinavians who farmed and fished at home.

Finnic, Baltic, and Slavic Tribes

At the onset of the second millennium the local players in the eastern Baltic were ethnic groups—tribes—rather than states. The Finnic and Baltic peoples did not hold their ground against Slavs and Germanic peoples who pushed them into the narrow confines of the amber coast and then, in turns, dominated them for some eight hundred years. This brute fact says that most Balts were less fit than their encroaching neighbors. Estonian, Latvian, and most other tribes on the amber coast were subjugated by invaders from the north and west; some tribes, such as the Old Prussians, disappeared—killed or assimilated by others. The exception were the Lithuanian tribes, who united and formed one of Europe's most powerful states for several centuries until they too were subdued.

Still, Estonians and Latvians as well as Lithuanians were sufficiently fit to inhabit the eastern Baltic for at least two thousand years before Christ and to survive until the twentieth century, when they formed states. Their fitness is underscored by numbers: there were more speakers of Estonian, Latvian, and Lithuanian in the late twentieth century than at any time in history. Thus, at the height of Lithuanian power (approximately 1350–1430), there were probably about 590,000 ethnic Lithuanians; when Russia absorbed Lithuania in 1795, this number had increased to about 1,540,000; it reached 2,000,000 in 1923; and, despite losses in the 1940s, some 4,000,000 as the twentieth century ended—including more than 1,000,000 abroad.[2] Similar growth trajectories characterized Latvians and Estonians.[3]

The Baltic peoples before 1200 represented a military culture in which young men and aspiring chieftains demonstrated their courage and ability in raids against their neighbors. They took booty and slaves. They believed that their pagan gods justified this militarism: the gods had to approve every expedition; the gods shared in the booty; they welcomed the dead who rode straight to them from the funeral pyre. When Viking energies subsided, raiders from the eastern Baltic raided Denmark; in 1187 they burned the capital of Sweden.

Why were Baltic tribes vulnerable to outside domination? Many tribes exalted violence and bravery. Communist historians have referred to the Baltic peoples as "military democracies."[4] But this is a romanticized misnomer. They were closer to *military oligarchies*. Elders and large landowners made the big decisions, which the mass of tenant farmers followed. Most Balts identified with their own village and clan— not with their own language group or some other larger principle.

Discord among Baltic peoples helped foreigners—from Scandinavia, Germany, and later from Russia—to divide and conquer. Relations between Baltic peoples were not cooperative. There was a kind of pecking order: Estonians bullied Latvians, while Lithuanians raided both Estonians and Latvians. Lithuanian tribes were reported to have captured more than a thousand slaves in a single battle, later selling some to Byzantine and Turkish traders.[5]

When German and other crusaders besieged the amber coast in the thirteenth century, Balts showed little solidarity with one another. By contrast, Swiss cantons fighting the Habsburgs at that time had the political wit to submerge their political, cultural, religious, and linguistic differences. Balts seldom did. As a result, they could not raise the money or men needed to build forts far from their fields, and they could not wage preventive war or initiate preemptive attacks. Tribal leaders often failed to persuade clan elites to surrender power to them.

Lack of social differentiation and central political direction made it difficult for Baltic tribes to defend against encroachments from outside. These conditions also impeded development of advanced military technologies. Orientation toward one's own village made it difficult to organize extensive and reliable cross-village strategic cooperation.[6]

The subjugation of Baltic tribes by outside forces was far more total than that contemporaneously suffered by the patrimonial principalities of Russia. Baltic organization was rudimentary. Because social roles overlap in tribal societies, change—when it comes—tends to overthrow the old ways. Outsiders, when they take control, tend to rule from the top down rather than depend on local agents. In contrast to the Baltic peoples, when Russians paid tribute to the Golden Horde, Moscow and other Russian principalities continued to live in their familiar ways.

In 1342–1343, however, many Estonians rose up against Danish-German rule and religion. So individualistic were the Estonians that, instead of uniting behind one commander-in-chief, they chose four local "kings" to lead the revolt. The Estonians nonetheless destroyed Danish control outside Tallinn, but were eventually crushed by the German knights, who then purchased northern Estonia from the Danish king. The revolt failed in part because Estonians in some regions did not take part and because help from Sweden, arranged in advance, arrived too late.[7] Also, as noted below, Lithuania's grand duke spurned Estonian overtures for collaboration.

Most Baltic tribes failed to cope with the complex challenges to their security. Their internal order was too rigid. The class structure of haves and have-nots prevented tapping the full energies of each tribe. Their "us-first" orientation blinded them to possibilities of strategic cooperation among kinfolk and neighboring tribes. A value-claiming orientation led to myopia and, in time, servitude. The Swiss Forest cantons, by contrast, fought off outsiders and never made war on each other—a model of democratic peace for hundreds of years.

The Baltic Crusades: A Knightly-Clerical-Mercantile Consortium

Crusader orders of monk-knights, most of them German-speakers, conquered and governed the amber coast for centuries. They blended top-down centralization with some self-organization. The Brothers of the Sword Order was founded in 1202 to protect missionaries and merchants in Livonia—what is now Latvia and Estonia; protect converts to Christianity; and repress if not extirpate piracy, highway robbery, polygamy, infanticide, human sacrifice, and worship of pagan gods.

Blessed by a distant pope and Holy Roman Emperor, the Sword Brothers relied fundamentally on their own wits and muscles. The Livonian knights elected a grand master (*Hochmeister*) who, in turn, appointed a supreme bailiff and other top officials responsible for logistics, finances, and hospitals and consulted with them on important decisions.[8] Western technology, organization, and ideology helped the knights to vanquish rapidly the tribal peoples living in what is now Latvia and Estonia. When the knights moved southward, however, their advance spurred Lithuanian tribes to unite. The tribes defeated the Sword Brothers in 1236. More than five hundred years passed before the Lithuanians too fell to Germanic and Russian onslaughts.

Another crusading order, the Teutonic Knights, was founded in 1190–1991 in the Holy Land. Driven from Jerusalem, they were invited by a Polish duke in 1226 to put down the people now called Old Prussians. Fighting for some fifty years, the knights wiped out or enserfed the Old Prussians, took their land, and invited settlers from Germany.

The realm of the German knights became one of the best administered polities of the Middle Ages. The knights' grand master was not only a territorial lord in Prussia, but the sovereign head of an ecclesiastico-political institution whose activities extended from the Mediterranean through all of Europe. The Order organized efficient mail services and intelligence gathering, for example, on the rise and fall of Jeanne d'Arc. The Order's representatives at the Vatican were among the first standing ambassadors in Europe.[9]

Following their defeat by the Lithuanians in 1236, the Livonian Knights merged with the Teutonic Order to their west. Lithuanian territory separated the two orders, however, and each remained a separate state. The Livonians' eastward expansion was stopped in 1242 by Prince Alexander Nevsky of Novgorod in a battle on the ice of Lake Pcipsi between today's Estonia and Russia.

Initially alien rule was tempered by expediency: the knights needed Balts to fight with them as well as to till the fields. Within a few centuries, however, the knights and their vassal landlords enserfed native Balts—sometimes selling them like cattle. What the vassals gained, the yeomen lost.

No other German state in the fourteenth and fifteenth centuries could rival the Order in political or economic power. The knight-monks often partnered with the Hanseatic towns and shared with them a German-speakers' community of interests. The Order backed Hanseatic merchants abroad in ways the Holy Roman Emperor no longer could. The Order's grand master in 1451 was addressed in England as head of the Hanseatic League.

The knights and the merchants in Tallinn, Riga, and other Baltic towns such as Gdansk shared an interest in trade: grain from the knights' estates filled the cargo ships sailing from Baltic ports to London, Edinburgh, Boston, Bruges, and even Cadiz. But the knights overreached. They received permission from the pope to engage in trade, not for a profit, but to overcome their poverty. When the knights encroached, merchants in the port towns complained and began to buy grain directly from those yeomen who still controlled their own produce. Some Hanseatic towns even sided with Lithuanians and Poles against the Order. And some bishops objected to the increasingly brutal treatment of the peasants by the knights.

At times the amber coast was a confused condominium in which many actors asserted their rights—the knightly orders, bishops (local and Scandinavian), town councils, provincial assemblies, overseas potentates—all subject to a distant pope and, under him, the Holy Roman Emperor. Such chaos splintered Germanic unity.

The Order was often at odds with Riga's archbishop and the town's merchants.

Tallinn and its overlord for many years, the faraway king of Denmark, usually backed Riga against the knights. The knights were strong militarily, but Riga had a trump card: it could align with the pagan Lithuanians against the Order.

When war erupted between Riga and the Order early in the fourteenth century, the two sides agreed to make peace. To arbitrate unresolved issues, the conferees selected the archbishop of Lund. But Riga spurned his judgment and instead negotiated a deal directly with the Order.[10] Riga would buy the Order's fort at the mouth of the Dvina (Daugava in Latvian) River for one thousand silver marks and promise that for one year they would not join the Lithuanians against the Order or sign a peace treaty with the Lithuanians without the Order's approval. Both sides agreed in the future to make common cause against the pagans and do nothing harmful to each other. A year later, however, Riga again allied with the Lithuanians against the knights, who had retaken the fort.[11]

Such internecine struggles persisted among the Germans.[12] They weakened the Order and facilitated its defeats by combined Lithuanian-Polish forces in 1410 and again in 1466. The 1466 Treaty of Thorn transferred to Poland full sovereignty over most of west Prussia, leaving only a fragment of east Prussia to the Order. The Order moved its headquarters to Königsberg (after 1945, Kaliningrad).

The Order's death blow came from within: in 1525 the grand master accepted the Reformation, declared Prussia a secular duchy, and was invested as duke by the king of Poland.[13] In Livonia the Sword Brothers held on until the mid-sixteenth century, when Tsar Ivan IV invaded. Soon Livonia was partitioned among Russia, Sweden, and Lithuania-Poland. The Livonian Order was disbanded in 1561; its grand master became the duke of Courland under Lithuanian-Polish suzerainty.

Strange as it may seem, an order of monkish knights acquired fitness sufficient to dominate Baltic life for hundreds of years. The knights transformed the region while keeping their own tongue and values. Their belief that God was on their side gave them courage, but also reinforced their tendency to claim and seize values rather than work with others for mutual gain.

The Hansas

As cities grew larger across Europe, they wanted the grains, timber, wax, skins, and furs abundant in the Baltic region and its Slavic hinterlands. German merchants—*die Hanse,* as they came to be known—transported heavy cargos in the largest type ship of the time, *die Kogge,* with a shallow draft (useful in rivers) but much sturdier than Viking craft.[14]

Hanseatic merchants settled in the Baltic, converting port towns such as Tallinn, Riga, and Gdansk into vital hubs in a network of transnational trade.[15] The Hanseatic city-states rose in the twelfth and thirteenth centuries and flourished for some five hundred years—into the seventeenth century. Here was the first European economic community—more than one hundred Hanseatic towns and outposts, led by the cities of Lübeck and Rostock on Germany's northern coast, extending to Novgorod in the east and to London in the west.

The Hansas had four great trading posts (*kontore*): in London for wool and cloth; in Bergen for fish and timber; in Bruges for cloth; and in Novgorod for furs. In Bruges and other Flemish towns, the Baltic traders converged with those from the Mediterranean who brought spices, silks, and fruit.

The Hansas offered the leading model of self-organization in Baltic history, at least until the twentieth century. Their fitness was demonstrated by an ability to master complex challenges at home, regionally, and in distant places. They promoted mutual gain—not just for the merchants who ruled each town but also for those with whom they traded in distant ports. They also benefited some local Estonians and Latvians who, escaping serfdom, became artisans in Hanseatic towns such as Tallinn.

The term "Hansa" meant "flock," but it came to apply to the foreign trade merchants, mostly Germanic, who banded together in the Baltic Sea and beyond to promote their mutual security and commercial interests.[16] Had a stronger German state existed, the Hansas would have had neither the need nor the freedom to act as they did. But they served as the merchant class of the Holy Roman Empire. They sought market access—not territory. They armed for defense—not for attack. For the Hansas, international relations were trade—not war.

The merchants helped to break the rigid ways of medieval Europe. They resided in towns—"nonfeudal islands in a feudal world."[17] The Hanseatic city-states were virtually independent from the principalities, kingdoms, and empires that struggled for power in other parts of Europe and Russia.

The Hansas embodied some features that Immanuel Kant forecast in his booklet, *On Perpetual Peace* (1795–1796), would generate perpetual peace. They lived by the "spirit of commerce" and supported the development of law and cosmopolitan ways. Their politics were neither republican nor authoritarian. Each town was governed by a patriarchate elected by the top merchant families. The system's rigidity sometimes spawned revolt as up-and-coming merchants and prosperous artisans sought admission to the ruling class. The ruling class responded by coopting a few of the rebels, who then deserted their fellows.[18]

Peace prevailed among the Hanseatic republics for three and a half centuries. The Hansas, like the Swiss Forest Brother cantons and nations of the Iroquois Confederation, never fought one another. The Hanseatic republics were not democracies but oligarchies, but they shared a set of common commercial values and respect for the law—*das Recht*—the legal code of Lübeck or a variant thereof.

The seal of Lübeck depicted a ship on which stood two men taking an oath—symbolizing the republican myth of a sworn community of equals in a lordless wilderness. Indeed, the cities of Lübeck and Hamburg swore in 1230 to treat each other's citizens under identical legal conditions. Commerce made for peace and peace made for commerce. The Hansa city-states extended their common domestic legal order—its ideals and practices—to the "international" relations among them.

If Hanseatic states could not resolve their disputes by direct negotiation or by mediation (for example, by another Hanseatic city-state), they submitted the issue to the judgment of a Hanseatic assembly. Hanseatic cities fought, usually in self-defense, against every kind of neighboring autocracy. But they maintained peaceful relations with each other and with other German city oligarchies in the Rhineland and with Dutch republics.[19]

When the shopkeepers and artisans of Braunschweig seized power from the ruling

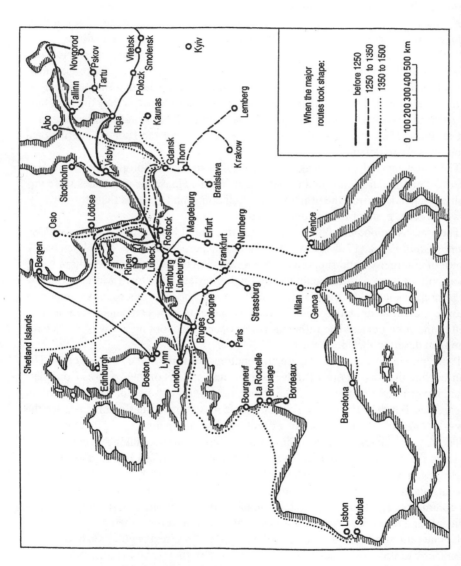

The expansion of Hanseatic trade from before 1250 to 1500. Adapted from Klaus Friedland, *Die Hanse* (Stuttgart: Kohlhammer, 1991), p. 223.

Map labels:

Shetland Islands

Bergen, Oslo, Lödöse, Stockholm, Åbo, Tallinn, Novgorod, Pskov, Tartu, Vitebsk, Smolensk, Polozk, Riga, Visby, Kaunas, Lemberg, Kyiv

Edinburgh, Boston, Lynn, London, Ripen, Lübeck, Rostock, Hamburg, Lüneburg, Magdeburg, Erfurt, Nürnberg, Gdansk, Thorn, Bratislava, Krakow

Bruges, Cologne, Frankfurt, Strassburg, Paris, Milan, Genoa, Venice

Bourgneuf, La Rochelle, Brouage, Bordeaux, Barcelona

Lisbon, Setubal

When the major
routes took shape:

— before 1250
--- 1250 to 1350
···· 1350 to 1500

0 100 200 300 400 500 km

patriarchate in the 1370s, oligarchs in other Hanseatic states worried lest mob rule spread. But they did not use military force against Braunschweig. They severed its commercial privileges until economic duress compelled Braunschweigers to modify their regime.

By contrast, the Italian city-states were conflicted at home and with each other. Rival clans and authorities fought each other in Genoa, Pisa, and Florence as vigorously as each city-state fought its rivals.

The German-speaking upper class did little to foster mutual gain with native Balts. German-speakers dominated not only the towns' external trade but also their local artisan guilds, the Church, and local government. No locals joined the clergy until after the Protestant Reformation. But the towns served as a refuge for runaway serfs, many of whom became artisans. Reliable social statistics are hard to come by, but a 1688 census of Tallinn (total population 12,500 to 13,000) showed the upper and middle classes composed mainly of ethnic Germans and a few Swedes; Estonians and a few Swedes made up the lowest class. Of business people and hand workers in Tallinn, only 3 to 4 percent were from Estonia, Latvia, or Courland. The largest percentage of hand workers (19 percent) came from Saxony, while 67 percent of the business people were local Germans, followed by 12 percent from Lübeck.[20]

The towns' major export, grain, came from estates ruled by Germans but worked by the indigenous peoples. The prosperity of the upper-class Hansas trickled down to the German-speaking middle classes, but barely percolated to the natives. Hanseatic fitness and self-organization were formidable, but Hanseatic prosperity depended ultimately on exploitation of native Balts, whom many Germans saw as inferior, even subhuman. Had the Hansas done more to bring native Balts into a system of joint value-creation, the city-states' independence and prosperity would have stood on broader foundations.

Some authors speak of a Hanseatic "League" or "Confederation," but these terms exaggerate the ties binding the Hanseatic city-states. The Hanseatic towns had no unifying covenant, no regular time and place to council, no regular mode of taxation, and no established military force. Still, when confronted with a serious external threat, they often self-organized to meet the challenge.[21]

The Hansas' spirit of commerce, we should also note, did not include free trade. Merchants from different towns sought monopoly control over trade in certain commodities, for example, herring from Norway.[22] More generally, they sought to prevent merchants from non-Hanseatic towns from trading in basic commodities important to Baltic producers and consumers.

In the fifteenth century Hansa patriarchates passed laws to exclude competitors. In Livonia foreigners were at times forbidden to learn Russian, so as to prevent their dealing with the natives of Pskov and Novgorod. Foreigners could not stay in Livonian towns more than three or four months, so no colony could be formed. Foreigners could not become citizens of any Livonian town. Foreign merchants in Novgorod were prohibited from entering joint ventures with Russians.[23]

Hansa efforts to prevent foreigners from trading in the Baltic achieved some successes in the fifteenth century but eventually failed. They backfired when rivals such as Amsterdam and London became powerful and ended the privileges once extended to Hanseatic merchants.

But size *plus* organization is an advantage. As European kingdoms became larger and better organized, the Hanseatic towns found it harder to maintain their independence and to compete in commerce. Threatened by Denmark and Poland, Tallinn put itself under Swedish protection in 1561. Enriched by the Dutch East Indies, Amsterdam became far richer and more powerful than Lübeck or Gdansk. The Americas, revealed by Columbus, promised riches far greater than Baltic grain. Hanseatic towns and their hinterlands were attacked and wasted by invaders in the Thirty Years War (1618–1648) and the Great Northern War (1700–1721).

In the seventeenth century the Hansa towns lost their vitality and their independence. They fell to the monarchs of Poland, Prussia, or Russia. They were not invited to sign the 1648 Treaty of Westphalia. The Hanseatic diet met one last time in 1669, but Hanseatic were never formally dissolved. In the 1990s Riga and Tallinn boldly recalled their Hanseatic past; Hamburg and Bremen boasted that they were Hanseatic Free Cities.

Lithuania and Poland

In the second millennium Lithuanians met challenges better and maintained their independence much longer than the other Baltic peoples. In the thirteenth century Lithuanian tribes formed a duchy. This state became an empire, then a confederation, and then a junior partner to Poland. With Poland's partition, Lithuania was submerged in the Russian empire, but it reemerged independent in the 1920s–1930s. It became a Soviet "union-republic" for half a century but regained independence in 1990–1991.

Even before Christian missionaries and knights landed on the Baltic coast, Lithuanians were regional hegemons. They bullied neighbors to the west and north and pressed against Slavic peoples to the east and south. Unlike Latvians and Estonians, the Lithuanians banded together and kept the German crusaders at bay.

Lithuanians were shielded by their forested, often marshy perimeter—what Germans called the *Wildnis*—difficult for outsiders to penetrate and master. Lithuania benefited also from an influx of skilled warriors fleeing Germans, Muscovites, or Tatars.

Lithuania took part in the great game between Teuton and Slav, Catholic and Orthodox, European and Mongolian, pope and "Holy Roman" emperor. Lithuanians' maneuvers, however, were complicated by their clan-based infighting. Some Lithuanians allied with Muscovy, others allied with the Tatars fighting Slavs, and some others with German crusaders.

Still, the pressure to cooperate against the Sword Brothers in the north and the Teutonic Knights in the west goaded Lithuanian tribal leaders in 1253 to form a kingdom—later a dukedom. Lithuanian diplomacy relied on force and an opportunistic realpolitik—allying with others against foes, jumping on the winners' bandwagon, dividing the opposition. The grand duke married his offspring to control rival princedoms. Lithuanian rulers repeatedly used the prospect that they would accept Christianity to win favors from Catholic and Orthodox powers. The West saw Lithuania as a buffer against the East; the Orthodox realm saw it as protection from the West.

In the fourteenth century Lithuania became a multicultural empire under Grand Duke Gediminas (scion of a family that ruled Lithuania and later Poland from about 1289 until 1572). From his citadel in Vilnius, Gediminas governed not only ethnic

Lithuanians but also Slavs in the western principalities of Orthodox Rus'. Vilnius ruled more Rus'ian territory than did Muscovy. The grand duke's realm straddled the major trade routes between the Baltic Sea and the rivers Dvina and Dnepr. He taxed the traffic in food, iron, horses, and wax and used this income to fuel his military campaigns. A *pax lithuanica* safeguarded the commercial routes between northern Germany and Rus' and between the Christian-pagan Baltic and Muslim Tatar Black Sea. Across the river from the Lithuanian outpost in Kyiv was camped the Golden Horde.

Lithuania's openness to other cultures helped it attract traders, artisans, and scholars from other lands. Many of the duke's subjects followed the Orthodox Church in Constantinople, but the Lithuanian realm promised room for Catholic missionaries from the West. In the second half of the fourteenth century ducal documents in Vilnius were written by Orthodox scribes in a west Rus'ian dialect, in part because the duke had to deal with Rus'ian political and church leaders.[24]

Cultural and political lines hardened in the fourteenth century. In 1385 Lithuania's rulers opted for a dynastic union with Poland and for Roman Catholic Christianity. The Lithuanian Grand Duke Jogalia, a grandson of Gediminas, married the ten-year-old queen of Poland and became Wladyslaw II Jagiello.

The Jagiellan dynasty lasted until 1572—nearly two hundred years. The Polish and Lithuanian states held sway from Silesia to Smolensk, from the Baltic Sea to the Black Sea. Partnership with Poland brought some geopolitical gains to Lithuania, but also real costs. The duke's acceptance of Catholicism alienated many of his pagan subjects and his Orthodox subjects to the east. Lithuania's cultural fitness suffered. The alliance with Poland cost Lithuania its pagan faith and led to the Polonization of the ruling classes, who embraced not just Roman Catholicism but the Polish language. Lithuania's class structure also came to emulate that of the Baltic barons in Courland.[25]

Lithuania failed to balance its eastern and western traditions and still maintain a national identity. This failure left its mark in the 1990s as Lithuanians glorified their military past *and* portrayed themselves as perpetual victims.

Another problem: the Protestant-Catholic split in the sixteenth century put the Baltic peoples on different trajectories that endured into the twenty-first century.[26] The Catholic Counter Reformation curtailed Protestant inroads in Poland and Lithuania, while most other Baltic peoples became Protestant.

As Sweden and Russia became stronger in the sixteenth century, and as the Jagiellan dynasty had no heir, Lithuania drew closer to Poland. The 1569 Union of Lublin established a confederation often called the Polish-Lithuanian Commonwealth. Both the Polish and Lithuanian terms for this entity, however, were translations of the Latin *res publica—Rzeczpospolita* and *Zecpospolita*. Though Lithuania remained nominally independent, it had to transfer to Polish control some western lands and the southern half of the Lithuanian empire, including Ukraine.

The 1569 Union specified joint Lithuanian/Polish *sejms* (diets) that elected the king of Poland, who was also the grand duke of Lithuania. When the last Jagiellan died, the next kings-dukes elected were foreigners: first, a French prince, then a Hungarian, and then a scion of Sweden's Vasa dynasty. The Swedish connection triggered more than half a century of warfare, beginning in 1599, between the Catholic Commonwealth and Protestant Swedes, each of whom tried to subdue if not convert the other.

Sweden and Poland fought over Livonia. Sweden took Narva in 1581 and dominated the trade routes to Novgorod and Pskov, while Poland in 1582 occupied Riga and southern Livonia. Soon, the Swedish-Polish rivalry extended all the way to Muscovy, where a succession crisis generated a "Time of Troubles" from 1598 to 1613. Poland backed pretender claimants to the Kremlin throne in 1605 and, more forcefully, in 1608–1611. Some Russians invited the son of the Polish king to take the throne in 1611. Unwilling to see Poland gain power, Sweden promised relief to Muscovy. But the Polish *sejm* decided the matter: it would not pay for the mercenaries needed to occupy Russian lands. The succession crisis ended in 1613 when Russian nobles installed a Romanov on the Kremlin throne, but Polish forces threatened Muscovy once more in 1618.

While Sweden became more powerful in the seventeenth century, the Commonwealth's fitness withered. Few Polish or Lithuanian nobles adjusted creatively to complex challenges at home or abroad. The nobles' greatest experiment in self-rule was the *liberum veto,* which allowed any representative to block a law, dissolve the *sejm,* and annul its previous decisions. Deputies applied this privilege recklessly in the seventeenth and eighteenth centuries. Paralyzed, the *sejm* could not take the decisions needed to cope with peasant uprisings and with external attack from all directions. A constitutional reform in 1791 came too late.

Both Poland and Lithuania soon disappeared from the map. In 1772, 1793, and 1795 Russia, Prussia, and Austria partitioned the Commonwealth. They compelled Poles and Lithuanians to live under alien rule for more than a century. Indeed, Russian authorities sought intermittently in the nineteenth century to obliterate Lithuanian language and culture.

In 1918–1920 an independent Poland and an independent Lithuania emerged from the ruins of three empires. When Poland seized Vilnius in 1920, however, the unresolved conflict prevented Lithuania and Poland from cooperating against threats from the east and the west. As in the mid-sixteenth century, there was no obvious hegemon in the eastern Baltic after World War I. Germany proper was separated from East Prussia by the free city of Danzig and the Polish corridor. In 1939, however, Berlin and Moscow again partitioned Poland and Baltic lands.

In the 1940s Lithuania became a Soviet union-republic and Poland after 1945 became a Soviet client state. Anti-Soviet Poles and Lithuanians again found themselves on the same side. Poles stepped forward boldly in the 1970s and early 1980s; Lithuanians did so in the late 1980s, having learned something about nonviolent resistance from Poland's "Solidarity" movement—a model of self-organization against repression. Each country regained real independence with the demise of the USSR.

Swedish Absolutism

In the wake of the Protestant Reformation Sweden filled the vacuum left by the collapse of the German knightly orders before an expanding Russia could do so. Starting in 1561, Sweden dominated large reaches of the Baltic's southern and eastern shores until driven back by Peter the Great in 1710–1721.

Swedish kings understood the importance of the Baltic provinces: they would be a granary for Sweden, a source of revenue and of manufactures, and a barrier to Russian expansion. Dominion over the Baltic provinces would permit Sweden to control trade between Europe and Eurasia.[27]

Swedish rule on the amber coast sharply qualifies the thesis that self-organization is more effective than autocracy. The Swedish kings were modernizers: they did much to break feudal restraints and give greater power to government bureaucrats and to the rising bourgeoisie. Absolutist kings promoted a modern state with an educated population. Sweden required all its subjects to become literate. In the language of complexity theory, the Swedish monarchy sought to upgrade the fitness of its subjects at home and abroad (including New Sweden in America) and create values generally—not just claim values for royal enrichment. Its doctrine was "cameralism"—the idea that a state must be strong to protect the interests of all subjects. In Tallinn, for example, Swedish King Charles XI in 1687 abolished the city council and autonomous guilds and gave full powers to a trusted mayor.[28]

An authoritarian state aims to provides stability against the forces of chaos. But an enlightened authoritarianism, oriented to creating new values, can do more: it can relegate a decrepit order to the dust bin of history. The Swedish kings tried to do so, though their actions often fell short of their aspirations.

Enlightened absolutism is not self-organization. Indeed, the Swedish kings labored to weaken the self-organization of feudal lords.[29] But Swedish absolutism opened the way to self-rule at a later stage.[30] This was the sort of enlightened despotism of which Malinovskii dreamed a century later in St. Petersburg, but did not get.

In the 1680s King Charles XI imposed the "Great Reduction." He seized more than half the lands controlled by the German lords in Estonia and Latvia. The king declared that the peasants on his estates were no longer the personal property of the landlords but the subjects of the king. Sweden increased grain levies, thus creating more burdens for peasants, but loosened the bonds of serfdom in the Baltic provinces. Most important, Sweden initiated schooling in the local languages for peasant Estonian and Latvian children and reopened the University of Dorpat (Tartu) in 1690.

Entire regiments of Estonian and Latvian troops took part in the Great Northern War. The Swedish king forced the provinces to pay for a great defensive wall against Russia—upgrading the old crusader fort at Narva and the Danish-German fortifications at Tallinn.

Swedish rule was far from ideal for Balts, and Swedish aspiration often exceeded Swedish action. Still, Swedish governance was far more progressive than what went before and came after Peter the Great obtained Russia's "window on the west."

The Patrimonial Russias and Baltic Independence

The principalities of Russia—from the ninth to the sixteenth centuries—were patrimonies. Unlike tribes, a patrimony has a fairly strong, centralized government, some social differentiation, but less communal loyalty than is typical in tribal life. The princes of a patrimony view the state as their personal property. The Russian princes' "my-patrimony-above-yours" attitudes made it difficult to mobilize strategic cooperation against the better-organized invaders who, for centuries, swept into the Russian steppe. Hence, Kyiv and other Russian patrimonies were vulnerable to Mongols and other outsiders with fewer material assets.

Beginning in the sixteenth century, however, the principality of *Moskva* became the heart of an expanding Russian empire. But even the empire was a veritable patrimony—the property of the tsar or tsarina, whose formal powers, at least until the first Duma (1906), were nearly unlimited.

Tsarist rule in the Baltic, as elsewhere in the Russian empire, was absolutistic—autocratic and top-down. In the Baltic lands, however, St. Petersburg chose to restore the unlimited powers of the Germanic barons over the peasantry. A closed corporation of 324 families enjoyed a monopoly of landholding. Then, in 1816–1819, St. Petersburg abolished serfdom in Estonia, Courland, and Livonia, long before ending it throughout the empire in 1861. Former serfs were legally free but had no land. Many stayed on as farm workers but many moved to cities, where a radicalized working class began to take shape.

In the second half of the nineteenth century the Tsarist Empire mounted several campaigns aimed at Russifying its western reaches, where Germans, Poles, Estonians, Latvians, Lithuanians, Ukrainians, and others still spoke their own languages and where many experienced a nationalist awakening.

Tsarist rule ended in 1917 but the patrimonial tradition continued. Communist leaders, especially Stalin, viewed all humans and land under their control as their possessions. They surrendered the Baltic and other borderlands to Germany in 1918 to promote Soviet Russia's security by the Treaty of Brest-Litovsk.

In August 1939 negotiations with Germany, Stalin claimed Estonia, Latvia, and Finland but left Lithuania to Hitler. A short time later, however, the USSR got Lithuania as well in exchange for concessions further south. Stalin, bowing to Franklin Roosevelt's request, promised a show of democracy in the Baltic lands but clearly assumed that these lands too were again part of the Russian patrimony.[31] Stalin and his successors flooded the Baltic region with Slavic settlers, sharply altering the ethnic balance in Estonia and Latvia.

Russia's post-Soviet rulers in the 1990s continued the patrimonial tradition. The "oligarchs"—former ministers or those close to President Boris Yeltsin's Kremlin—took what had been publicly owned factories and resources and turned them into privately owned enterprises. A new class of millionaires and even billionaires took shape while most Russians became poorer. Post-Soviet Russia had a few pockets of creative enterprise such as Novgorod—an outpost of commerce and relatively stable self-rule, as it had been in Hanseatic times. But the rouble devaluation of August 1998 wiped out many small and medium-sized businesses across Russia. Only the super-rich had stashed their wealth safely in foreign banks.

At the end of the millennium, Russia continued to oscillate between order and anarchy—lacking the fitness that copes effectively with complex challenges. This was the context in which Russians in March 2000 elected a new president, Vladimir V. Putin, who promised a "dictatorship of law."

The Baltic Republics

For centuries Balts were ruled by others. But Russia's defeat by Japan in 1905 unleashed revolutionary movements across tsarist Russia. Popular assemblies—one thousand delegates in Riga, eight hundred in Tartu, two thousand in Vilnius—

demanded autonomy for the Latvian, Estonian, and Lithuanian regions of the tsarist empire. In 1917–1918 Balts again demanded autonomy and then independence. By 1920 the imperial German, Baltic German, and Soviet Russian troops had retreated. The three Baltic republics, along with Finland and Poland, emerged as the first nation-states on the eastern and southeastern shores of the Baltic.

Considering that they were arising from centuries of autocratic repression, Estonia, Latvia, and Lithuania made a good start toward self-organized fitness in the 1920s.[32] But circumstances were not favorable for achieving this goal. Democracy in the new republics was aborted by a weak democratic political culture, political inexperience, the world depression, the rise of authoritarian regimes in most of Europe, the Stalin-Hitler partition of Eastern Europe, Soviet occupation, and World War II.

It is difficult for a single society to be fit—especially when relatively small—if its neighbors are unfit or if the overall international system conduces either to despotic order or to anarchy.

NARROW SELF-SEEKING VERSUS SELF-ORGANIZATION FOR MUTUAL GAIN

By A.D. 2000 none of the great Baltic empires remained. The expansive realms of Vikings, Danish and Swedish kings, Lithuanian and Polish dukes, Hanseatic patriarchies, Germanic knights and kaisers, tsars, a Führer, and various commissars were gone. Why?

Exploitation backfired. Narrow self-seeking kept most Baltic peoples from combining their strengths against external threats. Unlike Estonians and Latvians, Lithuanians managed to unite—only to overreach. Allied with Poland, they sought to dominate even Russia. In time the *liberum veto* undermined Poland and Lithuania from within and helped Russia to advance. Swedish kings also suffered imperial overstretch as they fought to rule the Baltic littoral as well as all Northern Europe. A latecomer based in Brandenburg-Prussia, imperial Germany also went too far—its imperial expansions defeated in 1918 and 1945.

Tsarist Russia and Soviet Russia outreached the other overreachers. They ruled one-sixth of the earth's surface but antagonized many of their own subjects and most of their neighbors. The Soviet empire practiced exploitation far more than mutual gain. Lenin's system offered a kind of Social Darwinism. He taught that the question of politics is *kto kovo*—"who will destroy whom?" Such a system could not prosper. Too late did Soviet reformers perceive that true fitness must come from self-organization—not centralized commands. Even when Mikhail S. Gorbachev sought to "restructure" Soviet life, he wanted all parameters to be set by the center—the Kremlin.

The near absence of self-organized democracy before 1920 helps explain why most actors on the amber coast sought one-sided rather than mutual gain. Political and economic life on the Baltic shores seldom integrated material power with efficient self-organization. The least efficient were the Russian and Soviet empires—autocratic masters of vast resources which they used poorly. The most successful were the Hansas who, with few material assets, prospered thanks to self-organization.

The indigenous Baltic peoples—Estonians, Latvians, Lithuanians—generally lacked both material power *and* a capacity for self-organization. Their double weakness helped foreigners to pillage the amber coast for most of the second millennium. Balts self-organized briefly in the 1920s and 1930s, but not optimally. Only in the last fifteen years of the second millennium did native Balts begin to organize—within each state, regionally, and with the rest of Europe—in ways that effectively leveraged their limited material assets. Of all peoples in the USSR, Balts had the most recent memories of self-rule. Not by accident, they played David to the Soviet Goliath.

Caption for Chapter 2 Photo: Fifteenth-century Hanseatic merchants with a cosmopolitan crew refit a ship meant to carry grain and furs from Baltic ports such as Tallinn, Riga, and Klaipeda to England, Belgium, and Norway. Hanseatic trade was profitable but dangerous. Death contemplates whom to hit with his crossbrow. Like the Hansas, the reborn Baltic republics aspire to be part of a prosperous and secure Europe.

NOTES

1. Francis Fukuyama, "How to Re-Moralize America," *Wilson Quarterly* 23 (summer 1999), pp. 31–44 at 38; elaborated in his *The Great Disruption: Human Nature and the Reconstitution of Social Order* (New York: Free Press, 1999); critiqued in Paul Berman, "Reimagining Destiny," *Wilson Quarterly* 23 (summer 1999), pp. 45–55.

2. V. Stanley Vardys and Judith B. Sedaitis, *Lithuania: The Rebel Nation* (Boulder, Colo.: Westview, 1997), p. 6; Rokas M. Tracevskis, "Lithuanians Abroad Saluted in Vilnius," *Baltic Times,* September 23–29, 1999, p. 2.

3. By 1200 Estonia had a population of 150,000; in 1550, about 250,000; in the 1990s, about a million Estonian speakers in Estonia and more abroad. See Rein Taagepera, *Estonia: Return to Independence* (Boulder, Co.: Westview, 1993), pp. 6, 14, 19.

4. Joachim Herrmann et al., *Wikinger und Slawen: Zur Frügeschichte der Ostseevölker* (Neumünster, East Germany: Karl Wachholtz Verlag, 1982).

5. From the account of Henry of Livonia quoted in William Urban, *The Baltic Crusade* (DeKalb, Ill.: Northern Illinois University Press, 1975), pp. 21–22.

6. On tribes and patrimonies, see Michael W. Doyle, *Empires* (Ithaca, N.Y.: Cornell University Press, 1986), pp. 130–33.

7. Heinz von zur Mühlen, "Erober, Stammbevölkerung und Nachbarn Livlands bis 1561," in *Tausend Jahre Nachbarschaft: Die Völker des baltischen Raumes und die Deutschen,* ed. by Wilfried Schlau (Munich: F. Bruckman, 1995), pp. 39–46 at 42–43.

8. The grand master was aided by a supreme bailiff (*Grosskomtur*), below whom were grouped *Landmeisters,* under whom *Hauskomturs* ruled their *Komturei,* the groups of at least twelve knights who acted as seigneurs over their peasants.

9. Eric Weise, chief keeper of the archives (ret.) in *Two Expertises relating to the Archives of the Teutonic Order and the Ancient Prussian Duchy* (Göttingen: Academy of Sciences [mimeograph], 1949).

10. Speaking from Rome a short time later, the arbiter announced his judgment: the German Order could call a conference only once a year in Riga that could be attended by no more than fifty delegates. But the Bishop of Riga, representing the town council, rejected the ruling. He complained that the knights forced local bishops and lower prelates to attend such conferences "or lose everything they owned."

11. The February 25, 1304, meeting (*Versammlung*) of the Latvian and Estonian Assem-

blies (*liv- und estländischer Stände*) was attended by the bishops and church vassals from Tartu and Saaremaa, the land marshal and twelve representatives of the Order in Livland, a representative of Lund, and vassals of the Danish king in Estonia (*Estland*). See documents and commentary in Oskar Stavenhagen, ed., *Akten und Recesse der Livländischen Ständetage,* vol. 1, *1304–1460* (Riga: J. Deubner, 1907), pp. 1–10.

12. In 1309 and in 1313 delegates from Tallinn (representing the bishop, town council, and vassals of the Danish king) and from Saaremaa delivered ultimata to Riga and to the Order: make peace with each other and make common cause against the Lithuanians. Whoever refused would have to fight the forces of Tallinn and Saaremaa. Submission was to be signified by sacred oaths, delivery of hostages, and official seals. The documents implied that not only the Order but also the citizens of Riga were subjects of international law. Ibid., pp. 11–12.

13. Martin Luther addressed a letter: "An die Herren Deutschen Ordens."

14. Perhaps exaggerating, the *Cologne Chronicle* asserted that such a ship carried some fifteen hundred crusaders and their provisions from Cologne to Palestine in 1188. Archaeologists found a *Kogge* 23 meters long—not longer than some Viking ships, but higher (4 meters at midships) and wider (7.8 meters). Its single mast was 24 meters, its four-cornered sail 160 square meters. It could carry a cargo of 120 tons and had a crew of fifteen. Uwe Ziegler, *Die Hanse: Aufsteig, Blütezeit und Niedergang der ersten europäischen Wirtschaftsgemeinschaft* (Bern: Schwerz, 1997), pp. 304–308.

15. The German-speaking Hansas knew Tallinn as Reval, Tartu as Dorpat, Memel as Klaipeda, Gdansk as Danzig.

16. The first recorded usage of "Hansa" was in a sermon in A.D. 370; later it appeared in *Beowulf*. But it was not applied to traveling German merchants until the twelfth century. See Klaus Friedland, *Die Hanse* (Stuttgart: Kohlhammer, 1991), p. 21.

17. Nathan Rosenberg and L. E. Birdzell Jr., *How the West Grew Rich: The Economic Transformation of the Industrial World* (New York: Basic Books, 1986), pp. 78, 135.

18. S. E. Feiner, *The History of Government from the Earliest Times,* 3 vol. (New York: Oxford University Press, 1997), 2: p. 954.

19. Spencer R. Weart, *Never at War: Why Democracies Will Not Fight One Another* (New Haven: Yale University Press, 1998), pp. 242 ff.

20. From a population of 13,000 Tallinn formed a militia of 732 men. Tallinn's mayor told the ruling Swedish king that the *Undeutschen* were undependable. The highest placed *Undeutschen* ranked no higher than gang foreman (*Rottmeister*). Heinz von zur Mühlen, ed., *Die Revaler Münster-Rolle Anno 1688: Ein Verzeichnis der Bürger und Einwohner* (Lüneburg: Verlag Nordostdeutsches Kulturwerk, 1992), pp. 3–11, 18, 30, 36.

21. The 1370 Treaty of Stralsund ending the Hansas' war with Denmark was negotiated by twenty-three Hanseatic city-states reaching from Tartu, Tallinn, and Riga to Hamburg and ten Netherlands towns. Denmark was represented by two bishops and a spokesman from Rügen. Heinz Stoob, *Die Hanse* (Graz, Austria: Verlag Styria, 1995), p. 183.

22. The Hansa monopoly was facilitated by the fact that herring spawned off the coast of Scania and was preserved using salt supplies controlled by Lübeck and its allies. See Archibald R. Lewis and Timothy J. Runyan, *European Naval and Maritime History, 300–1500* (Bloomington: Indiana University Press, 1985), pp. 128–30.

23. Philippe Dollinger, *The German Hansa* (London: Macmillan, 1970; originally published in French, 1964), pp. 202–203.

24. Rus'ian refers to an area of common political, religious, and literary culture before the rise of Muscovites over Rus'ians in Ukraine and Belarus. The analysis here follows S. C. Rowell, *Lithuania Ascending: A Pagan Empire within East-Central Europe, 1295–1345* (Cambridge: Cambridge University Press, 1994).

25. The barons of Courland were long vassals of the Kettle dynasty of Poland. Many noble families from Courland acquired estates in Lithuania. There was heavy trading across the border. The Russo-Polish upper class in Lithuania resembled that of the Baltic German upper class in Estonia, Livonia, and Courland.

26. Nonetheless there were points of contact. For example, following the dissolution of the Teutonic Order, first Livonia and then Riga swore allegiance to the Polish crown and, for more than sixty years, belonged to the Lithuanian part of the Polish-Lithuanian Commonwealth. When Livonia was conquered by Sweden, however, Livonia's eastern region of Latgale (sometimes called "Polish Latvia") remained part of the Union until Poland was partitioned. Most of its people remained Catholic. Georg von Rauch, *The Baltic States: The Years of Independence, 1917–1940* (New York: St. Martin's, 1995), pp. 4–5.

27. See essays by Aleksander Loit and twenty-four other scholars in *Die schwedischen Ost-seeprovinzen Estland und Livland im 16.-18. Jahrhundert,* ed. Loit and Helmut Piirimäe, Acta Universitatis Stockholmiensis, Studia Baltica Stockholmiensia, no. 11 (Stockholm: Almqvist & Wiksell, 1993); for a bibliography, see Stig Appelgren, comp., *Estlands Svenskar och Svenskbygd: Bibliografi Sammanställd* (Stockholm: Almqvist & Wiksell International, 1997). The lag between Swedish aspiration and action is emphasized in Toivo U. Raun, *Estonia and the Estonians,* 2d ed. (Stanford, Calif.: Hoover Institution, 1991).

28. This was the origin of the military census of 1688. See Von zur Mühlen, *Die Revaler Münster-Rolle,* p. 9.

29. Determined to integrate the north German as well as the eastern shores of the Baltic into the Swedish empire (*rik*), King Charles X assured German nobles that their privileges would remain intact under Sweden. In time, however, Swedish kings sought to reduce the German nobility's voice by weakening the Holy Roman imperial diet (*Reichstag*), the provincial estates (*Provinzstände*), and town assemblies (*Stadträte*).

30. The approach anticipated the path taken in Taiwan from the 1950s into the 1990s: Absolutism → mass education → economic growth → self-rule.

31. For documentation, see Walter C. Clemens Jr., *Baltic Independence and Russian Empire* (New York: St. Martin's, 1991), pp. 296–98.

32. Unsure of Latvians' capacity for self-rule, a Latvian diplomat in November 1918 sounded out the French embassy in London about installing a Frenchman as king of Latvia. Huges Jean de Dianoux, "Un roi français pour la Lettonie en 1918," in *Independence of the Baltic States: Origins, Causes, and Consequences. A Comparison of the Crucial Years 1918–1919 and 1990–1991,* ed. Eberhard Demm et al. (Chicago: Lithuanian Research and Studies Center, 1996), pp. 75–81.

3

Leo Moks

Nonviolent Revolution: How Three Davids Undermined Goliath

Baltic independence movements were as weighty as any factor in subverting the USSR. Balts yoked the strengths of nationalism and nonviolence. Their achievements remind us that material power does not assure influence; that small states can sometimes defy larger ones; that intangible assets, well channeled, can sometimes best tangible.

Beginning in the mid-1980s, Balts used reforms sponsored by Soviet leader M. S. Gorbachev to assert their rights to protect their environment and their historic monuments and, later, their claims to sovereignty and independence. When Balts withstood outside threats, they exposed an irresolute Kremlin. Bolstering separatism in other republics, Balts triggered multiple challenges to empire. Partnered with Russian leader Boris Yeltsin, Balts asserted their sovereignty and Russia's. Gorbachev's counter—a planned "Union of Sovereign States"—ignited the August 1991 putsch that effectively ended the USSR. Following the abortive coup, the world recognized Baltic independence.

HOW COULD BALTIC DAVIDS CHALLENGE GOLIATH?

Few observers anticipated the rapid and relatively nonviolent collapse of the Soviet system in 1989–1991.[1] Fewer still thought that some of the smallest units of the USSR could spearhead its dissolution. If any union-republic could break from Moscow's grip, it might be Ukraine—large, industrially developed, with abundant resources. Still, one expert reasoned, Ukraine would not rebel because it could not. Its economic interdependence with other Soviet republics was too deep. Soviet spies and agents would thwart any moves to organize against Moscow.[2] Yes, Ukraine and other borderlands escaped Russian domination for a few years after World War I, assisted by foreign intervention against Soviet power. But no such external agent loomed in the late 1980s.

Baltic real estate was valuable to Moscow. The Kremlin would not surrender it lightly. And Balts were in a far weaker position in the 1980s than Ukraine. Not only were their lands and peoples tiny in the Soviet context, but many of their assets had been depleted by half a century of Soviet rule. Many of their most creative people disappeared in the 1940s—executed, deported to Siberia, or had fled to the West. Many Balts died fighting the Red Army or the Nazi Wehrmacht. Their economies were tied to and dependent on a larger system controlled by Moscow.

Foreign occupations devastated Baltic spirits. As one Latvian wrote: "I like everything that is light and the colour of the sun, but I am oppressed by the fate of Latvia. In waking in the night I dare not think about it, for fear of falling into despair and thus suffering sleeplessness."[3] Nations with just one, two, or even three million members speaking a unique tongue had reason to fear extinction by Sovietization and Russification.

Still, Balts had leverage that other peoples in the Soviet realm lacked. Soviet rule in the Baltic had even less legitimacy than in other parts of the USSR. The three Baltic states were independent from 1920 until 1940. No other Soviet peoples, except Russians, had exercised an independent statehood for more than a few years in the twentieth century. Balts' sovereign rights had been violated by the Soviet takeover.

Balts were among the richest and best-educated of Soviet citizens. One might have expected the poorest—not the richest—to take risks for independence.

Balts compared themselves not with Russians but with Finns, who had similar living standards in the 1930s but whose material conditions were among the best in the world by the 1980s.

Because many Soviets knew that Balts were "more advanced," they expected them to be different. Gorbachev hoped Balts would form the avant-garde of *perestroika*—economic reform. But their independent ways provided a dissident example attractive to Georgians, Ukrainians, and even Russians.

Baltic dissidents took advantage of the 1975 Helsinki Final Act signed by the USSR, the United States, Canada, and most countries of Europe. The subsequent "Helsinki Process" fostered international scrutiny of human rights observance in each signatory country. Emboldened, Baltic activists protested Soviet militarization of their region and other Soviet practices. Many dissidents were imprisoned, but others took their places. Balts made common cause with Andrei Sakharov and other campaigners for human rights in the USSR.

Baltic activists won only modest encouragement in the 1980s from Western governments, but Balts benefited from Washington's steadfast refusal to recognize Soviet annexation of the Baltic republics. Each pre-1940 Baltic state continued to have a legation in Washington. U.S. State Department official Jack F. Matlock reminded an assembly in Latvia in 1986 that Washington had never recognized Baltic absorption into the USSR.

Geography and demography also helped. Had Balts been further from the West, the prospects of Western support would have been lower. Had there been fewer Baltic émigrés living in Sweden, Finland, Canada, and the United States, Western politicians might have given less notice to Baltic affairs.

Despite deportations and repression, gifted political leaders arose to champion

Baltic independence. Despite political and other differences among them, these individuals managed to cooperate against Soviet and Russian imperialism.

EXPLOITATION AND IMPERIAL OVERREACH

When and how the Soviet empire would collapse was not predetermined. Had Soviet living standards improved, the Kremlin might have been more confident and its subjects more content. Had fresher minds and spirits gained power before 1985, the Soviet regime might have kept its empire longer by deft manipulation of carrots and sticks.

But the Soviet body politic was the sick man of Eurasia. Starting in the 1960s, infant mortality rose and life expectancy declined. Top Kremlin leaders concluded that rejuvenation of their economy and technology required steady inputs of Western assistance. Farms around Moscow were being depopulated and the Aral Sea was shrinking, but Soviet power reached out to Angola, Afghanistan, Grenada. Like the Habsburg and other deceased empires, the Soviets neglected internal reform and multiplied their foreign adventures. Here was classic imperial overreach.

In the 1970s many observers wrote of Moscow's strong "imperial will." They contrasted Soviet dynamism with America's inward orientation after Vietnam. But the burdens of empire and defense on the Soviet economy led other scholars to predict that the USSR would eventually lose the Cold War to the less-burdened United States. Still, such analysis could not specify just when Goliath would falter.[4]

Like other imperial metropoles, Moscow ignored the wise counsel of Diodotus to the Athenians:

> The proper basis of our security is in good administration rather than in fear. . . . The right way to deal with free people is this—not to inflict tremendous punishment on them after they have revolted, but to take tremendous care of them before this point is reached, to prevent them even contemplating the idea of revolt.[5]

Fitness is the ability to cope with complexity. But the USSR suffered more than it gained from its complex ethnic makeup. The United States, on balance, benefited from its ethnic complexity. Most immigrants wanted to live in the United States and learn its language; most non-Russian regions of the USSR were subjugated to Moscow by force. Nearly half the Soviet population had a mother tongue other than Russian. Few learned Russian except under pressure. These and other differences between the United States and the USSR are summarized in table 3.1.

Three variables determined the strength of the Soviet realm: the vitality of the "Center" (the highest organs of the Communist Party and Soviet government); the behavior of units on the periphery, especially the union-republics; and the links between Center and its agents and subjects on the periphery.

The Baltic republics on the northwestern tip of the empire became stronger while the core grew weaker. Portrayed as a fitness landscape, the Baltic peak rose and the Soviet declined. In this process, the ties that once bound—the imperial compact— frayed. By word, deed, and example, Balts subverted the core and buttressed independence movements elsewhere on the periphery and in Russia itself.

Table 3.1
Comparing U.S. and Soviet Integration in 1990 (before the USSR broke apart)

	USA (1990)	USSR (1990)
Population Size	Large: 250 million	Large: 291 million
Civilizations	1 + others in an evolving synthesis	Several distinct
Major ethnic groups	75% Anglophone white; 12% black; 9% Hispanic; 4% others	51% Russian; 15% Ukrainian; 6% Uzbek; 4% Belarus; many others
Languages	1 official + some bilingual education	1 countrywide official language plus official language of each republic
Government	Federal democracy	Authoritarian "Union" under Communist dictatorship
How formed?	Mainly voluntarily	Unity imposed by Moscow
Ethnic segmentation by political unit	None except for Indian reservations	Each Union-Republic named for an ethnic group
History of ethnic conflict	Yes—especially whites against Indians and blacks	Yes, with genocide in 1930s and 1940s
GDP per capita	Very high	Low to medium

THE HISTORICAL FACT: BALTS PLAYED A DECISIVE ROLE

The key role played by the Baltic independence movements in undermining the Soviet system is attested in the statements by Eduard Shevardnadze, Soviet foreign minister from 1985 to 1990; the recollections of the U.S. ambassador to Moscow, 1987–1991, Jack F. Matlock Jr.; and the memoirs of party leader M. S. Gorbachev and his major rival for a time, Yegor Ligachev.

Shevardnadze told U.S. Secretary of State James Baker in 1989 that nationality issues were the "greatest problem" faced by the Soviet government. Moscow was looking for a new approach to these issues, he said, but would not use force against the border republics. For the Balts to break their economic ties with Moscow would mean "suicide." But if Balts tried to quit the USSR, the peoples of the Transcaucasus might do the same. When Baker suggested a referendum, Shevardnadze allowed that it might be feasible in the Baltics, "where people are generally calm," but could ignite a civil war in the Caucasus.[6]

Matlock's *Autopsy on an Empire* details the great force exerted by developments in the Baltic. Shevardnadze several times told Matlock that the Soviet Union's nationality problems were more difficult to solve than its economic weaknesses. One such occasion took place on March 7, 1990, less than an hour before leaders of the Lithuanian independence movement were scheduled to visit Matlock. Shevardnadze begged Matlock to try to forestall any Lithuanian declaration of independence until after the USSR

Congress of People's Deputies could establish a presidential system strengthening Gorbachev's hand. Otherwise, Shevardnadze warned, a civil war might commence and the Soviet military establish a dictatorship in Lithuania and perhaps even in Moscow.[7]

When Matlock met Lithuanian leaders later that morning, he listened and offered little advice. But on March 11 the Lithuanian Supreme Council voted unanimously (with six abstentions) to restore formally the country's independence. Four days later, Gorbachev became the USSR's president. But neither he nor other Soviet officials took steps then to repress Lithuania. As Matlock perceived the unfolding events of 1990–1991, the impetuous Balts—sometimes bolstered by U.S. diplomacy—immobilized the Kremlin's will to crush nationalist dissent by armed might.[8]

The importance attached by the Gorbachev regime to the Baltic was reflected in Politburo instructions to Shevardnadze for his meetings with high U.S. officials in April and May 1990. Shevardnadze's talking points gave priority to Baltic issues over Germany and arms control.[9] When Matlock urged Gorbachev to curtail military action against Lithuania in January 1991, Gorbachev asked the ambassador to help President George Bush understand that "we are on the brink of a civil war." In March 1991, as in August 1990, the Communist Party of the Soviet Union's (CPSU's) Central Committee publicly condemned U.S. aid programs and radio broadcasts that, Moscow charged, sought to subvert Soviet rule in the Baltics.

Gorbachev's archrival Ligachev wrote in 1992 that nationalist separatism had undermined the entire Soviet state. Lithuanian nationalism led the Communist Party there to split from the CPSU. Ligachev blamed Gorbachev and his aide Aleksandr Yakovlev for ignoring the dangers of separatism.[10]

Answering Ligachev and other critics, Gorbachev claimed to have known from the outset that perestroika could not succeed unless it took into account the interests of the many nations and nationalities living in the USSR. Still—writing as if someone else were in charge—Gorbachev wrote that Soviet reformists did not fathom the scale of the rapidly gestating national problems and stuck to traditional methods, even after unrest among Kazaks and Crimean Tatars in 1986 and 1987.[11]

The "most vulnerable element in the Union," according to Gorbachev, was the *pribaltika*. As of 1987, he recalled, there were no demands for secession except in the Baltic, the "vanguard" of nationalism, where "extremist" groups were active in each republic.[12]

When Matlock revisited Russia in 1992, he asked more than a dozen political leaders who or what killed the Soviet system. Liberals condemned Gorbachev for permitting or authorizing force against nationalists; they blamed him for the loss of life in Vilnius. Hard-liners blamed him for not using more force.

Several respondents pointed to other manifestations of nationalism:

- Russia's declaration of sovereignty and the formation of a separate Russian Communist Party in the summer 1990;
- The republics' taking control of tax collections in January 1991;
- Ukraine's move toward complete independence in 1991.

Some respondents blamed pervasive economic and social malaise. Some said the Soviet system was genetically doomed.

Matlock concluded that it was individuals and their decisions—not abstract forces—that sped the demise of the Soviet system. KGB (Committee of State Security) chief Vladimir Kriuchkov was the individual most responsible for wrecking the system, because he organized the August 1991 coup against Gorbachev.[13]

Gorbachev whined that the West gave him insufficient support. Ultimately, however, Gorbachev lost power because of his own acts and failures to act.[14]

HOW THE THREE DAVIDS ASSERTED THEMSELVES AND WEAKENED THE CENTER

The Soviet Union weakened as a result of actions and inactions by the Center as it confronted a multifaceted campaign by Baltic activists for independence. Tables 3.2 and 3.3 summarize the main points.

Let us try now to flesh out these processes and suggest how they reinforced one another. The chronology on page viii includes the key events.

Balts Utilized the Center's Espousal of Perestroika

The Gorbachev regime after 1986 permitted and even encouraged some self-organization of society from below. Elements of civil society had developed in the USSR since the mid- and late 1950s. Their emergence was a cause as well as an effect of Gorbachev's reforms. These institutions often had a nationalist character as they endeavored to protect the local history, culture, and environment. In the Baltic as in Russia and other republics, nationalism and democratic self-assertion through mass organizations and demonstrations reinforced one another. Their synergy cut away at the foundations of imperial rule.

In 1988 popular fronts were established in each Baltic republic—the first in Estonia, founded by Communist and non-Communist intellectuals. A Comintern slogan

Table 3.2
How the Center Lost the Periphery

Actions by the Center	Inactions of the Center
1. Exploit the periphery for generations	1. Fail to generate a sense of mutual gain between rulers and the ruled
2. Provide legal-political structures for incipient, nationality-based states in the union and other republics	2. Fail to create a homo soveticus
3. Align Communist-style modernization against every traditional value (religion, local culture, etc.)	3. Fail to recognize the power of nationalism
4. Promise perestroika and other reforms, but then retreat or renege	4. Fail to assuage demands for self-determination, e.g., by turning over state-owned property to republics or by liberalizing the union treaty until too late
5. Tolerate separatist behavior until crisis conditions develop and then fail to use decisive force	5. Fail to sustain imperial will and to maintain a compact between the core and compradors

Table 3.3
Actions by the Baltic Independence Movements

1. Challenge the center on safe issues (preserving historical monuments, protecting the environment) and gradually escalate to demand independence
2. Adopt regime slogans such as perestroika, glasnost, and legality
3. Coopt or pressure local Communists to join the nationalist cause
4. Mobilize moral strengths while avoiding violence with nonnative settlers, the Soviet Army, and the Kremlin
5. Exploit leeway offered by the Soviet Constitution
6. Multiply strengths by aligning with Yeltsin and anti-Soviet nationalists in other republics, including Russia
7. Mobilize foreign backers

from the 1930s, the term "popular front" was used in Estonia and Latvia, but Lithuanians called their group a "movement"—*Sajudis*. The inaugural congress of each Baltic front was held in October 1988.

Initially the popular fronts avoided any direct challenge to the metropole. The fronts claimed to support perestroika, glasnost, and legality—watchwords of the Gorbachev regime—but the fronts soon became vehicles for nationalism. They tapped long-suppressed ethnic and civic identity and accumulated anger toward perceived repression past and present.

Seeking to encourage but channel Baltic energies, Gorbachev unloosed powers he could not control. His regime welcomed the popular fronts as partners in economic reconstructing. Gorbachev hoped for Baltic innovations to test and apply the principles of perestroika. Gorbachev probably reasoned that, of all the peoples in the USSR, the Balts had the best prospects to devise constructive economic policies. After all, Balts were the most westernized, most affluent, and most widely educated, as well as the least Sovietized. Just as several tsars gave Finland a long leash, Gorbachev loosened the reins for the Balts. But the Balts pushed further and faster than he wanted. Less than two years separated the founding of Estonia's Popular Front in April 1988 and Lithuania's declaration of independence in March 1990.

From the empire's perspective, these new, informal organizations embodied the wolves of nationalism in sheep's clothing. Balts worked within the system to exit the system. Both Gorbachev and the fronts fueled expectations that could not be satisfied by temporizing. The new wine could not be contained by old skins. Thus, in October 1988 the Lithuanian movement, Sajudis, demanded sovereignty within the Soviet federation; by April 1989 it asserted that "a sovereign country cannot be part of another country." Ligachev aptly summarized Baltic trends: one could graph how unofficial movements there turned to "radical nationalism," how they moved from realistic accounting (*khozrashchet*), a necessary ingredient of economic reform, to secession.[15]

Balts Utilized the Center's Espousal of Glasnost

In late 1987 authorities in Moscow instructed Baltic newspapers to apply the principles of glasnost to nationality issues.[16] Accordingly, the Communist-controlled press in Estonia promptly began a series of frank reports on Russians' and Estonians' differences and what to do about them. Open discussion of ethnic conflicts in the Baltic was probably essential if a solution was to be found. But the regime had stalled too long. Following the decades of repression, candor cut deep and reopened wounds hard to heal.

Some Baltic publications, especially those in the local languages, took advantage of glasnost to go far beyond what its sponsors had anticipated. Ligachev complained that the newspaper of the Baltic popular fronts became "battering rams, shaking the pillars of socialism and the Union state." He charged that Baltic "radicals" used glasnost and democracy to "incite social tensions, disorient the public consciousness, and destabilize the state." He allowed that old-style dictatorship could no longer be used to control the press, but regretted that Soviet authorities did not stop the radical media from "running amok with their attacks" on the system.

Ligachev contended that separatist entrepreneurs played on past "distortions" of national cultures and languages to foment trouble. "National awareness always leads the way, acceding to civic concepts only as the working class acquires political experience." The problem, as Ligachev saw it in 1988, was how to encourage political activism without allowing it to turn into a nationalistic, anti-Soviet movement."[17]

Balts Utilized the Soviet Constitutional Framework

When Balts demanded self-determination, they did so at first within the framework of perestroika. Later, when they insisted on outright independence, they presented this as a right long established in the Soviet Constitution.

In 1988 Balts began to demand sovereignty in specific domains, for example, control of resources, but gradually broadened their demands to sovereignty in general. Even when they demanded independence, however, this did not necessarily signify secession to Kremlin minds. Thus, Gorbachev's memoir states that Baltic demands for restoring their interwar anthems and flags and achieving "real autonomy (*samostoiatel'nost'*) of the republics" conformed with the Baltic constitutions, the USSR Constitution, and the ideas of the XIX Party Conference — "without any demand for withdrawal from the [Soviet] Union."[18]

When Estonia's Supreme Soviet declared that its laws could override those of the USSR, however, the Presidium of the USSR Supreme Soviet declared the Estonian moves to be unconstitutional and invalid. Still, Gorbachev softened the decree by including a phrase calling for development of mechanisms whereby the unionrepublics could expand and protect their "sovereign rights in the USSR."

When Estonian resistance stiffened in 1989, Gorbachev looked for ways to accommodate nationalist demands. In August 1989 the Gorbachev team produced a draft CPSU platform on nationalities that called for a transformation of the "Soviet Federation" to provide meaningful "national autonomy." The proposal also broke ground by raising the possibility of a new Union Treaty. Gorbachev's support for a revised, more liberal "Union of Sovereign States" proved to be a major catalyst of the coup that virtually unseated him in August 1991.

Balts profited from the lack of clarity in Russian minds about the distinctions between "sovereignty," "independence," "union of states," and "confederation." For much of 1991 Gorbachev recommended that a Union of Sovereign States replace the USSR. An association of *sovereign* states, however, is not a "union" but a confederation.

Baltic independence did not materialize until rival hard-line and reformist imperialists in Moscow each gave a fatal blow to the other's aspirations. Recognition of Baltic independence by Russia, by other countries, and then by the USSR State Council came only in the days and weeks after the August 1991 coup. Antipathy among the rivals in Moscow had been fueled by the challenge of nationalism on the periphery, especially in the Baltic. The hard-liners feared that the reformists would soon enact a new compact that turned the USSR—into not a "Union" but a weak confederation of "Sovereign States." The putschists struck just days before Russia, Ukraine, and Belarus were expected to sign a new Union Treaty. Three of the plotters may also have been galvanized by Gorbachev's private pledge to Yeltsin to replace them after the treaty was signed.[19]

Gorbachev later complained that in September 1991 Russian president Yeltsin proposed neither a federation nor a confederation but an even looser grouping resembling the European Union. In November 1991 the USSR State Council debated whether to adopt a "union state" (favored by Gorbachev) or a "union of states" (endorsed by Yeltsin). But the options became hopelessly muddled. Thus, one option was "a union with centralized state power—either federative or confederative."[20]

As the USSR dissolved, a Commonwealth of Independent States (CIS) was established in December 1991 by Russian president Yeltsin and the presidents of Ukraine and Belarus. Led by Kazakstan, most of the other former Soviet Republics immediately joined the CIS. Georgia refused to be represented except by "observers" and Azerbaijan later withdrew. The three Baltic republics refused to take part in any way. They feared that the CIS could be a vehicle for a revived Russian imperium. In the 1990s, however, the Commonwealth remained nearly so loose as its British namesake. The CIS adopted many resolutions but implemented few.

BALTS MOBILIZED MORAL POWER AND ESCHEWED VIOLENCE

Balts followed a path of nonviolence.[21] Like Indians inspired by Gandhi and like the Polish movement Solidarity led by Lech Walesa, Balts became free in part because they acted as though they were free. Their independence movement was called a Singing Revolution because it eschewed violence and because each Baltic republic produced huge music festivals that manifested and mobilized national consciousness. "The sounds of hundreds of thousands of voices symbolize[d] national harmony in every sense, like Rousseau's 'General Will' set to music."[22]

As the Singing Revolution built momentum, the numbers of demonstrators increased dramatically. In 1987 some three to five thousand Latvians commemorated deportations of their countrymen by Soviet invaders in 1941. In 1988 this event was memorialized by about one hundred thousand people. A quarter million people took part in Estonia's September 1988 music festival—roughly one in four of the Estonian-speaking population! Several Latvian demonstrations in 1989 and 1990 involved a quarter to a half million people.[23]

One of the Balts' strongest moral-legal cards was their demand for publication of the secret protocols of the Treaty of Nonagression between Germany and the Soviet Union, dated August 23, 1939. Beginning in 1987, demonstrators in all three Baltic republics began to mark the anniversary of the 1939 Nazi-Soviet treaty, which set the stage for their annexation. The largest single demonstration took place on August 23, 1989 (fifty years after the Hitler-Stalin accord), when one to two million Estonians, Latvians, and Lithuanians—one-sixth to one-third of the total Baltic population—formed a 370-mile human chain from Tallinn through Riga to Vilnius.[24]

After years of denial and delay, the Center acquiesced and organized a commission to study the matter. The commission concluded that Stalin and Hitler had in fact partitioned Eastern Europe. The USSR Congress of People's Deputies in December 1989 declared the secret protocols invalid from their inception. For Balts, this admission undercut Soviet legitimacy in the Baltic. One member of Congress shouted at the commission chairman: "You are giving a green light to the dissolution of the Soviet Union!" Russian diplomats later maintained, however, that Soviet incorporation of the Baltic republics in 1940 was a legal act not dependent on the protocols.

The greatest tests of Baltic willpower took place in late 1990 and early 1991. Pro-Soviet Committees of National Salvation appeared and sought to replace the ministers and legislatures that, by that time, were working for independence. The National Salvation committees moved in unison with Soviet troops, who seized public buildings, including the television station and tower in Vilnius and the Ministry of the Interior in Riga, killing about fifteen Lithuanians and five Latvians. One Soviet officer died and another lost a leg. Some Balts wanted to fight and some armed themselves with hunting rifles and shotguns, but nonviolent resistance prevailed. Soviet troops did not attempt to break through the lines of civilians surrounding the parliament building in Vilnius. Soviet commanders in the Baltic or their bosses in Moscow were unwilling to kill enough Balts to install the Committees of National Salvation.

The attempted Soviet takeovers in Vilnius and Riga took place just before and after the opening salvos of the UN offensive against Iraqi forces in Kuwait. Moscow may have hoped that Soviet support for UN policy would purchase Western acquiescence in the Baltic crackdown. But Western news channels did not neglect the bloody events in Vilnius and Riga. Balts used each incident to embarrass the Gorbachev regime, welcoming foreign television crews to record any use of brute force against Balts. The Singing Revolution was also a "CNN Revolution," because Western news channels covered these events. Western leaders called on Gorbachev to halt violence against Balts.

In mid-January 1991 Russian president Yeltsin arrived in Tallinn and urged Soviet forces not to shoot at Baltic demonstrators. Major General Dzhokhar Dudaev, commander of Soviet forces in Tartu, Estonia, from 1987 through March 1991—who was elected chairman of the executive committee of the Chechen National Congress in December 1990—did likewise. Indeed, his views on Chechen independence reflected his observation of events in Estonia.

There were a few street fights between Balts and Russian-speaking settlers in the late 1980s and early 1990s. So far as is known, however, all deaths in the movement toward Baltic independence were inflicted by Soviet troops upon basically passive resisters in the streets of Vilnius and Riga and at Baltic border posts. Total deaths—most of them in 1991—numbered several dozens.

Box 3.1. Origins of Resistance[1]

Vytautas Landsbergis, a renowned professor of music, led Lithuania's independence movement. Elected chairman of Lithuania's Supreme Council in 1990, he was the country's de facto head of state as it declared its independence from the USSR. In January 1991 Landsbergis hunkered down in the Supreme Council building with other parliamentarians as Soviet troops and local Communists sought to restore Moscow's rule.

In May and June 1996 Landsbergis told me about the factors that shaped his world view.
W.C.: *What influences shaped your politics? Why did you have hope that change was possible?*
V.L.: My father fought in the Lithuanian army in the struggle for liberation after World War I. Our family library was rich in the history of our country. I was eight years old when the Soviets occupied Lithuania in 1940. I remember their occupation, followed by the German, followed by the Soviet again. My elder brother was a member of the anti-German underground and distributed leaflets.
When did you first think about liberating Lithuania from Soviet rule?
I never thought that I alone could do this. But when I became an educator, I met with other educators who thought we should try to liberate the country from Stalinism. We met in small groups and talked frankly with each other. We took hope from Hungary 1956, the Prague Spring 1968, and from Poland. Other musicians and I were in Poland the very day that its Communist government gave in and made an agreement with Solidarity.
How did you learn about nonviolence?
We learned about nonviolence from reading a Soviet-era book about Gandhi translated into Lithuanian. We also read about Henry David Thoreau in the 1970s. But we knew little about Martin Luther King Jr. until later. Soviet propaganda treated King as an opponent of U.S. imperialism rather than as a force for brotherhood.

Most of our ideas about nonviolence grew from our own thinking. We knew we should take a human approach to our enemies and see them as brothers—*confused* brothers.

But we were not absolute pacifists. The persons who guarded our parliament building in January 1991 were ready to fight with primitive weapons if need be. We were with them when they took a solemn oath.

---

[1]For a detailed account, see Vytautas Landsbergis, *Lithuania: Independent Again* (Seattle: University of Washington Press, 2000).

BALTIC COMMUNISTS: FROM FAITHFUL LACKEYS TO "NATIONAL DEMOCRATS"

Baltic Communist leaders tried to dampen local nationalism. They tended to support the status quo even when Gorbachev launched perestroika. Gorbachev's memoir castigates the Communist Party for remaining aloof and treating every manifestation of nationalism with caution or hostility. Gorbachev seemed to blame the republican party apparatus rather than the central organs, where he had more influence.

Gorbachev wrote that Balts began to see their popular fronts as alternative to the Communist Party. The fronts confronted the questions that were troubling society, and "quickly became stronger in influence than the Party organizations."[25]

Soon, however, many Baltic Communists began to shed their ties with the Center and jump on the nationalist bandwagon. As Ligachev saw it, many Communist leaders in the Baltic republics changed their stripes and became " 'national democrats,' pinning national colors to their lapels to hold on to power and privileges." Thus, Algirdas Brazauskas chaired the withdrawal of the Lithuanian Communist Party from the CPSU and became a "classic Liquidator."[26]

INDECISION AT THE CENTER VERSUS BALTIC INTRANSIGENCE

In February 1988 Gorbachev announced a future plenum of the Communist leadership to consider "the national question," to which he proposed no answer. Since the Soviet leaders claimed to have "solved" the "national question" long ago, none of them had an immediate answer for what they had presumed to be a nonproblem.

Balts emasculated Soviet power by refusing to bow to threats of military or economic coercion. When Balts held firm, the Center usually pulled back, did nothing, or offered an olive branch. Thus, after Balts formed a human chain across the Baltic on August 23, 1989, the CPSU Central Committee accused the Balts of nationalist hysteria and threatened to crush them by force. When Baltic opposition leaders repudiated this accusation, the Kremlin was silent and then conciliatory.

Ligachev sought to tighten discipline in the Baltic, but Gorbachev ignored his warnings and kept them from the Central Committee. Not until the December 1990 plenum of the Communist Party did Gorbachev call a spade a spade. Referring to Baltic claims to national "greatness," Gorbachev told the plenum that "today" the country faced no greater danger than "the extremist nationalism that stirs up interethnic discord." Ligachev lamented that Gorbachev had ignored this danger for so long.

When the Lithuanian Communist Party split into a nationalist and a pro-Moscow faction, some Kremlin leaders urged reconciliation. A draft resolution of the CPSU Central Committee plenum in February 1990 urged people in Lithuania to "smooth things over." This kind of "benign approach," Ligachev said, "inevitably leads to disaster." He managed to have the draft rewritten so as to support the pro-Moscow faction. Still, the dominant faction of Lithuanian Communists continued its nationalist orientation.

Backed by Moscow and sometimes by Soviet armed forces stationed in the Baltic, some Slavic-speakers in the Baltic formed "International Fronts" to resist Baltic independence. By 1989 native speakers of Russian, Ukrainian, Belarusian, or Polish made up nearly half of the population of Latvia, nearly two-fifths that of Estonia, and one-fifth that of Lithuania.

Some Slavic-speakers had lived in the Baltic for generations, most since the 1940s. Many believed, like Americans, that they had the right to live anywhere in their country and speak the dominant language. But many believed that they would become more prosperous in an independent republic not attached to the USSR. Thus, some Slavs backed Baltic independence. More than half of non-Latvians voted for Latvia's independence in March 1991. However, following Baltic independence, as we shall see in chapter 7, many non-Balts complained that they were treated unfairly by the new governments of Estonia and Latvia.

SOVIET DEPENDENCY AND WESTERN DIPLOMACY

One reason why the Center failed to use decisive force against dissident nationalists was that Moscow wanted détente and trade with the West. The United States did little to foment separatism in the USSR, but any Soviet repression of human rights risked cutting off the infusions of Western credits and technology that Kremlin leaders hoped would energize perestroika. Thus, in January 1991, Ambassador Matlock, on instructions from Washington, warned Gorbachev that armed intervention to crush Lithuania would sever movement toward détente and trade in East-West relations.[27]

But Gorbachev's reluctance to use a mailed fist continued a secular trend toward delay and restraint:

- 1953: The Kremlin immediately crushed uprisings in East Germany with tanks;
- 1956: Moscow deliberated for weeks before taking military action against Hungarians, causing many deaths;
- 1968: Moscow temporized for eight months before intervening in Czechoslovakia, causing few deaths;
- 1979: The Kremlin agonized for more than a year before invading Afghanistan in 1979, resulting in a long war followed by a Soviet retreat;
- 1980–1981: The USSR did not use force against Solidarity but depended upon Polish troops to restrain Polish dissidents;
- 1986–1991: Soviet regular, interior, or special forces were deployed briefly against Kazaks, Georgians, Azeris (who suffered the most deaths), and Balts.[28] But the big picture was that the Gorbachev regime pulled Soviet forces from Afghanistan and let Eastern Europe go without a fight. By the late 1980s Balts could infer that their steady but calm demands for sovereignty ran little risk of provoking a forceful Soviet response—especially if compared to the dangers that dissidents faced in earlier decades.

The trend toward restraint probably evidenced the ebb of imperial will and the Kremlin's perception of mounting Soviet dependency on the West. Seeking to justify the use of force in Azerbaijan in 1990, Gorbachev's memoir asserted that force must sometimes be used, but only as a last resort in emergency situations. Later, however, countering charges that he "lost" Eastern Europe, Gorbachev averred: "The losses are imaginary, the gains are significant—most important, the realization that Russia oppresses no one and does not hold by force its friends and allies. We have often quoted Marx: 'No people can be free that oppresses other peoples.' Giving freedom to those who were counted in the 'Soviet camp'. . . we followed that maxim. Their freedom and our own—this is the main defense of my policies." Gorbachev's focus here was Eastern Europe but he applied this defense to Ukraine and other former Soviet republics as well.[29]

THE BALTIC EXAMPLE

The Baltic independence movement influenced other republics—even Russia. Encouraged by the election victories of popular front candidates in the Baltic in 1989, Gorbachev notes, Georgians established a popular front in June, Uzbeks in May, Ukrainians in September. Similar stirrings took place in Moldova and Armenia. "Balts, as the most experienced and organized, supplied their ideological materials and tried to establish coordination. . . . The activities of the popular fronts escalated, and separatist tendencies began to prevail more and more frequently."[30] Dissidents in Kazakhstan told me in 1990 that their leaflets were printed in Latvia.

As Ligachev saw it, Lithuania's situation in April 1989 "suggested a scenario of action for nationalist forces in other republics." Lithuania's Sajudis set out the path that Georgia's nationalists followed.[31]

Balts, said Gorbachev, succeeded in persuading Yeltsin's followers to clone Russia on the Baltic model. When Russians too demanded sovereignty and withdrawal from the Union, this undermined any prospect for saving the Union. Yeltsin was elected Russian president in May 1990; in the summer and fall 1990 the Russian legislature (followed by the Ukrainian) asserted that its laws took precedence over Soviet; in October the USSR Supreme Soviet declared such assertions invalid but took no other action. The "sovereignization" of Russia scuttled the search for a new formula for relations with the Baltic republic in a reformed Union. It caused a chain reaction in all the union-republics and later in autonomous republics. "A 'parade of sovereignties' had begun."[32]

THE UPSHOT

In 1989 Hungarians and other Eastern Europeans breached the Iron Curtain. Before the late 1980s, however, no entities so small as the Baltic peoples had by their *peaceful* actions done so much to undermine a large polity.[33] Most national self-determination movements had to fight their way to independence—from the United Provinces against Spain to Eritrea against Ethiopia. Poles and other Eastern Europeans gained independence as the Russian, Austro-Hungarian, and German empires collapsed in World War I. India and other Third World nations won their independence from European countries exhausted by World War II or, like Algeria, in hard fighting.

What if Balts had not challenged the Center but dedicated themselves to Gorbachev's program? Balts would not then have led the "parade of sovereignties." They might have raised hopes perestroika could revitalize the Soviet system. But Balts did not take this fork. Instead, their actions exacerbated all the challenges facing the Soviet system. Without the Baltic drive for independence, it is unlikely that the USSR would have disintegrated so soon or so peacefully.

Weakness at the Center permitted and encouraged self-assertion on the periphery. Had the Kremlin ruled with enlightened grace or an iron hand, Balts might have remained quiescent. But Moscow did neither. Hence, resolute Davids showed that Goliath towered on feet of clay

Caption for Chapter 3 Photo: The Singing Revolution included political demonstrations. In 1992 Estonian leaders Tunne Kelam and Mari-Ann Rikken Kelam were among those demanding an end to Russia's military presence in the Baltic republics a year after they regained independence. In the late 1980s Tunne Kelam helped organize the Estonian National Independence Party. As a new century began, he was vice-

president of parliament and a candidate for president of the republic, and Mari-Ann Kelam was a member of parliament.

NOTES

1. In the 1990s more than one hundred thousand people died from ethnic fighting in Tajikistan, Georgia, and other parts of the former Soviet Union. But such numbers paled next to the casualties when other empires crumbled and when Pakistan split from India.

2. Alexander J. Motyl, *Will the Non-Russians Rebel? State, Ethnicity, and Stability in the USSR* (Ithaca, N.Y.: Cornell University Press, 1987). A classroom simulation at Boston University in the 1980s postulated Soviet military action against Ukrainian separatists. While Moscow was engaged in Ukraine, Balts asserted their independence. In reality, these roles were reversed. Moscow focused on the Balts, giving some respite to dissident Ukrainians.

3. Quoted in Vieda Skultans, *The Testimony of Lives: Narrative and Memory in Post-Soviet Latvia* (London: Routledge, 1998), p. 45.

4. The burden of empire argument is implicit in A. F. K. Organski and Jacek Kugler, *The War Ledger* (Chicago: University of Chicago Press, 1980). The Kremlin's weak response to Solidarity and the Poles' decision to proselytize in neighboring countries provoked the present author in 1981 to ask: "Will the Soviet Empire Survive 1984?" *Christian Science Monitor,* July 10, 1981, op-ed page.

5. Diodotus versus Cleon in Thucydides, *Peloponnesian War,* Book Three.

6. James A. Baker, III, *The Politics of Diplomacy: Revolution, War & Peace, 1989–1992* (New York: G. P. Putnam's, 1995), pp. 145–48, 203. Shevardnadze's memoir details his dismay at the use of force against demonstrators in Tbilisi in April 1989 and Gorbachev's refusal to let him speak to the Congress of People's Deputies on this matter. See Eduard Shevardnadze, *Moi vybor: v zashchitu demokratii i svobody* (Moscow: Novosti, 1991), pp. 320–27.

7. Jack F. Matlock Jr., *Autopsy on an Empire: The American Ambassador's Account of the Collapse of the Soviet Union* (New York, Random House), pp. 323–30.

8. On March 8, 1990 Shevardnadze told Matlock that he would resign if he saw a dictatorship coming. "I'll not be part of a government with blood on its hands." Matlock, *Autopsy,* p. 329.

9. The Politburo instructed Shevardnadze to explain Soviet policy in the Baltic region and warn against U.S. encouragement of Baltic separatism. See *direktivy* and *ukazaniia* to the Soviet foreign minister for his meetings with President George Bush and Secretary of State James Baker in April 1990 and with Baker in May 1990, cited in Celeste A. Wallander, "Did the West Contribute to the Collapse of the Soviet Union," paper prepared for the Olin Critical Issues Series, Harvard University, Cambridge, Massachusetts, February 25, 1997.

10. Yegor Ligachev, *Inside Gorbachev's Kremlin* (New York: Pantheon, Random House, 1993), pp. 172–78. Originally published as *Zagadka Gorbacheva* (Novosibirsk: Interbuk, 1992).

11. Mikhail S. Gorbachev, *Zhizn' i reformy,* 2 vols. (Moscow: Novosti, 1995), 1: pp. 498–501. This passage appears in chapter 15 of Gorbachev's one-volume English *Memoirs* (New York: Doubleday, 1995). The two-volume Russian version contains much omitted from the one-volume English version.

12. For Gorbachev's most systematic discussion of Baltic issues, see his *Zhizn',* 1: pp. 500–501, 510–17; *Memoirs,* pp. 326–31.

13. *Autopsy,* pp. 665–67.

14. Alfred Erich Senn, *Gorbachev's Failure in Lithuania* (New York: St. Martin's, 1995), p. 153.

15. Ligachev, *Inside Gorbachev's Kremlin,* p. 174.

16. Author's discussions with Aleksandr Ivanov and other editors in the Tallinn offices of *Sovetskaia Estoniia* in January 1988; for the 1987–1988 press treatment of nationality issues, see Walter C. Clemens Jr., *Baltic Independence and Russian Empire* (New York: St. Martin's, 1991), pp. 77–80.

17. Ligachev, *Inside Gorbachev's Kremlin*, pp. 100–101, 172.

18. Gorbachev, *Zhizn'*, 1: p. 510, and *Memoirs*, p. 340.

19. Matlock, *Autopsy*, p. 578.

20. Gorbachev, *Zhizn'*, 2: pp. 588–93, and *Memoirs*, pp. 655–66.

21. For a global survey of nonviolent techniques and this author's essay on nonviolent action in the Baltic, see Roger S. Powers and William B. Vogele, eds., *Protest, Power, and Change: An Encyclopedia of Nonviolent Action* (New York: Garland, 1997).

22. Anatol Lieven, *The Baltic Revolution: Estonia, Latvia, Lithuania and the Path to Independence* (New Haven: Yale University Press, 1993), p. 113. Such festivals had been held periodically since the nineteenth century. Nationalist themes were muted under Nazi and Soviet rule but reemerged in late 1980s.

23. Rein Taagepera, *Estonia: Return to Independence* (Boulder, Colo.: Westview, 1993), p. 142; Olgerts Eglitis, *Nonviolent Action in the Liberation of Latvia* (Cambridge Mass.: The Albert Einstein Institution, 1993), p. 14.

24. For 125 documents from 1939 and January 1940, see *Ot pakta Molotova-Ribbentropa: do dogovora o bazakh: Dokumenty i materialy* (Tallinn: Periodika, 1990).

25. Gorbachev oversimplifies here. Baltic Communists initially took part in the fronts. Estonians informed Gorbachev that theirs was the "Popular Front of Estonia in Defense of Perestroika" (see the documentary collection *Narodnyi Kongress: Sbornik materialov kongress Narodnogo fronta Estonii 1–2 okt. 1988 g.* [Tallinn: Periodika, 1989], p. 221). Many anti-Communist Estonians viewed the Popular Front with disdain and set up rival organizations, such as the Estonian National Independence Party.

26. Ligachev, *Inside Gorbachev's Kremlin*, p. 174.

27. Matlock, *Autopsy*, pp. 469–71.

28. *Chernyi ianvar' Baku—1990: Dokumenty i materialy* (Baku, Azerbaijan: Azerneshr, 1990). A novel describing an earlier Soviet Army bloodbath in Baku, *Ali and Nino* by "Kurban Said," began to be serialized in *Azarbayjan* (Baku) beginning with no. 1, 1990. It was first published in German in 1937 and in English in 1970.

29. Gorbachev, *Zhizn'*, 1: p. 520; 2: p. 476.

30. Gorbachev, *Zhizn'*, 1: p. 514, and *Memoirs*, p. 342.

31. Writing about the April 1989 Soviet military action against demonstrators in Tbilisi, in which nineteen Georgian civilians died, Ligachev said that the Georgians inflamed nationalist passions and incited attacks on the Soviet army, saving Georgian blows against the central authorities until later. Ligachev, *Inside Gorbachev's Kremlin*, pp. 141, 189; for a different perspective, see Shevardnadze, *Moi vybor*, pp. 320–27.

32. Gorbachev, *Zhizn'*, 1: p. 520 ff., and *Memoirs*, p. 347.

33. Soon, however, Slovenia seceded from Yugoslavia and precipitated its disintegration. Later, Slovakia parted from the Czech lands without violence. But the old ways prevailed elsewhere. Demands by Tamils, Kurds, East Timorese, Abkhazians, Tibetans, and Uigurs for greater self-determination were met by force in Sri Lanka, Iraq, Indonesia, Georgia, and China. Hong Kong could conceivably have played a role in China similar to Estonia in the USSR, but the PRC absorbed Hong Kong in 1997 and began to curtail its freedoms.

4

Walter C. Clemens Jr.

Creating Good Government: Who Won What When?

CHALLENGES TO GOOD GOVERNMENT

Governments in the reborn Baltic states would have to master myriad tasks to strengthen societal fitness: provide security from foreign and internal threats; generate a sense of shared identity among citizens; earn respect and obedience of citizens; and establish their legitimacy and exert their authority across the land. They would also have to enhance their country's image abroad and contribute to world law and order.

As argued at the beginning of chapter 2, no government or society is perfect. Good government and fitness are not absolutes, but points on a spectrum. While history seems to contradict those complexity theorists who contend that the proclivity to cooperate is encoded in our genes, humans can be mobilized to cooperate from the top down or by self-organization.

But effective self-organization is rare. To be sure, self-rule spread across the globe in the twentieth century. As the twenty-first century began, however, some three-fifths of humanity still lived in unfree or partly free societies. Freedom House reported in late 1999 that 36 percent of humanity lived in "not-free" countries; 25 percent in "partly free" societies; and 39 percent in "free" societies.

Lithuania ranked as free throughout the 1990s, while Estonia moved from partly-free to free by 1993, followed by Latvia in 1994, when Russian troops withdrew from Estonia and Latvia. By 1995 political rights in Lithuania were ranked as 1—the highest grade on a scale from 1 to 7—with civil liberties ranked as 2. Estonia reached this same 1 and 2 ranking in 1996, Latvia in 1997. In Russia, both political and civil liberties were constricted, but the country was judged partly free in the 1990s (4 to 5 in rankings), while some ex-Soviet republics such as Turkmenistan and Uzbekistan were not free (6 to 7). Ten years after the Berlin Wall came down, Eastern European countries such as Hungary and Poland were judged to be free (1 to 2); others, such as Albania and Yugoslavia, were partly free (4 to 5). One country still under Communist rule, China, held a quarter of humanity in not-free conditions.

DYNAMICS OF CHANGE

Balts in the 1990s created a system of self-rule to replace the mixtures of authoritarian and colonial rule they had long endured. Five decades of one-party dictatorship promptly gave way in 1991–1992 to multiparty democracy. For self-rule to work, Balts needed a participant political culture—discussed below in chapter 5. This chapter tells what happened; the next chapter tells why what happened was possible.

In the 1990s, as we shall see, a dialectical movement developed between nationalist, leftist, and moderate victories in each Baltic republic. Compared to the United States, the political scene in each Baltic republic was unstable in the 1990s—more chaotic even than in post–World War II Italy, where despite many parties a single party dominated elections for generations. Multiple parties contested in the Baltic, sometimes forging fragile coalitions that dominated and then lost control of parliament. Governments changed frequently. Many parties were deeply divided internally. There were "wandering deputies" to parliament who deserted their election-time affiliations. Voter preferences zigged and zagged. It appeared that party constellations were rather unstable—even kaleidoscopic. Coalitions formed and broke up over specific issues or personalities more than over basic worldviews and agendas.[1]

Former Communists now dressed as social democrats faced bitter anti-Communists, each disparaging the other's ultimate agenda. There were wild cards—émigrés such as University of California professor Rein Taagepera, Chicago Environmental Protection Agency administrator Valdas Adamkus, and Montreal professor Vaira Vike-Freiberga, who returned from abroad to compete in elections.

The terms "left" and "right" can mean many things. In Baltic politics in the 1990s "leftist" parties generally favored more state intervention for public welfare in economics, "rightist parties" free market liberalism. Some leftist parties sought to conciliate Moscow and help non-Baltic natives to become citizens. Rightist parties were more inclined to denounce the Soviet past, take a tough stand against pressures from Moscow, and demand that any would-be citizens be tested in the official language and civics. But inconsistencies abounded. For example, the Homeland Union in Lithuania tilted toward welfare economics while resisting any sign of Russian imperialism.

As in the 1920s, each Baltic country in the 1990s spawned multiple political parties tied to narrow interest groups and led by strong personalities. Whereas multiparty chaos paved the way to strong-man rule in the late 1920s and 1930s, Baltic voters eschewed authoritarian leadership in the 1990s. They often voted for strong personalities, but did not want any semblance of a dictator.

The number of parties contesting elections and winning parliamentary seats in each Baltic republic declined in the mid- and late 1990s—a sign of growing stabilization. Ruling coalitions began to last longer. In terms of complexity theory, an emerging fitness replaced the interwar extremes of chaos and order.

This chapter examines the nuts and bolts of Baltic politics in the 1990s. We begin with snapshots of the constitutional structures and presidential politics in each republic. We then examine who won what when.

STRUCTURES

Democratic constitutions do not ensure democracy. Weimar Germany and post-Soviet Russia had constitutions that appeared reasonably democratic. But authoritarian traditions coupled with other problems made these countries vulnerable to an authoritarian takeover. The Weimar constitution permitted the president to make Hitler chancellor and for the parliament to give him dictatorial powers. Sixty years later, Russia's 1993 constitution emasculated both houses of parliament and gave autocratic powers to the president.

But constitutions can encourage self-organization and restrain trends toward dictatorship or anarchy. The U.S. Constitution, with its checks and balances, its implicit ideals, and its safeguards against abuse, conduced to the world's most stable governmental structure in the last centuries of the second millennium.

Estonia and Lithuania adopted a constitution by referenda held in 1992, while Latvia revived its 1922 constitution. Estonia and Latvia became the only ex-Soviet republics to adopt a parliamentary system, with the prime minister as head of government and an executive president as head of state. Lithuania opted for a semipresidential system. Let us sketch the constitutional picture as it appeared in the late 1990s and early twenty-first century.

Each Baltic parliament consisted of just one house. The Estonian *Riigikogu* had 101 members, the Latvian *Saeima* 100, the Lithuanian *Seimas* 141. Parliamentary terms were four years.

All citizens aged eighteen and older could vote. The Riigikogu and Saeima were elected by proportional representation; in Lithuania the system was more complicated—seventy-one deputies to the Seimas were elected directly, seventy on a proportional basis through party lists.

To limit the number of parties in parliament, each republic required that a party (or coalition of parties) pass a 5 percent threshold to win a seat. (Lithuania waived this requirement for ethnic minority parties, but raised it to 7 percent for coalitions of parties.) The threshold made election results hard to predict. Many voters cast their votes for small parties with little prospect of winning a seat in parliament.

Each Baltic republic in the 1990s was a unified state—not a federation—divided into counties. Administration was divided into central government and local authorities, with no intermediate level of government. Each republic had a national police force under the Ministry of the Interior.

Each republic pledged to uphold the *human* rights of all its residents, citizens or not. Lithuania granted citizenship to all residents, while Estonia and Latvia (like all Western countries) made citizenship conditional, as discussed in chapter 7. Beginning in 1996, however, Estonia (but not Latvia) permitted resident noncitizens to vote in local elections, though only citizens could run for office and all political posters had to be in Estonian. This was not an empty gesture. In 1999 a party backed by ethnic Russian voters helped a right-center coalition to win control of the Tallinn City Council.

Each republic had an independent judiciary with a supreme court, lower courts, and a constitutional court. In the 1990s Baltic judicial systems were inefficient, and there were long delays in court hearings and the enforcement of decisions. Prisons were crowded; prosecutors and police were often harsh in their treatment of the accused.

STABILIZERS: THE PRESIDENTS

In the 1990s each Baltic president stood as a stabilizing force amid the whirlpool of party politics. The president in each Baltic country was head of state and presided at ceremonial functions. Each president also had important executive functions: each nominated the prime minister subject to approval by the parliament; each could delay if not veto legislation by returning bills to parliament; the Estonian and Latvian presidents could appoint the chief of the general staff but not the defense minister, who was chosen by the prime minister.

The Latvian and Estonian presidents were elected by parliament; the Lithuanian by popular vote.[2] The presidential term in Latvia, at first three years, changed to four years in 1997. In Estonia it was four years, in Lithuania five years. No Baltic president could serve more than two consecutive terms.

Estonia

Lennart Meri was elected president in 1992 and again in 1996.[3] The major contender against Meri each time was Arnold Rüütel, who had chaired Estonia's Supreme Soviet (later Council) from 1983 until 1992 and backed Estonia's demands for economic self-management in the late 1980s. Rüütel was popular in the 1990s, particularly in rural communities.

Box 4.1. Lennart Meri: European of the Year 1999

Born in 1929, Estonia's future president was the son of an interwar Estonian diplomat "repressed" after the USSR annexed Estonia in 1940. When political controls eased, Meri traveled widely in the USSR, filming and writing about the Finno-Ugric kinspeople of Estonians living in other parts of the country. In the last years of the Soviet regime Meri served as Estonia's foreign minister and as an ambassador. He made the case for his country's independence in Washington and to business executives and top officials at MIT, Harvard, and Boston University.

A man of great charm and erudition, President Meri did much to put Estonia on the world political map. His name, Meri, means "sea" in Estonian. In 1996 he campaigned on the theme, "Meri will take us to Europe" (*Meri viib meid Euroopasse*)—toward closer ties with European institutions. And he succeeded. In 1999 he was named "European of the Year." His popularity with the Estonian people was evident in July 1999 as marchers in Tallinn doffed their hats to him and the crowd later applauded as he addressed the country's Song Festival. But President Meri's popularity fell in 2000 as he intervened in many political issues instead of standing apart and conciliating partisan camps. Many Estonians resented that Meri often refused to explain why he acted as he did, for example, in dismissing Johannes Kert as commander-in-chief of the armed forces.

Latvia

Like the Estonian and Lithuanian presidents, the Latvian head of state could shape foreign as well as domestic policy. The president's right to dissolve parliament, however, was limited by the requirement to call a referendum before holding an early election. And the Saeima could overrule a presidential veto by a simple majority.

The Saeima twice chose Guntis Ulmanis as Latvia's president—in 1993 and again in 1996. Nephew of the interwar dictator, Karlis Ulmanis, Guntis Ulmanis belonged to the Farmers' Union and often took an active role in domestic politics. For example, he did much to strengthen minority rights in Latvia and improve relations with Russia.

In 1999 the Saeima chose a woman, Dr. Vaira Vike-Freiberga, to be Latvia's president. A dark-horse candidate, she was elected on the second ballot by fifty-three of the one hundred delegates. She was soon faced with a new law that would restrict the use—even in business—of any language save Latvian. In July 1999 the new president returned the bill to the Saeima, but she approved a revised law later in the year.

Lithuania

Lithuania's 1992 constitution established a much clearer division of powers than existed in Soviet times. The president of Lithuania would have more powers than those of Estonia or Latvia, as well as Germany, but less than the presidents of France or the United States. The Lithuanian president was empowered to set the main lines of foreign policy and help implement them; the president could dissolve parliament and initiate legislation.

Box 4.2. Vaira Vike-Freiberga

The first female president of a Baltic country, Vaira Vike-Freiberga was born in Latvia in 1937. A professor at the University of Montreal for many years, she returned to Riga in 1998 to head a nongovernmental organization promoting Latvia's image abroad. She resigned her Canadian citizenship one day before the Saiema elected her president in 1999.

In Montreal she wrote seven books on Latvian folklore and developed a database of Latvian folk songs. Her essay, "Similarity and Contrast as Structuring Principles in the Latvian Daina Quatrain," became the lead article in *Journal of Baltic Studies,* autumn 1999.

In 1999 some Latvians called their president "our iron lady," comparing her with former UK prime minister Margaret Thatcher. In September Vike-Freiberga met another "iron lady" born just to the east of Germany—U.S. secretary of state Madeleine Albright.

Vike-Freiberga addressed the UN General Assembly in September 1999, speaking first in French and then in English, to rebut criticisms by the Russian foreign minister regarding treatment of ethnic minorities in Latvia. At home she resolved to learn Russian and urged the country's Slavic residents to learn Latvian. I met the president at Harvard University in 2000, when she was honored by a forum for women leaders in world affairs. Like President Meri, Vike-Freiberga did not accept repeated invitations to comment on this book.

The Lithuanian constitution established a strong presidency because the anti-Communists who drafted it expected independence leader Vytautas Landsbergis to be elected president, but he lost to the former Communist Party leader. The Estonian constitution was also written by anti-Communists. They created a figurehead presidency because they feared that Soviet-era leader Arnold Rüütel would win the presidency, but Lennart Meri prevailed. In Russia, meanwhile, the 1993 constitution established the strong presidency that Boris Yeltsin wanted. That constitution was still in place when a much more dictatorial personality took charge in 2000.

THE PATTERNS OF BALTIC POLITICS IN THE 1990s

Nothing was simple, but a dialectical logic—thesis, antithesis, synthesis—underlay the zigs and zags of Baltic politics in the 1990s.

Thesis

Communists fell and nationalists rose to power in the Baltic in the late 1980s and early 1990s. Starting in 1988, each Baltic country had a "popular front" spanning many political viewpoints that did much to unite people against Soviet rule. Once

---

Box 4.3. Lithuania's Presidents

Two men, each born in 1932, contended for Lithuania's presidency in the decade before 1998—music professor Vytautas Landsbergis and longtime Communist politician Algirdas Brazauskas. As the USSR weakened in the late 1980s, the popular front Sajudis, led by Landsbergis, became the driving force behind Lithuania's struggle for independence. Moving in the same direction, Brazauskas in 1989 led the majority wing of the Lithuanian Communist Party to declare its independence from the Moscow-controlled Communist Party of the Soviet Union.

In 1990 Brazauskas briefly served as chairman of the Lithuanian Supreme Soviet presidium—in effect, as Lithuania's president—after the previous chairman resigned and named Brazauskas his successor. But later that year Sajudis won control of parliament and named Landsbergis its chairman.

In 1993 Brazauskas defeated Landsbergis and became Lithuania's first directly elected president. A cartoon in a German newspaper showed Lithuanians carrying a national flag bursting through an opening in a wall under the banner of Landsbergis and entering a voting booth, where they endorsed Brazauskas.

Five years later, Brazauskas chose not to run again and Valdas Adamkus, a Lithuanian-born American in his early 70s, won the 1998 presidential elections. Unlike Brazauskas and Landsbergis, Adamkus had no party affiliation. Above the partisan fray, he could more easily return unsatisfactory legislation to the Seimas and exercise other presidential prerogatives. Some voters hoped he would bring U.S. efficiency to Lithuania. However, Adamkus, the former head of the Environmental Protection Agency in the Chicago area, complained that the bureaucracy of Lithuania was ten times more obdurate than its counterpart in the United States.

In 2000 the tide of popular opinion shifted once more. Landsbergis apologized on television for sharp remarks he made toward political opponents, but his party did poorly in the October parliamentary elections.

independence was achieved, the popular fronts splintered and dozens of diverse political groupings took shape in each republic.

Antithesis

The nationalists were better at breaking from Soviet domination than at governing. Winning independence was different from managing a modern state and economy. Euphoria gave way to postindependence disenchantment. A reverse wave smashed the amber coast in the mid-1990s as voters in each Baltic republic turned against the very leaders who had led the liberation struggle. Most voters were disappointed that living standards fell for all but the newly rich; many were also angry that some politicians profited from the privatization of national resources; and some worried that nationalists were poking the Russian Bear so hard it might lash out.

In Estonia and Lithuania voters brought back leftists—even former Communist officials—to power. The Latvian electorate turned against moderate incumbents; many voted either for the far left or the ultra right. But many of the new leaders also proved inept or corrupt.

Synthesis

Soon the tides turned again. From 1996 to 1999 center-right coalitions regained power in each Baltic republic. Some of the same nationalist leaders who appeared too naive or radical early in the decade now seemed more pragmatic and skillful.

Many factors drove the dialectic—ideology, ethnicity, trust in charismatic politicians, and economic interests. Voter moods oscillated between hope and anger. The dialectical pattern was clearest in Estonia but variations also appeared in Latvia and Lithuania.

Estonia

Thesis

Estonian citizens approved a new constitution in June 1992 and went to the polls in September 1992 to elect 101 deputies to the one house of the Riigikogu, the new parliament. A nationalist coalition led by the Pro Patria Union won the largest number of seats. The Riigikogu subsequently elected the cultural historian and diplomat Lennart Meri as president. Meri called on a thirty-two-year-old historian, Mart Laar, to head the new government.

Prime Minister Laar's government quickly created the most open, free-market economy of all former Soviet countries and reoriented trade away from Russia toward Finland and other Western countries. Russia strongly protested when the Riigikogu passed a citizenship law in 1992 that disenfranchised most residents who were not native to Estonia. Still, bowing to sticks and carrots offered by the West, Russia finally withdrew its remaining troops from Estonian soil in August 1994.

Antithesis

Prime Minister Laar's nationalist government lost popularity as economic hardship persisted, and was discredited by internal splits and scandals. The March 1995 parliamentary election brought to power a center-left alliance of Tiit Vähi's Coalition

Party, Rüütel's Rural Union, and Edward Savisaar's Centrist Party. Vähi became prime minister. The Centrists were soon forced out of the government, however, following a wire-tapping scandal. The Reform Party joined the coalition in their place, but left it again in November 1996 after discovering that Vähi was still cooperating with the Centrist Party. This left Vähi's government without a parliamentary majority. Vähi resigned in February 1997 and was replaced by Mart Siimann.

In late 1997 the Reform Party and several other parties buried their differences and formed the United Opposition. This development augured well for democratic stability, but the United Opposition was not entirely united: it expelled a right-wing grouping early in 1998.

Despite political feuding, the Riigikogu functioned. In June 1998 I watched the proceedings at Toompea Castle—an ancient building now wired for the computer age. Representatives of many parties conducted a civilized debate on Estonia's relations with Europe, each speaker keeping to his allotted time.

Synthesis

A center-right, majority coalition won 53 of 101 Riigikogu seats in the 1999 elections. Thirteen parties or coalitions contested these elections—down from thirty parties in 1995. This was a plus for stability, but voter turnout was comparatively low in 1999—only 57.4 percent. Some potential voters were apathetic and some were confused by a system which banned electoral alliances in 1998 but in 1999 permitted parties to cooperate on a single list.

Box 4.4. Party Politics in Estonia

The major parties shaping Estonian politics in the 1990s were:
- *United People's Party* represented the interests of ethnic Russian citizens and residents.
- The *Center Party* was dominated by its leader, Edgar Savisaar (b. 1950), a founder of the Popular Front in 1988. Savisaar was Estonia's prime minister from April 1990 until January 1992. Savisaar became chairman of Tallinn City Council at the 1996 municipal elections but lost this post in 1999.
- The *Rural Party,* led by Estonia's last Soviet-era president, Arnold Rüütel, sought government subsidies for agriculture and protective tariffs to limit food imports.
- The *Coalition Party* led a center-left coalition government from 1995 to 1999.
- The *Moderates* modeled themselves on Western European social democratic parties.
- The *Reform Party* was the strongest supporter of free-market economics on Estonia's political spectrum.
- The *Pro Patria Union* was the country's strongest force for Estonian national identity. The party's leader, Mart Laar, was described by former British prime minister Margaret Thatcher as her "favourite pupil." President Meri appointed him prime minister in the early 1990s and again in 1999. When I lunched with Maar in the Riigikogu cafeteria in June 1998, he was still an MP, but said he was happy to be out of government so he could concentrate on teaching history at Tartu University, where his students had conducted an extensive oral history of life under Soviet rule.

The coalition government led by Mart Laar in 1999 was composed of the Pro Patria Union (18 seats), the Reform Party (18 seats), and the Moderates (17 seats). Some observers saw Laar's cabinet as a "center-right dream team." Free marketers applauded when Siim Kallas, head of the Reform Party, again became finance minister. He won notoriety and respect when, as governor of the Bank of Estonia in 1991–1995, he introduced the kroon (crown) as Estonia's currency and pegged it to the German mark. However, as finance minister, he was later accused of misconduct for guaranteeing a loan to a private bank and for continuing his ties with the central bank. Moderate Party member Toomas Ilves again became foreign minister, a post he had resigned to contest the elections.

Other key ministers were: Aver Padar (Moderates), agriculture; Juri Luik (Pro Patria Union), defense; Mihkel Parnoja (Moderates), economic affairs; Tonis Lukas (Pro Patria Union), education; Heiki Kranich (Reform Party), environment; Signe Kivi (Reform Party), ethnic affairs; Tarmo Loodus (Pro Patria Union) internal affairs; Mart Rask (Reform Party), justice; and Eiki Nestor (Moderates), transport and communication.

Although the Center Party won the most seats (28), the center-right coalition won more votes and kept the Centrist leader, Savisaar, from power. Savisaar vowed to combine forces with the other opposition parties in the Riigikogu—the Coalition Party (7 seats), Rural Union (7 seats); and the United Peoples' Party (which represented Russian voters, 6 seats).[4] But Savisaar's authoritarian style did not make it easy for other groupings to collaborate with him. The Centrists at the end of the 1990s offered the only substantive policy changes to those enacted by Estonia's two previous postindependence governments. The Centrists demanded replacement of the flat-rate tax system with a progressive one, the doubling of child benefits, and a more inclusive citizenship policy toward ethnic Russians. Savisaar's party often kept other deputies up all night in 1999 and 2000 trying to block budget cuts proposed by Prime Minister Laar.

Laar's government had a tiny majority and could collapse if any party defected and open the way for a center-left administration led by the Center Party. But the majority coalition partners agreed on basic economic and foreign policy issues. Like its predecessors, Laar's government pursued membership in the EU and NATO. The Pro Patria Union favored tightening Estonia's citizenship law and language requirements, but any Estonian government would feel pressure to harmonize its citizenship laws with EU norms.

Table 4.1
The 1999 Election Results for the Riigikogu

Party	% of votes	No. of seats
Center Party	23.41	28
Fatherland Union	16.09	18
Reform Party	15.92	18
Moderates	15.21	17
Coalition Party	7.58	7
Rural Peoples' Party	7.27	7
United Peoples' Party	6.13	6

Box 4.5. A Husband and Wife Team in the National Cause

The United States, Canada, and Israel gained from talented and energetic immigrants. The Baltic countries after independence benefited from small streams of returning native-born sons and daughters and, sometimes, their offspring. A few retired U.S. military officers took leading positions in the Baltic defense establishments.

One returnee, Mari-Ann Rikken Kelam, had represented Estonia on the Joint Baltic American National Committee. Lobbying to promote restoration of Baltic independence, she testified before Congress and met with presidents Ronald Reagan and George Bush, and traveled Canada and Europe. A graduate of Oberlin College and the University of Toledo, she also edited documents on Estonian history and circulated news on Baltic affairs.

Moving from Virginia to Tallinn, Kelam in 1993 became spokesperson for the Foreign Ministry. In 1996 she became international secretary of the Pro Patria Union. In 1999 she was elected to the Riigikogu along with her husband, Tunne Kelam.

Trained in history and languages, Tunne Kelam had long pressed for Estonia's liberation from the USSR. He founded the first opposition party and chaired the Congress of Estonia, organized in 1990 to supplant Estonia's Supreme Soviet. He became vice chairman of the Pro Patria Union in the 1990s and served as deputy speaker of the Riigikogu. He placed third in the runoffs for Estonia's presidency in 1996 and led Estonian delegations to the Council of Europe in Strasbourg and the EU in Brussels.

The photo at the beginning of Chapter 3 shows the Kelams in a 1992 demonstration for the withdrawal of Russian troops from the Baltic countries.

Latvia

Thesis

Latvian politics in the 1990s saw much fractious bickering and heard many allegations of corruption in high places. The Popular Front-led government that took power in Latvia in 1990 rapidly lost popularity after independence as the Latvian economy fell into a deep recession. Still, a spin-off from the Popular Front, a party known as Latvia's Way, won the largest number of votes in the 1993 elections for the 100 seats in the parliament—the Saeima. Latvia's Way, led by Anatolijs Gorbunovs, formed a coalition government with the Farmers' Union, which championed agricultural interests. Valdis Birkavs, another leading member of Latvia's Way, became prime minister.

The Farmers' Union left the coalition in April 1994, after Latvia's Way refused to raise agricultural tariffs, and was replaced in government by the Political Union of Economists. This change occurred at a sensitive time for the government, which was overseeing the completion of Russian troop withdrawals as well as the introduction of a controversial citizenship law designed to restrict naturalization of the Russian minority. By August 1994, however, most Russian troops left Latvia, though some remained until 1999 at a leased radar station. However, any semblance of a honeymoon for Latvia's Way ended in 1995, when Latvia's largest bank collapsed amid allegations of fraud.

Box 4.6. Party Politics in Latvia

Latvia's political landscape shifted often in the 1990s. Here are the major players in the 1990s, arranged roughly from left to right:

- The *Equal Rights Party* aimed to integrate Russian speakers into Latvian society.
- The *National Harmony Party* also defended minority rights and supported reconciliation with Russia. At times it allied with Equal Rights.
- The *Democratic Party Saimnieks* ["Master of the House"] contained many members of the former Communist establishment. Accused of corruption, it faded in the late 1990s.
- The *Latvian Social Democratic Alliance* and its leader, Juris Bojars, next took over the left wing of the political spectrum. Banned from public office because of past affiliation with the KGB, Bojars attracted votes by denouncing corruption.
- *Latvia's Way* was the major right-of-center party and was committed to free-market reforms and integration with the West.
- The *People's Party* was organized by Andris Skele in 1998 after his first stint as prime minister ended and before his second began in 1999. Its backers hoped that Skele and other businessmen could make government more efficient and less corrupt.
- *For Fatherland and Freedom* and the *Latvian National Independence Movement* represented the nationalist right.
- The *People's Movement for Latvia,* founded by Joahims Zigerists, had a nationalist platform but appealed to the poor. It lost favor after Zigerists's rightist past in Germany became known.

Antithesis

The general election of September-October 1995 changed the political landscape once again. Voters turned out in large numbers—72 percent of those eligible. Many were angry because five of the country's ten largest banks had folded that year, causing thousands of depositors to lose their savings. Nearly one-third of Latvia's voters vented their frustration by rejecting the incumbents and endorsing either the left or the right—the recently formed Democratic Party Saimnieks (DPS) led by former Communist officials or the ultra-right-wing/populist People's Movement for Latvia, financed by an eccentric German who claimed Latvian descent. Each group won about 15 percent of the vote, as did the moderate incumbents, Latvia's Way. A distant fourth place went to the center-right party For Fatherland and Freedom (FFF). A half-dozen smaller parties also won seats.

To keep extremists from power, President Ulmanis selected the nonpartisan businessman Andris Skele for the post of prime minister. Skele managed to hold together a coalition of six parties of widely differing political ideologies for eighteen months. During this time he gave a big push to Latvia's reform program, focusing on economic policies such as revitalizing the privatization program and balancing the budget. But his energetic/aggressive style alienated many in the political establishment. He resigned in July 1997.

Guntars Krasts, of the center-right FFF, took over a largely unchanged government coalition and political agenda. Formerly an academic economist, Krasts was a weak PM. Without Skele, the coalition quickly disintegrated.

Bad news for the government continued. In July 1997 the European Commission recommended not to include Latvia in the first round of EU accession negotiations — in part because Latvia's minority issues were unresolved. The Fatherland Front's stance toward the Russian minority worsened Latvia's relations with Russia in 1998. In March 1998 the Kremlin intensified its charges that Latvia was abusing its Russian-speaking population, and Russia threatened economic sanctions. In April the DPS left the government, following quarrels over minority rights and privatization. Krasts's minority government limped along until the October 1998 general election, in which both his own FFF and the DPS suffered losses.

Synthesis

In the late 1990s Latvia was sharply criticized by Moscow for its treatment of Russian-speakers — far more sharply than was Estonia or Lithuania. But there was a stronger pro-Russian constituency in Latvia than in the other two Baltic countries. First, there was a powerful business clan in Ventspils, headed in the late 1990s by Aivars Lembergs, mayor of the port city. Hungry for Russian oil and oil revenues, it favored closer ties with Russia than with the EU. Second, Riga became a safe haven for Russian money. Banks in Riga such as Parex, headed by two Russians who obtained Latvian citizenship without passing the usual language exams, had close ties to Russia in the late 1990s. Parex placed ads on Russian television showing the dollar bill with the words, "We are closer than America." Third, the Latvian agricultural sector, where one prime minister had major holdings, depended heavily on Russian purchases.

Center-right parties won a decisive majority in Latvia's October 1998 elections. Some 72 percent of eligible voters participated — more even than the 68 percent that turned out for the 1998 referendum revising the country's citizenship law. Candidates from six of twenty-one contesting parties won seats in parliament. Radical right-wing parties and ultranationalists were punished in the 1998 parliamentary election. They were blamed for bringing Latvia to the brink of economic war with Russia.

A plurality of votes went to the People's Party, organized in the spring 1998 by former PM Skele. The People's Party pledged socially acceptable economic reform plus rapid integration with the West.

The second largest number of votes went to Latvia's Way, led by Valdis Kristopans. As transport minister from 1995 to 1998, Kristopans gained popularity for improving the country's transport system. His refusal to resign in 1997, despite corruption allegations, had contributed to Skele's resignation as prime minister.

Kristopans became the new prime minister after the 1998 elections. But tensions between the two leading parties kept them from forming a majority government. The policy goals of Skele and Kristopans were similar, but their rivalry was too strong.

Kristopans formed a minority center-right government. He brought the Fatherland Front and the New Party into a coalition with Latvia's Way. FFF leader Krasts returned to power as deputy prime minister for European integration. Together, Kristopans and Krasts kept Skele from power. To win a parliamentary majority, however, Kristopans's coalition needed the votes of the Latvian Social Democratic Alliance. The Alliance, in turn, insisted on the post of agricultural minister and on revisions in the economic reform program.

In early 1999 Latvia had forty-eight registered political parties. To stabilize the system, the larger parties in the Saeima voted in March 1999 to raise the minimum membership requirements for new political parties from two hundred to one thousand.

Kristopans resigned in 1999 over charges that he was manipulated by the transport lobby and by financial powers in Ventspils, center of the oil industry.[5] In July 1999 Andris Skele became Latvian PM once more. Of the parliament's 100 deputies, 60 voted to support a three-party coalition comprising Skele's People's Party, the center-right FFF, and Latvia's Way.

Skele told the Saeima in July 1999 that Latvia faced an economic crisis and needed to focus on balancing the budget. But the Social Democrats challenged any budget cuts likely to hurt pensioners, teachers, and local governments. Skele replied by quoting former West German chancellor Konrad Adenauer: "There is no better social policy than a thriving economy."

Latvia's economy in 1999 grew by less than 1 percent, but private investors bid high for shares in the Latvian Gas Company in a March 2000 auction, while no buyers were found for the Latvian Shipping Company.

Following nine months of disputes over privatization and Skele's personal wealth, he resigned as prime minister and was replaced in May 2000 by the former mayor of Riga, Andris Berzins, a member of Latvia's Way.[6] The centrist orientation remained. Nearly half the ministers in the previous government stayed on. The former coalition of the People's Party, Latvia's Way, and FFF was joined by the New Party, headed by Raimond Pauls, a popular musician who publicly declared there was insufficient evidence to prove that Latvia had been occupied by the USSR. But the coalition between Latvia's Way and the New Party shuddered in August 2000, when Pauls resigned from the party and became an independent MP.

The deep enmities driving Latvian politics erupted in 2000, when MP Janis Adamsons accused Skele and two former officials of links to pedophile gangs. After six months of investigation, however, the Prosecutor General's Office closed the case for lack of evidence and considered prosecuting Adamsons for libel.

Though Latvia's trade imbalance remained high, it appeared in late 2000 that Latvia's economy was expanding and its tax collections improving. The IMF worried, however, when Latvia's government promised increases in minimum wages that could set back fiscal discipline and economic growth.

Prime Minister Berzins had moderate views toward Russia, but he had to interact with President Vike-Freiberga, who minced no words when speaking about Russia. As mayor of Riga, Berzins had behaved more like a fixer than a strong-willed reformer. Still, Berzins committed himself to selling the big state-owned enterprises for cash so as to exclude the existing managers and their cronies. As of 2000, however, Latvia had privatized few big enterprises and carried out much less restructuring than Estonia had.

Most Latvians in the 1990s endorsed parties with a market orientation. By 2000, however, the government risked a backlash over perceived corruption, unfairness, and inefficiency—all seen in its failure to collect taxes from the rich as well as the poor.

Lithuania

Thesis

The first free elections ever held in Soviet Lithuania took place in spring 1990 as voters chose deputies for the new 141-seat parliament—the Seimas. They overwhelmingly favored candidates sponsored by Sajudis, which then dominated the Seimas and chose Landsbergis its chairman. But there was a kind of parallel government, because the Seimas also elected a prime minister, Dr. Kazimiera Prunskiene. She served from March 1990 until January 1991, when she was pushed out of office over differences with Landsbergis: she favored compromise with Moscow while Landsbergis was intransigent. Some Lithuanians thought her opportunistic, some thought Landsbergis too rigid.

Antithesis

The dominant fact shaping the 1992 parliamentary elections in Lithuania was a severe fuel shortage in the winter 1991–1992. At times the Russians simply cut the flow of oil. Many Lithuanians blamed Sajudis and its leader, Landsbergis, for alienating the Kremlin.

The nationalist Communists, renamed the Lithuanian Democratic Labor Party (LDLP), challenged Sajudis in the 1992 elections. A dozen or so other parties took part, but most voters backed either Sajudis or the LDLP, which won a working majority in the Seimas.

The LDLP's early period in office was marked by economic stabilization and better relations with Moscow. All Russian troops withdrew from Lithuania in August 1993 (a

---

Box 4.7. Gender Politics

The first female prime minister of a Baltic country, Dr. Kazimiera Prunskiene, was born in 1943. She studied economics in Vilnius and in Frankfurt, Germany, and then taught at the University of Vilnius. In 1988 she joined Sajudis; she was elected in 1989 to the People's Congress of the USSR and in 1990 to Lithuania's parliament. She challenged party orthodoxy in a dialogue, "To Listen to One Another," published in *Kommunist,* theoretical journal of the Soviet Communist Party, in April 1989. She published several books, including two in German: *A Life for Lithuania* (1991) and *The Baltic Market* (1994). She founded the Lithuanian Women's Party in 1995, but it won only 4 percent of the votes cast in the 1996 Seimas elections.

The Soviet Government and Communist Party admitted no women to top decision-making posts, but paid obeisance to gender equality. They used decrees and quotas and arranged the one-party slates so that in the 1980s women won roughly one-third of the seats in Baltic legislatures. But many people thought politics should be a males-only activity. As in most formerly Communist countries, the percentage of women deputies in Baltic legislatures and other official posts declined after independence was regained. This share declined in 1993 in Latvia to 15 percent and in Lithuania to 7 percent. In the late 1990s, however, the three Baltic countries had a greater share of women in government—from one-tenth to one-fourth at most levels—than in any other country in the former Soviet realm except for the Czech Republic, Slovakia, and Slovenia.

Box 4.8. Party Politics in Lithuania

- The *Lithuanian Democratic Labor Party (LDLP)* won the 1992 elections but lost power in 1996. The LDLP was formed from the Communist Party of Lithuania. Unlike the Communist parties of Estonia and Latvia, the Lithuanian Communists had not been dominated by ethnic Russians and had resisted Sovietization. Lithuanian voters could consider the LDLP as a vehicle for promoting the national interest. Estonia and Latvia, by contrast, banned their former Communist parties, which had opposed independence.
- The *Lithuanian Social Democratic Party* shared the left-of-center platform with the LDLP. The Social Democrats opposed many of the privatizations that took place in the 1990s.
- The *New Union of Social Liberals* presented themselves as liberals with a social conscience. They joined the centrist coalition dominating the Seimas after the October 2000 elections.
- The *Liberal Union* organized by Rolandas Paksas after he resigned as PM in 1999. It placed second in the 2000 elections and led a centrist coalition in the Seimas.
- The *Homeland Union* was built by Vytautas Landsbergis from the Sajudis movement. These conservatives generally favored government intervention in the economy and sought Lithuania's membership in NATO and the EU. The Homeland Union was marginalized by the October 2000 elections.
- The *Christian Democratic Party* championed a free market. Dating back to 1905, it was reestablished in 1989 by Algirdas Saudargas, who became foreign minister in 1990 and again in 1996, when the Christian Democrats became a junior partner of Homeland Union in government.

year before they left Estonia and Latvia). In opposition, Sajudis restyled itself the Homeland Union. It charged that the LDLP government was both corrupt and irresolute — supinely allowing Russia to use Lithuania as a military transit corridor to Kaliningrad.

The LDLP found itself in hot water as two of Lithuania's largest banks collapsed in December 1995. The Homeland Union charged that Prime Minister Adolfas Slezevicius and other LDLP ministers had received preferential interest rates at one of the banks; forewarned, they had withdrawn their deposits just before the bank closures. But there was scandal in Sajudis ranks, too. The Sajudis defense minister in 1990–1991, Audrius Butkevicius, was accused of fraud related to arms purchases; for his part, he accused his former patron, Vytautas Landsbergis, of having been a KGB agent.[7] While Butkevicius was convicted and sentenced to five and a half years in jail, an official investigation cleared Landsbergis; Butkevicius claimed that he was framed.[8] Paroled in 2000, he continued to denounce Landsbergis.

Synthesis

In the October-November 1996 election Lithuanian voters turned from the left to the center. Center-right parties won control of the Seimas in the late 1990s and faced little effective opposition from the left-of-center parties. Some thirty parties took part in Lithuania's 1996 parliamentary elections, but only five won more than 5 percent of the vote—the necessary minimum to take part in parliament. The threshold rule thwarted potential chaos.

The Homeland Union returned to power with 70 seats in the Seimas, and the LDLP was beaten into fourth place with a mere 11 seats (down from 73 in 1992). With Gediminas Vagnorius back as prime minister (he was PM when Sajudis was defeated in 1992), the Homeland Union formed a government with its political allies, the Christian Democrats, who won 14 seats, the second largest number. The moderate Center Union also won 14 seats. It received one ministerial post in return for parliamentary support, but did not officially join the coalition. The two main leftist parties, the Lithuanian Social Democratic Party (10 seats) and LDLP (11 seats) were in opposition. The Womens' Party gained 1 seat. A party representing Polish voters won 2 seats—down from 4 in 1992.

The center-right coalition followed a strategy of gradual reform, but large-scale privatization was plagued by delays; also, the government had repeatedly to fight allegations of sleaze and corruption.

Despite the westward orientation of its foreign policy, Lithuania was excluded from the first round of expansion by both NATO and the EU. In Vilnius in 1998 I watched the government juggle a visit on the same day from the president of Iceland, a proponent of Baltic membership in NATO, and Russian foreign minister Evgenii Primakov, an opponent.

When his presidential term expired, Brazauskas chose not to run again, and Valdas Adamkus was elected president in January 1998. After an initial honeymoon, the new president's relations with Prime Minister Vagnorius deteriorated. Amid mutual recriminations, Vagnorius resigned in April 1999, and President Adamkus proposed the mayor of Vilnius, Rolandas Paksas—a member of the Homeland Union—as the new prime minister. Parliament approved Paksas in May 1999 by a vote of 105 to 1 with 12 abstentions. Christian Democrats ended their formal coalition agreement with Homeland Union in June but left their ministers in the cabinet.

But Paksas and two ministers resigned in late October 1999. As we shall see in chapter 8, they objected to the financial burdens on Lithuania written into a deal with a U.S. oil company. The opposition parties saw blood and perceived a chance to overthrow the Homeland Union. Adamkus named a woman, Social Care and Labor Minister Irena Degutiene, as interim PM, but she did not want the job full time. On November 3 the Seimas accepted Adamkus's next nominee for prime minister, Andrius Kubilius, by an 82 to 20 vote with 18 abstentions—much less support than it had given Paksas. Kubilius, also from the Homeland Union, had been deputy chairman of the Seimas.

Municipal elections across Lithuania in March 2000 saw the decline of both major parties—the Homeland Union and the LDLP. Two left-leaning parties gained the most votes—the New Union of Social Liberals and the Peasants' Party. The New Union was headed by Arturas Paulauskas, rival to Valdas Adamkus in the 1998 presidential elections. Both the New Union and the Peasants' Party resisted Lithuania's early entry into the EU and NATO. Their victories pushed the Homeland Union into third place: it won just 10 percent of votes in the municipal elections.

Splitting from a Homeland Union still dominated by Landsbergis, former PM Vagnorius early in 2000 formed a "Moderate Conservatives" faction in the Seimas. In Vilnius, meanwhile, the Liberal Union formed by Paksas after his resignation as

---

Box 4.9. An American-style Politician as Lithuania's Pilot

Rolandas Paksas was approved as Lithuania's PM in 1999 but soon resigned, as we shall see in chapter 8, because he opposed government subsidies to an American investor. Paksas earlier had become well known as mayor of Vilnius because he did much to restore the capital's Old Town and rebuild its roads. Trained as an engineer and an airplane pilot, Paksas was twice the acrobatic flight champion of the USSR. Weeks after becoming PM in 1999, Paksas opened an international festival in Vilnius by performing stunt flights to the sounds of classical music, which was followed by fireworks. Like some U.S. politicians of note, Paksas often pledged: "No new taxes."

Forty-two years old in 1999, Paksas was born in western Lithuania, where his parents retained a five-liter bottle of apple wine made the day he was born. Paksas's wife, Laima, was educated as an engineer and an economist. The model couple had a daughter, Inga, and a son, Mindaugas.

Paksas became prime minister for a second time in October 2000, as his new party, the Liberal Union, mobilized a coalition of centrist parties against social democrats and conservatives.

PM joined with Polish Electoral Action, a party representing Polish voters, to win control of city hall.

Lithuania's parliamentary elections in October 2000, contested by more than twenty parties, generated a paradoxical outcome. The left-leaning Social Democratic Coalition stitched together by Algirdas Brazauskas won 51 of the 141 seats—more than any other party. The coalition united the Democratic Labor Party, the Social Democratic Party, and two smaller parties, the Russian Union and Party of New Democracy, the former Women's Party, headed by Kazimiera Prunskiene. But an alliance of centrist parties dominated the new Seimas. The center-right Liberal Union headed by Rolandas Paksas won 34 seats. It combined with the center-left New Union of Social Liberals of Arturas Paulauskas, which won 29 seats, and several smaller parties. With the blessing of President Adamkas, Paksas again became prime minister. Paulauskas replaced Landsbergis as chair of the Seimas.

The Home Union of Landsbergis won just nine votes in the October 2000 elections and was marginalized. Landsbergis warned that the new centrist coalition was "a soup where every ingredient can be found." The Liberal Union, for example, favored laissez-faire economics; the New Union of Social Liberals favored far-reaching state intervention. Both groups agreed, however, on the need to join the EU and NATO, and both were also willing to legalize casinos, as in the four neighboring countries.

TOWARD POLITICAL FITNESS

The transition to self-rule in the Baltics was not easy. Voters proved fickle or apathetic; many politicians proved venal or inept; many individuals and factions proved corrupt. Private enrichment often crowded out the common good. Still, a deep political transformation took place. Laws proved more powerful than any personalities, political patronage, or partisanship. When voters chose to replace one set of politicians with another, change took place peacefully. Even those politicians with deep grudges against one another bowed to democratic procedure.

Baltic politics in the 1990s resembled more the fledgling democracies of the Czech Republic, Poland, and Hungary than Russia or other former Soviet union-republics. There were deep differences as well as similarities in each Baltic republic. But some facts stood out: no strong man (or woman) dominated any Baltic country after the Soviet breakup; no armed battles took place between president and parliament; the worst corruption scandals in the Baltic did not approach the gravity of those that dominated Russian politics or that flared in Belgium and Japan.

The synthesis in Baltic politics did not mark the "end of history." The political pendulum would continue to swing, although it might change speed and direction. Whether democracy could be consolidated would depend heavily on the political culture of each Baltic country, discussed in chapter 5.

Caption for Chapter 4 Photo: The building housing Estonia's parliament and government stands on a hill from which Danish, Sword Brother, Swedish, Tsarist Russian, Nazi, and Soviet authorities tried to rule Estonians.

NOTES

1. This characterization of Estonian politics probably applies to party formation in Latvia and Lithuania as well. See Bernard Grofman, Evald Mikkel, and Rein Taagepera, "Fission and Fusion of Parties in Estonia, 1987–1999," *Journal of Baltic Studies* 31 (winter 2000), pp. 329–59 at 331; also see their previous "Electoral Systems Change in Estonia," ibid. 30 (fall 1999), pp. 227–49, and David Arter, *Parties and Democracy in the Post-Soviet Republics: The Case of Estonia* (Aldershot, England: Dartmouth, 1966).

2. Estonia's first post-Soviet president was to be elected in 1992 by direct popular vote. Since no candidate won more than 50 percent of the vote, the election was decided in the Riigikogu.

3. In 1996 the Riigikogu failed to provide a two-thirds majority for any presidential candidate so an Electoral Assembly consisting of parliamentary members plus representatives of local governments — more than five hundred delegates — convened to select the president.

4. Five parties failed to breach the 5 percent barrier: the Estonian Christian Party (2.4 percent), the Russian Party in Estonia (2 percent), the Blue Party (1.6 percent), the Farmers' Assembly (0.5 percent), and the Progressive Party (0.38 percent).

5. Another issue concerned privatization of the energy giant Latvenergo. Kristopans (joined by the privatization agency) wanted the firm broken up into subsidiaries; a dissident minister of economics wanted 25 percent of the shares to go public.

6. Skele, as a private citizen, had purchased 100 percent of the shares in the Ave Lat food conglomerate in April 1999. As he became PM, Skele turned over the Ave Lat firm to a blind trust proxy to avoid any conflicts of interest. But in early 2000 he sold his shares in the firm (renamed New Technology and Business Development Corporation) for $29 million in promissory notes.

7. Butkevicius mobilized a human shield to protect Landsbergis and the parliament from Soviet troops in January 1991. Trained as a psychiatrist, Butkevicius wanted to train the entire Lithuanian population in techniques of civilian defense. This exemplar of nonviolent resistance and member of parliament was caught in 1997 with $15,000 of a $300,000 "loan" he demanded from Dega, Ltd. for mediating its financial problems with the government.

8. Butkevicius was not impeached and so remained a member of parliament. In 1999 he asked Landsbergis, chairman of the Seimas, to send him documents in jail and to afford him the opportunity to attend sittings and votes. "Lithuanian convict Butkevicius ready to rule," *Baltic Times,* July 1–7, 1999, p. 6.

5

Self-Organization and Social Capital

A VIRTUOUS CIRCLE

Good government is a necessary but not a sufficient condition for high societal fitness. For that, broad and deep structures of self-organization are also required. Self-organized fitness depends not just on constitutions and free elections but on social capital, a democratic political culture, civil society, and human development. All these factors are interlinked. Movement in each variable strengthens or weakens the others. Social capital and political culture are discussed in this chapter, human development and integration in chapters 6 and 7. To enhance societal fitness, each Baltic government had to enhance all components in a virtuous circle of self-organization.

Social Capital

The term social capital sums up a society's capacity for self-organization—its capacity to promote and coordinate efforts for collective goods or shared profits. Like money in the bank, social capital is an asset available to produce more wealth. Social capital can foster good government, a vital economy, and creativity in other spheres. It motivates and permits people to create values for mutual gain. It makes things work and also helps to heal social wounds. Financial capital is a building block for investing in development. But social capital is more important than cash or credit. It is fundamental to societal fitness.

Why is social capital critical? A society with little social capital may be rich in educated human beings, knowledge, natural resources, and financial assets, and yet fail to use them efficiently or justly. This has been and will long remain the problem of Russia.

Social capital fosters and benefits from a democratic political culture, civil society, trust, integration, and rising levels of human development.

A Democratic Political Culture

Every political culture arises from and conditions a society's entire way of life. It is an orientation toward political life—attitudes, symbols, norms, and expectations about politics. Political culture shapes political structure and imparts pattern to political behavior. It builds upon and perpetuates tradition.

Electoral systems and divisions of power are important, but political culture is more fundamental than political constitutions. The key to a stable democracy does not lie in choosing a presidential or a parliamentary form of government. A presidential system works reasonably well in the United States, while parliamentary systems provide good government in Northern Europe. But neither presidential nor parliamentary systems can guarantee democratic stability. In the second half of the twentieth century, presidential systems often crashed in Latin America while parliamentary systems often failed in Africa and in parts of Asia; between the world wars parliamentary systems collapsed in Italy, Spain, Germany, and most of Eastern Europe—including the Baltic republics.

Democracy is not something that one "gets" once and for all in a constitution. Rather, democracy—like all ingredients of fitness—must be fought for and won on an ongoing basis. If citizens do not engage in this fight, there will be no democracy—and little fitness.

Why did urban reform fail in Aalborg (see box 1.2), even though Danes for two centuries had pursued modernity and democracy? A Danish scholar concluded that the old rationality of power had deeper roots than modern forms of rationality. Democracy, with its expectation of administrative neutrality, was young and fragile next to premodern traditions of class and privilege, consolidated in centuries of daily practice. Modernity and democracy, the Aalborg case suggests, are not end points but tools of power.[1]

Indeed, Bent Flyvbjerg concluded that greed and power tend to overpower reason—even in Denmark, a bastion of enlightened self-rule—that claims to "rational discourse" are often just rationalization, tactics in a campaign to bolster one's narrow self-interest. On the other hand, Flyvbjerg also inferred that conflict is natural and that its suppression—as in the former Communist states—throttles creativity.

In a democracy, each citizen must balance three roles. Each is a *participant* in the political process, but each is also a *subject* of government—required to perform duties and obey laws. Outside the political process, each is also a *parochial*—a member of family, cultural, and other groups. The parochial role helps moderate conflict by setting limits to politicization.

Complexity theory does not prescribe the optimum degree of centralization for any institution or society. Self-organized fitness could be decentralized (as in the early Swiss confederation) or coordinated from the center (as in a federal system). But it would avoid both poles—random chaos and the kind of top-down order by which the Soviet Communist Party directed all governmental and nongovernmental institutions.

Authoritarian regimes such as the former USSR try to promote passive, subject political cultures—blind obedience rather than thoughtful participation. They restrict decision making and the information needed for decision making to a narrow elite.

Top-down, authoritarian rule can sometimes mobilize public enthusiasm, but it rarely taps the deep strengths inherent in self-organization.

A democratic political culture fosters and requires self-organization, informed participation, political competence and skills, and a widely shared conviction that the system is just and merits support. The system posits majority rule combined with respect for minorities; it also requires a willingness by minorities to accept majority rule.

Civil Society and Trust

Civil society is a "realm of organized social life . . . autonomous from the state, and bound by a legal order or set of shared rules."[2] A civil society is rich in institutions that stand between people and government and shield people from the raw forces of a market economy. Communist and other totalitarian systems generally seek to limit such institutions; social capital and political democracy nurture and need them. Such institutions are the essence of self-organization.

In totalitarian dictatorships, the government controls all institutions. No independent institutions can challenge the ruling elite. By contrast, a modern democracy is self-organized on many levels. It spawns nongovernmental organizations (NGOs) that function independently of government. Some NGOs *bond* like-minded people or those with common interests; other NGOs look outward and strive to *bridge* diverse mind-sets and interests. The range of NGOs extends from parent-teacher associations to the Red Cross to environmental action groups. Some stand between individuals and government; others (such as trade unions, consumer advocacy groups, and Greens) protect individuals from the raw power of free market economics.

Civil society can exert a negative check on bad government. But it also generates social capital—cooperative energies that enhance the public good. NGOs contribute to self-organization—a key ingredient of fitness.

Trust is a vital ingredient in social capital, democratic politics, civil society, and economic vitality. Trust undergirds the capacity for self-organized fitness. Trust plus self-organization makes it possible to cooperate for mutual gain.

Without trust, people cannot organize for common purposes. As in southern Italy, one might trust a Mafia clan as part of one's extended family, but not the rest of society or the government, unless they were Mafia-controlled.

Some distrust, however, is to be expected in a democracy. Indeed, the U.S. Constitution's system of checks and balances (separated branches of government, each sharing power) exists because America's founding fathers distrusted human nature. Politics turns on interests as well as on competence and other factors. So long as people have divergent interests, they can be "trusted" to follow what they see as their interests.

Surveys suggest an erosion of trust in government among individuals and between groups in many Western polities. But democracy builds on recognition that politics does not provide a natural terrain for robust trust relations. Democratic systems institutionalize distrust by providing opportunities for citizens to oversee those empowered with the public trust. Still, democracy cannot do without trust, because it is a necessary building block for collective action. Democratic institutions depend on a trust among citizens sufficient for representation, resistance, and alternative forms of governance.[3]

Chapter 5

SOCIAL CAPITAL AND POLITICAL CULTURE
IN THE BALTIC REPUBLICS

An Authoritarian Heritage

Repressed for centuries, Balts began to self-organize in the nineteenth century. Both music festivals and popular assemblies demanding autonomy nourished social capital and the saplings of civil society.

After World War I Estonians, Latvians, and Lithuanians achieved independent statehoods and democratic constitutions. But none had a strong democratic political culture. Multiple political parties emerged—too many for political stability. Starting with Lithuania in 1926, each Baltic republic sought relief from chaos in authoritarian order, as happened in many countries between the wars.

Soviet rule attempted to destroy Baltic democracy and civil society. The Kremlin attempted to deracinate Balts—root out any identity save "Soviet." Communists tried to extirpate religious belief or, if that proved difficult, to infiltrate and control the churches. The Soviets flooded Estonia and Latvia with Slavic immigrants and raised up Baltic collaborators willing to serve Moscow.

The Kremlin claimed to foster democracy but the USSR practiced an authoritarian culture of obedience, with constricted access to information needed for self-organization. Communist leaders and collaborators were schooled in Lenin's view that politics is a zero-sum struggle—"*kto kovo*" or who [will destroy] whom? Mutual gain between classes, they learned, was impossible.

Against the odds, independence-minded Balts survived and gained strength in the late 1980s. Music festivals and a human chain from Tallinn to Vilnius demonstrated the general will for independence. After independent statehood was regained, however, the hard work of rebuilding and building a democratic polity began. Governing oneself could be more difficult than defying others.

After Soviet rule collapsed, what political culture or cultures would emerge in the Baltic region? Could political and economic freedoms flourish where authoritarian ways had prevailed in recent decades and in earlier centuries? Balts could adapt a wide range of democratic models to build their governments. The more difficult challenge would be to cultivate a democratic political culture. This task would be more important than deciding how to divide powers among the parliament, the prime minister, and the president.

The preconditions for democracy in the Baltic were weak,[4] but a participant political culture quickly took hold in each reborn Baltic state. Majority rule prevailed. Governments changed often, but they did so peacefully.

When political euphoria prevailed in the early 1990s, voter turnout was extremely high. As voters became disenchanted in the mid- and late 1990s, turnout declined. Still, far more than half the electorate continued to vote—less than in Soviet times but a much larger share than in most European democracies. More than 68 percent of eligible voters turned out for Estonia's 1995 election. Nearly 72 percent of eligible voters took part in Latvia's 1998 parliamentary elections. In Lithuania some 72 percent of eligible voters took part in the 1992 elections, but only 53 percent did so in 1996.

Many Baltic voters in the 1990s denounced their politicians as corrupt or incompetent. Unlike Soviet times, Baltic voters could throw the rascals out. Democracy was still the worst political system except for all others.

Whether right-of-center or left-of-center coalitions ruled in Estonia, Latvia, and Lithuania, the "ins" continued the mainstream consensus. They took few if any actions deeply offensive to the "outs."

Baltic democracy looked very strong compared to conditions in other parts of the former USSR. In the Baltic, no strong man dominated politics for years, as happened from Minsk and Moscow to Tashkent and Bishkek. In the Baltic, no one died in an ethnic or political battle. Governments came and went, obedient to electoral procedures.

Participation versus Alienation

On the whole, each Baltic state in the 1990s made substantial progress in rebuilding and building institutions of civil society. But many deep problems persisted or got worse. Independence regained, Baltic societies became more atomized as individuals and interest groups focused on their private good. Social capital was undermined by apathy, narrow self-seeking, and mutual distrust.

The past lay heavily on the present. For decades Communist regimes sowed distrust everywhere—within families, among colleagues, between generations, and between ethnic groups. Pervasive distrust would not be vanquished overnight—especially when a few Balts suddenly became rich while most became poorer. As the gaps between nouveaux riches and have-nots expanded, suspicions grew that government officials and their favorites were enriching themselves at public expense.[5] If evidence of corruption were strong, however, Baltic politicians resembled the Japanese more than Russians: they resigned instead of stonewalling, and none had rivals or critics assassinated.

Box 5.1. Is Disgust with Politics Normal in a Democracy?

Dissatisfaction with politics and politicians is common in the democratic world. No serious observer damned Baltic politics in terms so negative as some thoughtful Canadians directed at their country's political culture. On July 1, 1997, Canada's 130th birthday, the Toronto *Globe and Mail* editorialized: "If the land is strong today, the spirit is weak. Canada is suffering from a fading sense of community, an erosion of self-awareness and a retreat into sectionalism and ethnicity. . . . [We have] noxious envy, anger, ignorance and indifference. Against this corrosion, our leaders are helpless."

Other observers complained that Canada could define itself only in negative terms—not American, not English, not French, not a real country but a nationless state—at best, a postmodern society.

If Canada—repeatedly ranked as the most agreeable country in the world by the UN Development Programme—elicited such criticism from its citizens, what kinds of self-appraisals could be expected from poverty-stricken Baltic peoples emerging from fifty years of Communism?[1]

---

[1]These perspectives come from Modris Eksteins, a professor born in Latvia and brought up in Canada. Eksteins, *Walking Since Daybreak: A Story of Eastern Europe, World War II, and the Heart of Our Century* (Boston: Houghton Mifflin, 1999), pp. 17–18.

Box 5.2. Elite Democracy in the Baltic?

One study concluded that the three Baltic countries were governed in the 1990s by an elite democracy that denied voice to diverse groups. New elites replaced Soviet officials and manipulated the reborn states from the top down. Elites framed most issues as "technical"—beyond the competence of ordinary humans. Lacking a development strategy, the elites kept their rivalries within bounds and did whatever they could to retain power.[1]

Anton Steen interviewed Baltic elites and found that they saw themselves as important; often talked to one another, especially to the prime minister; showed solidarity against common threats; and sometimes intermarried. But was this a surprise?

In reality Baltic elites and parties competed intensely. Yes, most elites strongly favored free markets, but others demanded stronger social safety nets. In Latvia, where Steen says the elites colluded to keep Russian speakers from politics, major parties sought equal rights for the Slavic population. Many anti-Communists saw former Communists as opportunists. In each Baltic country, ruling coalitions often fell apart over charges that some leaders favored one business interest or another.

While Steen focused on elites, the UN Development Programme (see chapter 6) studied broad trends shaping political culture. Neither perspective is complete. To gain a full understanding, we must analyze society at large as well as what happens in the halls of power.

---

[1]See Anton Steen, *Between Past and Future: Elites, Democracy, and the State in Post-Communist Countries: A Comparison of Estonia, Latvia and Lithuania* (Aldershot, England: Ashgate, 1997).

Distrust bred apathy, undercutting the political culture of democracy. Baltic citizens in the 1990s lost much of their drive to learn about and take part in the political process. If citizens were ignorant and indifferent, they could be subjects but not participants in politics.

Estonia

The UN Development Programme in Estonia lamented the weakness of civil society.[6] It reported that grand causes did not greatly interest Estonians or noncitizens—not environmental protection, not historical traditions, and not religion. Indeed, three-fourths of Estonians and half of noncitizens expressed no interest in the church. Few Estonian workers joined trade unions. Noncitizens found it hard to organize politically and so tended to take to the streets with their complaints.

Only one-tenth of Estonians in 1995 reported that they took an active interest in politics or thought they could influence politics by voting. Two-thirds of the public deemed the state unable to cope with its tasks. Half the public charged that government representatives accepted bribes; two-thirds thought the government kept important information from them.

Other studies, however, suggested a high degree of public spirit. Surveys in 1995 showed that more than 80 percent of citizens and noncitizens in Estonia saw it as their duty to do military service, learn the official language, pay income taxes, respect the flag, and obey the law. A follow-up survey in 1997 showed a decline of 5 to 7 percent in positive replies by citizens and noncitizens. But three-fourths of the noncitizens (mainly Slavic speakers) still saw it as their duty to perform military service and pay their taxes. And more than 90 percent accepted the obligation to respect the flag and abide by the law.

A survey published in 1997 showed that only one-tenth of Estonian citizens and noncitizens yearned for a return to the Soviet era—fewer than in Latvia or Lithuania. At least two-fifths of Estonians and half the noncitizens, however, were ready to exchange the parliamentary system for an "iron fist."

Former Communists and anti-Communists found themselves coexisting in the same political milieu. What should nationalists and liberals, some of them former political prisoners, think about former Communist leaders who had donned nationalist attire? In Lithuania Vytautas Landsbergis often pressed for broader lustration—laws to prevent former Soviet officials from any role in public life. Pressed by the Home Union, Lithuania passed a law in November 1999 on confession, registration, and protection of former KGB collaborators. The law offered an amnesty to those admitting their past collaboration by August 5, 2000. Some fourteen hundred persons registered by this date, but a government official estimated that a total of four thousand to five thousand collaborators were still living in Lithuania. Before their names would be published, however, the government would have to prove their guilt in court.

But many Baltic voters did not object to previous Communist connections. As we saw in chapter 4, left-of-center politicians swept back into power in the mid-1990s. Baltic political cultures were not riven by a Manichean divide.

Latvia

At the end of the 1990s Latvians—both citizens and noncitizens—placed little trust in political parties, the parliament, or the cabinet of ministers. Latvian schoolchildren told a German visitor in 1996 that the only way to get rich in Latvia was by stealing.[7]

Latvians' confidence in their institutions remained low throughout the decade. In 1992 only 5 percent of the Latvian population expressed confidence in political parties; by 1997 this share rose only to 10 percent. Individual leaders scored higher than

---

Box 5.3. Was the Glass Half-Full or Half-Empty?

As in the United States and elsewhere, trends in Baltic societies were contradictory in the 1990s and difficult to interpret. In 1991 one-fourth of all Estonians and one-sixth of Slavic speakers attended political rallies, but by 1996 only 3 percent of Estonians and 2 percent of non-Estonians did so. If public demonstrations were smaller and less frequent, did this mean that people had become apathetic or that they now trusted in institutions and elections?

Most of the public opinion surveys cited here are taken from UN Development Programme reports based on some of the best social science research conducted in the Baltic countries. Nonetheless they should be ingested with several grains of salt. Survey research is problematic because moods change, samples may be atypical, and questions may be loaded. Even if the data are accurate, more than one interpretation is usually possible. If half the public is disenchanted, should we say that the glass is half-full or half-empty?

their parties in public opinion polls—a sign that personalities counted for more than institutions.

Latvian citizens in 1997 expressed high confidence in television (79 percent), radio (77 percent), and in the most trusted institution, education (83 percent). Next most trusted were the church (69 percent) and the press (64 percent); much lower on their trust spectrum came local government (52 percent) and the Bank of Latvia (47 percent); at the very bottom were the Saeima (21 percent) and political parties (11 percent). The confidence curve of noncitizens followed the same trajectory, but was generally lower. For example, 65 percent expressed high trust in television, compared to 79 percent among citizens. But there were two large and two small exceptions. Noncitizens showed more confidence than citizens in the police (47 versus 41 percent) and the courts (36 versus 31 percent); noncitizens also showed 1 percent more confidence than citizens in the National Human Rights Office and the Saeima.[8]

As the decade ended, one survey showed that nearly two-fifths of the Latvian population agreed with the proposition that "the best way for people like myself to achieve success is to strive for mutual goals together with other people." But civil society remained weak. A Latvian NGO affiliated with the transnational European Movement enlisted some corporate support but attracted no more than five hundred people to its activities in 1999. Better living standards were more important to most Latvians than political participation. Few understood that the former might depend in part on the latter. Few expected that private citizens could influence government or that government would act to improve their lives.

The legacy of the past could not easily be undone. Communism weakened trust in the law, lawyers, and courts across the former Soviet realm. To be sure, the Baltic constitutions of the 1990s proclaimed the judiciary independent of government. But there was little separation of powers in Latvia. The executive sometimes abused its ability to dominate both the legislative system and the judiciary. American advisers suggested reform, often oblivious to local traditions and Continental legal systems.

Lithuania

Few Lithuanians became involved in politics or civil society. In 1994 only 6 percent of native Lithuanians and 2 percent of Russians claimed to be "very interested" in politics; half of Lithuanians and 60 percent of Russians had no interest. In 1996 some 38 percent of Lithuanians deemed it their duty to vote; 32 percent thought voting not important or a waste of time.[9]

Asked to rate their own abilities to shape politics on a scale from 1 (no effect) to 10 (great effect), Lithuanian teenagers gave the most optimistic replies, but averaging only 3.52. The most negative replies came from young adults aged twenty to twenty-nine, who averaged just 3.17.

Lithuanians' confidence in their political institutions increased from 1994 to 1996: in government, from 25 to 39 percent; in parliament, from 22 to 39 percent; in the president's office, from 26 to 30 percent. Trust in tax inspection increased from 13 to 16 percent, trust in commercial banks from 2 to 5 percent.

After the 1996 elections some 50 percent of Lithuanians expressed confidence in parliament. But fewer than one-fifth found reason to trust the police, the courts, or the tax inspectors; and only 7 percent trusted commercial banks.

Lithuanians registered more confidence in the mass media than in any other social institution—even the church—in the mid-1990s. (Education, the institution that elicited the most confidence in Latvia, was not an option in the Lithuanian polls.) Confidence in the mass media rose from 72 percent in 1994 to 74 percent in 1996 and confidence in the church rose from 66 to 69 percent.

With the exception of the country's historical past, few Lithuanians in the mid-1990s were proud of any aspect of their country. Some 60 percent took pride in Lithuania's past; 30 percent in its spiritual values; 30 percent in its architecture; 22 percent in the Lithuanian people; 7 percent in Lithuania's international standing; and from 1 to 3 percent in its courts, the government, the economy, and the parliament.[10]

No wonder Lithuanians and Latvians in 1998–1999 chose returnees from North America to serve as presidents!

Why Apathy and Alienation?

When hopes were high, Balts readily joined hands for shared goals. After independence was regained, however, the transition to a new way of life proved painful—for individuals, for firms, for political movements, for governments, for entire societies. There was no recipe for success. What worked in Poland might fail in Lithuania.

As living standards declined, many Balts became disenchanted. Many blamed their new governments for failing to generate more jobs, produce more low-cost housing, mend a broken safety net, and curb a high dropout rate in schools. Balts found it hard to accept that things might have to get worse before they got better.

Lithuanian president Algirdas Brazauskas wondered out loud in 1996 if there was a flaw in the political training within families and in schools. For his part, Vytautas Landsbergis pointed to the psychology of selfishness and dependency left over from Soviet times. "Many people think in a collectivist manner. They subordinate themselves to authority. They expect authority to distribute goods to them and are angry if this does not happen." This pattern, Landsbergis said, "has taken place not just in the Baltic but in much of Eastern Europe and in Russia itself."[11] Supporting Landsbergis, a 1996 survey showed that some 72 percent of Lithuanians believed the state should guarantee material well-being and 43 percent said it should control moral standards.

Asked why former Communist officials had won elections in the Baltic states, Landsbergis replied: "Thousands of persons took part in the independence movement, but now millions of people vote in elections. Their outlook has been colored by blockades, by the problems of transition, by a decline in living standards."

Was he disappointed in the moral character of the Lithuanian people? Were they less altruistic, less cooperative than he had hoped? "To some extent, yes." But he noted that a similar pattern had taken shape not just in the Baltic but in much of the former Soviet realm.

Landsbergis worried in 1996 that few young people in Lithuania "take an active role in politics now. Many think: 'Let the politicians decide.'" But Landsbergis rejected comparisons of Baltic quiescence with youthful energies in Latin America or the Middle East. "There," said Landsbergis, "politics is by physical demonstrations. Our politics is by voting and by other intellectual acts."

The UN Development Programme pointed to eight reasons why many Balts felt alienated from their governments:[12]

1. Lack of horizontal ties between individuals after the market economy replaced the old Soviet networks.
2. Low self-esteem among many individuals, compounded by their belief that they know little about governmental affairs.
3. Lingering collectivism at odds with market liberalism—the problem to which Landsbergis alluded, that is, cleavage between liberal elites favoring free markets and publics wanting extensive state intervention in the economy.
4. Profound disagreement and distrust among political elites.
5. Failure of governments to foster feedback from society, for example, by surveying public opinion before deciding on new policies.
6. Perceived corruption in high places (reflected in the various public opinion surveys cited in this chapter).
7. The tendency of central government to grow at the expense of local government.
8. Delayed reforms leaving the civil service unresponsive to public needs.

The centralized governments were to delegate extensive powers to the local communities. Following decades of strong Communist rule from the center, true self-governance presented great challenges to local elites. Most of the nearly three hundred local governments in Estonia could not meet these challenges efficiently. Faced with wide scale tax evasion, they depended on funds from the center sufficient to do little more than repair roads and pay municipal workers. Government in rural areas often became welfare institutions for the local elite. Self-seeking and bureaucracy prevailed over value-creating for mutual gain. Atomization contributed to crime and to alcoholism. The *Estonian HDR 1999* recommended merging municipalities but doubted that this would overcome the main weaknesses in the country's rural life. It viewed the development of private farming as the most acute problem in the country's future.

These problems would be difficult to change, but there was hope. Social capital, like other endowments, can be enhanced as well as spent. Political cultures are not immutable. If Germany and Japan could change in the 1950s, and Spain and Portugal in the 1970s, why not the reborn Baltic republics in the twenty-first century?

INSTRUMENTS OF CHANGE

The Media

Estonians and Latvians cherished newspapers from the time of their national awakenings in the nineteenth century. In the second half of the nineteenth century, Estonians became among the world's leaders in information consumption. As Soviet controls slackened, Balts in the late 1980s bought and read more newspapers and magazines than most Western Europeans or Americans in the late 1980s and early 1990s.[13]

In 1988–1990, the zenith of political activism, the media united and helped mobilize Balts for independence. After 1991, however, newspaper sales plummeted in the Baltic. Interest in public affairs waned even as newspaper prices jumped. Demand was elastic. As the price went up, sales went down. Still, many Balts continued to be avid consumers of information. Many read papers and journals at work or borrowed them from neighbors.

The good news was that Baltic media were much freer than they had been in the Communist past. After 1991 Baltic papers and electronic media did not depend upon unholy alliances of financial and political oligarchs as in Boris Yeltsin's Russia.[14] Sales of newspapers in the Baltic states declined in the 1990s, but the number of papers published increased, permitting a wide variety of viewpoints to be expressed.

Television viewing outpaced newspaper reading. In the late 1990s the average Estonian viewed television for 255 minutes per day, the average Russian in Estonia 285 minutes. Radio-listening declined somewhat in the 1990s, but Estonians listened to the radio an average of 230 minutes per day in 1997, Russian speakers 162 minutes.

Some media users were highly active, seeking information or entertainment. Active readers, viewers, and listeners also tended to use the Internet actively. Other media users were more passive. They included many middle-aged and retired persons, the unemployed, those with low incomes, and non-Estonians who could follow programs only in Russian. Those Estonians and noncitizens who read more tended to be wealthier than those who read less. But the correlation with TV watching was less positive. Many who watched a wide variety of TV programs were poor.[15]

Except for National Radio and Television, the mass media in Lithuania were independent of the state. Laws adopted in 1996 obliged journalists to present information honestly, but slander and defamation cases increased in the mid-1990s.

Baltic citizens and noncitizens expressed very high confidence in the accuracy of their electronic media and newspapers. Since those over thirty had been brought up to believe there was no truth (*pravda*) in *Pravda* or news (*izvestiia*) in *Izvestiia,* this was a sign that the media were doing a good job.

Nongovernmental Organizations

Civil society in Soviet times was very weak. The Communist Party dominated not just the government but nongovernmental organizations. This situation changed in the 1980s as three types of NGOs—Popular Fronts, citizens' movements, and music festivals—mobilized people from many social strata and regions. Only the Popular Fronts, however, welcomed nonnatives. Citizens' movements such as the Congress of the Estonian People (1990) sought to restore self-rule for the indigenous people, while music festivals celebrated the local culture.

The number and diversity of NGOs mushroomed but then plateaued in each Baltic republic in the early 1990s. Unlike the Popular Fronts of the late 1980s, few of the new NGOs cut across societal divisions to represent the public at large. Few NGOs linked both citizens and noncitizens in some shared endeavor. Most joined special interest groups such as pensioners, persons with specific health problems, apartment owners, taxpayers, and hobby and sports clubs. Few if any NGOs helped people to fight corruption or official abuse of power. Many NGOs were instigated by foreign NGOs, and generated subsidies and free foreign travel. The Open Society Institute and other Western foundations cloned local self-help groups that sought progressive change for entire societies. But bonding associations outpaced those seeking to bridge diversity.

Special interests utilized NGOs for their narrow objectives and local needs. The NGOs filled gaps left by local governments that were weak, poorly funded, and inspired little confidence. Was parochial NGO activity a sign of maturing democracy or a civil society desert? The bare facts could be read either way.

The UN Development Programme in Estonia portrayed many NGOs there in a negative light. Of 750 not-for-profit organizations in Estonia in the mid-1990s, most focused on national activity and international ties rather than on practical measures at the local level. Thus, the Estonian Hearing-impaired Association belonged to an international federation of such groups. Other Estonian NGOs were linked to the European Folk Art and Handicrafts Association, the World Esperanto Association, the European Young Geographers Association, and Youth for Christ. Nearly all these organizations denied any connection with a political party, though many claimed to have influenced legislation.

The *Latvian Human Development Report* for 1998, on the other hand, found some reasons to cheer. It noted that more than four thousand NGOs were registered in Latvia by 1998, though only 6 percent of Latvians—those directly involved—claimed to know much about NGOs. The Latvian report analyzed a local self-help NGO—the Pensioners' Social Assistance Fund of the City of Talsi. This NGO provided health care plus cultural, sport, and social programs for its members, and linked them with other groups fostering adult education and music. The fund got support not only from the Talsi City Council but from the Queen Juliana Fund in the Netherlands.

The *Lithuanian Human Development Report 1997* reported that in 1996 there were more than 700 NGOs registered with the Ministry of Justice, covering a wide range of activities. In 1997, however, the number of registered NGOs fell to 604, as many NGOs ceased to function. Among the most influential NGOs in Lithuania were those associated with the Catholic Church, the mass media, the Industrialists' Confederation, and the Association of Industrial, Business, and Trade Centers. At least nine nontraditional religious communities were also registered.

The trade union movement in Lithuania was reviving in the 1990s after being discredited in Soviet times, when it was seen as a tool to enforce labor discipline. There

---

Box 5.4. An NGO Nonprofit Foundation for Liberal Change

In the 1990s the Open Society Institute, funded by George Soros, sought to enhance civil society in the former Soviet realm. Institute programs sought to computerize universities and link them to the world through the Internet. The Institute also sponsored the writing of new history texts. Soros demonstrated how one determined individual could use his resources constructively—in tandem with or against the preferences of his own government. In the late 1990s the dollar value of Open Society programs in the former USSR exceeded those of the U.S. government. Soros showed how self-organization could nourish self-organization.

were 362 trade unions representing over two hundred thousand members—some 10 to 15 percent of the working population. A Tripartite Council was formed in 1995 with representatives from government, employers, and trade unions. But there was no central agency to coordinate union activity across the country.

The greatest country-wide NGOs in each Baltic country were the music and dance festivals. Attendance declined after independence was regained, but in the late 1990s thousands of well-trained dancers, singers, and musicians continued to take part in these festivals—energizing and energized by huge crowds who applauded, sang, danced, and rejoiced with them in the beauty of their own culture.

Not everyone was enamored of traditional and classical music. In August 2000

Box 5.5. The Greatest NGO

Tallinn July 2–4, 1999: the 16th All-Estonian Dance Festival took place at the Kalev Stadium, where some eight thousand dancers ranging from seven to seventy leaped in unison, adorned in the blouse and skirt, or jacket and slacks, of their native regions. The girls' hair was garlanded with flowers, all faces with smiles. In high spirits, it seemed they could have danced all night.

The 23d All-Estonian Song Festival began on a Saturday afternoon as festival choirs paraded for four hours from Tallinn's medieval towers, past the modern city center, and then along the seaside to the festival grounds. Each choir, dressed in the costume of its region, doffed their hats, played their horns a bit louder, did a jig, or just shouted "hurrah" as they passed President Lennart Meri and his wife, who reviewed the parade from a sidewalk.

The summer sun was still high when the last marchers reached the festival grounds at 7:15 P.M. Near the stadium, Estonian army mobile stoves, fueled by trimly cut logs, steamed vats of green pea soup, served up with chunks of dark bread, for everyone present.

In weeks before the festival, runners carried a torch from one county of Estonia to another. Now a runner carried this flame up a tower, pausing at each level as trumpets blared to honor each of fifteen counties. President Meri then addressed the audience of several hundred thousand seated in a natural amphitheater.

The 1999 Song Festival included two evenings of choral and symphonic music by Estonian and other composers. More than a dozen conductors took turns leading the concerts. For example, Neeme Järvi (b. 1937), who left Estonia in 1979 and now directed the Detroit Symphony, led the festival orchestra in excerpts from "Carmina Burana," by Carl Orff, and "Sanctus," by Estonian composer Rudolf Tobias (1873–1918). There was also music to the Estonian epic tale "Kalevipoeg"; to poems by the contemporary writer, Jaan Kross; and from Estonian and Italian operas.

Järvi told me he would return in 2000 to conduct on the anniversary of the Congress of Estonia (which he did). At the intermission Järvi sat with President Meri, PM Mart Laar, the Kelams, and their families. A few rows back sat Rein Veidemann (b. 1946), whom I met in pre-independence days, when he edited a literary journal and became one of the first public figures to say in print that Estonia might exercise the right to self-determination. Next to Rein was his wife, Andrea, Estonia's minister of integration until her party lost the 1999 elections. Now, Rein often sang along with the chorus; in autumn he would return to Tartu University to teach literature.

The sun did not go down until 11 P.M.—half an hour after the concert ended. Many people hummed and skipped as they made their ways back to town.

many Estonian fans of pop singer Tina Turner and some ten thousand of her admirers from Latvia, Russia, Lithuania, and Finland crowded into Tallinn for her concert. The musical comedy *The Flintstones in Viva Rock Vegas,* a takeoff on the American cartoon, had a successful run in Riga. Despite Estonians' avowed support for their own culture, Tonu Kaljuste, chief conductor of the Estonian Philharmonic Chamber Choir, announced his resignation, protesting the government's failure to provide stronger financing for Estonian culture. His professional singers received no more than the average Estonian wage of five thousands kroons ($288) per month.

Acculturation

Political cultures are not fixed in granite. Younger, better-educated persons who have suffered less from life may have a more optimistic and more cooperative attitude than others in their society.

In June 1999 I conducted several experiments with a group of university students (mostly in their twenties) from around the Baltic Sea—from Estonia, Latvia, Lithuania, Poland, Russia, and Sweden.[16] The results were suggestive, even though the samples were too small to prove anything. The experiments supported my expectations about social capital in each country; they harmonized with the theoretical views set out in the first pages of this chapter; they also implied an agenda for future research.

To begin, the students were asked to rate as "high," "medium," or "low" the abilities of their compatriots and ethnic minorities in their countries on three dimensions: their capacity for mutual trust; their competence for coping with complex problems; and their inclination to pursue mutual gain.

As expected, the scores for trust, fitness, and cooperation dovetailed, and they paralleled the ranking of these countries in both wealth and political stability. Thus, Sweden scored high; Poland, medium (except in Krakow, high); Russia, low. Estonia, Latvia, and Lithuania placed low to medium—higher than Russia but below Poland and Sweden. Nearly the same lineup took shape when researchers asked Lithuanian business executives to evaluate the reliability of foreign partners.[17]

As for minorities, the student respondents reported that Balts distrusted Slavs; that Russians distrusted all minorities except Ukrainians, and that Swedes distrusted guest workers and immigrants. Except for Poland (with no sizable minorities), ethnic minorities in each country got lower scores for competence than the ethnic majority.

Most of these students gave low or medium grades to their compatriots on trust issues. But their own performance in two role-playing exercises showed not just an ability to trust each other but a disposition to look for ways to generate mutual gain.

Prisoner's Dilemma

Our first exercise required each student to carry out sequential plays of Prisoner's Dilemma (PD), each time with a different partner. Each partner plays an isolated prisoner who must choose whether to cooperate with the other (be silent) or defect (confess to an alleged crime). If each prisoner cooperates and does not confess, each goes free (valued as $+10$); if one defects by confessing and the other remains silent, the defector wins freedom and a reward ($+20$) while the "suckered" cooperator gets a long jail term (−40); if both defect and confess, however, each gets a medium jail term (−10). The paradox is that narrow self-interest and caution instruct each player to defect, but if each does so, each loses.

Trust and openness cost nothing by themselves, but they risk abuse by others. Caution is necessary lest one become a sucker or a martyr, but excessive cynicism makes mutual gain impossible. It condemns each party to the inevitable losses suffered by the diffident players in PD.

In the first round of our exercise, each pair of prisoners jointly cooperated, except for one player who confessed while her partner remained silent. The players were not allowed to talk with one another during the play, but each could observe how the others had played. Each could see how dangerous it could be to count on cooperation. In five additional rounds, nonetheless, most pairs cooperated, despite occasional defections. Their cooperative behavior was optimal for mutual gain, but it ignored the dire consequences if one party defected.

One or Two School Houses?

Next, our students simulated the decision making process in two towns facing a choice whether to build two separate schools or one they could share. Both Town A and Town B had five hundred families with two children and another five hundred families with no children. The towns were twenty kilometers apart, linked only by a bad road.

A single school would cost 150 million euros, while separate schools would cost 100 million euros each. A single school with its library and equipment would be more cost-effective than two and need fewer employees than two schools, but roads and bus service between the two communities would have to be improved. The regional government would continue to contribute the same monies for education and roads as in the past. Any savings or additional costs for the new school or schools would go to local taxpayers.

The students played the roles of one governor, two mayors, and leaders of each community's teachers' union, parents' association, taxpayers' NGO, construction firm, and transport company. There was also one representative of the Open Society Institute. All these parties could talk, lobby, and negotiate with one another in private sessions before coming together for a master negotiation.

We planned to conduct this exercise twice. In the first round, each player would labor to *claim values*—seek his or her narrow interest; in a second round, each player would try to *create values* for mutual gain. But we never got to the second round because, even when told to claim values, players were driven to mutual gain by enlightened self-interest. Already in round one they decided to build a single school with shared facilities. If some parties suffered, such as redundant teachers, they would be compensated from the overall savings. The Open Society representative added a decisive consideration: she offered to fund a high-quality computer system for one school but provide only modest facilities for two. This player also focused the deliberations by taking it upon herself to lay out on paper the costs of alternative strategies. (In Estonia she attended a technical institute, but found time to organize and lead children in orienteering exercises—at no cost to anyone except parents, who had to buy compasses and maps.)

Beyond Machiavelli?

None of these Baltic rim students had read about how to negotiate for mutual advantage in handbooks such as *Getting to Yes* or *Beyond Machiavelli*. Most seminar participants came from countries where mutual trust was weak. They had known one another for only one week in Sweden. Still, their combination of intelligence and good will, deployed in a friendly environment, pushed them toward cooperative problem solving. The real world, of course, is not an ivory tower. If real money or security were at stake, perhaps the players would have been less trusting, more self-protecting, more narrowly egotistical. Still, the classroom exercises gave reason for hope.[18]

Given favorable conditions, perhaps people can intuit or learn the advantages of creating values for mutual gain. Still, social capital in the three Baltic republics appeared weak or, at best, medium strong as a new century began. This shortfall fed on and contributed to deficiencies in human development, as we see in chapter 6.

Caption for Chapter 5 Photo: The style and content of architecture frames our thought and feeling. Public buildings help to inspire or limit the growth of social capital. Riga's architecture spans many centuries and styles—Gothic, Baroque, Classical, Art Nouveau. The "Three Brothers" (just two of them shown here), built in the fifteenth to the eighteenth centuries, recall times when self-governing Riga was a prosperous and cosmopolitan hub of East-West trade.

NOTES

1. Bent Flyvbjerg, *Rationality and Power: Democracy in Practice* (Chicago: University of Chicago Press, 1998), pp. 5, 90.

2. Larry Diamond, "Toward Democratic Consolidation," *Journal of Democracy* 3 (July 1994), p. 5.

3. See essays in Mark E. Warren, ed., *Democracy and Trust* (Cambridge: Cambridge University Press, 1999).

4. Having studied many cases, one scholar concluded that, in industrial countries, stable democracy correlates with relatively high incomes and a Protestant culture, and in less developed countries, with exposure to British rule, as in India and Trinidad. Seymour Martin Lipset, "The Centrality of Political Culture," in *The Global Resurgence of Democracy,* ed. Larry Diamond and Marc F. Plattner (Baltimore, Md.: Johns Hopkins University Press, 1993), pp. 134–37.

If this view were correct, the cultural preconditions for democracy were nearly absent as the Baltic peoples regained independence. None was wealthy by European standards; none had experienced British rule. Estonians and Latvians had lost much of their Protestant heritage after fifty years of communism; Lithuanians' Protestant connections were even more tenuous.

5. *Latvia Human Development Report 1997* (hereafter *Latvia HDR* for a given year; Riga: UN Development Programme, 1997), p. 44.

6. *Estonian Human Development Report 1998* (hereafter *Estonian HDR 1998;* Tallinn: UN Development Programme, 1998), pp. 38–41, 45, 48.

7. Reinhard Krumm, "People Need Trust," *Baltic Times,* March 21–27, 1996, p. 21.

8. *Latvia HDR 1998,* pp. 38–39.

9. If some problem arose, 27 percent of Lithuanians would appeal to the government and

30 percent would appeal to the media. Only a handful would turn to the courts or to a political party. Some 9 percent, however, said they would form a group to solve the problem and 28 percent claimed they would join such a group. *Lithuanian Human Development Report 1997* (hereafter *Lithuanian HDR* 1997) (Vilnius: UN Development Programme, 1997), chapter 7.

10. The data in the preceding paragraphs are from *Lithuanian HDR 1997,* chapter 7.

11. Interviews with the author in Chicago and Washington, May 1996.

12. *Latvia HDR 1998,* pp. 39–45.

13. In Soviet Estonia in 1987 there were 406 newspaper copies per 1,000 inhabitants. By 1990 there were 529 newspaper copies for every 100 persons. Russian-language newspapers reached a circulation of 95,000; Estonian-language, up to 200,000. By 1997, however, average circulation of national newspapers had dropped to one-fifth of what it had been in 1990. Even so, Estonians claimed to read an average of six newspapers regularly or occasionally, while non-Estonians read three.

14. Russian newspapers in the 1990s were no longer censored by a central authority, but many did their master's bidding. There was no longer a single "Party line" but the lines of many parties and factions. Objective reporting was hard to find—especially on state television, which was slanted to serve the top occupants of the Kremlin.

15. More than half the Estonians displayed the traits of active seekers of knowledge— watching a variety of TV programs, reading many periodicals, and, when possible, searching the Internet; less than half of Estonians were passive watchers of television. Of non-Estonians, some 85 percent appeared to be passive. They included many factory workers and pensioners in Tallinn and northeast Estonia, most of whom lived in apartment blocks rather than separate homes with gardens. Those who watched TV programs in Russian, locally produced or beamed from Russia, were less inclined to seek integration in Estonian society. *Estonian HDR 1998,* pp. 35–37.

16. "Trust and Voluntarism," Baltic Sea Foundation Summer School, Södertörns University College, Sweden, exercises held on June 21, 1999.

17. Of nineteen countries, business people from Sweden, Denmark, and the United States were placed at the top; next came those from Estonia, Latvia, and Poland—all of whom were judged "very reliable" by more than half the respondents. By contrast, only 13 percent of respondents thought Russians very reliable. Belarusians and Russians placed at the bottom. All the rankings except Poland's fit the rank order suggested by my student respondents. Perhaps the business respondents' lower estimate of Polish reliability reflected Lithuania's troubles with Poland between the world wars. See *The Baltic Times,* April 12–19, 2000, p. 11.

18. Human development—or lack thereof—was tested in August 2000 when fifteen Balts (five from each country) spent a month on an isolated Estonian island doing a Baltic version of the *Survival* program that attracted many U.S. television viewers earlier that year. The Baltic program, however, differed from the American. First, it adapted a format already used in England and Sweden: it was called *Robinson*—from *Robinson Crusoe,* a tale of cooperation more than conflict. Second, the players came from three countries, compelling them to communicate in a foreign language. Third, the program ran as a cross-media event, with a web site that permitted viewers to take part. Fourth, the show did not take place on a lush, fruit-laden tropical island but on a desolate Baltic island. The program aired on thirteen Saturdays at 9 P.M.

6

Milda B. Richardson

Human Development: Winners, Losers, and the Internet

WHAT IS HUMAN DEVELOPMENT? HOW CAN IT BE MEASURED?

Human development is both a goal and an instrument of social capital. Developing human capacities can expand human choice and tap human potential. The Communist system provided no choice for citizens and little choice for consumers. Could the new way of life in the Baltic republics do better?

Human development can be assessed in many ways. The United Nations Development Programme (UNDP) in the 1990s based its Human Development Index (HDI) on three variables: health, education, and per capita incomes.[1] The HDI measured health by life expectancy at birth; educational attainment by adult literacy and enrollments in primary, secondary, and higher education; and real per capita income by purchasing power parity (PPP).[2]

CHANGING HUMAN DEVELOPMENT RATES IN THE BALTICS

The Baltic republics had the highest HDI scores in the former Soviet Union and probably, had such records been kept, in tsarist Russia. In 1990, for example, life expectancy at birth for Lithuania was 71.5, Estonia 70.0, Latvia 69.6, and Russia 69.3. Had the Baltic republics been independent in 1990, Lithuania would have ranked 29th among the world's states on the HDI, Estonia 34th, Latvia 35th, and Russia 37th.[3]

Infant mortality was much lower in the Baltic republics than in the other Soviet republics.[4] In the late 1980s, according to Soviet statistics, infant mortality in Estonia was 12.4 deaths per 1,000 live births; in Latvia, the number was 11; in Lithuania, 11.5; and in the United States, less than 10. The average for the USSR was 24.7.

Estonia and Latvia were the most urbanized republics in the USSR. Characteristic of modern, urban economies, fertility rates in the Baltic republics were among the lowest in the USSR in the 1980s. Latvia, Russia, and Estonia led in divorces, followed by Ukraine and Lithuania.

Material conditions were better in the Baltic republics than in most parts of the USSR, but this situation did not make Balts content with Soviet rule. Estonians recalled that their living standards had been as high or higher than Finland's in the 1930s. By the 1980s, however, Finland's per capita income was more than three times as high as Estonia's.

Independence regained did not magically liberate the Baltic republics from problems accumulated in Soviet times. Instead, many economic and social challenges became more acute. The shift toward self-rule and free enterprise gave Baltic citizens and consumers many choices, but their options were constrained by insecurities and inequalities. Some Balts became rich, but many more became poorer.

Balts suffered less than most other peoples in the former USSR, but gross domestic product (GDP) in each Baltic state dropped in the early 1990s. For most people incomes fell while prices increased. Unemployment was high. Rural living standards lagged urban. Social welfare nets disintegrated. As incomes fell, a wide range of social ills became more acute. Health problems became more severe. Crime increased. Societal tensions mounted.

Baltic HDI scores fell dramatically. The *Human Development Report* published each year by the UNDP ranked Estonia, Latvia, and Lithuania in the early 1990s among countries with "high human development"; by the mid-1990s they had fallen into the group with "average human development."[5] Thus, Estonia's life expectancy in the mid-1990s fell to just the world average—six years less than the average for industrialized countries. The rankings of Latvia and Lithuania fell even more sharply. As we see in table 6.1, however, each Baltic republic in the late 1990s moved up sharply relative to other countries. The *Human Development Report 2000* raised each of the Baltic countries much higher in global rankings and returned Estonia to the ranks of countries with "high human development" (46th out of 46).

But the year 2000 report said that life expectancy in the Baltic countries was lower in 1995–2000 than in 1970–1975. Life expectancy in Estonia declined from 70.5 in the earlier period to 68.7 in the latter; in Latvia, it declined from 70.1 to 68.4; and in Lithuania it declined from 71.3 to 69.9. In Russia things were even worse. Life expectancy declined from 68.2 to 66.6. By contrast, life expectancy increased in Sweden from 74.7 to 78.6, in the United States from 71.3 to 76.7, and in Japan—the world leader—from 73.3 to 80.0.[6]

Of course none of these statistics was handed down on Mount Sinai. Indeed, the global

Table 6.1
Baltic HDI Rankings in the World, 1993–2000

	1993	1994	1995	1996	1997	1998	1999	2000
Estonia	34	39	43	68	71	77	54	46
Latvia	35	30	48	55	92	92	74	63
Lithuania	29	28	71	81	76	79	62	52

SOURCES: *Latvia Human Development Report 1998* (Riga: UNDP, 1998), p. 12; United Nations Development Programme, *Human Development Report 1999* (New York: Oxford University Press, 1999), table 1 and technical note 1 (pp. 164–165) explaining rank changes between 1998 and 1999 due to revised methods and revised data; *Human Development Report 2000* (New York: Oxford University Press, 2000), table 1.

Human Development Report published in New York often gave a more negative appraisal of Baltic affairs than country reports by the UNDP offices in Tallinn, Riga, and Vilnius. Thus, the Vilnius office of the UNDP claimed in 1999 that life expectancy in Lithuania rose in 1998 to its highest level in forty years—71.78 (66.50 for men, 76.87 for women). And while the New York global reports suggested that infant mortality in Estonia and Lithuania rose by one-third in the late 1990s, the Vilnius UNDP held that infant mortality in Lithuania had steadily declined in the mid- and late 1990s. The World Bank reported in 2000 that infant mortality in Lithuania and Estonia declined by nearly half in the 1990s to 9 deaths per 1,000 births and in Latvia by one-quarter to 15 deaths per 1,000 births. These and other statistical inconsistencies are discussed in the appendix to this chapter.

Another measure of human development is the percentage of people *not* expected to survive to age 60. The UNDP in New York reported that this percentage in Sweden was 8.5 in 1998; in the United States it was 12.4. In the Baltic region, Lithuania did best at 22.9, followed by Estonia at 23.3 and Latvia at 24.6. Many Eastern European countries did much better than Balts, while Russia did much worse at 29.5.[7]

A range of other human development measures is shown in table 6.2. This table compares health and living standards in the three Baltic countries with trends in Russia, Hungary (one of the most successful Eastern European countries), Sweden (one of the most prosperous small countries), and the United States. We shall return to those four countries later in the chapter for comparative perspective.

Let us now examine in more detail the key indicators of human development in the reborn Baltic republics.

INCOMES, JOBS, AND WELFARE

One determinant of HDI is real income. Pauperization was widespread in the former Soviet empire. A relatively poor but secure life in Communist times gave way to instability and rapid change. In 1989 about 14 million people in Eastern Europe and

Table 6.2
Comparative Health and Living Standards, 1997–1998

	Lithuania	Estonia	Latvia	Russia	Hungary	Sweden	USA
Life expectancy (years)	70	69	68	67	70	79	77
Infant mortality (per 1,000 live births)	13 (9)	13 (10)	16	20 (17)	10	4	7
Maternal mortality (per 100,000 births)	36	41	40	75	30	7	8
Urban population (% of total)	73	74	73	77	66	83	77
Primary school enrollment (% of relevant age group)	n.a.	99 (87)	99 (90)	99 (93)	98	99	99
Secondary school enrollment	(80)	86	81	88	97 (87)	99	96

SOURCES: United Nations Development Programme, *Human Development Report 1999* (New York: Oxford University Press, 1999), tables 1, 8, 10; numbers in parentheses are from the local UNDP reports or from reports by the Economist Intelligence Unit.

the former USSR lived on less than $4 a day. In the mid-1990s that number rose by ten times—to about 147 million. When Communist rule disappeared, the visible hand of centralized political authority suddenly became the invisible hand of the market. The shrinking of the state was not matched by institutional reform, by regulation, or by measures to protect the poor and help the sick when markets failed to do so.[8]

Table 6.3 shows the decline and gradual rise of incomes in the Baltic republics, in Russia, and the poorest of the former Soviet republics, Tajikistan. Incomes bottomed in Estonia and Latvia in 1993, in Lithuania in 1994, in Russia in 1995, and in Tajikistan in 1996. By 1997 only Estonia had regained its 1989 per capita income; the others were far behind. Untaxed and shadow businesses did not show up in these figures, but they added greatly to each economy—as much as one-third in Lithuania.

Each set of numbers, of course, demands interpretation. For example, Russia's per capita income included earnings on sales of oil, diamonds, and other natural wealth—the proceeds of which benefited only the privileged few. The table's last two columns contrast estimates based on PPP and on dollar exchange rates—a reminder that comparative estimates depend heavily on methodology.[9]

The spread of wealth was quite uneven throughout the Baltic—within as well as across countries. Jobs and wages tended to be higher in the capitals than elsewhere.

Table 6.3
GDP and GDP Per Capita in the Baltic Republics, Russia, and Tajikistan (at Purchasing Power Parity, except for final column, at $ exchange rate)

	1989	1990	1991	1992	1993	1994	1995	1996	1997	1998
Estonia										
GDP										
$ bn	7.9	7.6	7.0	6.2	5.8	5.8	6.2	6.5	7.4	4.9
$ per capita	5,033	4,816	4,471	3,998	3,803	3,859	4,162	4,452	5,094	3,360
Latvia										
GDP										
$ bn	13.6	14.6	13.6	9.1	8.0	8.2	8.3	8.8	9.7	6.0
$ per capita	5,094	5,469	5,114	3,460	3,070	3,213	3,313	3,516	3,920	2,430
Lithuania										
GDP										
$ bn	20.3	20.1	19.7	16.0	13.7	12.7	13.4	14.3	15.4	8.4
$ per capita	5,505	5,412	5,278	4,268	3,681	3,409	3,612	3,853	4,164	2,260
Russia										
GDP										
$ bn	865.0	875.4	864.7	759.7	711.9	636.3	623.6	613.1	629.5	395.0
$ per capita	5,871	5,919	5,833	5,122	4,805	4,300	4,210	4,150	4,280	2,680
Tajikistan										
GDP										
$ bn	9.9	10.2	9.7	6.9	5.2	4.5	4.0	3.9	4.1	2.0
$ per capita	1,914	1,920	1,768	1,247	915	782	693	665	678	330

SOURCES: UN Development Programme, *Human Development Report 1999* (New York: Oxford University Press, 1999), table 11; ibid., *2000,* tables 7 and 13; for percentage changes in real GDP, 1990–1997, see *Human Development Report for Central and Eastern Europe and the CIS, 1999* (New York, UNDP, 1999), table 2.1. See also periodic reports by the International Monetary Fund and the Economist Intelligence Unit.

In Lithuania, besides Vilnius, the interwar capital Kaunas and the port of Klaipeda also had good job prospects. Besides Riga, in Latvia the port city of Ventspils prospered. But each country also had regions with high unemployment, as in northeastern Estonia, where many Russian speakers were concentrated. Unemployment was common among persons unable or unwilling to acquire the skills needed to work in a market economy.

GENERATIONAL DIFFERENCES

Wealth and opportunity were also skewed by age and education. Of course there were sharp differences *within* every age cohort, but sociologists discerned three generations: Winners, Losers, and the New Young.[10]

The Generation of Winners consisted of persons in their mid-twenties to late thirties when Communist rule ended. Educated in the 1980s or early 1990s, many were computer literate and business smart. They got their foot in the door of new enterprises in 1988–1993. Some Winners employed other people at low wages and made good profits, lightly taxed. Winners benefited from a free market with a minimum of government intervention, taxes, and social welfare. They favored right-wing or liberal parties and wanted their countries to join the EU.

The Generation of Losers included persons born between World War I and the 1950s. Older than age fifty when Communism expired, they found that their knowledge and experience counted for little. When state enterprises folded, they could not find new jobs. They could not readily compete with younger people.

The lifetime savings of older people were wiped out as new currencies replaced the Soviet rouble. For retirees pensions fell far behind prices—especially in the early 1990s. The safety net for the elderly, the disabled, single-parent families, and the unemployed was porous or nonexistent. Governments transferred large sums to welfare, but transfers did not keep up with need. Lithuania was slower than Estonia and Latvia to reform its pension system.

Many older persons, along with farmers, wanted more state intervention in economic life—more social insurance, more subsidies, more tariffs against foreign goods. They favored rural parties and those advocating a social market economy. Many opposed joining the EU.

The New Young were in their late teens and early twenties in the 1990s. This generation was not so individualistic, and not so enthusiastic about free markets as persons one or two decades older. By the mid-1990s the Winners had already found a place in the new society, while the New Young had to struggle. The young did not remember the worst of the Soviet past, and so were much open to government intervention in economic life. They wanted to improve education and reduce its cost. The New Young wanted to join the EU *and* have better relations with Russia.

The Winners and some of the New Young enjoyed and nourished the exuberant city centers of Tallinn, Riga, and Vilnius, while Losers such as Mikhail and Alik (see box 6.1) languished in depressed city slums and much of the countryside.

Here is how the World Bank pictured the economic and social health of the Baltic countries at the end of the 1990s: Estonia ranked highest in GDP per capita at $3,940,

Box 6.1. Old and Cold in Riga

Riga, July 1998. On a balmy Saturday evening I walked from the harbor toward the old town center. The sounds of rock music played at outdoor restaurants drifted over the ancient city walls, punctuated by the occasional screech of a sports car careening across cobble stones. Seeing two men on a park bench reading Russian newspapers, I stopped to ask how they got along with Latvian-speakers.

"Our problem is not nationality but age," said one. "At age fifty nobody wants to hire us." Mikhail explained: In the Soviet Army he had been a professional soccer player; later, in civilian life, he became a master plasterer. In 1992 the state-owned firm where he worked closed down. For six years now he had lived hand-to-mouth, with no prospect of a pension, however miserly, for the next decade. He could no longer climb scaffolds like younger men, but believed that his overall ability to plaster was much better.

His buddy Alik had tried "trading" in the early 1990s. At first he made some money, but then he lost huge sums. Now he was afraid to try new things.

"Do people in your situation commit suicide?" I asked. "I've heard of some," said Mikhail.

Alik told how a friend, also age fifty, had to sleep outside the year round. One night he got frost bite. The hospital doctors asked if he had private insurance. No? Since nobody would pay for sophisticated treatment, they simply amputated his leg. Next winter, even less able to cope, he froze to death.

Alik's older sister and her husband had a dacha outside Riga. They put off renovating it until he retired. But he died in 1991, just before prices skyrocketed. On her pension she could not pay for the needed materials or labor.

followed by Lithuania at $2,620 and Latvia at $2,470; by purchasing power parity (PPP) Estonia was first at $7,826, followed Lithuania at $6,093 and Latvia at $5,938. Hungary's PPP was $10,479; Russia's—boosted by oil sales—was $6,339. Income inequality in Estonia (Gini index, 40.0) was similar to that of the United States (40.8) but much less than that of Russia (48.9). Latvia and Lithuania (both 32.4) had less inequality than Estonia but more than did Hungary (30.8) or Sweden (25.0).[11]

In 2000 the average monthly pension amounted to $95 in Latvia, $87 in Estonia, and $78 in Lithuania. The Baltic republics experienced high levels of joblessness, among the young as well as the elderly, with women often laid off before men, as overstaffed state enterprises shed labor which the emerging private sector was slow to absorb.[12] Real levels of unemployment may have been much higher than the official figures suggested, because governments reported only the number of persons registered with official employment agencies. Many persons stopped searching or looked for jobs outside official channels. In Lithuania 30 to 40 percent of the working-age population was engaged in unofficial employment (earning income while collecting welfare) or hidden unemployment (part-time work). The effectiveness of government policies was difficult to gauge because labor statistics did not capture the full picture.

THE BODY POLITIC: PUBLIC HEALTH AND DEMOGRAPHICS

The Soviet system provided universal health care funded by the state. But public health started to decline in mid-1960s. Why? Ecocide. Alcoholism. Increased smoking—by women as well as men. Psychological stress. Disasters such as Chernobyl. Fewer public services, as the military-industrial complex leached funds from all other sectors.

Male life expectancy in Russia declined from 64.6 years at birth in 1964–1965 to 61.4 in 1979–1980; it then rose to 64.9 in 1986–1987, declined to 57.3 or 57.6 in 1994, and climbed to 59.6 in 1996 and 60.7 in 1998. The life expectancy for white males born in the United States in 1996–1997 was 73; for U.S. black males, it was 65.[13]

Environmental pollution continued to affect public health in the post-Soviet Baltic countries. Some forms of pollution decreased in the 1990s as Russian military forces withdrew, as energy became more expensive, and as factories produced fewer goods. But oil and chemical wastes in the soil and water remained, and would be expensive and difficult to remove.

The reborn Baltic republics were free, in principle, to devote more resources to health services than the old regime. But the new governments were strapped for cash and they wanted to privatize whatever institutions they could. Health care suffered from low funding. Public health care expenditures in the Baltic republics ranged from 4 to 7 percent of GDP in the 1990s, comparable to Western Europe. But Balts spent relatively little for private medical care or private health insurance.

The supply of health services shrank while the need for them mounted as public health worsened. The number of doctors per capita, the number of hospital beds, and the number of hospitals all declined. Budgetary constraints meant that medical personnel continued, as in Soviet times, to be paid poorly, and that few hospitals could replace old, Soviet-designed equipment. Services would get worse before they got better.

The consequences were cruelly evident: between 1990 and 1994 the mortality rate (the excess of deaths over births) in Estonia increased by 16 percent; in Latvia it increased by 27 percent, in Lithuania by 17 percent.

Fertility rates fell sharply from 1975 to 1997: in Estonia, from 2.1 to 1.3 children per woman; in Latvia, from 2.0 to 1.3; in Lithuania, from 2.2 to 1.4; and in Russia, from 1.9 to 1.3. By 1998 Latvia had one of the lowest rates in Europe—1.09. The likely declines in population by 2015 are shown in table 6.4. The UN Economic Commission for Europe forecast in 2000 that in fifty years the populations of Estonia and Latvia would decline by one-third, while that of Russia would fall by nearly one-fifth.

The combination of lower living standards, more alcoholism, and poorer health care led to a higher death rate. Life expectancy in each Baltic country reached its lowest point in 1994–1995, before rising again. Even so, life expectancy across the Baltic

Table 6.4
Population in the Baltic Republics and Elsewhere (millions)

Country	1975	1997	(projected) 2015
Estonia	1.4	1.4	1.2
Latvia	2.5	2.5	2.1
Lithuania	3.3	3.7	3.5
Russia	134.2	147.7	142.9
Hungary	10.5	10.2	9.4
Sweden	8.2	8.9	9.1
United States	220.2	271.8	307.7

SOURCE: UN Development Programme, *Human Development Report 1999* (New York: Oxford University Press, 1999), table 16.

was still lower at the end of the 1990s than in the late 1980s. Men died significantly younger than women on average. In Lithuania men of working age were four times more likely to die than women of similar age.

The deterioration in living standards after the collapse of communism made it more costly to bring up children. Birth rates fell in the 1990s and more children were born out of wedlock. Couples preferred smaller families. In 1999–2000, however, fertility rates in Estonia and Latvia showed a slight uptick.

Each Baltic country also lost population due to emigration by disaffected Russians and other minorities, but the outflow tapered off after 1994–1995.

As in other developed countries, Baltic populations became grayer. But Balts depended upon social insurance programs much weaker than those typical in Western Europe. Below are some specifics on health conditions in each country.

Estonia

In the 1980s Estonia's population grew by an average of 0.8 percent per year. After independence, however, the entire population declined—by 2.3 percent in 1993, by 1.3 percent in 1994, and by 1 percent in 1995 and 1996. Estonia's population at the beginning of 1998 was estimated at 1,453,200—a fall of 7.2 percent since 1991.

Maternal mortality rose steeply in the mid-1990s and then declined. But it was still twice as high in 1997 as in 1992—41 deaths per 100,000 births. This was very high compared to Sweden (7 deaths), Slovakia (8), or the United States (9). But it was low relative to Russia (75 in 1997), Pakistan (340), or Sierra Leone (1,800).[14]

The state remained the main health-care provider in the 1990s, but private medicine established a toehold in the system, with many private practitioners working under contract to state providers. Funding remained a problem, although the central health insurance fund swung into small surplus in 1997.

In the late 1990s the first point of access for patients was still the hospital. The government resolved to establish a general-practitioner system responsible for primary health care, referring patients to specialists only as necessary.

Latvia

Latvia's population declined by more than 10 percent in the 1990s. Infant mortality rates rose quickly after independence, to a high of 18.5 per 1,000 births in 1995, but subsequently fell back to 15.2 in 1997. Women lived nearly twelve years longer than men, with the result that females outnumbered males by nearly 15 percent in 1997. There was a rise in poverty-related diseases, such as tuberculosis and viral hepatitis, as well as in sexually transmitted diseases. In 2000, Latvia had the highest rate of diphtheria in all the former USSR. HIV infections increased from about six hundred to over nine hundred.

The decline in health services was reflected in two indicators: at the beginning of 1999 there were 95 hospital beds per 10,000 inhabitants—down from 130 in 1992—and one physician per 307 persons, compared with one per 244 persons seven years earlier.

In 1996 the government launched a new health-care policy emphasizing primary health care and preventive measures, rather than hospital-based treatment; in 1998 the government made private health insurance compulsory. Because private firms were slow to implement this requirement, however, the State Health Insurance Fund remained the main source for funding health expenses.

Lithuania

Lithuania's population declined by 1.2 percent in the 1990s. The main reason for the decline was emigration to Russia early in the decade, but higher mortality and lower birth rates also contributed. Most infectious diseases declined in the 1990s except for tuberculosis. Official statistics showed that alcohol-related diseases stabilized around 1994, but this impression may have resulted from abolition of compulsory treatment for alcoholism.

Life expectancy reached its nadir in 1994: 62.7 years for men, 74.9 for women. By 1997 it had risen to 64.3 and 75.6 respectively—a gender gap greater than eleven years. But there were fewer births than deaths. So the percentage of persons over age sixty-five increased from 10.8 percent in 1990 to 12.7 percent in 1998.

As in Estonia and Latvia, the government initiated reforms intended to shift the focus from specialist care to primary health care and general practice. Unlike Estonia and Latvia, the number of physicians in Lithuania did not decline in the 1990s. The number of paramedical personnel and hospital beds decreased by one-fifth in the early 1990s, and then stabilized.

EDUCATION

Starting with the Reformation and Counter Reformation, many forces nourished Balts' devotion to learning. Even Communist rule made a positive contribution: it did not encourage free-thinking but promoted universal literacy and first-class technical institutes. In 1990 the three Baltic republics ranked among the highest in the USSR by percentage of the population completing secondary education and by percentage entering or completing tertiary education.

When Communist rule disappeared, Balts were again free to think and say what they wished. In the 1990s many became "wired" with the world.

Secondary school enrollments dropped in each Baltic country in the 1990s—in Estonia from 100 percent to 86 percent of the relevant age group and in Latvia from 90 percent to 81 percent; Lithuania also declined to 81 percent. Hungary and the Czech Republic, by contrast, experienced increases to 97 and 100 percent, respectively. Declining births meant fewer pupils and many school closings. In Estonia the number of pupils attending schools in 2000 was 216,000—down by 5,000 from 1999. Officials expected the school population in 2008 to be only 60 percent of its 2000 level.

In the late 1990s there were more Latvians being admitted to college than graduating from secondary schools. One factor was a minor baby boom in the 1980s followed by a decline in births in the 1990s; another was a widening belief in the utility of higher education. In 1996 the number of Latvians over age sixty exceeded the number under fourteen.

Enrollments in higher education fell in the early 1990s and then rose. Soviet institutions of higher learning had emphasized sciences and technical subjects. Baltic colleges in the 1990s began to offer more courses in business, law, information technology, social work, and psychology. Retraining schemes were established to help people adjust to changing skill requirements.

The Baltic countries in the 1990s reported large and growing numbers of students enrolled in colleges and universities—at least one-third the rate in Canada and half the U.S. rate. Estonia claimed in the mid-1990s that 29 percent of its population aged twenty-five and older had graduated from college—more than the 23 percent in the United States.[15] School dropout rates, however, increased in each Baltic state, depressing incomes and contributing to poor health.

As in medical services, funds for education fell short in each Baltic country. Public expenditures for education in the late 1990s reached 5.4 percent of GDP in Lithuania, 6.3 percent in Latvia, and 7.2 percent in Estonia. These percentages were as high as or higher than in the United States, with the important difference that Americans also paid out huge sums for private schools and private universities. Private schools and colleges in the Baltic states and Russia picked up enrollments in the 1990s, but exceeded the financial reach of most residents.

Each Baltic republic required nine years of schooling starting at age six or seven. Special-needs schooling, neglected under communism, got more attention and funding in the 1990s.

In the 1990s Estonia and Latvia operated parallel school systems using the national language or Russian as the primary means of instruction. Latvia also had a small number of schools for Poles and Ukrainians. The Estonian and Latvian governments wanted to phase out schools in which Russian was the medium of instruction early in the twenty-first century. Children of Russian-speaking parents whom I met in Estonia and Latvia in the late 1990s were comfortable using the national language.

Lithuanian was the main language of instruction in Lithuania, but there were also schools for the Polish, Russian, Jewish, Belarusian, and other ethnic minorities.

In Lithuania nearly 40 percent of children also attended preschool. School attendance was required from age six to sixteen, but at age fourteen students could opt for vocational schools or comprehensive teaching in science and the humanities. A growing number of children, mainly boys, left school between ages fifteen and eighteen. Many went on to vocational training schools, but there were not enough such schools to meet needs. Starting in 1994, employers' organizations played a greater role in shaping the vocational schools' curricula.

Estonia had seven universities, eight public and thirteen professional colleges, and five vocational colleges. Latvia also had a large number of universities and colleges relative to its population. By 1997–1998 around sixty-five thousand students in Latvia were pursuing higher education—an increase of 41 percent since 1990–1991.

Lithuania had seven universities in 1996 (up from four in 1990), seven academies, two institutes, and three seminaries. Around 40 percent of secondary-school graduates continued their studies, with females much more likely to do so.

GENDER DIFFERENCES

Within a single country, human development may differ by region, by ethnic group, and by gender. The UNDP constructed two ways to compare attainments by gender. The Gender Development Index (GDI) showed gender inequalities in the same three variables that constitute the HDI. The greater the disparity, the lower a country's rank. The Baltic countries, Russia, and many countries in Eastern Europe scored higher on the GDI than on the HDI: women outlived men, got more education, and received nearly the same incomes.

The Gender Empowerment Measure (GEM) analyzed women's participation in decision making in professional, economic, and political domains. At the top of the GEM rankings in the late 1990s were Norway, Sweden, and Denmark. The Baltic countries scored even higher on this measure than on the GDI. Indeed, they had more women in administration and professional jobs than Sweden! As we see in table 6.5, Latvia and Lithuania had higher rates of women's representation in their parliaments than did most of their neighbors, but they did not approach Sweden's level.

Table 6.5 Gender Issues in the Baltics and Elsewhere in 1998 (with data for 1997 in parentheses)

	Estonia	*Latvia*	*Lithuania*	*Russia*	*Hungary*	*Sweden*	*USA*
Human Development Index	46 (54)	63 (74)	52 (62)	62 (71)	43 (47)	6 (6)	3 (3)
Gender Development Index	43 (49)	51 (62)	47 (55)	54 (61)	38 (43)	6 (5)	4 (3)
Female and male life expectancy	74.7 (74.5) 63.4 (63.0)	74.5 (74.4) 62.8 (62.5)	75.7 (75.6) 64.7 (64.3)	72.9 (72.8) 60.7 (60.6)	75.1 (74.9) 67.1 (66.8)	81.0 (80.8) 76.4 (76.3)	80.2 (80.1) 73.5 (73.4)
School enrollment ratio	87/82 (83/80)	76/73 (72/69)	78/74 (77/73)	81/75 (80/74)	75/73 (75/73)	108/95 (100/95)	97/91 (97/91)
Female share of earned income (%) (in 1995)	41.9	44.0	40.9	41.3	38.5	44.7	40.3
Gender Empowerment Measure	27 (46)	25 (30)	29 (28)	53 (n.a.)	42 (48)	3 (2)	13 (8)
Seats in parliament (%)	17.8 (10.9)	17.0	17.5	5.7 (7.5)	8.3	42.7	12.5
Female administrators and managers (%)	33.5 (36.5)	41.0 (37.5)	35.7 (35.2)	37.9 (n.a.)	35.3 (32.8)	27.4 (27.9)	44.4 (44.3)
Female professional and technical workers (%)	70.3 (66.8)	64.1 (66.4)	69.7 (67.5)	65.6 (n.a.)	60.4 (60.9)	48.6 (63.7)	53.4 (53.1)

SOURCES: UN Development Programme, *Human Development Report 2000* (New York: Oxford University Press, 2000), tables 2 and 3; ibid., 1999; 1995 data are from ibid., 1998, pp. 132, 135.

Box 6.2. Female Empowerment on the Amber Coast

The Baltic-rim countries were among the first in the modern world to empower women in politics. Finland in 1906 became the first European country to extend suffrage to women, though New Zealand had done so in 1893. Estonian, Latvian, and Soviet Russian women were allowed to vote and run for office in 1918; Lithuanian women received these rights in 1921. An Estonian woman was elected to parliament in 1919.

In the 1990s women had a modest share of seats in Baltic parliaments and held few cabinet-level jobs. But the first female prime minister in the former Soviet realm took office in Lithuania in 1990, while Latvians inaugurated the first female president in Eastern Europe in 1999. Literacy had helped Baltic women for centuries, and the first female PM and president held Ph.D.s.

Life expectancy for women in each Baltic republic was about nine years longer than that for men in 1990. As we also see in table 6.5, this gap increased to more than eleven years by the late 1990s! Among the reasons, men were more violent than women, took greater risks, and drank more alcohol.

Some critics charged that power in the Baltic lands was virtually a male monopoly, that male politicians cared mainly for their own well-being (and, for short intervals, that of their female subordinates), and that they were indifferent to women's needs such as maternity leave. Governments did little to change conditions in which abortion was still the most common form of birth control. In Lithuania, for example, there were 149 abortions for every 100 live births in 1996!

The Communist system opened educational doors for women as well as men, though it tended to shunt women into medicine, teaching, and other fields deemed "female professions." After communism fell, females continued to outnumber males at all levels of education in the Baltic countries and in Russia.

Once women finished their schooling, however, they earned less than men for the same jobs. In 1995, for example, Estonian female managers earned about three-fourths as much as male managers; female skilled agricultural workers earned three-fifths as much as men's wages; female machine operators four-fifths. When firms downsized, they tended to lay off women before men. The employment rate for Estonian men was 68 percent, for women 56 percent.[16] In 1998 Lithuanian women earned on average just 77 percent the amount earned by men. Female teachers outnumbered males in the Baltic, as in many countries, but male secondary school principals outnumbered female. Education suffered as men and women left the teaching profession for better-paying jobs.

In 1998 the Seimas adopted a Law on Equal Opportunities, the first such law in Eastern Europe. It defined and banned gender discrimination. Lithuania also set up an ombudsman and agencies within government ministries to promote equal opportunities for and advancement of women. A number of NGOs and a Woman's Information Center also worked for women's interests. Meanwhile, violence against women remained a pressing problem. A network of shelters to assist female victims of violence was expanding.

Box 6.3. Beyond the Numbers: Private Miseries

Some miseries do not show up in the numbers. Nearly all the older women I talked to in Estonia in 1999, whether Estonian citizens or Russian residents, had a story about a man who left them and their children, sometimes turning them out of their dwelling to boot. Thus, a Russian woman selling embroidered hats on a street corner in Tallinn told me she had endured two Russian husbands who drank heavily and beat her; for the last ten years, however, she had been living with an Estonian man.

"Is he better than the others?"

"No, he doesn't work and drinks everything I earn."

"You must love him."

"No," she said, "I pity him."

How to integrate Russian-speaking women into local life—especially widows and divorcees of ex-Soviet military personnel, many of them with young children, no spouse to support them, and little knowledge of the local language? A program called Integration through Training for Estonian and Non-Estonian Women was launched in 1998 by an NGO known as the International Organization for Migration, the OSCE, and the U.S. embassy in Tallinn. The program selected 170 women from over 300 applicants for language, vocational, and cultural training. They studied Estonian in Narva, where most of them lived, and in a summer school on the Estonian-speaking island of Hiiumaa. Nearly 140 passed the Estonian language proficiency test. For job training, the program offered instruction in computer use, bookkeeping, sewing, and hairdressing. It offered small-scale business grants and it backed a sewing company in Narva that gave jobs to five disabled women and a handicraft shop in Sillamäe that employed seven persons. The cultural program brought eighty women from Russian-speaking enclaves to a workshop in Tartu on Estonian history. The program also assisted more than one hundred Russian-speaking children to learn Estonian in summer camps.[17]

SOCIAL MALAISE

Opposing sets of forces resulted in gains and losses in the fitness of Baltic societies in the 1990s. One set contributed to fitness, the other eroded its very foundations. Constructive forces generated a virtuous circle in which social capital reinforced democracy, civil society, and trust. Pitted against this movement were vicious circles of poverty, poor health, and alienation. Self-perpetuating, they served as cause and consequence of a deep social malaise. They undercut the capacity for self-organization and a democratic political culture; they bred cynicism and despair—even among the young.

Income was the single variable that seemed to explain a welter of other social trends. Low incomes generated a nest of persistent social problems in nearly every post-Soviet society. As we have seen, Baltic incomes fell sharply from 1991, bottomed out in 1994–1995, and then slowly improved. When material conditions deteriorated, fewer babies were born and more people died or emigrated. In 1994–1995 life expectancy dropped to its lowest point in decades. Those years also marked the highest rates of maternal mortality, road accidents, homicide, suicide, and rape. Housing issues were critical for low-income families, squatters, persons evicted, and those without proper "papers." School dropout rates increased for children of poor or asocial families and those living in remote areas.

With lower incomes, Balts worried more and died earlier. They married later or not at all, and had fewer children. They consumed more alcohol and drugs. They knifed, shot, and bludgeoned one another at higher rates; suffered more road accidents; and committed suicide in greater numbers. More teenagers—especially males—dropped out of school. The good news was that, by 1996, average incomes and life expectancy began to rise. University enrollments increased dramatically in each Baltic republic. Life in the present was tough, but many people bet on education for their futures.

To be sure, some social indicators ignored or lagged behind the ups and downs of income. In Estonia, for example, infant mortality decreased and life expectancy rose in 1994–1996, even though each year there were fewer doctors per capita and public expenditures on health changed little. Divorce rates peaked in 1995 but were still higher in 1996 than in 1994. Births outside of marriage continued to increase even after incomes began to rise.

On the other hand, the crime rate in Estonia did not decline as incomes improved. Drug-related crimes shot up from 1.4 per 100,000 people in 1992 to 7.8 in 1996. Crime rates in Tallinn increased by one-fifth in the first quarter of 1999 compared to the previous year. Violent crimes and robberies also increased sharply in the late 1990s. In Ida-Virumaa county (home to many Russian speakers), however, crime declined in the late 1990s, but remained well above the national average.[18]

Drug abuse and, with it, HIV infection increased in Lithuania. The number of registered drug addicts increased by nearly 70 percent between 1995 and 1997. Unlike in countries in the EU, the majority of registered drug dependency cases in Lithuania were intravenous drug users, drug-related morbidity was increasing, and the number of HIV-infected drug users was growing. Nearby Kaliningrad was a hub of drug use and HIV infection.

Drugs were easily available at many schools and on many streets throughout the Baltic. A survey conducted in July 2000 found that 75 percent of youths in Riga had tried drugs, and that many were regular users. Prices for marijuana and other narcotics in Riga were only one-fourth the prices in Sweden, thanks to Baltic links with sources in Central Asia. Some observers blamed the lack of state funding for police, teachers, and other agents who might stem the tide.[19] In August 2000 Latvia's interior minister called on the government to invest more in its criminal police, fighting a present danger, rather than on armed forces being prepared for NATO and some hypothetical conflict.

That same month, however, Lithuanian authorities broke up a network smuggling drugs from laboratories in Poland to all three Baltic countries and Belarus. Police arrested three Lithuanian citizens, though the ringleader remained abroad.

Crime in Lithuania increased by more than 5 percent in 2000. Police officials blamed poverty and budget cuts for law enforcement. In some police districts, telephone service was cut off and police patrolled on horseback because they lacked funds to purchase gasoline. In the city of Panevezys, three police inspectors were assassinated gangland style in 1999–2000.

The U.S. Congress earmarked $3 million in 2001 for the Federal Bureau of Investigation (FBI) to open an office in Vilnius to fight organized crime. The interior ministry of each Baltic country stepped up cooperation with the FBI in 1999–2000. Interpol units in each country could access the FBI database, including its records of wanted or missing persons and stolen property, including autos and heavy equipment. Officials hoped to stem the trade in vehicles stolen in the West and shipped through the Baltic to Russia. Also, at the Estonian police college in Paikuse, the FBI provided training courses for Baltic police in safe-arrest methods, antibomb techniques, and DNA analysis.

Estonian authorities said that the country suffered a shortage of trained policemen—especially in the capital. In June 1999, however, I witnessed the arrest in Tallinn's Old Town of three young men in jeans by a female police officer and her male colleague, neither of whom drew a club or pistol. The officers simply ran from their vehicle to a wall where the three were hiding, handcuffed them, marched them to the car, and drove away. When I expressed surprise at the nonviolent outcome, several bystanders said, "Our police are well trained."

But who would guard the guardians? Estonian police chiefs met in August 2000 to discuss aberrant behavior by off-duty police. Five of one hundred traffic fatalities in Estonia that had occurred so far that year were caused by off-duty police, four of whom were intoxicated and one of whom was driving at eighty miles per hour in Tallinn. A sixth death was caused by an off-duty policeman who shot a man who was unwilling (or unable?) to move his car from a pedestrian promenade.

Alcohol scourged the former Soviet Union. The consumption of alcohol in Russia doubled between 1990 and 1995. Contraband alcohol—smuggled and home brewed—caused many deaths. In St. Petersburg as many as nineteen of every twenty bottles of vodka sold came from illegal sources.

Alcohol-related problems rose in Latvia in the late 1990s. Deaths from cirrhosis of the liver shot up from 12.5 percent of all deaths in 1997 to 15.2 percent in 1998. Workplace surveys showed that many Latvians—14 percent in Riga, and 20 to 29 percent in rural regions—had alcohol-related problems. Medical authorities blamed the government for lax controls and low prices on alcohol. In May 1999 two Latvian policemen were shot to death and two others wounded when they sought to search a suspected bootlegger's house.

Contraband alcohol, some experts said, was Lithuania's social disaster, accounting for about 60 percent of Lithuanian consumption in the mid-1990s.[20] In Lithuania in 1996 there were 1,300 cases of alcoholic psychosis and 9,400 cases of alcoholism. In 1997 some 76,000 people were registered with health authorities as suffering from alcoholism and alcoholic psychosis.

In each Baltic country socially induced nonmedical factors caused many deaths. In Lithuania they caused 80 percent of the deaths among men age fifteen to twenty-nine. Between 1990 and 1994 more than 40,000 Lithuanians died from accidents, poisonings, and injuries—19 percent of them from road accidents, 25 percent from suicide, 7 percent from murders, and 9 percent from drowning. Alcohol played a role in many of these incidents—including drowning. In 1997–1998 the incidence of alcohol-related psychoses was nine times greater in the Lithuanian countryside than in cities.

In Lithuania, the total number of crimes grew by 3 percent in 1998, but the number of murders decreased. Still, the number of premeditated murders in Lithuania exceeded 10 per 100,000 population—2.5 times the rate in Germany. Some 25,000 criminal offenders were registered in Lithuania in 1998—mostly males, and over half of them unemployed or not attending school. Most were arrested for stealing. Lithuania had strict laws and its courts gave long sentences. The number of prisoners in 1999 was 329 per 100,000 population—compared with 85 per 100,000 in EU countries. The *Lithuanian Human Development Report 1999* urged programs to keep young people productively occupied and called for systematic liberal reform of criminal policy.

Table 6.6 provides much grist for analysis. Homicide rates in each Baltic republic were about the same in 1991—between 9 and 11.4 per 100,000 of population. In just two years homicide rates more than doubled in Estonia and Latvia, and increased by one-half in Lithuania. By 1995 homicides declined in Lithuania but exceeded the 1991 level by one-third; in Estonia they remained twice the 1991 level and in Latvia they remained one-half greater. In Russia homicides were much more common in 1991 than in the Baltic, and doubled in frequency by 1994–1995.

Suicides took place at comparable levels in the four countries in 1991—two or three times as frequent as homicides. In each country they increased by about one-half but remained at comparable levels in 1995, though Lithuania led the others.[21]

HDI was a good predictor of homicide and suicide rates in the countries surveyed in table 6.7, though it is not reliable in many other countries. For example, while the United States and Sweden ranked high in HDI and had comparatively few homicides or suicides, Finland and Denmark, notwithstanding high HDI scores, had high rates of suicide.[22] The Baltic countries and Russia ranked much lower in HDI and had far higher rates of murder and self-murder. Anomalies: Estonia had a very high homicide rate and Hungary a very low rate. Lithuania's suicide rate was one of the highest in the world, though Catholic countries usually had low suicide rates. As incomes rose and boosted HDI, crime if not suicide could be expected to decline.

WHO OR WHAT TO BLAME?

Why did social problems become more acute in the Baltic countries? Serious difficulties were bound to occur as Balts faced the challenges of transition. But the depth and duration of social malaise were not preordained. Responsibility lay with humans—in and out of government.

Table 6.6
Homicide and Suicide Rates in the Baltic States and Russia (per 100,000 population)

	Homicides					Suicides				
	1991	1992	1993	1994	1995	1991	1992	1993	1994	1995
Estonia	10.8	19.6	25.2	28.3	22.2	27.0	32.2	38.2	41.0	40.1
Latvia	11.4	16.1	24.7	23.0	17.9	28.5	34.9	42.5	40.5	40.5
Lithuania	9.1	10.5	12.5	13.4	11.7	30.5	34.6	42.1	45.8	45.6
Russia	15.2	22.8	30.3	32.3	30.7	26.5	31.0	37.8	41.7	41.4

SOURCE: Based on Arvo Kuddo, *Social Transition: Social and Economic Policies in the Former Soviet Union States* (Washington, D.C.: World Bank, draft manuscript, 1998), appendix 38.

Table 6.7
HDI, Homicide Rates, and Suicide Rates (per 100,000 people), 1900–1995

Country	HDI Rank	Homicides	Male Suicides	Female Suicides
USA	3	9.0	19.8	4.5
Sweden	5	9.5	21.5	9.2
Hungary	47	4.3	50.6	16.7
Estonia	54	24.4	67.6	16.0
Lithuania	62	14.2	79.1	15.6
Russia	71	21.8	72.9	13.7
Latvia	74	14.7	70.8	14.7

SOURCES: UN Development Programme, *Human Development Report 1999*, tables 23, 24; *Statistical Abstract of the United States 1996* (Washington, D.C., U.S. Government Printing Office, 1996), tables 310–313.

Priorities

Some leaders counted on marketization and wrote off the older and marginal groups as beyond help. Like former Communist officials, some Baltic leaders enriched themselves and followers at the public trough. They cared for their own perks and ignored the needs of persons who could not hurt or help them.

Uncertainty

Untested leaders, new to the job, did not foresee the consequences of their policies. Economists did not know whether it was best to proceed gradually or overnight ("cold turkey") into a market economy.

Little Trust in the Law

Balts expressed little confidence in their legal systems, which even if honest were slow and inefficient. This situation weakened social capital, facilitated corruption, and put off investors.

Noncompliance

Soviet life did not prepare Balts to pay taxes or contribute to the common good. The shadow economy amounted to 30 to 40 percent of GDP in each Baltic country in the mid-1990s. In many cases profits that should have been taxed in Tallinn, Riga, or Vilnius were instead banked in Liechtenstein or another tax haven. The Baltic became a conduit for Russian money launderers.

Criminal elements were of many types—aggressive youth, graduates of Soviet prisons, the former privileged class of Communist elites. They exploited the lack of accountability in the newly freed economies. The drug trade from Central Asian poppy fields to Baltic ports to Western and Northern Europe made the criminally rich even richer. Traders exploited porous borders to smuggle oil, spirits, tobacco, and seekers of asylum to Sweden. One Lithuanian wag proposed a way to raise the living standards of all citizens: "Require each to work a month in the customs office." Huge sums passed from Moscow to Riga en route to Zurich.

Communism

A half century of communism weakened self-reliance and bred fear of free enterprise. The longer and more intrusive the rule of Big Brother, the more that human values suffered. Never annexed by the USSR, some Eastern European countries raised their living standards as they began the transition to market economies. The years 1990–1994 saw life expectancy increase and infant mortality decrease in the Czech Republic, Slovakia, Hungary, Poland, and Slovenia. The post-Communist governments in those countries gave a gentler, kinder touch to some policies than did their counterparts in the Baltic.[23]

Quirks of the Nomenklatura

Confident of premium care in clinics and spas for themselves, Soviet officials designated for patronage and privilege, the *nomenklatura,* did not esteem ordinary physicians. About two-thirds of Soviet physicians were female and poorly paid. Even after the fall of communism, medical personnel continued to receive low pay in the Baltics and much of Eastern Europe. The best treatment now went to newly rich who could afford it.

Gender

Some observers suggested that male domination of Baltic power structures gave government policies a tougher edge than would be the case if women had a larger voice. Perhaps, but the thesis is difficult to test. Many women who excel in politics are "iron ladies."

HOW TO BREAK THE VICIOUS CIRCLES?

The Potential of Education: Self-Organization

Balts in the 1990s inherited the Communist disposition to distrust other humans, but they still trusted education. The reborn Baltic republics debated how to orient education in the twenty-first century. Here are four different approaches that could unite or divide Baltic societies by 2010.

- *Scenario 1:* Traditional schools promote passive learning and national values. They strengthen the identity of the ethnic majority in each republic but leave Baltic societies divided and ill-suited for the Information Age and global interdependence.
- *Scenario 2:* A back-and-forth competition between different educational philosophies leaves Balts spinning their wheels, going nowhere.
- *Scenario 3:* Private schooling generates an elite equipped for modern life, but public education is neglected, leaving most people to flounder. The upshot: polarities deepen between social-economic haves and have-nots.
- *Scenario 4:* Proactive learning fuses tradition with the needs of the Information Age; generates lifelong learning, harnessing the energies of youth and wisdom of experience; understands and respects the past but also searches out new knowledge to solve current problems. The Baltic republics in the 1990s laid the foundations for pursuit of scenario 4.

Information Technology: Self-Organization

Proactive learning can use advances in information technology (IT) to promote the synergies of openness—scientific discovery, technological innovation, and a democratic political culture.

The World Bank in 1998 analyzed "knowledge for development." It reported on successful applications of IT to spread health knowledge in Costa Rica, create an African Virtual University, and generate the world's most efficient port in Singapore. Just as Singapore created a networked information system to accelerate customs procedures, so Balts might compensate for their small size and late entry into world commerce by cultivating one of the great equalizers—IT.

Estonia ranked among Europe's most computerized societies. In 1998 more than 10 percent of Estonians used the Internet—a proportion similar to that in France and Germany. This percentage did not rival Iceland, Sweden, or the United States, where more than 40 percent of the population used the Internet, but it was far higher than in Russia (0.8 percent in 1998) or Austria (5.4 percent).

The number of Internet hosts in Baltic countries per 10,000 people increased dramatically from 1996 to 1998: in Estonia it went from 45 to 209, in Latvia it increased from 21 to 57, and in Lithuania it rose from 7 to 34. Sweden, however, had 670 hosts per 10,000 in 1998, Finland more than 1,200, and the United States nearly 2,000. In 1998 Estonia had 34 personal computers for every 1,000 people, Lithuania had 34, Finland had 182, Sweden 361, and the United States 362.[24]

In the late 1990s, according to the UN Development Programme in Riga, some 8 percent of Latvian children had a computer at home—10 percent in urban areas. In 1996 there was one computer per 101 students in schools, two years later there was one per 45. Overall, however, television was king. Most homes had TV and young people watched more than two hours a day. Many Latvian boys claimed to read nothing except school assignments. And many did not finish secondary school.

Latvia was less "wired" than Estonia or Lithuania. But in 2000 the Latvian government worked with Microsoft to prepare the legislative base for digitizing Latvian society—new laws treating electronic documents and signatures as fully valid. The government sought to create an electronic portal from which a citizen could access any government service, get information, or make payments—as in Singapore and in parts of the United States.

The reborn Baltic republics ranked high both in political and civic freedoms and in Internet involvement. The Baltic republics also led in the quality of information conveyed on government web sites—hard facts, texts of laws and other documents. Each ranking—for quantity and for quality of information—correlated strongly with the "Freedom in the World" rankings by Freedom House, as the table illustrates.

Greater access to information may foster democracy and commerce, but only if reliable communications networks and computers are widely available, and if people use the information received. If different levels of access to online information exist, there may develop classes of information haves and have-nots.[25] Where access is equalized, the gaps between winners and losers will be easier to narrow. This is a feasible goal for proactive education in the Baltic region.

Table 6.8
Measures of Internet Involvement and Democracy, 1997–1998

	Estonia	Latvia	Lithuania	RF	Ukraine	Tajikistan
Number of hosts per 10,000 adults	206.8	57.3	34.4	14.7	5.4	0.4
Combined quality score for gov't web sites	308.8	226.5	321.1	204.8	73.1	0.0
Freedom House composite score for political rights and civil liberties*	1.5	2.0	1.5	3.5	3.5	7.0

*1 = highest rating; 7 = lowest rating. Source: Erik S. Herron, "Democratization and the Development of Information Regimes: The Internet in Eurasia and the Baltics," *Problems of Post-Communism* 46 (July/August 1999), pp. 56–68 at 66, and *World Development Report,* 2000/20001, table 9.

If these conditions are met, the Internet can be an exemplar of self-organization for sharing information and solving problems together. This kind of Internet engagement illustrates two themes of this book. It shows how self-organization can enhance fitness and also how openness can promote mutual gain. The more decisions reflect the interests of each actor, the greater the chances that they will create values for all concerned parties. The more that all parties communicate, the greater the prospect of finding solutions useful to all sides.

Self-organized generation of knowledge can buttress self-rule in politics. Both kinds of self-organization can nourish each other.

Proactive learning could also build a cohesive society in which Slavic speakers can become bicultural. How Balts and ethnic minorities interact is the focus of the next chapter.

APPENDIX 6.1: MEASURING HUMAN DEVELOPMENT

The UNDP *Human Development Reports* probably overstated the decline and rise in Baltic living standards in the 1990s. The UNDP's HDI gave equal weight to each of the three variables considered. Compared to other countries, the Baltic rankings were boosted by relatively high educational attainments but depressed by low purchasing power. To compare purchasing power across borders is extremely difficult. For some countries, the UNDP calculated PPP from World Bank estimates; for others it used Penn World Tables. Comparisons developed within Europe gave still different results. When the *Human Development Report 1999* measured per capita incomes by dollar exchange rates rather than by PPP, this made Baltic incomes look about one-third less than did World Bank and other calculations.

The Estonian UNDP office charged that the UNDP in New York often ignored the official statistics of the Baltic republics.

The global UNDP reports produced some findings hard to explain except by methodological weaknesses or statistical inconsistencies. For example, Lithuania fell forty-three places in HDI ranking from 1994 to 1995; Latvia fell thirty-seven places from 1996 to 1997. But then each Baltic republic made a dramatic advance in 1998–1999. The trends depicted may have been accurate, but the UNDP exaggerated their steepness.

The UNDP global *HDR 1998* probably erred even on relative rankings. It assigned a higher HDI ranking to Russia in 1995 than to any Baltic country. It ranked Latvia behind Macedonia and just one notch ahead of Kazakstan.

The *HDR 1999* highlighted changes in HDI values and ranks based on new previous formulas and revised data (pp. 164–67).

Whatever their shortfalls, both the global and national human development reports were a boon to researchers and a valuable platform for further study.

Caption for Chapter 6 Photo: In the late 1990s each Baltic country had a generation of winners, of aspiring winners, and of losers. Many losers were elderly; many lived in the country. This woman in the village of Kretuonai in eastern Lithuania walks home with an apron full of eggs she has stored with a neighbor, one of the few villagers to have a refrigerator. As the twenty-first century began, many rural Lithuanians still drew water from a well.

NOTES

1. See United Nations Development Programme, *Human Development Report* (hereafter *HDR;* New York: Oxford University Press, various years).

2. If calculated correctly, PPP would express the number of "international dollars" required to purchase the same basket of goods and services that a U.S. dollar could buy in the United States. For less-developed countries, PPP is usually higher than the gross national product per capita translated into dollars at official exchange rates.

3. Uzbekistan, Kyrgyzstan, and Tajikistan would have placed 80th, 83d, and 88th in the world. Arvo Kuddo, *Social Transition: Social and Unemployment Policies in the Former Soviet Union States* (Washington, D.C.: World Bank, unpublished manuscript, 1998), appendix I.

4. In 1980 infant mortality in Estonia was 17 deaths per 1,000 live births; in Latvia and Lithuania, it was 20; in Russia, 22; in Tajikistan, 58; in the United States, 13; in Finland, 8; and in Sweden, 7. World Bank, *World Development Report 1998/99* (New York: Oxford University Press, 1999), pp. 202–203.

5. The report for 1994 was published in 1995 and based on statistics from 1991–1992. Similar lags characterize each year's publication. Other methodological problems are discussed in the appendix to this chapter.

6. *HDR 2000*, table 9.

7. *HDR 2000*, table 5.

8. United Nations Development Programme, *Transition 1999: Human Development Report for Central and Eastern Europe and the CIS* (New York: UNDP, 1999), pp. iii–iv.

9. The so-called European comparison program showed that Lithuania reached almost the same PPP as Estonia in 1995. *Lithuanian HDR 1997* (Vilnius: UNDP, 1998), chapter 2.

10. This analysis is based on sociological studies of Estonia but probably applies broadly to Latvia and Lithuania as well. See *Estonian Human Development Report 1998* (hereafter *Estonian HDR 1998;* Tallinn: UNDP, 1998), pp. 14–16; also see Mikk Titma et al., "Winners and Losers in the Postcommunist Transition: New Evidence from Estonia," *Post-Soviet Affairs* 14 (May-June 1998), pp. 114–36.

11. Statistical tables in *World Development Report 2000* (New York: Oxford University Press, 2000), pp. 274 ff.

12. Unemployment increased in Estonia from 3.7 percent in 1992 to 10 percent in 1997; in Latvia it rose from 5.8 percent in 1993 to 7.2 percent in 1996, and fell to 7 percent in 1997; in Lithuania it grew from 1.3 percent in 1992 and peaked at over 8 percent in early 1997, before stabilizing at 6–7 percent. Unemployment rose again in 1998, as companies affected by the Russian economic crisis scaled back production and laid off workers, but the trend subsided in 1999.

13. Murray Feshbach, "Comments on current and future demographic and health issues," distributed by e-mail on the Johnson Russian List, June 10, 1997; see also *HDR 1999*, table 2.

14. Averages for 1990–1996 are from World Bank, *World Development Report 1998/99* (New York: Oxford University Press, 1999), p. 203; 1997 data are from *HDR 1999*, table 8.

15. See *HDR* for each Baltic country and U.S. Bureau of the Census, *Statistical Abstract of the United States: 1996* (Washington, D.C.: U.S. Government Printing Office, 1996), pp. 150–51; also see global *HDR 1998*, p. 190.

16. Kuddo, *Social Transition*, appendices 29 and 32.

17. Report by U.S. ambassador to Estonia Melissa Wells in Sillamäe on May 5, 2000. The ambassador was born in Estonia but left with her parents in 1936 at age four for New York and Hollywood. See the interview by Nele Laanejärv in *Global Estonian* 1 (summer 1999), pp. 16–21.

18. Dennise Albrighton, "Crime Soars in Tallinn," *Baltic Times,* May 20–26, 1999, pp. 1, 4; Rebecca Santana, "Officials Beat Path to Northeast," ibid., p. 4.

19. *Baltic Times,* August 31–September 6, 2000, p. 15.

20. Officially reported alcohol consumption in Latvia peaked in 1994. In 1996 it was 8.3 liters per capita, lower than in Estonia (11.5 liters). *Latvian HDR 1998,* pp. 101–103; *Estonian HDR 1998,* pp. 125. But French and German people also consumed more than 11 liters per capita, while Russians reported only 5.2 liters in 1995—home brew omitted.

21. Suicides in Lithuania fell in the run-up to independence but then rose steadily from 1992 through 1996, with rural men twice as likely to kill themselves as urban. In the late 1990s traditionally Catholic Lithuania had one of the highest suicide rates in the world—46 per 100,000, four-fifths of them by men.

22. Of large, highly developed countries, Japan and Canada suffered the fewest deaths from aggregated homicides and suicides. The U.S. murder rate rose from 7.9 per 100,000 people in 1984 to 9.8 in 1991 and then declined to 9 in 1994 and even lower later in the decade. In 1994, however, Washington, D.C., and New Orleans had seven to eight times more homicides than the U.S. average. In Finland in 1994 the rate was 10.5 per 100,000 for homicides, 38.7 for male suicides, and 10.7 for female suicides.

23. From 1990 to 1995 the Czech Republic and Hungary lowered infant mortality substantially. See Arvo Kuddo, "Determinants of Demographic Change in Transition Estonia," unpublished manuscript (World Bank, 1996), tables 2 and 3. In 1991–1996 family and maternity allowances in the Czech Republic, Slovakia, and Hungary consumed from 2.5 to 4 percent of GDP, compared with 1 to 2 percent in the Baltic republics and less than 1 percent in Russia. Kuddo, *Social Transition*, appendix 26.

24. Compare table 19 in *World Development Report 1998/99* with that in *WDR 2000/2001,* where some data on Latvia are missing.

25. Erik S. Herron, "Democratization and the Development of Information Regimes: The Internet in Eurasia and the Baltics," *Problems of Post-Communism* 46 (July/August 1999), pp. 56–68; also see the thoughtful discussion in *Estonian HDR 1998,* chapter 5.

7

Walter C. Clemens Jr.

Integration: Coping with Ethnic Complexity

The movement toward self-organized fitness in the Baltic republics had an Achilles' heel in the 1990s: more than one-fourth of the persons living in Estonia and Latvia were not citizens. For most noncitizens, their first and often only language was a Slavic tongue—most commonly Russian—not the official, "titular" language. Many native Balts resented the Russian speakers as an unwelcome remnant of a repressive empire. Many non-Balts, in turn, were indignant at what they saw as "discrimination." Ethnic-cultural conflicts were aggravated by the economic shortfalls and social issues discussed in chapter 6.

In the last years of Soviet rule, the Baltic republics sometimes teetered on the brink of civil war between ethnic Balts wanting to split from Kremlin rule and Russian speakers upholding the Soviet Union. In March 1990, for example, I watched as thousands of Russian speakers—civilian workers and uniformed military—demonstrated in central Tallinn against Baltic independence. Their banners proclaimed that "The Army and People Are One." On previous occasions their signs declared that "The Party and People Are One," but in 1990 they counted on the army—not the Party— to maintain the Union.

After the Soviet breakup, some 25 to 27 million Russians resided in erstwhile Soviet republics outside the RF—more than a million in the *pribaltika*. As we shall see in chapter 10, the RF claimed a right and duty to protect these "compatriots" (*sootechestvenniki*).

THE IDEAL OF THE NATION-STATE: HERDER AND HEGEL TO WILSON

Nationalism is a relatively new force in world affairs. It comes in many forms—liberal and tolerant, aggressive and closed. Nationalism can energize but also divide peoples.

A statue of Johann Gottfried von Herder in Riga reminds Balts of the Prussian linguist who worked in Latvia as pastor and teacher in 1764–1769 and taught that the spirit of every nation, imprinted in its culture and song, has value. He saw the human race as a whole in which all nations should dwell in harmony.

Herder planted seeds of cultural nationalism; another German, Georg Hegel (1770–1831), fostered political nationalism. Herder idealized folklore, Hegel the state. Hegel argued that no people has meaning as such unless embodied in its own state.

A third German, Friedrich List (1789–1846), nurtured economic nationalism—a force that often reinforces cultural and political nationalism.

Long before nationalism, however, there was ethnic pride—a belief that one's own tribe or culture is superior. For centuries the Baltic barons looked down on Estonians, Latvians, and others as "non-Germans." Estonians and Latvians, their masters thought, were not nations but lower social orders. Despite Herder, many nineteenth-century Germans regarded Estonian and Latvian as peasant vernaculars—not vehicles for literature or culture. Nonetheless, Balts experienced a national awakening in the nineteenth century.

A growing national spirit helped cultivate a sense of shared identity within each subject people in the nineteenth-century Europe. It inspired many of them to seek statehood after World War I. Woodrow Wilson became the foremost voice for national self-determination as the war ended. When the victors deliberated Europe's postwar boundaries, however, Wilson discovered that Eastern Europe was a patchwork quilt of ethnic and cultural complexity. He felt compelled to compromise. For example, the victor states approved a "Czechoslovakia" that contained not only Czechs but many Germans, Slovaks, Hungarians, and Roma.

The new Baltic republics were far more homogeneous than Czechoslovakia, but they contained Russian, German, Polish, Jewish, Swedish, and other minorities, some of whom had lived in the Baltic region for centuries. All three Baltic states granted their minorities not only cultural and educational autonomy but the right to form political parties and contest national elections. Ethnic issues in Lithuania, however, were complicated by two border disputes that festered from the early 1920s until 1939. On the Polish border, the government in Kaunas never accepted Poland's annexation of Vilnius. On the border with Germany, Lithuania seized from League of Nations administrators the Klaipeda (Memel) region, populated mainly by Germans.

ETHNIC-CULTURAL TRANSFORMATION OF THE BALTIC, 1940–1991

Cataclysmic changes ensued in 1939–1940. Hitler took back the Memel region from Lithuania but summoned "home" all Germans from Estonia and Latvia. The USSR annexed what remained of the three Baltic republics in 1940, returning Vilnius to Lithuania.

The ethnic composition of the Baltic states, especially Estonia and Latvia, changed significantly from 1940 through the 1980s. The number and proportion of Balts declined due to mass arrests, executions, deportations; World War II deaths; and "biological" losses—babies not born because prospective parents died young. After the war, however, reduced numbers of Balts were more than offset by soldiers, sailors, and settlers from other parts of the Soviet Union.

Most newcomers moved to the Baltics in response to orders or to material incentives from Soviet authorities. Few settlers had any desire to learn the local language or ways. The situation was quite different from the United States, where most immigrants came voluntarily, wanted to assimilate, and eagerly learned the language.

The share of Estonians in Estonia's population decreased from 88 percent in the late 1930s to 61 percent in 1989; the percentage of Latvians in Latvia's population decreased from 77 percent before World War II to 52 percent in 1989. As we see in table 7.1, the titular populations increased very little in Estonia and Latvia in decades between 1959 and 1989, while the numbers of Slavs (mostly Russian speakers) roughly doubled.

Russians were the largest minority in each Baltic republic in 1989, followed by Ukrainians in Estonia; Belarusians in Latvia; and Poles in Lithuania, as shown in table 7.2.

In 1989, when the last Soviet census was taken, nearly half of Latvia's population and two-fifths of Estonia's consisted of persons whose first language and cultural identity were Slavic. Estonians made up barely half the population in Tallinn and only a few percent in Estonia's northeast. Russian speakers outnumbered Latvians in seven of Latvia's eight largest cities.

Slavs and other minorities made up only one-fifth of Lithuania's population, because Soviet leaders did not target Lithuania for industrialization, as they did Estonia and Latvia, and dispatched fewer workers there. Many Slavs in Lithuania were Poles. Unlike most Russian speakers in Estonia and Latvia, Poles in Lithuania descended from persons who had lived for generations—even centuries—in or around Vilnius. As if to protect their genes and languages, endogamy prevailed among Balts. In the last decade of Soviet rule some 80 percent of Latvians married other Latvians, more than 90 percent of Estonians married other Estonians, and some 94 percent of Lithuanians married other Lithuanians.[1]

Table 7.1
Ethnic Composition of Baltic Populations, 1959–1989 (in thousands)

	1959	*1970*	*1979*	*1989*
Estonia				
Estonians	893	925	948	963
Slavs	267	381	468	551
Others	37	50	49	51
Latvia				
Latvians	1,298	1,342	1,344	1,388
Slavs	647	853	1,000	1,117
Others	148	169	162	109
Lithuania				
Lithuanians	2,151	2,507	2,712	2,924
Slavs	279	339	393	452
Poles	230	240	247	258
Others	51	42	40	41

SOURCE: Viktors Ivulis, ed., *Latvians: Fight for Survival* (Riga: University of Latvia, 1993), p. 13.

Table 7.2
Ethnic Groups in the Baltic Republics, 1989 (in thousands)

	Estonia	Latvia	Lithuania
Titular nationality	963	1,388	2,924
Russians	475	906	345
Ukrainians	48	92	45
Belarusians	28	120	63
Poles	—	60	258
Lithuanians	—	35	—
Latvians	—	—	4

SOURCE: 1989 census of the USSR.

Few Balts chose to live in Russia. In 1989 there were only 46,000 Estonians, 47,000 Latvians, and 70,000 Lithuanians there.

Unlike Ukrainians, Belarusians, and Moldovans, very few Balts adopted Russian as their mother tongue. Unlike most Central Asians, Baltic intellectuals did not accept Russian as the language of scientific or literary discourse. Most Balts sent their children to kindergartens and schools where the medium of instruction was the titular language. The Baltic republics published many more newspapers and books in the titular languages than in Russian—many times more than warranted by population size. But library collections contained an excess of Russian-language books relative to local demographics. The numbers of newspapers and books in Baltic kiosks and libraries were skewed by Russian-language publications from the Russian Republic.[2]

HOW TO COPE WITH THE NEW SITUATION?

How could the reborn Baltic republics deal with ethnic diversity without losing their own national cultures? Each country and political party groped for answers. But they found no simple formula both just and efficient. Their search puzzled some outsiders. Americans, whose language, culture, and dollars were the common currency of McWorld, were often slow to empathize with peoples who felt they were on the endangered species list.[3] Given the ethnic composition of their populations in 1991, what model should the reborn Baltic republics pursue in the post-Soviet era?

- A multinational state dominated by one major group, as in the former USSR and Yugoslavia?
- A bilingual, bicultural "consociation"—power-sharing on the Belgian or Swiss model?
- A pluralistic melting pot, U.S.-style, where ethnicity usually plays only a minor role?
- A cosmopolitan state in which "anything goes"—any language and any way of life, whatever serves to communicate and do business in a globalized "McWorld" where borders represent administrative conveniences more than "national" differences?
- A nation-state that finds political expression in statehood with an official language, symbols, and culture?

This last option was favored by leaders of the reborn Baltic republics. They wanted to restore the nation-state. But ethnic cleansing was not a morally or politically acceptable option.

Basic Options for Baltic Governments

The Baltic states could deal with minorities by what David Laitin termed a civic or a culturalist program. The civic program would accept minorities as citizens regardless of their language and culture. If the central government opted for a civic program and it was accepted by minorities, the outcome could be a form of pluralism or consociation.[4]

Without using Laitin's terms, Lithuania in effect embraced a civic strategy, while Estonia and Latvia embraced a culturalist one. The Lithuanian civic program promoted pluralism, though it also allowed some legislative representation for minorities unable to win even 5 percent of the total vote. Estonia and Latvia, however, denied citizenship to minorities who arrived after 1940 unless they acquired the official language and accepted the constitution. If the Russian speakers did so, the titular language would over time be standardized—"rationalized," in Max Weber's phrase.

All residents of Lithuania could become citizens just by applying. Lithuania could endorse the civic approach more readily than Estonia and Latvia because its culture was more secure. As noted earlier, only one-fifth of Lithuania's residents were non-Lithuanian. By contrast, titulars in 1991 barely exceeded half Latvia's population and three-fifths of Estonia's.

Options for Nontitular Peoples

Between 1988 and 1991 some Slavs also wanted Baltic independence. In Latvia, for example, the percentage of non-Latvians favoring Latvian independence rose from 9 percent in May 1989 to 26 percent in June 1990 and 38 percent in March 1991. Ethnic Latvians, however, were far more positive—55 percent in May 1989, 85 percent in June 1990, and 94 percent in March 1991.[5]

Some Russian speakers were disappointed when they were not automatically enfranchised in Latvia and Estonia. Still, most preferred to remain—if only because economic conditions in Russia, Belarus, and Ukraine were going from bad to worse.

Some Slavs were highly educated—engineers, military officers, scientists, lawyers. Most Slavic factory workers were less so. Some—especially in northeastern Estonia—had criminal backgrounds, having been released from Russian jails and denied a residence permit for St. Petersburg or Moscow. As noted earlier, many criminal gangs in the Baltic lands had Russian connections.[6]

Under Soviet rule, Balts were pressured to conform to an alien culture imposed from outside. After 1991, however, their situations were reversed: Russian speakers and other minorities had to consider how to relate to Balts. Here is the spectrum of their choices:

1. Exit: Go to Russia or elsewhere.
2. Revive Russian: Stay and promote the Russian language in certain regions.
3. Accept marginalization: Lose contact with Russia and stay disengaged from the titular culture.

4. Embrace consociation: Practice self-rule in Russian-speaking regions and share power in national politics. Use Russian in the region as well as at home.
5. Integrate: De-emphasize identity issues and participate in pluralist politics. Ally with other interest groups on particular issues. Use Russian mainly at home.
6. Assimilate: Children and many adults acquire the local language and culture.

The more determined a person was to live in a Russian-speaking culture, the more likely she or he would exit, revive Russian, endure marginalization, or share power. The more willing to accept the titular way of life, the more likely a person would be to share power, integrate, or even assimilate.

A number of Russians, Ukrainians, and Belarusians did exit the Baltic countries, especially in the early 1990s. Their departures served to increase the native element, in Estonia's population from 61 percent in 1991 to 65 percent in 1998 and in Latvia from about 52 to 56 percent. In the late 1990s there was also slight movement in the other direction, as several hundred Slavs emigrated or returned to Baltic countries.

PRACTICE

Lithuania's Civic Program

With a population that was more than 80 percent Lithuanian, the Sajudis-led government had the confidence in December 1991 to grant citizenship to all residents who applied for it, took a loyalty oath, and showed proof of having renounced any other citizenship. The 1991 law was amended in 1995. It provided citizenship to persons born within the borders of the republic who themselves, or whose ancestors, were citizens of Lithuania before 1940, or who became citizens under previous legal authority. In the 1990s more than 90 percent of Lithuania's Russian, Polish, Belarusian, and Ukrainian inhabitants received citizenship.

For persons not qualifying under these categories, naturalization required a ten-year residency, a permanent job or source of income, knowledge of the constitution, renunciation of any other citizenship, and proficiency in Lithuanian. In the first half of 1998 some 248 such persons applied for citizenship and 220 received it after passing the required exams.

Many nonethnic Lithuanian public-sector employees were required to attain a functional knowledge of Lithuanian within several years, but deadlines were usually extended. Vilnius claimed that no one was fired solely due to failure to meet language requirements.

Vytautas Landsbergis told me in 1996 that every citizen "must feel in favor of the country." He endorsed coexistence (integration)—not assimilation. He and his followers backed laws that supported schools in the language of every minority, including Jews and Belarusians, if only Sunday schools.

Lithuanian was the main language of instruction, but in the late 1990s nearly 15 percent of Lithuanian schoolchildren received their education in a minority language. Some schools catered to the Polish, Russian, Yiddish, Belarusian, and other ethnic minorities. In 1999, however, some Polish speakers complained that they were being pressured to learn Lithuanian.

While few complaints arose about citizenship issues in Lithuania, human rights groups reported that discrimination against women and abuse of children were widespread.

In 1994 the Lithuanian government established a Department of International and Human Rights within the Ministry of Justice to assure compliance with Lithuania's international obligations. But the Ministry of the Interior refused to discuss with outsiders charges of police brutality and corruption.

Slavic speakers presented little threat within Lithuania, but Russia continued to menace the country from outside. As we shall see in the next chapters, Russia threatened Lithuania by manipulating the oil spigot, by exploiting waters claimed by both sides, by military maneuvers, and by closer ties with Belarus.

Culturalist Policies

Intent on restoring a nation-state and fearful that their cultures could disappear in a Slavic sea, Estonia and Latvia established procedures for naturalization that required several years of residency, some knowledge of the local language and constitution, a legal source of income, and a loyalty oath. Certain classes of persons were not eligible for naturalization, such as criminals, former agents of a foreign intelligence service, and career soldiers in the armed forces of a foreign state.

These culturalist programs (to use Laitin's term) offered many concessions to minorities. Deadlines were extended. Some rules were watered down. Forums for dialogue were broadened. Political parties representing minority interests took part in elections and won seats in national governments as well as local councils. The governments gradually devoted more resources to helping minorities learn the titular language and culture.

Noncitizens of Estonia and Latvia were free to do business and make money. In Estonia they could even purchase land; in Latvia they could own shares in companies that purchased land. The Estonian and Latvian governments paid the same pensions to noncitizen residents as to citizens. Latvian noncitizens, however, received fewer privatization certificates than did citizens.

Balts were often pressed not just by Russians but by Western Europeans to liberalize naturalization procedures. But who deserved to preach? France, Germany, Italy, and the United Kingdom—torn by ethnic politics even though minorities made up no more than 5 percent of their populations? Austria—where the anti-immigrant Freedom Party entered the government in 2000? Naturalization and residence requirements in Estonia and Latvia resembled Canada's. They were much easier for nonnatives to satisfy than similar provisions in Switzerland, Germany, or Malta.[7]

The Estonian and Latvian governments pointed out that respect for human rights need not entail a grant of citizenship. Most human rights groups concurred that no Baltic country in the 1990s violated the *human* rights of its residents, except perhaps in the case of Latvia's refusal until 1998 to grant citizenship to all children born there after 1991.[8]

Intermarriage between Balts and Russian speakers was not common, but in Estonia and Latvia there were celebrated (or notorious) cases where the spouse of a titular man or woman could not become a citizen without the usual residence period and exams, even though they had lived in the country for years and knew the language. Several Estonians struggling for independence from the USSR whom I met in the late 1980s were married to Russians.

Estonia

The status of any residents who arrived before 1940 was relatively unproblematic. But Estonia's citizenship laws left some half million non-Estonians with the status of noncitizens. They had either to apply for Estonian citizenship through naturalization or opt for the citizenship of their country of origin.

A 1993 law required noncitizens in Estonia to apply for temporary or permanent residence permits. The deadline for noncitizens to file for permanent residency was extended twice but expired in 1996. Some people never got permits but the law was not strictly enforced.

Critics said that Estonia in the early 1990s became one state with two societies. The identity of Estonians was defined by law, the identity of non-Estonians, fluid and uncertain. Many Slavic speakers lived in Tallinn; others were concentrated in the northeast county of Ida-Virumaa (197,000 residents in 1999) and its main city, Narva (74,572 residents). The county had Estonia's highest unemployment rate in 1999— between 15 and 25 percent. When a Swedish firm purchased a huge textile mill in Narva, it improved the machines but laid off workers. Greater efficiency meant fewer jobs, at least in the short run. Many observers feared that social decay in the northeast could help trigger trouble with Russia.

The Estonian Supreme Court in 1993 declared unconstitutional a referendum calling for an autonomous government in northeastern Estonia without supervision from Tallinn. Unlike Latvia, however, Estonia in the 1990s permitted noncitizens to vote in local elections, though only Estonian citizens could run for office. Local governments in predominantly Russian-speaking communities conducted most official business in Russian in the 1990s. Where more than half the population spoke a language other than Estonian, the inhabitants were entitled to receive official information in that language. Noncitizens of Estonia could express their concerns at a presidential roundtable on ethnic affairs and in local roundtables. In 2000, a party representing Russian interests helped form the ruling coalition in Tallinn's municipal government.

In 1998 and 1999 the Estonian government committed itself to a process of integration so that non-Estonians could take part fully in Estonian life. The government planned to enhance the economic development of northeastern Estonia to improve material conditions and reduce the isolation of Slavic speakers concentrated there.

The official policy sought to accelerate the naturalization of noncitizens in the years 2000–2007. The Estonian government sponsored programs that aimed to raise children born in Estonia as Estonian citizens, regardless of ethnic origin. One program helped children of Russian-speaking families (especially children from one-parent homes) to spend summers in the countryside with Estonian families. More than half of monies appropriated for integration would go to Estonian-language instruction.

Estonia changed its citizenship law in 1998 to permit children of noncitizens born after February 26, 1992 to apply for citizenship without first taking a language test. But this change did not immediately promote a stampede.[9]

In December 1998 the Riigikogu amended Estonia's language laws to require that parliamentary deputies and local government representatives be proficient in Estonian. The amendments also made it tougher for nonspeakers of Estonian to work even in the private sector. They required all persons dealing with the public, including private businesses and nongovernmental organizations, to speak Estonian. The amendments banned the use of any language save Estonian on all public signs, ads, and notices—even election posters. The amendments were sponsored by the Pro Patria Union and signed into law by President Meri in February 1999—despite objections from Moscow, from Estonia's Russian parties, and from international figures such as Max van der Stoel, high commissioner for national minorities, Organization for Security and Cooperation in Europe (OSCE). Replying to critics, Director of the National Language Board Ilma Tomusk declared: "You can say that in Narva there are only 4 percent Estonians, but those 4 percent have the right to be served in Estonian."

Though Narva had more unemployment than other Estonian towns, when I visited there in 1999 it looked prosperous—with supermarkets, outdoor cafés, an amusement park, and McDonald's. People there lived much better than in Narva's sister city, Ivangorod, across the Narva River in Russia. For some details, see box 7.1.

Estonia's population minister announced on November 20, 2000, that the republic had 1,115,000 citizens. Less than one-fourth of the population consisted of noncitizens (down from one-third in 1998). Noncitizens included 110,000 persons with passports from other countries (75,000 of them with RF passports—not 100,000 as claimed by the RF embassy). There were also some 175,000 stateless persons and about 35,000 illegal residents.

More than 400,000 of Estonia's noncitizens—at least two-thirds of the total—opted to remain in the 1990s. More than 100,000 were naturalized. Nearly 150,000 others received Estonian permanent residence permits. Many stateless persons had gray passports that permitted them to visit Russia without formalities. Nearly half had no work permit for Estonia and did not plan to acquire one. Many noncitizens were not registered in any way and had no health insurance or other social support.[10]

Applications for naturalization increased in 1999–2000. Why? Because pressures mounted to show proficiency in Estonian for jobs in the public sector. The language exam was restructured to indicate beginning, intermediate, and advanced language skills. A five-year resident who passed the history and civic exams could apply for citizenship after passing only the beginning level language exam. Exam fees were reduced. So many Russian speakers took the language test in the first half of 2000 that the state exam center exhausted its budget for administering the tests.

Having visited Narva again in August 2000, OSCE High Commissioner Van der Stoel issued an optimistic assessment: the ethnic majority and minorities in Estonia were collaborating. The number of stateless persons—some 200,000—would decrease. Ever more Russian speakers were acquiring a working knowledge of Estonian, and this would help them complete the naturalization process.[11]

Still, a survey by the Integration Foundation in 2000 found that half of ethnic Estonians believed their country would benefit if non-Estonians left. Some 45 percent of

Box 7.1. One River, Two Ways of Life

Though poor compared to Tallinn, Narva in the late 1990s looked prosperous to Russians living in Ivangorod just across the Narva River. Some five hundred Russians in Ivangorod in 1998 petitioned Moscow to allow their city to secede and join Estonia, but their efforts got nowhere.

Dependent on utilities in Narva for water purification and electricity, Ivangorod failed to pay its bills for long periods in the late 1990s. For a time Estonian authorities extended humanitarian assistance, but then shut off sewage treatment, whereupon Ivangorod let its sewage go untreated into the river and thence to the Baltic Sea.

After Russian prices collapsed in August 1998, many Estonians and Russian residents of Estonia crossed the bridge from Narva into Ivangorod to shop—by one count, some ten thousand per day in May 1999. These shopping sprees in a foreign land drained the life blood from many businesses in Narva. Starting in 2000, however, all Estonians needed visas to visit Russia. Those with kin on the other side could obtain multiple entry permits.

By the late 1990s both sides had check points. The Russians often tried to block Estonian imports, while Estonians generally fostered two-way trade. Press accounts in the late 1990s reported that Russian customs inspectors often delayed trucks from Estonia and Latvia for more than twenty-four hours.

Not just toll offices but ancient forts faced one another on each side of the Narva River. The Hermann Fort on the Estonian side was built by German knights and later upgraded by Swedish kings; the Russian fort in Ivangorod was built to match or surpass the Swedish. Russians attacked the Hermann Fort in previous centuries and again in 1944, when Estonian soldiers, armed by Germany, used the fort to keep the Red Army at bay for many months.

In the late 1990s Estonian authorities tried to work out an arrangement by which tourists could visit the forts on each side of the Narva River without a special visa, but the Russians said "nyet."

In July 1999 some high-school students from St. Petersburg drove across the bridge from Russia to visit the Narva fortress. Their guide to the Hermann Fort was a native Russian educated in St. Petersburg (then called Leningrad) who had married an Estonian and lived in Narva for more than twenty years. Speaking to the students from St. Petersburg, she kept referring to Narva as "our city" [*nash gorod*]. Did "our" refer to Estonia or to Russia? This was not clear, but when I spoke to her alone, she lashed out against Estonians who, she said, "think all of Europe should know their language" even though they number just one million.

Estonians believed Russian speakers were not loyal to the state and did not support its reported development.[12]

Children whom I met in Narva, born to Russian parents, seemed to think very little about national identity, as reported in box 7.2.

The policies begun in the late 1990s would not strip non-Estonians of their Russian or Ukrainian identities. These minorities could be bicultural and bilingual, but not binational. Where only one language was officially recognized, however, it was unclear how long biculturalism would last.

Latvia

Ethnic issues in Latvia were more troubled than in Estonia. In October 1991 Latvia granted citizenship to all who were citizens of pre-World War II Latvia and their descendants, regardless of ethnicity. As a result, nearly two-thirds of the population

---

Box 7.2. Multiple Identities

"Are you Estonians or Russians?" I asked some ten and eleven year olds in Narva who gathered around a visiting American. "Half and half" they replied in Russian. "And we study not just Estonian and Russian but also English and German."

"Have you been to Russia?" I inquired.

"No." None had ever been to Russia, even though the Russian town of Ivangorod stood a few hundred yards away on the opposite bank of the Narva River, easily reached by a short bridge. These children, whose first language was Russian, had lived in Narva their entire lives without visiting the land from which their parents and their culture originated!

Olga explained, "It's hard for us to get a visa—unless we go for a relative's funeral, and then it's allowed only on certain days." She wanted to know my favorite movie.

"Bambi," I replied.

Olga was delighted, because she had *Bambi* on video, but she was crestfallen that I had not seen *Titanic,* which she had viewed seven times.

Igor wanted to correspond with someone in the United States. "Do you have any pen pals in other countries?" I asked.

"I have one in Russia," he said. "Her family is coming here for a visit next week." Russia, for him, is another country.

(including many Slavic speakers) became citizens, but one-third became noncitizen residents of Latvia.

Latvia's 1994 law on naturalization established a "window system," whereby the naturalization board considered applications from people belonging to a specific age group at the time of application. Lawmakers said they wanted the naturalization process to be completed in an orderly way by 2002. Critics said this system prolonged the process of obtaining citizenship and was unnecessary, because relatively few residents were applying for citizenship anyway.

OSCE High Commissioner Van der Stoel urged Latvia to drop its window system, grant citizenship to children of non-Latvians born in Latvia after August 1991, and simplify the citizenship examinations on Latvia's constitution and history.

The Latvian government, in response, amended its laws in 1998 to make naturalization easier. But the For Fatherland and Freedom party demanded a referendum. The result was that a majority of ethnic Latvians voted against the liberalized amendments, but the referendum passed by 52 percent, thanks to the "yes" votes of Russian speakers who were already citizens.

The revised law encouraged more Russian speakers to apply for Latvian citizenship, but exclusionist forces became stronger on the language front. On July 8, 1999 the Saeima voted (73 of 100 members in favor) to revise the Language Law so as to exclude the Russian language from Latvia's public life and billboards and constrain its use even in the private sphere. (Allowances were made for Livonian, however, still spoken by about two hundred Latvian residents.) The measures were backed by every ethnic Latvian political party. Only the sixteen-member Harmony Bloc, representing Russian-speaking minorities, voted against them.

The revised law provided that no one could submit a document to a government agency in any language but Latvian. And private businesses would be required to provide a translation into Latvian of an internal discussion if just one participant requested it. The Council of Europe secretary said the laws violated Latvia's commitments to the Council, while the EU warned that the law could discourage foreign investors. Demonstrators in Riga carried signs in Latvian, Russian, and English with the warning "Linguistic dictatorship leads to Kosovo."

President Vaira Vike-Freiberga refused to sign the law and returned it to parliament on July 14. She said that Latvia had no choice but to accept EU criteria if the country wanted to join the organization. The Saeima could have overridden her refusal by a simple majority, but parliamentarians in December 1999 softened some rules and Vike-Freiberga signed the reamended law. The OSCE and EU accepted that the revised law met international standards, but officials in Moscow said the law was still "unacceptable." At the same time that Russian bombers were flattening Grozny and Moscow police were arresting many ethnic Chechens on sight, the Russian Foreign Ministry said that the revised Latvian law represented a "human catastrophe" that would deprive almost a million people of their basic rights and treat them as pariahs in what they considered their native home.

The Russian Foreign Ministry overstated the number of noncitizens in Latvia. In 1999 there were 687,000 noncitizens, of whom 65 percent were ethnic Russians. Latvia had 2.5 million inhabitants, of whom 1.1 million were not of Latvian ancestry. These included 765,000 ethnic Russians, 100,000 ethnic Belarusians, nearly 70,000 ethnic Ukrainians, more than 60,000 ethnic Poles, and small numbers of Lithuanians, Jews, Roma, Germans, Tatars, Estonians, and Armenians. More than 70 percent of Latvia's inhabitants were citizens, including 400,000 who belonged to ethnic minorities. As in Soviet times, however, Latvian passports identified the holder's ethnicity, which could invite discrimination.

In the 1990s nearly half of Latvia's schoolchildren continued to be taught in Russian, even though Latvian language education became compulsory in 1988, when Latvian became the state language. There were also a few schools where instruction was in Polish or Ukrainian. But the government resolved to shift all secondary school teaching to Latvian by 2004.[13] A government survey in 2000 showed that 62 percent of Latvia's residents said that Latvian was their native language, even though only 57.6 percent of the population were ethnic Latvians.

The Latvian Council of Ministers defended the new language laws adopted in September 2000 as necessary for forming a unified society. Critics said the laws were needlessly harsh. One asked why a roofer needed level-2 Latvian. Others said the state provided very little support for older persons wishing to learn Latvian.

Faith in the Latvian government was low among Russian speakers. How could it be otherwise when, in the late 1990s, three-fifths of Russian speakers had no or only a poor knowledge of the official language?

Some Russians in Latvia complained that authorities used the language laws against them to quash their political activities.[14] Thus, in 1997 Antonina Ignatane's name was struck from the list of candidates standing for election to Riga City Council after the State Language Center ruled that her Latvian language skills were too weak. But Ignatane had already received a top-level Latvian language certificate. The head teacher of a secondary school, Ignatane thought she was being persecuted because she had led a campaign against closure of her school, where Russian was the medium of instruction.

In 2000 the Latvian Youth Club, composed mainly of native Russian speakers, was fined one hundred lat ($161) by language inspectors for distributing leaflets translated from Russian into Latvian, but with many mistakes. When the club's protest was rejected by the Riga District Court, its members considered taking the case to the European Court of Human Rights.

Still, more Russian young people in Latvia were confident of their future economic success than were young Latvians—two-fifths versus one-third. Many Russian speakers, however, attended college in Russia.

Why Not More Naturalization?

Relatively few noncitizens of Estonia and Latvia applied for naturalization in the 1990s. Many Russian-speaking adults despaired of learning even the rudiments of a Baltic tongue. Many were unfamiliar with naturalization laws. Some balked at the fees—the equivalent of $53—for naturalization. An elderly museum attendant in Estonia told me in Russian that the language test—for citizenship or for employment—cost an amount equal to 15 percent of the minimum monthly wage. Language lessons, she added, were also expensive.

Some noncitizens complained that the language tests for naturalization were unreasonably demanding and arbitrary. But Estonian authorities in the late 1990s stated that 75 to 90 percent of applicants passed the language exam. The Naturalization Board of Latvia reported that nearly 95 percent of applicants passed the Latvian tests on their first try. A U.S. professor observing an exam in Latvia in September 1999 thought it quite easy. Fourteen of fifteen applicants passed—all except an elderly woman who passed the oral exam but not the written test, given in a multiple choice format. But she was encouraged to retake the written exam soon. The professor planned to give a similar test to his Latvian 103 students at the University of Washington.

For men, military service was another consideration—as suggested in box 7.3., Citizens had to serve; noncitizens did not.

Many noncitizens were content to use their old Soviet passports or gray "stateless" documents to visit Russia without having to apply and pay for a special visa. From 1991 to 1997 the Estonian and Latvian governments recognized the erstwhile Soviet internal passports held by many noncitizens. In 1997, however, the Estonian and Latvian

---

Box 7.3. Dodging the Draft and Other Complications

One evening in Riga in 1998 I met a well dressed, strong-looking law student in his twenties. Speaking in Russian, Viacheslav told me that he knows Latvian but has not sought naturalization because he would be conscripted. Latvian males were required to serve twelve months in the army immediately after secondary school. Noncitizens, by contrast, could enroll in college with no delay. By the time Viacheslav finishes law school, he might be too old to be inducted.

In Riga a recently married couple in their twenties told me they had no time to apply for naturalization. They had Russian passports and Latvian residence permits. This combination made it easy for them to go back and forth to St. Petersburg on business.

governments demanded that noncitizens exchange their old documents for new ones. They could ask Russian authorities for a Russian Federation passport or obtain a stateless (or "alien") passport from Estonian authorities. By late 1998 Estonia had received 174,000 requests for alien passports and honored 170,297.

RESULTS: TOWARD A MODIFIED NATION-STATE?

Gradually the nonnative elements in the Baltic were being co-opted rather than repressed or driven out. Time, social change, and government policies gradually tipped the balance of incentives in the 1990s toward integration and assimilation in the Baltic lands.[15] Some Russian speakers feared that neighbors might ostracize them for "defecting." But gradually Russian speakers lost incentives to resist integration. Some, especially older persons, accepted marginalization. Proponents of Russian rights or separatism got little real help from Moscow except sporadic rhetoric and on-again, off-again economic warfare. Russian meddling in Baltic affairs was quite limited by comparison with Moscow's military and other interventions in Moldova, the Caucasus, and Central Asia.

As the balance of incentives tipped toward integration and assimilation, more Russian speakers in the Baltic countries tried to learn the titular language and a different way of life. Many did so in a quiet way, so as not to offend neighbors.

To work in government or in some professions required a fair knowledge of the titular language, but most jobs did not. Still, more and more Russian speakers regarded proficiency in the local Baltic language as a condition for economic and social success. Children, in any case, had to study the titular language in school in the 1990s, while parents realized that all teaching in public schools would be in the titular tongue within the first few years of the twenty-first century. Children and teenagers whom I met in the late 1990s seemed comfortable using the titular language.[16] Many children of Slavic-speaking families were becoming bilingual or trilingual. English and German—not Russian—vied to become the region's lingua franca. In 2000 there were some private colleges taught in Russian, but they were expensive and might not endure for long.

Many factors affected adaptation. *Jobs:* The unemployed and persons dissatisfied with their work or living standards were quite likely to be marginalized. *Gender:* In Estonia in the mid-1990s Russian-speaking women were twice as likely as men to integrate. *Age:* Younger people were twice as likely to integrate as the elderly. Some 20 percent of the elderly leaned toward staying in Estonia but apart from Estonian culture, but few young (2 percent) or middle-aged (5 percent) Russian speakers did so. *Region:* Adaptation also varied from one city to another. Integration was nearly twice as common in the university town of Tartu as in the northeastern town of Lasnamäe, whereas marginalization was twice as common in Lasnamäe as in Tartu. Russian speakers in the town of Pärnu occupied a middle range between these extremes.[17]

Reading between the lines of Estonia's Russian-language newspapers in the late 1990s, one could perceive both an "end of ideology" and an "end of history" but no clash of civilizations. Estonia in the late 1990s had two privately owned Russian-language daily newspapers and several weeklies. *Estoniia* and *Kupecheskaia gavan'*

(*Merchant Harbor*), both published in Tallinn, carried articles in 1998 on how to make money, win at the lottery, furnish a new flat, go abroad on holiday, be healthy (for example, through a "Mediterranean diet"), and generate personal pleasure—plus ads for "cultivated" and "exotic" partners. On July 3, 1999 *Estoniia* gave front-page coverage, with a color photo, to the song and dance festival taking place in Tallinn. On page 2 it reported on the first one hundred days of Mart Laar's second turn as prime minister, headlining that the "young Estonians" running the government had become "older, wiser, and lazier." There was nothing to suggest any trouble between Russian speakers and titulars in Estonia. The most sensitive foreign news concerned terrorists in the north Caucasus: "Guarding Russia against Russia."[18]

The Russian-language newspaper *Molodozh' Estonii (Youth of Estonia)* on July 5, 1999, also gave front-page coverage of the song and dance festival. Inside were articles on choosing a profession, on unemployment, on the "inconvenient Latvians who cruelly" trounced the Russians in basketball, on a clinic in Arizona that treats sex addictions, and on the community of 4,500 Estonians living in St. Petersburg—down from 20,300 in 1905. Russian-language programs, most of them produced in Estonia, were broadcast over state and private television channels. Television programs from Russia were available by cable.

The Latvian newspaper *Diena* (daily except Sunday) helped bridge gaps between Latvian and Russian speakers. It gave well-balanced political reportage—local, national, and international—in Russian and Latvian editions. The costly Russian edition, however, was discontinued.[19] But Latvia had other newspapers as well as independent television and radio outlets in the Russian language. Satellite television broadcasts in Russian increased in the late 1990s.

Lithuania also had a wide range of newspapers and magazines, many noted for their objectivity, in Russian and other languages. In the late 1990s state television and radio were being transformed into public stations independent financially from government.

In late 1999 the Russian television company NTV shut down its Baltic bureau. NTV director Vladislav Andreyev explained that little happened in the Baltic to interest viewers in Russia. Not much more could be said about how Russian speakers lived in the *pribaltika*.

Assimilation and integration are easier as society becomes more individualized—less dominated by group consciousness. Successful adaptation can occur quickly for young people but require decades for entire societies. Some individuals, however, refuse to take their identities off any peg; they themselves tailor what they wear; they insist on creating their own personae—their *auto-couture*.[20] Thus, an Estonian scientist I know is quite at home in the laboratories, cafés, and jogging paths of Tallinn, Bordeaux, Moscow, and Cambridge, Massachusetts. By day he researches ocean currents and ocean depths (in the 1980s to assist Soviet submarines); evenings he reads the *Bhagavad Gita* or *Walden*.

A person may live with multiple identities until circumstances force a choice. A concatenation of forces could push the scales one way or the other. Until and unless a choice became necessary, many Baltic residents could thrive in ambiguity, as we see in box 7.4.

Box 7.4. A Russian Estonian or an Estonian Russian?

A blonde woman cleaned the dining tables of the passenger ship "Regina Baltica" as we sailed into Stockholm harbor following an overnight cruise from Tallinn. I asked her in English where the ship had been made. "Germany," she replied.

"Are you Swedish or Estonian?" I asked.

"Russian," she replied—still in English.

Switching to Russian, I asked if she enjoyed seeing the world. She replied that she wanted to travel as much as possible before beginning university in September. Where? In Tartu, the old Estonian university town, where she planned to study Finno-Ugric linguistics.

"Have you read President Meri's field studies of Finno-Ugric peoples around the Soviet Union?" No, but she had heard of them and planned to read them.

"Are you an Estonian citizen?"

"Yes" (though before she said she was a Russian—not a Swede or an Estonian).

"Have you been to Russia?"

"Yes, often."

"Why does Estonia do better than Russia economically?"

"Better? Estonia doesn't do well at all. People go hungry. Things get worse all the time. But the leaders get a lot of foreign money."

Though an Estonian citizen, Irina considered herself a Russian. And though she looked on Estonians with disdain, she planned to specialize in the study of their language family.

This encounter reminded me of a meeting between a U.S. Navy officer and a young woman in a Crimean port. "Do you speak Russian or Ukrainian?" he asked a young woman. "I speak Russian," she replied—in Ukrainian.

ANTI-SEMITISM AND FASCISM

There are currents of anti-Semitism and fascism in each Baltic society—as in most of Europe, Russia, and the Americas. As in Poland, most Jews in the Baltic countries perished in the Holocaust. Some Balts killed Jews or helped Nazis to do so—especially in Latvia and Lithuania, which had large Jewish populations. But other indigenous Balts risked their lives to save Jews.[21] The heroes of tolerance are sometimes forgotten. Half a century passed before the story emerged of a Japanese consular officer in Kaunas who risked everything to create travel documents for Jews to escape the Holocaust.[22] President Vike-Freiberga in July 2000 awarded the country's highest honor to four Latvians who helped save Jews from the Holocaust—one of whom hid more than thirty persons under his barn. The president called on Latvians to fight the evil that was and that still existed in the motherland. She lamented the recent desecration of two memorials to Jews.[23]

The strength of anti-Semitism is hard to gauge. What lies dormant may vent. "Jews Rule the World" screamed the cover of the August 2000 edition of *Kapitals,* a business magazine published in Riga. The cover showed a hook-nosed, dark-skinned, hatted man with a gold watch, a gold earring, and gold cuff links, clasping the globe with effeminate claws. The ten-page article by Normunds Isovskis recapitulated anti-Jewish slurs found on neo-Nazi web sites. The author allowed that Jews excelled in business but suggested they had brought the Holocaust on themselves. Faced with a storm of criticism,

Kapitals editor Guntis Rozenbergs resigned, protesting he did not understand why people were upset.

The *Kapitals* article generated more than a thousand messages on an on-line discussion board. Most of the messages "equaled or exceeded the sentiments of the piece in neo-Nazi flavor."[24] Latvia's foreign minister Indulis Berzins, however, denied that anti-Semitism was a problem in Latvia, while a spokesman for the prime minister suggested that the article may have been a "provocation"—a favorite if ambiguous term in Soviet times.

The *Latvia Human Development Report 1999* warned that "the absence of political tolerance is a serious threat to the development of democracy" in Latvia. However, the same document reported that Latvians of all ages ranked "tolerance" as the most or second-most important value that families should cultivate in their children. Respondents age twenty-five and younger ranked tolerance above the work ethic and good manners. Middle-aged and older Latvians ranked it just below the work ethic. (The next most valued qualities were perseverance and independence, with the least support for frugality and obedience—values esteemed, respectively, by half and one-quarter of older Latvians.)

One commentator opined that both Latvia and Lithuania have a minority of Nazi sympathizers and a majority "whose acceptance of ethnic stereotypes and ignorance of history make them vulnerable to hate."[25] Some critics wondered why Latvia had still not extradited two elderly Latvians accused of collaborating in Nazi crimes.

An Estonian observer objected to simplistic generalizations. She recalled that a Jew had torn down the Estonian national flag when Soviet troops occupied Estonia in 1940, but said this individual was remembered not as a Jew but as a Communist.

The wartime context was crucial. Balts were occupied by the Red Army, overrun by the Germans, and reinvaded by the USSR. A few Balts were Communist, some were Nazi, even more were anti-Semitic, and still more were nationalist. Some Estonians and Latvians joined Nazi SS-Legions; Lithuanians did not. But Lithuanians as well as Estonians and Latvians joined German-organized Police Battalions. Later, in 1944, more than forty thousand Estonians—several thousand arriving from Finland—took up arms to resist the Soviet advance. In August 2000 some fifty Estonians who fought with German troops in 1944 held a clandestine reunion to recall their fallen comrades. But their leader told reporters that they fought for Estonian independence—not for the German Reich. An historical museum in Pärnu displayed Waffen-SS uniforms worn by some Estonians during World War II. Estonians and Latvians were not alone. A majority of Waffen-SS troops were non-German. Belgian, Norwegian, Finnish, and other Europeans joined SS Legions.[26]

While President Vike-Freiberga honored past heroes, the government in Lithuania was planning to rebuild the Jewish quarter of Vilnius—the "Jerusalem of the north" before World War II. A Jewish member of parliament, Emanuelis Zingeris, headed the state commission for this project. He said that the reconstruction of the historic district would be the best monument to victims of the Holocaust.[27] In September 2000 police raided the headquarters of the unregistered Lithuanian National-Socialist Party in Siauliai. The country's Ministry of Justice refused to recognize the party and said that its statute did not comply with the Lithuanian constitution and incited "ethnic discord."

A BALANCE SHEET

Ethnic troubles in the Baltic countries ebbed more than they flowed in the 1990s. Unlike the years just before independence, Russian speakers staged few demonstrations in the post-Soviet Baltic countries. The year 1998, however, was tense in Latvia. Two Latvians died in the blast they set off to attack a Soviet war memorial.[28] Elderly women who were noncitizens demonstrated for higher pensions; other noncitizens demanded that the government speed up its issuance of passports. In May 1999 some two thousand persons demonstrated at the Soviet Victory Monument in Riga and applauded speeches denouncing NATO. Later in 1999, some Russian speakers protested the proposed language law revisions.

But no one died in the Baltics in the 1990s from ethnic or other political fighting, except for those killed by Soviet troops in 1990–1991. The Baltic republics in the 1990s were spared the violence that killed and maimed in much of the Balkans, Caucasus, Central Asia, and Moldova—not to mention Northern Ireland, the Congo, or the United States. The situation of noncitizens in Estonia and Latvia was nothing like that of Tamils in Sri Lanka, where when imperial Great Britain withdrew, Sinhalese politicians used majority-rule to reverse the favored status previously enjoyed by Tamils, provoking a civil war in 1983 that raged into the next century.

In the Baltic, habits of nonviolence served accommodation, compromise, and healing. In the late 1990s both Latvia and Estonia made it easier for Slavic speakers to become citizens. At the onset of the twenty-first century most Slavic-speaking residents were adjusting to their changed milieu. Few planned to exit. Most Baltic leaders deemed it unwise and unnecessary to treat Slavic minorities as foes—better to nourish them as potential partners. The citizenship issue seemed to lose salience.

LESSONS FROM THE NORTH?

Balts could see in Norway, Denmark, Sweden, and Finland examples of moderate nation-states that maintained their own languages and cultures while adapting to modernity. Finland's case was especially relevant, because Finns were long ruled by Swedes and then, starting in 1809, by Russians. Finns asserted their independence from Russia in December 1917, a few months before Balts did. Finland lost valuable territory to the USSR in the 1940s and was often bullied by Moscow during the Cold War, but Finland remained independent. Finns remembered well this history but were not paralyzed by it. They traded with Russia and all the world during and after the Cold War. Both the conservative Swedish People's Party and the Leftists (Communists) won roughly 10 percent of the seats in the Finnish parliament in the 1990s. Finns continued to revere Jean Sibelius, a member of the Swedish-speaking upper class at the turn of the century who composed *Finlandia* (1900) and other nationalist music.

Despite the long shadow of Russian power, Finland became a modern country with gleaming office buildings, hotels, art museums, and concert halls. Finns in the 1990s manufactured one of the world's most popular cellular phones and sophisticated computer equipment. A larger percentage of Finns used the Internet than did Americans.

But Finland's example provided no reason to pursue binationalism in the Baltic. Finns could readily give official status to Swedish, a language spoken by only 6 percent of the population in 2000—down from 14 percent in 1917. (The Saami people, less than 1 percent of Finland's population, also received special privileges.) Estonians and Latvians could hardly be so liberal toward a minority making up 30 percent or more of the population. Because each Baltic population was so small, and each country so vulnerable to a large and often hostile neighbor, binationalism could spell chaos.

There was no good reason to dissipate the distinct Baltic cultures in a binational, multinational, or cosmopolitan state. A moderate version of the nation-state was probably the appropriate model for each Baltic republic. It would include:

- One official language to be learned by all citizens, with an option to use Russian or Polish in local governments where most residents depend on these languages;
- Cultural autonomy for citizens and noncitizens;
- Well-funded and generous programs to help nonnatives adjust, integrate, learn the official language, and appreciate the indigenous culture.

This model counts on time and compromise to close old wounds and learn new ways. It seeks to sustain the national culture, recognizing that national differences will lose their edge as Balts interact with Europe and the world. The moderate nation-state would allow individuals to create their *auto-coutures,* but invite all to share in community enterprises. The moderate approach rejects the radical nation-state as pursued in the 1990s, for example, by some Croat and Serb leaders.

Russians might wish the Baltic republics to become binational states. But binationalism risks civil and even international strife. The smaller "nation" may complain of discrimination, as in Quebec, or if its numbers increase relative to its guaranteed share of power, as in Lebanon. Both scenarios tempt intervention by outside powers.

Balts thought they needed to protect their cultures and statehoods, while many Russian settlers in their midst felt ill-treated. The fate of Russian speakers remained a flash point—a handy tool for neoimperialists in Moscow to stoke passions and divert public attentions from other issues. The entrepreneurs of ethnic strife could exploit the fact that ethnic differences were also embedded in a clash of civilizations.

Conflicts about material interests are usually easier to resolve than ethnic or cultural discord. As we see in the next chapter, reasonable people in the Baltic and Slavic countries could negotiate business deals to mutual advantage.

Caption for Chapter 7 Photo: Living in Narva, these children spoke Russian at home but used both Russian and Estonian in school. Their flats looked across the Narva River to the Russian town of Ivangorod. As of 1998, however, these children had never crossed over. For them, Russia was a foreign country. Children like these adjusted easily to life in Estonia. For many older Russian-speakers, however, it was not easy or pleasant to learn another language and way of life.

NOTES

1. Statistics from 1989 are summarized in Walter C. Clemens Jr., *Baltic Independence and Russian Empire* (New York: St. Martin's, 1991), pp. 66–67.

2. Algimantas Prazauskas, "The Influence of Ethnicity on the Foreign Policies of the

Western Littoral States," in *National Identity and Ethnicity in Russia and the New States of Eurasia,* ed. Roman Szporluk (Armonk, N.Y.: Sharpe, 1994), table 7.1.

3. A University of Toronto professor repeatedly termed the Estonian and Latvian policies toward the Russian speakers "hard." He accused Latvians of striving to assimilate a few Russians while encouraging the others to leave. See Aurel Braun, "All Quiet on the Russian Front? Russia, Its Neighbors, and the Russian Diaspora," in *The New European Diasporas: National Minorities and Conflict in Eastern Europe,* ed. Michael Mandelbaum (New York: Council on Foreign Relations Press, 2000), pp. 81–158 at 120.

4. Laitin compares policies toward nontitular peoples in Estonia, Latvia, Ukraine, and Kazakstan, but says little about Lithuania. See David D. Laitin, *Identity in Formation: The Russian-Speaking Populations in the Near Abroad* (Ithaca, N.Y.: Cornell University Press, 1998).

5. Rasma Karklins and Brigita Zepa, "Multiple Identities and Ethnopolitics in Latvia," *American Behavioral Scientist* 40 (September 1996), pp. 33–45 at 34.

6. Baltic countries also served as conduits for offshore money-laundering operations by Russian gangs. One deal ran from Russia to Lithuania to Hungary to Buffalo, New York, and the Cayman Islands. See *New York Times,* July 25, 1999, pp. 1, 4.

7. Voters in Emmen, an industrial suburb of Lucerne, voted in March 2000 whether to grant citizenship to applicants, many of them resident for decades, including some born and raised in Switzerland. Provided information about an applicant's salary, tax status, background, and hobbies, Emmen voters decided that only four families, all of Italian origin, were suitable to become Swiss—eight out of fifty-six applicants. Most of those rejected came from the former Yugoslavia. Swiss were also cool to Turks and Hungarians.

8. See, for example, the International Helsinki Federation for Human Rights report, "Protection of Ethnic Minorities," submitted to the UN Commission on Human Rights in 1998 and available at http://www.ihf-hr.org/reports/9804prot.htm.

9. Only eighteen children applied for citizenship in the first five weeks after the law went into effect in July 1999. *Baltic Times,* August 19–26, 1999, p. 3.

10. *Estonian Human Development Report, 1998,* chapter 2.3, and U.S. Department of State, *1999 Country Reports on Human Rights Practices. Estonia,* available at <http://www.state.gov/> with reports on Latvia, Lithuania, and other countries.

11. *Baltic Times,* August 31–September 6, 2000, p. 3.

12. *Baltic Times,* September 14–20, 2000, p. 4.

13. In 1997 some 94 percent of Russian pupils and 86 percent of other non-Latvians attended Russian-language schools. About half the graduates of these schools knew little or no Latvian. Rasma Karklins, "Ethnic Integration and School Policies in Latvia," *Nationalities Papers* 26, no. 2 (1998), pp. 283–302.

14. The following paragraphs are based on reports in the *Baltic Times,* September 14–20, 2000, p. 6.

15. For applications of tipping theory to ethnic identity, see Laitin, *Identity in Formation.*

16. Asked in 1998 about their knowledge of Estonian, three Russian teenage girls in Tallinn said they had been studying the language since age eight. Did they have Estonian friends? "Yes," all replied. One added that Estonian girls are easier to get along with than Russians, because they were less "jealous."

17. Tiit Tammaru, "Regional'nye razlichiia adaptatsii russkikh i faktory, vliiaiushchie na adaptatsiiu," *Raduga* (Tallinn), no. 1 (1998), pp. 121–36 at 124, 128, 132–34.

18. *Estoniia* on July 3, 1999, published one article with an anti-Soviet inflection: a translated report from the Estonian-language *Postimees* newspaper about an Estonian woman whose two sons had lived in the woods for thirteen years to avoid arrest by Soviet forces. The paper also covered the opening of the British film version of the Russian classic *Onegin* in the Russian city

of Tver'. *Estoniia* also discussed Barbara Streisand's reasons for investing in Viagra.

19. In 1998 demand for the Russian edition justified a run of only 9,553 copies compared to 85,466 in Latvian (figures from the June 12, 1998 edition).

20. Rushdie notes that "culture" can refer to a "squirm of germs on a glass slide . . . a laboratory experiment calling itself a society. Most of us wrigglers make do with life on that slide." We may even "feel proud of that 'culture.' Like slaves voting for slavery or brains for lobotomy, we kneel down before the god of all moronic microorganisms and pray to be homogenized or killed or engineered; we promise to obey." For the case of three persons who defied their upbringing, see Salman Rushdie, *The Ground Beneath Her Feet* (New York: Henry Holt, 1999), p. 95.

21. Romuald Misiunas and Rein Taagepera, *The Baltic States: Years of Dependence, 1940–1990,* expanded edition (Berkeley: University of California Press, 1993), pp. 55–64.

22. Hillel Levine, *In Search of Sugihara, the Elusive Japanese Diplomat Who Risked his Life to Rescue 10,000 Jews from the Holocaust* (New York: Free Press, 1996). See also Avraham Tory, *Surviving the Holocaust: The Kovno Ghetto Diary* (Cambridge, Mass.: Harvard University Press, 1990); Harry Gordon, *The Shadow of Death: The Holocaust in Lithuania* (Lexington: University Press of Kentucky, 1992); and analysis and references in Algimantas P. Taskunas, "Telling the Full Story," *Baltic Times,* November 23–29, 2000, p. 19.

23. For a balanced appraisal, see Andrew Ezergailis, *The Holocaust in Latvia, 1941–1944: The Missing Center* (Washington, D.C.: Historical Institute of Latvia and U.S. Holocaust Memorial Museum, 1996).

24. See the editorial "Negative Input, Positive Potential," *Baltic Times,* August 10–16, 2000.

25. Opinion piece by Ben Smith in *Baltic Times,* August 10–16, 2000, p. 15—denounced as a continuation of Soviet-initiated vilification of Latvia and Lithuania in a letter published in the August 31–September 6 edition.

26. The Harvard Widener Library has more than three hundred entries on the Waffen-SS including a few on Latvia and Bosnia but none on Estonia. See, e.g., Mirdza Kate Baltais, ed., *The Latvian Legion: Selected Documents* (Toronto: Amber, 1999), and Arturs Silgailis, *Latviescu legions: dibinasana, formesana un kauju gaitas otra pasaules kara,* 2d ed. (Copenhagen: Imanta, 1965).

27. In the 1990s, however, there was little movement in the Baltic countries to make restitution to Jews. See Elazar Barkan, *The Guilt of Nations: Restitution and Negotiating Historical Injustices* (New York: Norton, 2000).

28. In April a bomb exploded in a park across from the Russian embassy in Riga, damaging some embassy vehicles but injuring no one. In July Latvian police arrested Vilis Linins, chief ideologue of the ultranationalist Thundercross organization, suspected of bombing Soviet memorials and other targets. The prosecutor general's office launched an investigation into anti-Russian statements in the newspaper of the For Fatherland and Freedom party as possible violations of Latvia's national and racial equality policies.

8

Energy for a New Life: From Dependency to Interdependence

Port of Tallinn

THE CHALLENGE OF ENERGY

Challenge and response. How societies meet challenges can determine how they live—indeed, whether they survive. Many ancient societies organized their life around the control of water—for irrigation and flood control. Modern societies, too, tap water for energy, but they also utilize oil and other resources to meet the power demands of industrial and postindustrial civilizations.

In world politics energy can be both a means and an end. States with abundant energy possess a powerful tool for advancing their wealth, fitness, and influence. Energy have-nots, by contrast, often find themselves the targets of exploitation by energy haves.

The breakup of the Soviet Union left the Baltic republics heavily dependent on Russia for energy. Russia tried to exploit Baltic needs to dominate if not regain control of the *pribaltika*. Russians turned the oil spigot on and off to show Balts who was boss. When Balts were not cowed, Russia demanded a controlling share in Baltic energy firms. When this too did not happen, the Russians backed down and accepted whatever deal would permit them to ship oil to the Baltic republics for refining and transshipment to Europe.

It turned out that in energy matters, as in many issues of environmental protection and economic development, Balts and Russians became more interdependent in the 1990s. Each could help or hurt the other. Exploitation and dependency slowly gave way to efforts to generate mutual gain. In the twenty-first century, however, myopia and spite could still yield one-sided or even mutual pain.

SOVIET-ERA DEPENDENCY

All Soviet republics looked to Moscow. They looked to the Kremlin, inter alia, for decisions on how to allocate and utilize most forms of energy and other resources. All three Baltic republics, especially Latvia and Estonia, were rapidly industrialized under Soviet rule and needed fuel imports to keep their engines racing; all three, including Lithuania, depended heavily on Russian energy sources for heating, electricity, or transportation. In 1990 Latvia produced a mere 8 percent of the energy it consumed, Lithuania produced just 25 percent, and Estonia 51 percent. The Russian Republic, a net exporter, generated 41 percent more energy than it consumed.[1]

Subordination of the Baltic republics to the center was magnified by their energy needs. These needs reinforced the leverage Moscow enjoyed by virtue of Russian-speaking settlers and large contingents of Soviet armed forces in the Baltic region.

Despite Moscow's many control levers, however, the Gorbachev regime achieved only modest success in its carrot-and-stick use of energy supplies and military force to discourage Baltic deviance. For example, the Kremlin warned on April 13, 1990, that the USSR would sharply reduce oil and gas deliveries to Lithuania if its declaration of independence were not retracted within forty-eight hours. On April 18 the Lithuanians offered concessions on some issues but not on the principle of independence. The same day the Kremlin cut off all oil and most of the gas supplied to Lithuania. It even set up a naval blockade to keep foreign supplies from reaching the rebel republic. The Kremlin resumed deliveries on June 30, 1990—one day after Seimas voted a temporary suspension of its independence declarations.

Still, given the Baltic region's multifaceted dependency on Russia, many observers in 1991 doubted that the three Baltic republics could endure as independent states unless they bowed to the Kremlin. Reliant upon relatively cheap fuel from Russia since the late 1940s, would they not be compelled to accept Russian dictates in the 1990s?

Post-Soviet Russia in the early 1990s exploited many of the same tactics employed by the Gorbachev regime toward the Baltic region. Russia suspended and then released energy shipments in an effort to get the Baltic republics to follow Moscow's will.[2] Moscow in 1993 refused to sign a free-trade agreement with Vilnius on the ground that Lithuania did not belong to the Commonwealth of Independent States. In September 1993 Russia raised import duties on some Lithuanian exports to 100 percent.

Whereas Soviet-era oil prices were low, Russia began to demand payment in hard currency at near–world-market prices for its oil, natural gas, and nuclear fuel exports. Barter deals were ruled out by privatized Russian energy firms. They spurned, for example, any deal by which Lithuania's debts could be offset against the large sums owed by Kaliningrad for Lithuanian electricity and transport.

HOW BALTS OVERCAME DEPENDENCY

Even though the energy odds seemed stacked against them, the three Baltic republics in the 1990s generally followed their own policy preferences regardless of Moscow's demands. As in the run-up to independence, so afterwards: Balts continued to behave as if they were free.

Six factors helped Balts to surmount their longtime energy dependency on Russia and make the most of their growing ties with Europe: privatization, reduced consumption, indigenous energy sources, global interdependence, Baltic ports and infrastructure, and foreign investment. Let us review each one.

Privatization

Each Baltic state debated whether to sell stakes in its energy assets to foreign interests. Liberals in each Baltic country wanted markets—not domestic or foreign politics—to determine fuel prices. Liberals sought to privatize energy production and distribution. Partnerships with foreign investors would provide much-needed capital, technology, and know-how. Ties with Western firms would reduce Russian influence on the local economy and politics. But privatizers had to overcome internal resistance and convince outsiders that investments in Baltic energy could be rewarding. Antiprivatizers condemned selling out the native land ("Mother Daugava" in Latvia). Socialists feared higher energy prices charged by greedy capitalists. Many drivers, utilities, factories, and municipalities said it was the government's duty to provide cheap energy.

Liberals began to win in Vilnius and Tallinn. In 1999 the Lithuanian government sold a one-third interest in the nation's oil complex to a U.S. firm. In 2000 it announced plans to restructure the state-run energy utility Lietuvos Energija (Lithuanian Energy) and privatize two electricity distribution subsidiaries. The Swedish firm Vattenfall acquired some 5 percent of Lietuvos Energija and negotiated to buy more.

In August 2000 Estonia sold 49 percent of shares in Narva Power Plants (Elektrijaamad) to the U.S. company NRG Energy (though the parties gave themselves twelve months to finalize details). Center Party leader Edgar Savisar led opposition to the deal, but officials in Narva saw it as the best—indeed, the only—way to modernize the plants.[3]

Reduced Consumption: Belt-Tightening and Light Industry

In the early 1990s Balts coped with Russian economic pressures partly by tightening their collective belts—by enduring winter cold more and by driving less. Their consumption of electricity declined sharply in the early and mid-1990s.[4]

Baltic economic survival was made easier in some respects by the general decline in the region's industrial production in the early and mid-1990s. Whatever Russian oil and gas did get through could be used more for heating and transportation because the demands of local industry had declined.

Baltic trends resembled those in most of the former Soviet Union: industrial production declined and so did living standards. Still, Russia exported more energy in 1994–1995 than in 1992–1993, whereas the Baltic countries produced fewer goods and imported much less energy.

Most forms of economic activity in the former Soviet Union stagnated in the 1980s and then fell off sharply in 1990–1995. As we see in tables 8.1, 8.2, and 8.3, both Russia and the Baltic republics consumed less energy for commercial purposes and less electricity per capita in 1997 than in 1990. The four First World (OECD) economies in the tables consumed more energy in 1997 than in earlier years, while achieving higher GDP with fewer units of energy.

While the former Soviet republics lost ever more energy in transmission, the other four countries became more efficient. Latvia, with weaker indigenous supplies than Estonia or Lithuania, wasted the most energy. Why could it not become efficient like Singapore or Japan?

Table 8.1
Commercial Energy Use in the Baltic and Elsewhere

Economy	Thousands of metric oil equivalent			Kg of oil equivalent per capita			Per Capita Avg annual % growth
	1980	1990	1997	1980	1990	1997	1990 to 1997
Estonia	n.a.	10,163	5,556	n.a.	6,469	3,811	−7.4
Latvia	n.a.	3,274	4,460	n.a.	1,126	1,806	−1.1
Lithuania	8,953	17,224	8,806	3,326	4,628	2,376	−10.2
Singapore	6,049	13,357	26,878	2,653	4,938	8,661	8.4
Sweden	40,984	47,747	51,934	4,932	5,579	5,869	1.0
Russia	764,349	906,433	591,982	5,499	6,112	4,019	−6.2
Japan	346,567	438,797	514,898	2,968	3,552	4,084	2.2
USA	1,801,406	1,925,680	2,162,190	7,973	7,720	8,076	0.8

SOURCES: World Bank, *World Development Report, 1998/99* (New York: Oxford University Press, 1999), table 10; ibid., *2000/2001,* table 10.

When the Baltic economies turned upward in the mid-1990s, they achieved more GDP with less fuel expenditure than they had in Soviet times. The composition of each Baltic republic's GDP became far more oriented toward civilian demand than in the old days, when each republic and firm faced Moscow-set quotas unrelated to human wants.

Indigenous Resources: Shale, Water, Oil, Atomic Power

Despite reduced consumption, Balts imported much oil and natural gas in the 1990s. In the first half of 1998, for example, Estonia imported about $29 million worth of Russian natural gas, Latvia imported $40 million, and Lithuania imported $85 million.

Table 8.2
Energy Use, Imports, and Emissions in the Baltic and Elsewhere

Economy	GDP per unit of energy use 1987 $ per kg			Net energy imports % of commercial energy use			CO_2 Emissions per capita metric tons	
	1990	1996	1997	1980	1990	1997	1990	1997
Estonia	1.2	0.9	2.0	n.a.	47	32	13.8	11.2
Latvia	6.6	1.5	3.1	54	88	63	5.0	3.7
Lithuania	n.a.	0.8	2.6	98	72	55	5.7	3.7
Singapore	2.8	3.8	2.9	100	n.a.	100	15.5	21.6
Sweden	3.1	4.5	3.5	61	38	36	5.7	6.1
Russia	1.6	0.5	1.7	2	−40	−57	13.1	10.7
Japan	5.4	10.5	6.0	88	83	79	8.7	9.3
USA	2.9	3.4	3.6	14	14	22	19.3	20

SOURCES: World Bank, *World Development Report, 1998/99* (New York: Oxford University Press, 1999), table 10; ibid., *2000/2001,* table 10.

Table 8.3
Electric Power Consumption and Transmission Losses in the Baltic and Elsewhere

	Consumption per capita kilowatt hours			Transmission and distribution losses as a percentage of output			
Economy	1980	1990	1997	1980	1990	1996	1997
Estonia	3,433	4,332	3,466	5	7	19	16
Latvia	2,664	3,281	1,758	26	18	47	29
Lithuania	2,715	3,228	1,818	12	5	11	11
Singapore	2,412	4,792	7,944	5	3	4	4
Sweden	10,216	14,061	14,042	9	6	6	7
Russia	4,706	5,821	3,981	8	8	9	10
Japan	4,395	6,125	7,241	4	4	4	4
USA	8,914	10,558	11,822	9	9	7	6

SOURCES: World Bank, *World Development Report, 1998/99* (New York: Oxford University Press, 1999), table 18; ibid., *2000/2001*, table 18.

Hoping to reduce Russia's leverage, each Baltic republic sought to develop its own energy resources.

Each Baltic republic burns peat to generate power in thermal-electric stations. The largest hydroelectric plants in the region are near Narva in Estonia and Kaunas in Lithuania, but the flat terrain limits Balts' ability to harness water power. Surveying the forests that bedecked their lands, however, some Balts looked for ways to extract energy from biomass.

Estonia

Oil shale and hydroelectric power have long been important in the region—so much that they figured in the negotiations leading up to Soviet recognition of Estonian independence in 1920.[5]

Oil shale is difficult and costly to exploit. Nonetheless in the 1990s it generated most of Estonia's electricity plus some for export to Russia. The state energy company, Eesti Energia, in the late 1990s was Estonia's largest firm in terms of annual turnover (more than 3 billion kroons).[6] Liberal politicians pressed in the 1990s for privatization of Eesti Energia. Negotiations began with the American firm NRG, which proposed to buy 49 percent of Estonia's two oil-shale-fired stations for $67 million and a guaranteed share of the local electricity market.

Estonia produces no natural gas or coal. Dependent on imports from Russia, Eesti Gaas lost money in 1997. Still, there were foreign bidders. By April 1998 some 27 percent of Eesti Gaas was owned by the Estonian state—63 percent was owned by Germany's Ruhrgas and Russia's Gazprom. The Estonian government then sold 10 percent of the state's share to the Finnish oil group Neste Oy. In February 1999 the Estonian government sold a further 11.4 percent of its share to Ruhrgas, making the German company the largest shareholder, with nearly one-third.

Estonia's energy system comprised several power plants and seven transmission and distribution companies. Parts of the system were sold to Finnish, Dutch, and U.S. firms in joint ventures with Estonian governmental and private agencies.[7]

Estonia supplies electricity and water to the Russian town of Ivangorod, across the river from Narva. Unable to pay its bills in the 1990s, Ivangorod for a time accepted subsidies from Estonia. In 1998, however, Estonia reduced water pressure for Ivangorod to one-fourth of normal to induce the Leningrad Oblast' government to pay its outstanding debt (15 million kroons in August 1998).

Latvia

Latvia had by far the busiest ports of the three Baltic states, but the country was the weakest in energy sources. It imported electricity from Lithuania, oil and gas from Russia.

A promising sign came in October 1999: the U.S.-based companies CME International and Caterpillar Power Ventures announced that they would buy 75 percent of the heating utility in the western Latvian city of Liepaja; the other 25 percent would be owned by the state utility Latvenergo and the Liepaja City Council. The U.S. firms would buy $8 million in debt owed by the insolvent power station and invest $70 million in a new natural-gas-fired cogeneration power station.

Lithuania

Lithuania in 1997 extracted some 212,000 tons of oil locally but imported 5.8 million from Russia. It also had small offshore reserves, not yet tapped.

The bulk of Lithuania's electricity in the 1990s was generated by two Chernobyl-style nuclear reactors at Ignalina. In 1998 the Ignalina plants generated 77 percent of Lithuania's electricity, while thermal plants supplied 18 percent and hydropower supplied 5 percent. By some measures Lithuania depended more on nuclear power than any country in the world. Its electricity output doubled between 1994 and 1996—increasing from 6.6 billion kilowatt-hours to 12.7 billion. Residential users accounted for the greatest portion of total energy consumption in 1998 (around 34 percent), followed by transport (28 percent) and industry (23 percent).

Ignalina provided electricity even when Russian oil flows were reduced or interrupted. It generated surplus energy sold to Latvia, Kaliningrad, and Belarus—its biggest foreign customer but one that often failed to pay bills on time or demanded barter deals.

As we shall see below, Ignalina shared the stage with Lithuania's oil complex in October 1999 as local, Russian, European, and U.S. firms and politicians struggled to shape the country's power industries. The actors included:

- The European Commission. It had the final say on when Lithuania could begin negotiations for entry into the European Union, and insisted that Ignalina be closed in the next few years because its Soviet-era reactors were accident-prone.[8]
- The European Bank for Reconstruction and Development. It provided some funds to repair Ignalina, but also gave Lithuania a timetable for closing first one block of the plant and then the other.
- Free market, Western-oriented politicians in Lithuania such as conservative leader Vytautas Landsbergis and President Valdas Adamkus—opposed by nationalists and leftists content to depend on Ignalina.

Lithuania in the mid-1990s promised to close both reactors by around 2005 and received funds from the multilateral Nuclear Safety Account on condition that it not rechannel the existing reactors once they burned out. In 1998, however, the government of Prime Minister Gediminas Vagnorius had second thoughts. The head of the Nuclear Energy Division in Lithuania's Economics Ministry argued that there were no safety reasons to close the Ignalina plant. He suggested that EU officials were bowing to groundless fears of European voters. Rather than searching for alternative sources of energy, the Vagnorius government sought to export energy across Poland to Western Europe and looked for ways to extend Ignalina's life to 2015.

Faced with Lithuanian intransigence, EU officials in the late 1990s warned that continued operation of Ignalina would keep Lithuania from reaching "fast track" negotiation status. The EU could hardly compromise on Ignalina without setting a precedent for other aspirant countries, notably Bulgaria and Slovakia, with reactors widely viewed as dangerous.

Bowing to EU pressure, Lithuania's parliament agreed (63–31–1) in October 1999 to close one of Ignalina's two reactors by 2005. Expectations were that Lithuania would have to decide the fate of the second reactor by 2004. Landsbergis warned that to prolong the decision would only promote conflict with the EU. He assured the Seimas that the European Commission would contribute 500 million Euros ($538 million) to ease the cost of closing the two reactors. He also called for creating a plan to reconstruct the energy sector after closing the second reactor—perhaps building a new nuclear reactor near Ignalina.

Opponents said that shutting down Ignalina would spell economic suicide for Lithuania, because the plant supplied nearly 80 percent of the country's electricity. There was also an ethnic issue, for many workers likely to lose their jobs came from Russia, Ukraine, and Belarus in the 1970s to work at Ignalina. Critics said that the total costs to Lithuania from the shutdown would run into billions of dollars—far more than any aid tendered by the EU. Meanwhile, Euroskepticism nearly doubled: only 18 percent of Lithuanians opposed joining the EU in 1998; a year later, that share rose to 31 percent.

A week after the Seimas vote, Lithuania was included among the next six countries with which the European Commission would negotiate for EU membership. Commissioners praised Lithuania for implementing judicial reforms, increasing trade with the EU, establishing a market economy, and voting to close the first reactor. They stressed, however, that the second should be shut down by 2009.

International efforts to shut down the accident-prone Soviet-built nuclear power stations in Lithuania and elsewhere achieved contradictory results. Many Lithuanians who had wanted after the 1986 Chernobyl meltdown to close down Ignalina changed their minds in the 1990s, when Russia showed it could stop oil deliveries to Lithuania. More fearful of nuclear accidents than many Lithuanians, Western Europeans offered Lithuania inducements to phase out nuclear power. Vilnius, like several other Eastern European governments, pocketed this aid and then used it to extend the life of their nuclear plants. Such behavior—some called it nuclear blackmail—was abetted by a nuclear engineering lobby in the West anxious to make money in the East and improve the image of nuclear power. Thus, subsidies from the West prolonged the very transnational threat they were trying to remove. But incidents at

Soviet-made power plants in Lithuania and elsewhere became less frequent and less serious than before the safety upgrades.[9]

Future Wealth? Overlapping Claims

In the 1990s Lithuania, Latvia, Russia, and Poland claimed oil deposits under the Baltic Sea. Mindful of the wealth that such deposits brought to Norway and the United Kingdom, the Baltic states sought in the 1990s to explore and tap this potential. Whether actual oil finds would justify the costs of offshore drilling and extraction remained to be seen. Exploitation of these deposits would take years. Before serious exploration could begin, the parties needed to agree how to demarcate economic zones and the continental shelf. Lithuania's claims bordered the same deposits claimed not only by Latvia but also by Russia.[10] Latvia's deposits bordered not just Lithuania's but Sweden's.[11] Moscow gained bargaining leverage from the reality that, so long as the Baltic countries had any border disputes, they were less likely to be admitted into the EU or NATO.

Global Interdependence: Geonomics vs. Guns

Economic clout often trumps military muscle in an era of global interdependence. Unless states are willing to risk war, geonomics (geography plus economics) can outweigh guns and geopolitics. As a result, the tiny Baltic states could more readily defy external military threats. The USSR and, later, post-Soviet Russia had overwhelming military superiority, but could not use it to coerce Balts without jeopardizing Moscow's economic lifelines to the West. Russia's economic dependence on the West counted for more in Kremlin decisions than the losses to Russia from Baltic independence.

Ports, Pipelines, and Refineries

Baltic ports have been important for Russian exporters and importers for more than a thousand years. Soviet Russia did not wish to lose this access when the Baltic countries first became independent. The 1920 Tartu Treaty between Soviet Russia and Estonia committed the parties to negotiate a trade treaty with special provisions for storage facilities at Estonian ports and duty-free transit for Russia at low rates.

Soviet planners decided in the 1960s to develop three new oil export terminals—Ventspils in Latvia, Odessa in Ukraine, and Novorossiisk in Russia. When Latvia and Ukraine became independent, only Novorossiisk and the much smaller port of Tuapse belonged to Russia. Economic self-interest dictated that post-Soviet Russia take advantage of existing Baltic and Black Sea outlets. But political motives led the Yeltsin Kremlin to curtail Russian use of Baltic ports and to minimize Russian trade with the Baltic republics. Russians made greater use of Finnish ports in the 1990s and considered building new ports to the north of St. Petersburg—even though the Gulf of Finland is shallow, and ice-bound for months.

St. Petersburg's vast port area was used mainly for dry goods. Its business declined sharply in the 1990s because of botched privatization, lack of investment, poor service, and poor security.[12] Anyone who sailed past St. Petersburg's docks in the late

1990s would see mile upon mile of desolation—rusting cranes, mostly idle—quite unlike the more modern, clean, and busy ports of Tallinn or Riga, not to mention Helsinki or Copenhagen. As a new century began, there were big but unrealized plans to modernize the port conceived as Russia's window on the West. But Russian authorities in 2000 contracted with a Belgian firm to build on the Gulf of Finland north of St. Petersburg a $50 million liquid gas terminal to reload both gas and ammonia from trains to ships.

Despite Russian reluctance to use Baltic ports, transit trade probably accounted for 30 percent of Baltic GDP in the mid-1990s. Rising oil prices and the revival of Russia's economy could easily boost this share to more than 50 percent.

Estonia

Tallinn was a key Baltic port in Hanseatic and later times. Under Soviet rule, however, Tallinn languished, isolated from world commerce. Independence regained, Estonia's government made the port of Tallinn a state enterprise in December 1991 and a public company owned by the state in 1996. The government became the landlord responsible for management, infrastructure, and navigation while private firms handled the cargo.

The Port of Tallinn includes four harbors: the Old City, Paldiski South, Paljassaare, and the deep water port of Muuga east of Tallinn. In 1999 the total complex handled 26.4 million tons of cargo—20.2 million in transit. Total volume increased by one-fourth over 1998 and doubled over 1995. Liquid cargo—much of it oil—made up two-thirds of the cargo passing through Tallinn in 1998–1999. Little of the cargo was timber or grain—a radical change from Hanseatic times. Of the nearly 10,000 ships docking in Tallinn in 1999, nearly 4,000 were cargo ships, while 6,000 were passenger ships with 6 million passengers. These numbers warranted more quays and storage space, backed by better infrastructure.

The port's oil terminal was one of Estonia's most profitable firms. Its profits exceeded 60 percent of annual turnover in 1997. The operator was efficient and had good relations with Russian oil companies.[13] Estonia considered building another oil terminal, but such a facility would face stiff competition from other Baltic ports.

Latvia

Latvia's main energy ace in the 1990s was that its port at Ventspils stood at the end of a pipeline through which flowed nearly one-fifth of Russia's oil exports to Europe. Russian oil also reached Europe through the Czech Republic, Slovakia, the Ukrainian port of Odessa, and Russia's port of Novorossiisk.

Latvia's ports in the 1990s handled a greater volume of traffic than the ports of Estonia, Lithuania, St. Petersburg, and Kaliningrad combined. Three major ports— Ventspils, Riga, and Liepaja—were central to Latvia's transit trade. In the 1990s each port was being developed into a free economic zone to encourage further investment. Ventspils handled oil and petroleum products as well as potash, chemicals, and metals. Despite low prices for oil in 1998, Latvia's dominant oil reloading firm, Ventspils Nafta, chose to expand. In 1999 it installed new tanks that would increase its storage capacity by one-third.

Riga Port handled passenger traffic as well as commerce, fish, and commodities such as metals and timber. Its turnover increased threefold from 1993 to 1998. Liepaja, formerly a closed Soviet military base, shipped metals and timber.

Russia's dependency on Baltic outlets was reflected in a contradictory web of sticks and carrots directed at Riga. In 1996 Russia's energy and fuel minister demanded 30 percent of the shares in Latvia's oil terminal Ventspils Nafta when privatized. If Latvia agreed, Moscow pledged not to decrease oil shipments, even though Russia was building a rival terminal at Primorsk.

In April 1998 the Kremlin threatened that Russia might shift its oil exports from Ventspils because of alleged Latvian discrimination against the country's Russian speakers. Latvian foreign minister Valdis Birkavs immediately denounced the threats and asserted that in any future trade war, Latvia would survive.

But Russia did not speak with one voice. Within government ministries and within the oil industry there was a welter of interests and opinions. As in Soviet times, Russian officials tried to "exploit contradictions" among foreign actors and take advantage of shifting opportunities. Rivalries among Balts made them vulnerable to tactics of divide-and-rule. The Kremlin would seek the best terms for its oil deliveries, refining, and shipping by playing off one Baltic country against the other. It could reward one country for its treatment of Russian settlers and punish others for "abuse of human rights." However, the bob-and-weave tactics of Russian negotiators did not add to their credibility.

Having threatened Latvia in vain, Russian officials later in 1998 proposed the expansion of Russian pipelines through Latvia, thus bypassing Lithuania. This maneuver came at the same time that Moscow pressured Vilnius to sell its new oil handling facilities to Russian rather than U.S. investors. In March 1999, however, Moscow snubbed the Latvians and vowed to cut Russian exports through Ventspils by 20 percent—another effort, it appeared, to pressure Latvian politicians.[14]

Were Moscow to punish Latvia or Lithuania by turning off the spigot, they could also hurt Russian financial interests—unless alternative routes were developed to reach Western markets. This explains why, despite the Russian bluster, Ventspils Nafta could report in February 1999 that transit volume remained strong, and that the share of total Russian oil exports flowing through Ventspils had increased from around 13 percent in 1998 to 18 percent.

Electricity and gas also figured into the Latvian energy equation. Along with Ventspils Nafta, the Latvian state-owned electricity utility Latvenergo was among the largest firms in the entire Baltic region. It made large profits in the late 1990s and used them to upgrade its network and technology.

The gas supply and distribution monopoly, Latvijas Gaze, reported large profits in 1998—more than double those for 1997. Ownership was shared by the Latvian state, Russia's Gazprom, and Germany's Ruhrgas and Preussen Elektra.

Lithuania's Energy Showdown, October 1999

The importance of energy in Lithuanian economics and politics was underscored by the interplay of forces in October 1999. As we saw earlier, the Seimas agreement to shut down the Ignalina nuclear plant quickly improved prospects for Lithuania's admission to the EU. Decisions on oil were even more complicated. The key actors were the following:

- *Lithuania's Oil Complex: Mazeikiai Nafta.* The consolidated oil industry consisted of the refinery at Mazeikiai, the Naftotiekis pipeline network based in Birzai, and the oil terminal offshore from Butinge, near the Latvian border. These three units were merged in December 1998 into one company under the name Mazeikiai Nafta, which employed nearly four thousand people. Mazeikiai Nafta had the largest share of capital in Lithuania after the Ignalina power station and Lietuvos Energija company. Lithuania also had a small oil product terminal at Klaipeda, which the government took over in November 1998 in hopes of increasing the plant's efficiency.

  Mazeikiai Nafta imported crude oil from Russia through the Druzhba (Friendship) pipeline across Belarus. For much of the 1990s, for reprocessing Russian crude for export through Ventspils in Latvia, Lithuania was allowed to keep one-fifth of the reprocessed oil for domestic needs.

  The Mazeikiai Nafta complex greatly enhanced Lithuania's political and economic clout. With the 1999 completion of the Butinge oil terminal, which was supplied by four pumping stations near the Latvian border, Lithuania was able to divert oil formerly exported through the Latvian port of Ventspils. The complex enabled Lithuania to block the flow of Russian oil from Russia proper to Kaliningrad and to European markets. Lithuania depended on Russia for crude oil, but if Russia balked, other suppliers could be found.

  Mazeikiai Nafta exported two-thirds of its production to the West. Oil refining could make a major contribution to Lithuania's GDP, but in the late 1990s it became a wasting asset. The business accounted for one-fourth of Lithuania's industrial production in 1994, but declined to less than one-fifth in 1995–1996. The firm earned about $10 million in 1997 but lost $28 million in 1998. Landsbergis called it a "sinking ship." It lost $250,000 a day when its Russian supplier closed the tap—as happened three times in 1999, forcing the refinery to halt operations.
- *Williams International Company.* A diversified firm based in the United States, Williams negotiated in 1998–1999 to purchase one-third of Mazeikiai Nafta shares for $150 million; take operational control of the company; and receive an option to buy a majority stake in the future. But Williams claimed in October 1999 that Mazeikiai Nafta was insolvent, with debts exceeding $307 million, and insisted Lithuania cover them as part of the deal.
- *LUKoil.* Russia's major oil exporter wanted a controlling share in Mazeikiai Nafta or at least a share equal to Williams's. It spurned suggestions it accept just 10 percent of Mazeikiai shares. LUKoil had carrots and sticks. It offered to deliver oil to Mazeikiai at prices less than it charged to Ventspils in Latvia. But LUKoil often flexed its muscles. It often cut off crude oil supplies to Lithuania. Seeing that Williams would prevail, LUKoil stopped delivery of crude again in October 1999, causing Mazeikiai's share price to drop by 12 percent. Neighboring countries— Latvia, Belarus, and Ukraine—also suffered when Russian suppliers failed to reach Lithuania. LUKoil pleaded shortfalls in Russia or pipeline problems, but

Lithuanians found evidence that political authorities in Moscow were directing the zigs and zags of LUKoil negotiating behavior in Lithuania.[15]

- *The Kremlin.* The Russian government wanted to keep Lithuania dependent on Russia and away from U.S. and European business and membership in NATO. But Russian business interests wanted to expand their commerce with Lithuania. In any case, Russia needed Lithuanian and other Baltic refineries and ports to sell its oil to the West.
- *Free-market politicians in Lithuania.* Seimas chairman Landsbergis, President Adamkus, and other Lithuanian free-market politicians were determined to engage Williams International to make the oil sector more profitable and solidify Lithuania's ties with the West, facilitating entry into the EU and NATO. Without modernization and greater efficiency, Adamkus argued, Mazeikiai Nafta would not earn but lose enormous sums of money.
- *Nationalist and leftist forces in Lithuania.* Many Lithuanians wanted to protect the national patrimony and to avoid conflict with Russia. They included former president Algirdas Brazauskas, former prime minister Vagnorius, and leaders of the major leftist parties. In 1998 the Vagnorius government had sought tripartite cooperation with Russia as well as the West to upgrade the country's oil sector.
- *Prime Minister Rolandas Paksas.* A member of Landsbergis's Homeland Front, Rolandas Paksas was appointed by Adamkus in June 1999 to replace Vagnorius as prime minister. But Paksas worried that covering Mazeikiai debts for Williams would dislocate the country's overall finances.
- *Multilateral agencies.* The International Monetary Fund (IMF) worried that the Williams deal would raise Lithuanian government debt from 5.8 percent to 10 percent of GDP.
- *Other potential crude oil suppliers.* Lithuania, like Latvia, experienced frequent interruptions in Russian deliveries. Seeking to diversify, both Lithuania and Latvia sought to refine not just Russian oil but also oil from Europe and from the Caspian Sea.[16] Vilnius hoped to import oil from Norway in trade for Lithuanian peat, cement, furniture, and textiles. Lithuania's economics minister made inquiries in Iran in October 1999 but was immediately overruled in Vilnius.

President Adamkus signed the deal with Williams and the cabinet approved it by eleven to three on October 19, 1999. But Prime Minister Paksas and two key ministers objected to the terms and resigned. Paksas opposed the stipulation that Lithuania provide 1.4 billion litas ($350 million) in long-term financing to cover the refinery's existing debts. The state, Paksas said, could not spare so much money for this one project because it had other obligations. The cabinet would have to take the money from the new issue of Eurobonds, thereby depleting the government's reserves and bringing it to the brink of a financial crisis. Paksas had offered to spread the $350 million over several years or make state guarantees to Williams, but the Americans refused any compromise. "Negotiations are really difficult," Paksas said, "when our partners know there is no competition for them and they dictate the conditions."

Opposition parties protested the sale of Lithuania's patrimony to outsiders and demanded a national referendum on the deal. Several thousand students and pensioners gathered near the Seimas building to denounce the arrangement with Williams. Speakers called it "shameful" and "humiliating" and warned it would divert money from education to foreign pocketbooks.[17] The Lithuanian Industrialists' Confederation called for delay in finalizing the accord so it could be investigated by a commission of independent experts.

But Adamkus and the acting cabinet authorized the acting minister of government reform, Sigitas Kaktys, and the acting transportation minister, Rimantas Didziokas, to sign the contracts with Williams on October 29—the date originally scheduled. Kaktys, the head negotiator for Lithuania, said the U.S. firm at the last minute agreed to lower Lithuania's financial commitments by $9 million to $344 million and to extend the term for payments.

Williams pictured the deal as a short-term burden for Lithuania but part of a long-term solution to the country's financial woes. The Lithuanian government in 1999–2000 would cover the state-funded debt already incurred while Williams invested in plant modernization. This dual commitment was needed, Williams argued, to convince Western banks to invest in Lithuania. The 1.4 billion litas Lithuania provided to the oil complex was not a gift but a loan, to be paid back at 10 percent interest. Williams pledged to make Mazeikiai Nafta the most efficient oil company in Europe, producing high-grade products that would meet EU environmental standards, creating jobs, and earning billions of dollars that would circulate in Lithuania. The true risk would be for Lithuania to reject the deal with Williams and face the bankruptcy of Mazeikiai Nafta, a default on government guaranteed loans, and the loss of four thousand jobs.

The European Bank for Reconstruction and Development agreed to lend the Lithuanian government up to 20 percent of the financing needed to upgrade the Mazeikiai refinery if the Williams deal assured the plant's viability. The International Monetary Fund was expected soon to negotiate a structural stabilization loan.

Adamkus warned that he would call new elections in 2000 unless parliament installed a stable government. But the Seimas on November 3 accepted Adamkus's nominee for prime minister, Andrius Kubilius, by an 82–20 vote with 18 abstentions. Kubilius, also from the Homeland Union, had been deputy chairman of the Seimas.

If Russia could not dominate Lithuania's oil business, it might settle for a lesser share. While LUKoil fumed, Russia's second-largest oil exporter, Yukos, arrived in Vilnius for tripartite negotiations with the Lithuanian government and Williams regarding the purchase of 10 or 12 percent of stock in Mazeikiai Nafta in exchange for a guarantee to supply crude to the refinery for ten years. Earlier, Yukos had become one of the first oil companies to fill its tankers with oil from the offshore terminal at Butinge. A Lithuanian negotiator stated that Yukos never set any preconditions and never used threatening tactics.

There were other signs of good will on both sides. In late October 1999 the Seimas ratified agreements with Russia on the Kaliningrad border and the division of the continental shelf. In November former Russian prime minister Evgeny Primakov visited President Adamkus and assured him that the Russian Duma would also ratify the border accords. Primakov had no complaints about the Williams deal so long as Lithuania was open to Russian business. Primakov was said to be close to Russia's ambassador to Vilnius, an ardent promoter of Russian commercial interests in Lithuania.

LUKoil was down but not out. In 2000 there were also reports that Mazeikiai Nafta was negotiating with LUKoil to set up a joint oil supply and fuel a marketing network in Lithuania. Meanwhile, Mazeikiai Nafta entered a three-year crude oil supply deal with the Kazak firm KBM, operated by a Canadian company—an arrangement facilitated by Russian's doubling the transit quota for Kazak oil.

How important was Mazeikiai Nafta to Lithuania's economy? The taxes it paid in 2000 covered one-fourth of the state budget!

THE FUTURE OF BALTIC ENERGY

A host of factors—domestic, regional, international—would shape Baltic energy in the twenty-first century.

Safety and Environmental Issues

Past and present pollution created real and present environmental dangers in each Baltic republic. Estonian scientists reported in November 1998 that the bill for cleaning radioactive, petroleum, and chemical wastes in the Pakri peninsula, home to a former Soviet military base, could run to $5 billion. Until then, however, the Estonian government had allocated just $294,000 for cleaning all former Soviet military sites, an amount supplemented by some $97,000 from Finland for remedial action in the Baltic countries and Poland. On the positive side, Estonian and Russian scientists, with Danish assistance, began in 1998–1999 to study how both sides could clean up the water reservoir shared by Narva and Ivangorod.

Meanwhile, extracting energy from oil shale was a very dirty business. Estonians looked for a way to generate energy from the biomass in their forests, but no substantial quick fix was in sight.

When people want abundant energy, they often ignore the dangers in its production. Thus, many Lithuanians downplayed the risks inherent not just in their nuclear power but in their oil operations. Latvians complained that the Mazeikiai complex degraded air quality in both countries. Latvian monitors reported in September 1998 that benzol, a byproduct of oil refining, was twenty times higher than recommended in the atmosphere near Mazeikiai.

Lithuanian president Adamkus (elected in early 1998) had long served as an Environmental Protection Agency official in the United States. For much of 1998, however, he downplayed charges that the oil terminal being constructed at Butinge could pose a risk to the environment. Prompted by a deluge of press reports, however, Adamkus in August 1998 acknowledged that the pipelines leading to the terminal were poorly built and could easily break. The German builders were said to have buried the pipelines quickly to try to conceal structural flaws. Environmentalists demanded that the entire project be stopped until an independent environmental impact assessment could be completed. But the project went ahead and began operations in 1999.

Latvian as well as Lithuanian environmental groups expressed concern about Butinge, located little more than a mile from the Latvian coast, because a spill at the offshore terminal would pollute the sea and shore. Lithuania agreed in 1999 to permit a Latvian monitoring system near the terminal, but claimed that its facility was the safest in Europe, if not the world. When leaks occurred, Lithuanians blamed them on freak winds and waves.

Oil tanker traffic, of course, also risked pollution. Thus, a LUKoil tanker leaked two tons of diesel fuel in the Estonian port of Miiduranna on November 29, 1998. Yet all three Baltic states hoped for more tanker traffic.

Lithuania's Butinge oil terminal exacerbated the widespread problem of illegal discharge of oil contained in ballast and bilge water. Butinge had no facilities for such waste, motivating ships to dump at sea. The platform was located in the open seas—hours from cleanup vessels. By contrast, Latvia's terminal at Ventspils helped prevent discharges at sea by charging low waste-management fees. Since loadings at Ventspils took place within the harbor's sheltered waters, accidents could be contained. Most of the diesel fuel spilled in an accident at Ventspils on August 22, 2000 was quickly retrieved.

Balts, Russians, and others could use energy far more efficiently and reduce carbon emissions.[18] As we saw in table 8.3, Balts lost more energy in transmission and distribution even than Russia. If all parties became less dependent on nuclear power, this would make it easier to phase out dangerous reactors or upgrade them.

Environmentalists warned that the southern Baltic coast was in a catastrophic environmental situation, stressed by extensive and chronic pollution. A quest for enhanced environmental quality could unite EU countries, Balts, and Russians. International and transnational efforts in the 1990s gave a multiplier effect to each country's efforts. The Baltic republics gained from the knowledge, experience, and subsidies of their Western partners. The Baltic republics made better use of foreign aid than did Russia. For them, pollution of their environment was a major priority, not just one of many.[19] Small but centrally organized states could mobilize and concentrate efforts more readily than could the sprawling Russian Federation.[20]

The littoral states were able to hitch the solution of their own environmental and water-supply problems to multilateral efforts to clean up the Baltic Sea as a whole. Cooperation helped each party to achieve a much larger return on its investments in environmental infrastructure. Joint programs helped the parties to reduce organic wastes, chemical pollutants, and phosphorus flowing into the Baltic Sea, and to curtail nitrogen buildups. The supply and purification of drinking water improved for the Baltic countries.[21] Finland helped Estonia curtail sulfur emissions, but other European interventions prolonged the life of nuclear power stations in Lithuania and elsewhere.

Norway, the United States, and Japan in the 1990s acted to forestall further nuclear leakage by Russian vessels in Baltic and Arctic waters and the Sea of Japan, but did little about wastes and leakage already occurring in those waters. The scale of such problems challenged even the richest countries. For its part, the Kremlin was cash strapped and comparatively indifferent to the environment. In 2000, however, Moscow paid Norwegian divers huge sums to extract bodies from its sunken *Kursk* submarine.

Regional Cooperation

Cooperation among Baltic consumers and suppliers could redound to mutual gain. As the acting president of the European Bank for Reconstruction and Development put it in May 2000: "In the Baltics, each country has different advantages, so cooperation is essential in the energy field to maximize the potential of the region." In May the Estonian and Latvian governments approved a memorandum of intent on merging the power utilities Eesti Energia and Latvenergo. The Eesti Energia board chairman said neither utility was likely to survive on its own in a free market and that a merger could give the new company access to cheaper credit. The Latvenergo chairman said another goal was to stabilize prices. The U.S.–based firm NRG Energy endorsed the merger. Other voices called for gas pipelines between Estonia and Finland, and between Lithuania and Finland. J.P. Morgan investment analysts in New York said that a "united Baltic Energy Ring" would justify foreign investments. Latvian president Vike-Freiberga spoke in the same vein, noting at a Harvard University symposium in May that the power resources of Latvia and Estonia could complement each other. Hydroelectric power in Latvia, she observed, depended on the flow of the Daugava River. As the year 2000 ended, however, each Baltic actor went its own way. Eesti Energia was partially privatized while Latvenergo remained a state monopoly.

Like Estonia, Lithuania in 2000 was privatizing more of its energy industry. Vilnius sought "energy bridges" to Western Europe and in the region. But Lithuanian policies met resistance from environmentalists as well as from statists in Latvia. Meanwhile, Belarus gave regional cooperation a bad name, for it owed Lithuania huge sums for electricity. A Russian firm pledged to pay off some Belarusian debts by supplying nuclear fuel to Ignalina. But Vilnius feared a Kremlin-backed Trojan Horse.

The Baltic, Russia, and the World

The ideal world for Balts would include a healthy and friendly Russia—not a poor or angry one. But Russia in the 1990s often proved a hostile or undependable partner for the Baltics, due both to its internal weaknesses and to residual imperialist tendencies.

Privatization did not help Russian energy production. Crude oil production declined from 516 million tons in 1990 to 318 million in 1994 and 284 million in 1998. Natural gas production declined by 10 percent in this period. On the other hand, the wealth of those who managed LUKoil, Yukos, and other major companies jumped from a few thousands to millions or perhaps a billion dollars.[22]

Asia's economic slump in 1998 sharply reduced demand for oil, causing prices to fall. About one-fifth of the value of the Russian rouble depended on energy prices. Oil prices declined by 33 percent and gas by 16 percent. Russia's oil exports fell 13 percent in the first half of 1998. Russia's exports of natural gas rose but they earned one-fifth less than in 1997. Exports of gas as well as oil became unprofitable, even as domestic sales were plagued by widespread nonpayment. On August 17, 1998 Russia established a ninety-day moratorium on servicing foreign bank loans. Russian officials later conceded that they had deceived IMF officials about the country's hard currency reserves. In September 1998 Standard and Poor's lowered its rating for eight large Russian firms, including LUKoil and several other energy companies, from a B− rating to CC.

Global demand picked up in 1999–2000 and oil producers acted in concert to raise prices. Russia's stock market more than doubled. If Asian demand continued to rise, Russia would have reason to develop oil production and distribution networks aimed at China, Korea, and Japan. Moscow would then have to decide whether to cooperate with or try to bypass Kazakstan and other Caspian Sea producers. But if Asian growth were to slow, Russia's incentives to deliver its oil to Europe would mount.

If Russia felt shut out of Black Sea and Caspian oil development and distribution by U.S. interventions, this could add to Moscow's motives to cooperate with Baltic refineries and ports. If Russian sensitivities were deeply wounded, however, a xenophobic reaction could blanket Russian dealings with all Western firms and countries.[23]

In the Baltic, as in Central Asia and the Caucasus, Russia wanted to control not only energy production but refining and distribution. Still, some signs in 1998 and 1999 suggested that Russia would welcome cooperation with Balts. Even though Moscow talked of bypassing Baltic outlets, Russian officials continued to explore greater use of Ventspils and the Mazeikiai complex.[24] As LUKoil bowed out of Lithuania in late 1999, Yukos stepped in.

It was probably easier and more cost-effective for Russia to utilize Latvian and Lithuanian refineries and ports than to outflank them. By the same token, at least for the near or medium term, it was probably easier for Latvians and Lithuanians to process Russian oil than to exploit offshore deposits.

The last months of the millennium saw new challenges to Russia's energy and other economic interests as reports surfaced about money laundering and massive human rights abuses in the North Caucasus. The IMF and Western governments asked whether their credits were among the billions of dollars laundered by prominent Russians through foreign banks and whether they should loan more money to Moscow if it would be used to subsidize Russia's brutal invasion of Chechnya. While Russia justified its war in Chechnya as a crackdown on terrorism, the Kremlin certainly wanted to regain control over the oil routes of the North Caucasus. The prize of oil could motivate a brutal war as well as peaceful collaboration.

Politics hovered over economics. Romano Prodi, president of the European Commission, backed by Germany, promoted an Energy Partnership between Europe and Russia. In 2000 the Russian firm Gazprom joined a consortium with Gaz de France, the German firm Wintershall, and the Italian SNAM to build a $2 billion pipeline to supply Europe with natural gas from Russia. Europe would thus depend on suppliers noted more for their aggressive politics than for their dependability and transparency in commerce. The more that the West invested in Russia, the more Russians could dictate. Not only did Moscow demand that the gas line bypass Ukraine and go through Poland, it also urged Western Europeans to press Warsaw to participate in a scheme bound to hurt its Ukrainian neighbor. Moscow also insisted the EU not participate in the U.S.-sponsored Baku-Ceyhan (Turkey) pipeline project skirting Russia. The precedents were ominous: the August 27, 1918 Treaty of Berlin committed Soviet Russia to supply Imperial Germany with oil from Baku, provided Germany stop supporting an independent Ukraine, Azerbaijan, and Armenia. The Kremlin rewarded Britain with a trade treaty in March 1921 when London abandoned an independent Georgia. Eight decades later, Russian pressures helped sack Ukraine's foreign minister and its chief of military intelligence for tilting toward NATO. Having embraced the Energy Partnership with Moscow, German diplomats in 2000 fell silent on Russian actions in Chechnya but aligned with Moscow on Yugoslav issues and missile defenses. Germany's chancellor pledged in September 2000 that "Russia will be able to count on Germany."[25]

Energy issues would continue in the twenty-first century to exert a heavy influence in Russia's relations with the Baltic republics. Each party—the world's largest country and three of its smallest neighbors—needed the other. How would they deal with shared vulnerabilities? Enlightened self-interest argued for cooperation to mutual advantage. Thus, *Kapitan Putilov* was one of the first Russian tankers to lift at Butinge in 1999; it delivered Russian crude from the Lithuanian terminal to a British Petroleum refinery in the Dutch port of Rotterdam.

Three-sided cooperation in energy matters could lubricate overall cooperation among the EU, the Baltic republics, and Russia—as it had in the 1970s among Iran, Western Europe, and the USSR. But it could easily go awry due to the greed, nationalism, or ineptitude of any partner. Failure to cooperate, in turn, could fuel East-West discord. Each party could profit or lose.[26]

Caption for Chapter 8 Photo: If energy was Russia's ace, the Baltic countries held ports in spades. Here we see Tallinn's Old City harbor, used mainly for passenger ships. The Port of Tallinn included three other harbors: Paldiski South, Paljassaare, and the deep water port of Muuga east of Tallinn. Of the nearly 10,000 ships docking in Tallinn in 1999, nearly 4,000 were cargo ships, while 6,000 were passenger ships with 6 million passengers. In Soviet times very few passenger ships docked in Tallinn.

NOTES

1. Central Intelligence Agency, *Handbook of International Economic Statistics* (September 1997), p. 57.

2. After difficult negotiations, Russia in early 1992 agreed to supply Lithuania with only two-thirds the natural gas in 1992 that it had furnished in 1991: 4.1 billion cubic meters compared with 6.3 billion. Lithuania agreed to supply Russia with 70,000 tons of meat and 400,000 tons of milk.

3. In the 1990s Finnish assistance and subsidies helped reduce sulfur and other emissions from the two plants near Narva. See Robert G. Darst, *Smokestack Diplomacy: Cooperation and Conflict in East-West Environmental Politics* (Cambridge, Mass.: MIT Press, 2000), pp. 127–31.

4. Lithuania's electricity consumption per capita declined from 3,127 kilowatt-hours per capita in 1992 to 2,462 in 1993 but increased slightly, to 2,480, by 1995—still much lower than in 1992. Latvia's electricity consumption declined from 2,621 kwh per capita in 1992 to 1,973 in 1995. Russia's fell by a smaller fraction—from 6,107 in 1992 to between 4,171 and 5,108 in 1995.

5. In 1919 the Soviets demanded the entire oil-shale producing area near Narva, even though the region's population was more than 95 percent Estonian. The Soviets soon dropped that demand, but they did obtain an Estonian commitment in article 16 of the 1920 Tartu Treaty, which generally favored Estonia, to supply hydroelectric power from the Narva River to Russia, at prices to be negotiated later. The Soviets agreed to provide Estonia with a concession to build a railroad to Moscow and a concession to exploit certain forests from Petrograd to Pskov and north to Arkhangelsk. See Ministry of Foreign Affairs USSR, *Dokumenty vneshnei politiki SSSR* (Moscow: Gospolitizdat, 1959) 2: pp. 339–54.

6. Kairi Kurm, "Oil Terminal Heads Estonian Top 100," *Baltic Times,* December 3–9, 1998, p. 15.

7. In October 1998 the entire Laanemaa distribution network was sold to a joint venture between Finland's IVO and Uhispank, while 49 percent of the Narva grid was sold to a local company, Starteko. Subsequently 67 percent of Starteko was sold to the Dutch subsidiary of the U.S. company Cinergy Global Power. In 1999 the Estonian Privatization Agency announced that it was selling a further 18 percent of the Narva grid to Starteko, while the remaining 33 percent stake would be auctioned later.

8. Ignalina had no accidents like the Chernobyl meltdown in 1986, but its history was troubled. In the early 1990s security was lax and a consignment of uranium disappeared, only to be discovered several years later buried in a nearby forest. Thanks largely to Swedish assistance, security and safety improved. Still, the plant was closed twice in 1997. It experienced nineteen incidents in 1998—seventeen ranked as zero in terms of radiation emissions, and two incidents rated at one on a zero to seven scale (Daniel Silva, "Ignalina Shuts Down . . . Again," *Baltic Times,* December 3–9, 1998, p. 3). It shut down twice in early 1999.

9. On moral hazard and extortion, see Darst, *Smokestack Diplomacy,* pp. 164 ff.

10. An agreement was signed between Russian and Lithuanian negotiators in October 1997. It was ratified by the Seimas in October 1999 but had not been ratified by the Russian Duma.

11. In 1995 Latvia signed an agreement potentially worth $1 billion with the U.S. firm AMOCO and the Swedish company Oljeprospektering AB on exploration for oil in the Baltic Sea. Lithuania recalled its ambassador from Riga in protest, but Latvia said no work would take place until the border was determined. *OMRI Economic Digest* 1 (November 1995). Earlier that year Latvia, Lithuania, and Poland presented geological data on their potential oil deposits to potential foreign partners.

12. In April 1996 dock workers in some of northern Russia's ports staged a one-hour strike to protest conditions that encouraged Russian exporters to use Baltic and Ukrainian outlets. The Russian Union of Dockers estimated that Russia's ports were being used to only 60 percent of capacity due to high taxes, rail tariffs, and outdated equipment.

13. Kurm, "Oil Terminal Heads Estonian Top 100," p. 15.

14. In March 1999 Russia announced plans to cut oil exports by one hundred thousand barrels per day to comply with a recent agreement between oil exporting countries to curb production and thus raise prices from low 1998 levels. Many observers doubted Russia would forgo sales and fully comply with the agreement.

15. When Lithuanians showed an intercepted document to the Russian ambassador, he had no comment. Author conversation with Landsbergis at Harvard University, November 14, 2000.

16. Lithuania wanted to import crude oil, wheat, and nonferrous metals from Kazakstan and export meat, milk, and consumer goods to Central Asia and China. Lithuania's then-president, Algirdas Brazauskas, suggested in 1997 that Kazakstan participate in construction of the Butinge oil terminal. Kazak president Nursultan Nazarbayev endorsed this idea and said that Kazak oil could be shipped across Russia to Lithuania by existing pipelines or by rail. Each side saw the other as a gateway to huge markets beyond.

17. Speakers included former President Algirdas Brazauskas, the rector of Vilnius University, a former minister of energy, a poet laureate and a well-known philosopher, both of them founding members of Sajudis.

18. Using indigenous and imported energy, Lithuania in 1992 generated 1.60 metric tons of carbon (CO_2 emissions) per capita—slightly more than Latvia (1.51) and Romania (1.43), but much less than Russia (3.85) or Poland (2.43). None of these countries approached the United States, which produced 5.22 metric tons of carbon per capita. Statistics on Estonia's emissions are unavailable. See T. A. Boden et al., *Estimates of Global, Regional, and National Annual CO₂ Emissions from Fossil-Fuel Burning, Hydraulic Cement Production, and Gas Flaring: 1950–1995* (Oak Ridge, Tenn.: Carbon Dioxide Information Analysis Center, 1995).

19. But when a joint Estonian-Russian committee met in September 2000 to discuss discharge of water into Lake Peipsi, the Russian delegation held to higher standards than the Estonian. The Russian team wanted the purification of cooling water, which Estonia thought unnecessary.

20. Latvia imported Russian gasoline for automobiles, but planned to require the same ISO standards as Western Europe by 2002.

21. Darst, *Smokestack Diplomacy,* pp. 87–88.

22. Marshall I. Goldman, "Russian Energy: A Blessing and a Curse," *Journal of International Affairs* 53 (fall 1999), pp. 73–84 at 76–77. For an overview, see David Lane, ed., *The Political Economy of Russian Oil* (Lanham, Md.: Rowman & Littlefield, 1999), which, however, says nothing about Lithuania and gives just one sentence to Estonia and Latvia.

23. Martha Brill Olcott, "Pipelines and Pipe Dreams: Energy Development and Caspian Society," *Journal of International Affairs* 53 (fall 1999), pp. 305–324.

24. On June 29, 1999, Lithuanian prime minister Rolandas Paksas and Russian prime minister Sergei Stepashin signed accords to prevent double taxation and protect investments. They pledged to cooperate on Kaliningrad and begin talks on how to avoid interruptions of oil deliveries to Lithuania. Within months, however, Stepashin had been fired and Paksas had resigned.

25. Françoise Thom, "Le partenariat énergétique avec la Russie: les risque pours L'Union Européenne," *Le Monde,* November 1, 2000, p. 17.

26. Whether outsiders could count on Russia was not so sure. On January 1, 2001, Russia cut gas supplies to AES, an American firm responsible for gas distribution and electrical power generation in Georgia. the RF Ministry of Economics ordered the independent gas reseller INGS (Inertgazstroi) to halt shipments to Georgia. The U.S. State Department complained that "Russian authorities have abrogated a valid contract between AES . . . and a Russian firm, thereby substantially interfering in an international commercial transaction." Meanwhile, Moscow was pressuring Georgia to permit Russian military bases to remain on its soil, to allow Russian troops to attack Chechen guerrillas operating from Georgian territory, and not to serve as a transit route for oil and gas from the Caspian region to the West. Seeking to prevent a breakdown of its electricity network, Georgia on January 4 purchased a twenty-day supply of gas (to be paid for by AES) from Itera, a Russian firm linked to Gazprom, the Russian state-owned monopoly.

Commercial motives probably overlapped with power politics. Itera was becoming the largest gas supplier to most former Soviet republics, while the State Duma's audit chamber was investigating dealings between Itera and Gazprom as part of a larger audit of Gazprom's books. See *Financial Times,* January 4, 2001, p. 5, and January 5, 2001, pp. 13, 14.

9

Tigers on the Baltic: Can the Small Be Fit?

Daina Stankevics

In this chapter we begin to consider not just the past but the future. What are the prospects for Baltic fitness in the first decades of the twenty-first century? Let us assess alternative futures and the factors that make one scenario or another more likely. In chapters 10 and 11 we shall consider Balts' relations with their neighbors. Here we focus on Balts' domestic assets and liabilities. How do Baltic strengths and weaknesses in the early twenty-first century compare with those of other small states that have achieved high fitness?

When the world was dominated by two superpowers, it seemed that fitness required a broad array of assets including a large population and land mass. Only the United States and USSR possessed the required properties. The tiny Baltic countries were no match for their large eastern neighbor. When the USSR disappeared and Russia sulked, Balts still had to worry about external security but could focus on other dimensions of fitness and development.

Small can be fit. This lesson is implicit in Baltic history—in the record of Vikings, Sword Brothers, Hanseatic merchants, and others who have flourished on the amber coast. Hanseatic Tallinn and Riga, for example, maintained and enhanced their culture, independence, and wealth even though they were tiny city-states adjacent to large kingdoms and empires. For centuries the Hansas enjoyed extraterritorial privileges from London and Bruges to Novgorod. They were a model of self-organization.

Apart from the misty past, the post-Soviet Baltic republics could also find encouragement from recent trends on the faraway Pacific rim and the nearby northern Baltic rim. From Singapore to Sweden, the late twentieth century saw a variety of small states achieve high incomes, high human development, and high security in a world still replete with anarchy, competition, and conflict.

SINGAPORE TO SWEDEN: DOES FITNESS DEPEND ON SIZE?

Prosperity and quality of life do not depend on size. As we see in table 9.1, seven of the world's ten richest countries at the end of the 1990s were very small, with popu-

Table 9.1
Small Can Be Rich, Developed, and Free

Country rank by real GDP per capita in 1999 (1997 in parentheses)	Real GDP per capita in 1999 (1997 in parentheses)	GNP per capita % growth rate in 1998–1999 (1996–1997 in parentheses)	HDI rank in 1999 (1996 in parentheses)	Freedom rank in 1999	Population (millions in 1999)	Surface area (thousands of sq. km. in 1999)
USA 4 (2)	$30,600 (28,740)	3.1 (2.9)	3 (4)	Free	273 (268)	9,364
Switzerland 6 (3)	$27,486 (26,320)	1.2 (n.a.)	13 (16)	Free	7 (7)	41
Singapore 7 (1)	$27,024 (29,000)	3.6 (7.2)	24 (28)	Partly Free	3 (3)	1
Norway 8 (5)	$26,522 (23,940)	0.1 (3.5)	2 (3)	Free	4 (4)	324
Denmark 12 (7)	$24,280 (22,740)	1.0 (3.1)	15 (18)	Free	5 (5)	43
Belgium 13 (8)	$24,200 (22,370)	1.7 (n.a.)	7 (12)	Free	10 (10)	33
Japan 14 (6)	$24,041 (23,400)	0.8 (0.2)	9 (8)	Free	127 (126)	378
Austria 15 (9)	$23,808 (21,980)	2.2 (1.9)	16 (13)	Free	8 (8)	84
Canada 16 (10)	$23,725 (21,860)	2.8 (2.6)	1 (1)	Free	31 (30)	9,971
Hong Kong 26 (4)	$20,939 (24,540)	0.1 (2.1)	26 (25)	Partly Free	7 (7)	1
South Korea 49 (24)	$14,637 (13,500)	10.1 (3.8)	31 (30)	Free	47 (46)	99
Taiwan	$13,198	6.2	High	Free	22	32

SOURCES: World Bank, *World Development Report, 2000/2001* (New York: Oxford University Press, 2000), table 1; ibid., *1998/99*, table 1; UN Development Programme, *Human Development Report 2000* (New York: Oxford University Press, 2000), table 1; ibid., *1998*; freedom rankings from <http://freedomhouse.org/survey99/tables/indeptab.html>. Data on Taiwan are from *Free China Journal*, October 8, 1999, p. 8.

lations of ten million or less: Switzerland, Singapore, Norway, Denmark, Belgium, Austria, and Hong Kong. Six of the next ten richest countries were also very small: the Netherlands, Austria, Sweden, Finland, Israel, and Iceland. Mini-state tax havens such as Luxembourg and Lichtenstein had higher incomes even than Switzerland.

Human development index (HDI) rankings showed nearly the same pattern. Twelve of the top twenty countries had populations smaller than ten million. Among the top ten were Norway, Iceland, Sweden, Belgium, and the Netherlands; in the next ten were Finland, Switzerland, Denmark, Austria, Luxembourg, Ireland, and New Zealand.

Of course small size does not assure fitness. Of the world's twenty poorest states, seventeen had small populations, for example, Mozambique and Tajikistan. In short, population size does not predict income or HDI.

Neither does population density. Impoverished Russia in 2000 had only 9 persons per square kilometer while affluent Finland had 17 and Japan had 336. The most affluent Baltic republic, Estonia, had 34 persons per square kilometer, while Latvia had 39 and Lithuania had 57.

Neither does land mass predict income or HDI. Small Singapore and Hong Kong are fit, but so are the large-scale United States, Canada, and Australia. Germany occupies a smaller space than Sweden. The Baltic countries are not so small relative to many highly developed countries. The smallest Baltic country—Estonia—covers a larger area than do Denmark, Taiwan, or Belgium.[1]

Cultural heritage is a better predictor of development than size or natural endowment. Nearly all the world's top twenty countries ranked by income or by HDI spring from Western civilization—especially its Protestant wing. All but one of the thirteen least corrupt countries also come from this wing.[2] The highest-ranked Asian countries on these lists—Singapore, Hong Kong, Japan, Taiwan, and South Korea—weave Western into Eastern (mainly Confucian or Buddhist) traditions.

The top thirty countries in HDI included no Muslim, Hindu, African, Communist, or former Communist states except for Slovenia (29th). Despite its rising GDP, China's HDI remained low (99th). Of Orthodox Christian countries, the highest HDI rankings went to Cyprus (22d) and Greece (25th). Among traditionally Catholic countries, Spain placed 21st and Portugal 28th. In Latin America, the highest HDI rank went to Argentina, which was 35th. The one Jewish state, Israel, placed 23d.

The world's most corrupt country was Nigeria, followed closely by Ukraine, Azerbaijan, Indonesia, Angola, Cameroon, and Russia. The least corrupt countries in Latin America were Costa Rica (28th in the world), followed by Brazil (49th) and Argentina (51st).

Whether size is a liability or an asset depends on conversion power—the ability to convert hard and soft power into fitness and influence. In the Cold War one superpower tapped rather effectively the size and diversity of its population; the other did not. If all things are equal, of course, size is a plus. A large country has a large domestic market that permits economies of scale and attracts low-priced imports; it can field larger armed forces than a smaller rival can; it can more readily afford mistakes and absorb disasters.

Demographic diversity can also be a plus or a minus. The United States benefits from diversity, Japan and Germany from homogeneity. The former USSR had greater diversity than the United States, but ethnic conflict helped topple the Soviet system.

If we focus on the Baltic littoral (see table 9.2), we see again that overall fitness does not hinge on size. On the southern coast are Germany and Poland—each quite fit in its own way. German is medium-large, and for decades has been an economic dynamo. Poland is medium in size and, in the 1990s, grew faster than any former Communist economy. Russia, however, is large and, by most measures, one of the least fit countries in the world.[3] Russian Kaliningrad was the poorest area on the Baltic coast in the early twenty-first century, and suffered high rates of drug addiction and HIV infection.

Four of Europe's ten top performing companies in 1996–2000 were Swedish, led by the insurance firm Skandia Forsakring, and two were Finnish, paced by Nokia, the world's leading manufacturer of mobile phones.[4] Some Finns worried that Nokia accounted for 4 percent of Finland's GDP and 20 percent of Finnish exports. However, other companies sprang up around Helsinki to support Nokia. While critics earlier worried that Finland depended excessively on pulp and paper, by 2000 the country's economy stood on three pillars: forestry, metals/engineering, and IT.[5]

Balts could take heart also from the fact that each country on the northern shore of the Baltic Sea ranked among the world's richest and most democratic states, although none had a population greater than 8 million. The cultures and languages of Denmark, Sweden, and Finland remained strong even as they adapted to global interdependence and the information revolution.

THE EAST ASIAN TIGERS

The Nordic way of life evolved gradually from foundations laid down over centuries. But Balts could find examples of rapid development in East Asia, where the "Tigers"—Singapore, Hong Kong, South Korea, and Taiwan—set the pace for the world's newly industrializing countries (NICs) in the last three decades of the twentieth century. In the century's final decade, two of them, the Republic of Korea (ROK) and the Republic of China on Taiwan (ROC)—also became democratic. Each Tiger was unique, but each bore some resemblance to the Baltic republics.

Singapore in the late 1990s was a city-state with a population larger than Latvia's but a land mass smaller even than Estonia's. Hong Kong belonged to China but also resembled a city-state. Though small in land area, its population of 7 million approached that of all three Baltic countries combined. The other two Tigers were hardly small, for Taiwan had 22 million people and South Korea 46 million.

Small can be strong. Singapore in the late 1990s was ranked "most competitive" country by the World Economic Forum in Switzerland—just ahead of Hong Kong and the United States. It had the highest percentage of human skills as a component of real wealth. Its eighth-graders ranked first in the world for science and mathematics. Transparency International ranked Singapore one of the least corrupt economies in the world, though its business people often bribed others to win favorable treatment abroad.

Singapore's human development and gender-related development scores in the 1990s were among the highest for developing countries (just behind Cyprus, Barbados, and Hong Kong). Singapore scored somewhat lower in gender empowerment. A country with peoples who at home spoke Chinese, Malay, Tamil, and English, Sin-

Table 9.2
Size and Fitness on the Baltic Littoral

Country rank by real GDP per capita in 1999 (1997 in parentheses)	Real GDP per capita in 1999 (1997 in parentheses)	GNP per capita % growth rate in 1998–1999 (1996–1997 in parentheses)	Human Development Index rank in 1999 (1996 in parentheses)	Freedom rank in 1999	Population (millions in 1999)	Surface area (thousands of sq. km. in 1999)
Denmark 12 (7)	24,280 (22,740)	1.0 (3.1)	15 (18)	Free	5.3	43
Germany 21 (13)	22,404 (21,300)	1.2 (n.a.)	14 (19)	Free	82	367
Finland 25 (18)	21,209 (18,980)	3.5 (4.3)	11 (6)	Free	5	338
Sweden 28 (17)	20,824 (19,030)	3.8 (1.7)	6 (10)	Free	9	450
Poland 73 (46)	7,894 (6,380)	3.3 (6.7)	44 (52)	Free	39	323
Estonia 74 (50)	7,826 (5,010)	2.4 (7.7)	46 (77)	Free	1.4	45
Russia 80 (59)	6,339 (4,190)	1.6 (n.a.)	62 (72)	Partly Free	147	17,075
Lithuania 83 (56)	6,093 (4,510)	-4.0 (2.9)	52 (79)	Free	3.6	65
Latvia 85 (64)	5,938 (3,650)	1.3 (n.a.)	63 (92)	Free	2.4	65

SOURCES: World Bank, *World Development Report, 2000–2001* (New York: Oxford University Press, 2000), table 1; ibid., *1998/99*; UN Development Programme, *Human Development Report 2000* (New York: Oxford University Press, 2000), table 1; freedom rankings from <http://freedomhouse.org/survey99/tables/indeptab.html>.

gapore nonetheless had little evident social strife. The government resolved many ethnic tensions by using English as its major language. But Freedom House judged Singapore to be only "partly free." It was virtually the only authoritarian country in the world that also ranked high in per capita income. Singapore's political and economic growth was managed from the top down. It was not a model of self-organization or of creativity.

Hong Kong was also quite competitive. It benefited at first from low wages and later from high education. It was more laissez-faire than Singapore but also not democratic. As a UK colony and later as a special zone of China, Hong Kong was only partly free.

South Korea's economy was more like Japan's — directed and often subsidized by the government. From the late 1940s until the late 1990s South Korea was unfree or partly free.

The economy of Taiwan was directed from the top down in the 1950s and 1960s, but gradually became more market driven. In the 1990s Taiwan became a democracy based on a large middle class.

In the 1970s what many observers termed an "East Asian miracle" took shape. Hong Kong blazed the path. Its industrialization began with textiles. When industrial countries raised protectionist barriers, the city moved into more elaborate manufactures — clothing, then toys, and then electronic products such as quartz watches. In the 1980s Hong Kong entrepreneurs returned to Shanghai to recreate capitalism there. Hong Kong became a warehouse for Chinese exports to the rest of the world.

Singapore started with fewer advantages than Hong Kong. Its population had little education or experience in manufacturing. Industrialization did not begin until 1967, when Lee Kuan Yew became prime minister. His policies helped Singapore become the world's leading recipient of foreign investment. Like Hong Kong, Singapore at first focused on textiles, but then shifted to chemicals and oil, then to toys, then to electronics and computers, and in the 1990s to financial services.

Modifying the Japanese and Hong Kong experience for their own settings, Taiwan and South Korea also industrialized in the 1970s. The four Tigers advanced from low income to low-medium income ratings. As incomes rose and education broadened, their infant mortality declined.

Like Japan, each Tiger exported far more than it imported.[6] From the 1970s through 1990 tiny Hong Kong exported more than any other Tiger. U.S. exports led the world, but were only 4.8 times more than Hong Kong's in 1990. As the Singapore, Hong Kong, and Taiwan economies matured, services began to rival manufacturing. By 1992 Taiwan's Central Bank possessed foreign-exchange reserves of nearly $90 billion, more per capita than any other country.

Sources of Tiger Power

Let us review the Tigers' liabilities and assets for development and then compare them with those of the Baltic republics. Each Tiger was different, but they all shared some common features, as suggested in box 9.1.

One important factor in East Asia was probably the high rate of saving and investment. Table 9.3 shows that in 1998 Singapore's rate of savings was 51 percent and

Box 9.1. Tiger Power: Liabilities and Assets

Liabilities:
- Poor resource base: few minerals or cash crops; heavy dependence upon imported energy
- Vulnerability to destructive rains
- Dense population relative to area under cultivation
- Small domestic market
- Political tensions and little democracy
- Severe external threats to stability and independence
- Except in Hong Kong, the burden of large armies and heavy military spending

Tangible Assets
- For several decades, substantial economic aid from the United States for Taiwan and Korea; support for Singapore and Hong Kong from the United Kingdom
- Inducements to foreign capital including physical infrastructure, tax holidays, cheap energy, and low operational costs, coupled with safeguards (except in Hong Kong) against foreign ownership of vital national enterprises such as banking and steel
- Investment capital available from expatriots and the United States, United Kingdom, Germany, and Japan
- Financing by bank loans rather than stocks and bonds, conducive to long-term investment horizons

Intangibles:
- New societies starting afresh
- Strong work ethic[1]
- Cheap labor relative to advanced industrial countries, though higher labor costs and land rents later pressed some industries to set up cheaper facilities offshore
- Entrepreneurial spirit linked with long-term horizons
- Welcoming attitude to potentially useful innovations; quick assimilation and improvement of Western technology
- Wide support for education on all levels—elementary to postgraduate
- Many family-owned enterprises with decision flexibility and high employee loyalty
- A pliant and willing labor force, fostered by paternalistic company policies and profit-sharing bonuses; weak trade unions
- Ethnic homogeneity or, if ethnic differences existed, their suppression
- Land reform in Korea and Taiwan[2]
- Except in British Hong Kong, a strong government able to enforce rules and collect taxes
- Much autonomy for the economic sphere from politics combined with neomercantilist industrial and strategic trade policies that nursed infant industries while obtaining foreign capital and technology—except again in laissez-faire Hong Kong
- The Cold War, which led Washington to provide political-military support and cultivate dependable allies regardless of their potential as economic competitors
- A global environment in the 1970s-1980s favorable to expansion and free trade
- The Japanese model, which the NICs emulated in some but not all respects, adapting Japanese innovations and filling economic niches evacuated by Japan

---

[1]But an editorial in *Free China Review*, 3, 11 (November 1989) worried that affluence in Taiwan had weakened "traditional values . . . based upon thousands of years of extended family life in rural settings." It hoped that, with time and experience, traditional Chinese values would adapt and reemerge to fit the demands of new conditions.

[2]When I asked him in 1992 what lessons the ROC experience held for the Baltics, President Lee Teng-hui immediately cited Taiwan's land reforms (in which he played a major role). Meeting in Taipei on August 21, 1992.

Japan's 30 percent—compared to 22 percent in Sweden and 16 percent in the United States. Two-thirds of Singapore's growth resulted from its high savings rate—38 percent in 1980 and 51 percent in 1997. Hong Kong's rate for 1980 and 1997 were 30 and 31 percent, respectively, South Korea's were 24 and 34, mainland China's 35 and 40, and Japan's 31 and 30. Taiwan's rate declined from 38 percent in 1986 to 30 percent in 1990.[7]

Domestic inputs counted for far more than technological progress. The French economist Daniel Cohen concluded that, instead of being good students, the four Tigers were mediocre, "with the dunce cap going to Singapore," which registered little or no technological progress.[8] This sharp opinion is corroborated by table 9.6 below. Despite its well-trained eighth graders, Singapore had few scientists, filed few patents, and attracted few patent registrations by outsiders. In 2000 Chief Minister Lee Kuan Yew said that Singapore had achieved a great deal by orderly discipline but that it now needed to encourage creative risk taking.

From this perspective, there was no miracle in East Asia. As Martin Luther and Adam Smith observed, wealth repays each individual's efforts. The road to wealth is by savings, investment, and education. The Tigers' growth benefited from foreign aid and favorable circumstances, but depended ultimately on their own efforts.

The Tigers proved that less-developed countries could break from structural dependency. The Tigers did not rail at the world system but joined it. Each Tiger geared its production to the world market, its prices, and its regulations. Each began with an import substitution policy and gradually developed a strong export-led growth. Each acquired a dynamic conception of competitive advantage, shifting from cheap labor to rapid accommodation to foreign market demands. Each captured specialty niches in Western markets by satisfying consumer demand while maintaining competitive prices.

THE BALTIC BALANCE SHEET

How did the liabilities and assets of the Baltic states at the turn of the century compare with those of the Asian Tigers a generation before? Balts were poor relative to their northern and western neighbors. Despite the turmoil of the 1990s, however, they maintained the highest living standards in the former Soviet Union. They were the only parts of the former USSR to have a higher GDP per capita in 2000 than in 1990.

Location

In world affairs as in real estate, location counts. Baltic ports occupied the crossroads where Northern, Western, and Eastern Europe meet Russia, Belarus, and Ukraine. They could help Russian oil and Ukrainian grain make their way to the West. The Baltic states contained ports and communication infrastructures valuable to East–West trade.

In 1998 Estonia marked the 800th anniversary of Hanseatic Law in Tallinn, while Riga, for the ninth year, celebrated "Hansa Business Days." But the game had changed. For much of the second millennium ports such as Tallinn, Riga, and Klaipeda were dominated by Scandinavians, Germans, or Russians. From 1920 to

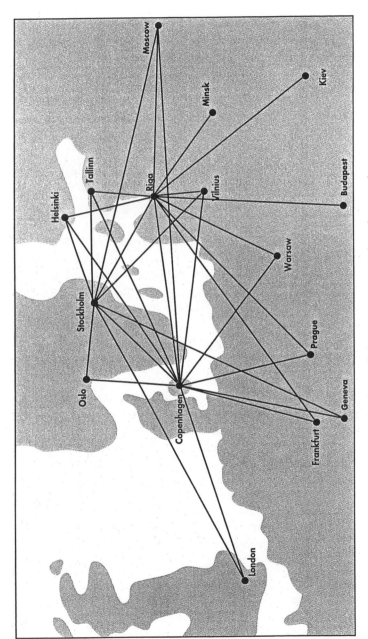

Expansion of Baltic air links, east to west and north to south

1940 and again after 1991, these ports belonged to Estonians, Latvians, and Lithuanians determined to make the most of their geographic and economic assets.

Whereas Hanseatic merchants sought and often obtained monopoly controls on Baltic trade, contemporary Balts had to compete in a world of relatively free trade. They had to win by offering better value than alternative suppliers.

Taken together, the three Baltic states had just under 8 million people in 2000, but they dealt with much larger markets. Counting the Baltic republics, Poland, and the Nordic countries, the Baltic basin provided a market of nearly 80 million people. Counting Germany and Russia, at either end of the Baltic, the market was several times larger.

Elites in Singapore and Hong Kong were well placed to mediate between mainland China and the West. Similarly, educated Balts understood the languages and cultures of Russia and the West.

Natural Resources

The Baltic republics' natural resources were meager but far richer than those of the Tigers. Balts had timber, minerals, and even some energy to spare. The region rarely encountered natural catastrophes such as earthquakes or typhoons. Unlike Hong Kong and Singapore, Balts could feed themselves and still have energy to spare. Their agricultural productivity, however, was very low in 2000 compared to that of more industrialized countries. Measured in U.S. dollars, each agricultural worker in Estonia and Lithuania added less than $3,500 per year; in Latvia it was only $2,500 per year. These levels exceeded Russia's productivity ($2,476) but were less than figures for Hungary ($4,771) and nowhere near Finland ($28,231) or the United States ($39,001).

Pollution

While Taiwan and South Korea did little about pollution, Singapore maintained an ultraclean environment. Japan showed that money, technology, and changed behaviors could improve a degraded environment.

Thanks to industrialization and militarization in Soviet times, environmental degradation in the Baltic was as bad as or worse than in East Asia. Soviet military units had often drained their leftover monthly fuel rations into the soil or water. Nuclear radiation left its mark on the Baltic as on other lands close to Chernobyl. Energy generation in the Baltic was still a dirty and sometimes risky affair.

As noted in chapter 8, enormous capital was needed to restore environmental quality in the Baltic. Even rich countries waited for someone else to do the job. But foreign aid could have paradoxical results, as at Ingalina.

Imperial Legacies

British imperialists took the lead in building the infrastructure of Singapore and Hong Kong; imperial Japan did the same for Taiwan and Korea. Similarly, tsarist Russia and the USSR developed the infrastructure and industry of the Baltic. Indeed, railroads set down by tsarist Russia facilitated the growth of Estonian, Latvian, and Lithuanian national consciousness, helping isolated country parishes to meet one another.

Though generations of Japanese rule weighed heavily on South Korea and Taiwan, Soviet imperial rule was much more onerous to the Balts than was foreign rule over Singapore, Hong Kong, Taiwan, and perhaps even Korea. Koreans and the Chinese of Taiwan kept their own languages and traditions intact; Chinese language and tradition lost ground in Singapore and Hong Kong, but this was the result of local choices more than British policy.[9] Some consequences of Soviet rule in the Baltic are listed in box 9.2.

The withdrawal of the Japanese and then the British empire left the Tigers hopeful but unsure about their futures. The shadow of communism did not stop investment or hard work in Hong Kong. Political insecurity diminished confidence in the future, but it also helped to unify each country against external threats.

Soviet controls were so extensive that in 1990—after some years of perestroika—Baltic banks had few direct links with the capitalist world but depended on the "center" (Moscow) to clear most transactions. Telephone lines with foreign countries ran through Moscow. The Estonian journal *Raduga* could not accept gifts of newsprint from Sweden without getting permission from authorities in Moscow!

Russian troops remained on Baltic soil for several years after Moscow recognized Baltic independence. It was as if Japanese troops had remained in South Korea or Taiwan after 1945, pleading that they and their families had no place to live back home! In the late 1990s, however, the threat from Russian imperialism to the Baltic republics was probably less than a PRC or North Korean threat was to some East Asian Tigers.

Balts shifted much of their external trade from Russia to the West in the 1990s, but were still heavily affected by developments in Russia. Baltic exports to Russia suffered when the rouble collapsed in 1998.[10]

Ethnic Strains

The Tigers faced fewer ethnic problems than the Baltic republics. Only Singapore had serious ethnic divisions. It used carrots, sticks, and an imposed language—English—to bring ethnic peace.

As we saw in chapter 7, Balts strove to fortify the local culture and language. They would not grant official status to Russian or adopt English or German as a common

---

Box 9.2. Costs of Soviet Rule to Baltic Fitness

- Large numbers of the most energetic Baltic citizenry killed or exiled, resulting also in "biological losses" of unborn children
- Suppression of private trade, farming, business, and banking for half a century, removing much useful know-how from living memory
- Disappearance or emigration of capital that could otherwise have been invested in the 1990s and earlier
- Indoctrination to disdain private property and expect state-fostered egalitarianism
- Policies undercutting expectations that hard work will be rewarded
- Immigration of alien workers disinterested in the local culture
- Some deracination caused by russification and sovietization
- Pollution so severe that it weakened public health and economic vitality

tongue. Pressed by the EU, Balts eased their policies toward minorities in the late 1990s and devoted more resources to helping Russian speakers to learn the official language.

Savings, Consumption, and Trade

Balts in the late 1990s saved at much lower rates than the Tigers or even Sweden. As we see in table 9.3, government consumption of resources was much higher than in Singapore or Japan, but less than in Sweden. Private consumption was much higher than in Singapore or Sweden, and compared with Japan and U.S. levels. On the other hand, Balts exported a far larger percentage of their goods and services than most of the other states surveyed. In doing so, they incurred a trade deficit of 10 percent or higher.[11] In 1980, however, even Singapore ran a trade deficit of 9 percent, while Sweden ran a deficit of 2 percent.

In the 1990s Balts managed to separate themselves from the unstable rouble zone. The Baltic states were the only former Soviet republics to achieve financial stability, as they kept their currencies at parity with Western currencies. Finland, Scandinavia, and Germany replaced Russia as the Balts' major trading partners. Balts removed the most egregious *dependencia* relationships of the Soviet imperial system.

But when the German and Scandinavian economies became sluggish and when Russia's nose-dived in 1998, Baltic economic growth slowed and budget deficits soared. At first the Baltic economies were little affected by Russia's August 1998 economic and financial tailspin, because Balts had shifted much of their trade westward.[12] When Russia's economic woes continued, however, Balts also suffered—especially in Lithuania, which depended far more on trade with Russia than did Estonia or Latvia.[13] A fourth of all Lithuanian meat and milk production went to Russia in the late 1990s. But Lithuania suspended meat and dairy exports to Russia on September 1, 1998, because consumers there could not pay.[14] As Russia's financial crisis unfurled, Latvian commercial banks announced that they had invested some $120 million in Russia—more than did their Estonian or Lithuanian counterparts. Latvia's trade imbalance doubled in 1998–1999.

How Ready Were the Balts for the EU?

As the twenty-first century began, the three Baltic republics were among a dozen or more states seeking admission to the EU. If EU membership increased, how could it make decisions? Could—should—the EU accept states whose economies were far less advanced than the existing members? Admitting all the new applicants would expand the EU's area and population by about one-third but add only 10 percent to its GDP. Some applicant countries—the Czech Republic, Cyprus, Estonia, Hungary, Poland, and Slovenia—seemed better prepared than others, like Bulgaria, Latvia, Lithuania, Malta, Romania, and Slovakia. Some EU officials said the first group should be admitted first and the others later. Some EU representatives said each country should be admitted whenever it qualified.

Table 9.4 permits us to compare economic and social development in the Baltic and other major applicant countries with the EU averages in 1999. Purchasing power

Table 9.3
Structure of Demand as a Percent of GDP: The Baltic States and Others, 1990–1999

Economy	Private consumption		General government consumption		Gross domestic investment		Gross domestic saving		Export of goods and services		Trade balance	
	1990	1999	1990	1999	1990	1999	1990	1999	1990	1999	1990	1999
Estonia	62	64	16	19	30	28	22	17	60	83	−8	−11
Latvia	53	68	9	22	40	20	39	10	48	44	−1	−10
Lithuania	57	63	19	25	33	24	24	12	52	47	−9	−12
Singapore	46	39	10	10	37	33	44	52	202	n.a.	7	19
Sweden	51	53	27	26	21	14	22	21	30	44	0	7
Russia	49	57	21	14	30	14	30	29	18	48	0	15
Japan (1980–1997)	58	60	9	10	32	29	33	30	11	11	+1	+1
USA	67	68	18	15	17	19	15	17	10	12	−1	

SOURCE: *World Bank, World Development Report, 2000/2001* (New York: Oxford University Press, 2000), table 13.

Table 9.4
Economic and Social Indicators for EU Applicants, 1999–2000

Economy	Population (millions)	Total GDP in euros (billions)	GDP per capita at PPP in euros (thousands)	GDP per capita as % of EU average	Average GDP % growth 1995–2000	Higher education outlays as % of GDP	Telephones per 100 people	Life expectancy at birth
Estonia	1.4	4.6	7,048	34.1	4.3	7.3	34.3	70.5
Latvia	2.4	6.2	5,946	28.8	3.7	6.5	38.3	70.3
Lithuania	3.7	9.8	5,975	28.9	2.7	5.6	30.0	71.4
Bulgaria	8.3	11.6	4,871	23.6	−1.7	3.3	32.9	71.1
Czech Republic	10.3	49.2	11,830	57.3	0.6	5.4	36.4	69.9
Hungary	10.1	46.2	10,384	50.3	4.0	4.7	30.4	69.3
Poland	38.7	145.4	8,061	39.0	5.4	5.2	22.8	70.2
Romania	22.4	32.3	5,512	26.7	−2.2	3.6	16.7	68.5
Slovakia	5.4	17.5	9,402	45.5	4.2	4.9	28.6	70.2
Slovenia	2.0	18.6	14,492	70.2	4.0	5.8	36.4	69.4
EU total/average	375.8	8,092.8	20,650	100.0	4.0	5.1	56.6	71.4

SOURCE: "EU Integration," *Financial Times*, October 24, 2000.

parity in Estonia was only 34 percent of the EU average; in Latvia and in Lithuania it was still less—29 percent. But Poland's PPP was 39 percent—not much higher than Estonia's. Even the Czech Republic's PPP was only 57 percent of the EU average. In Eastern Europe, Slovenia did best at 70 percent.

The average GDP growth rates in Estonia and Latvia approximated the EU average in the late 1990s, while Lithuania lagged.[15] Baltic spending on higher education exceeded the EU average. Life expectancy in the Baltic states nearly matched the EU average. Balts had far fewer telephones than did EU members, but that discrepancy could be remedied without major difficulty. As we saw in chapter 6, computer use in Estonia rivaled rates in France and Germany.

In 1992 Estonia tied its currency to the German mark but planned to switch to the euro upon accession to EU. Lithuania's currency board in 1994 fixed the exchange rate at four litas to the dollar. By 2000, however, Vilnius expected soon to transfer the lita's peg to the euro.

Big Government vs. Economic Freedom

Was government too big in the Baltic countries to succeed in the First World's free markets? Table 9.5 shows that government subsidies in the three Baltic countries were more than four times higher than in Singapore, but lower than in Sweden or the United States.

The corporate tax rate in the Baltic republics was about the same as in Singapore and Sweden—much lower than in Russia, Japan, or the United States—but in 1999 Estonia planned to eliminate corporate taxes altogether.

The average tax burden in the EU rose from 28 percent of GDP in 1965 to 34 percent in 1973 and 42 percent in 1996—in tandem with reduced GDP growth. The burden of taxation in the post-Communist countries was somewhat less than the EU average. In

Table 9.5
Government Subsidies, Credit Ranking, and Corporate Taxes

Economy	Government subsidies and other current transfers % of total expenditures		Institutional investor credit rating (in March)		Highest corporate tax rate
	1990	1997	1999	2000	1999
Estonia	73	47	38.9	49.4	26
Latvia	59	61	34.0	43.4	25
Lithuania	67	41	n.a.	40.8	29
Singapore	12	8	82.9	80.4	26
Sweden	72	71	77.1	83.9	28
Russia	49	n.a.	20.0	19.6	35
Japan	50	n.a.	86.5	86.9	35
USA	50	60	92.6	92.9	35

SOURCE: World Bank, *World Development Report, 2000/2001* (New York: Oxford University Press, 2000), table 17; ibid., *1998/99,* table 17.

1996 only Poland matched the EU rate; Hungary and the Czech Republic reached 40 percent, Estonia 37 percent. Lithuania rose to 34 percent in 1998. Indirect taxes such as value-added played a much greater role in Lithuania than in the EU, where direct taxes on incomes were more important—making it easier to impose progressive rates on higher incomes. But tax evasion was widespread in Lithuania and Latvia, undermining faith in government and limiting government's ability to function.

Some observers suggested that Estonia could teach the EU how to cut red tape. Tariffs in Latvia averaged just under 1 percent; in Lithuania they averaged just over 1 percent. But Estonia's tariffs were so low in 2000 that, if admitted to the EU, it would have to raise them on more than ten thousand items against non-EU countries—thus increasing food prices for Estonians. It would also have to favor EU producers of coal and steel, forgoing cheaper suppliers outside the EU.

Estonia abolished some corporate income taxes on January 1, 2000, and compensated by placing tariffs on imports from non-EU countries. In 1998 more than half the price of gasoline in Estonia went to taxes. Seeking both revenue and conservation, the Estonian government in 1998 raised taxes about 10 percent, so that one gallon cost slightly more than in the United States. The government wanted to keep raising taxes until the price of gasoline reached Swedish or Finnish levels.

Thanks to Estonia's very low tariffs and its favorable climate for investors, it placed 14th in the world among 161 countries on the Index of Economic Freedom compiled in 2000 by the Heritage Foundation—this was up from 18th in 1998. Latvia advanced to 46th from 61st in 1998, Lithauania rose to 42d from 72d, and Russia fell from 106th to 127th. The foundation rated all three Baltic economies as "mostly free" and Russia's as "mostly unfree." Less than half the world's economies were judged free or mostly free.[16]

The Baltic economies got much lower credit ratings than the advanced industrial economies. But Estonia in 1998 received foreign direct investment (FDI) amounting to $407 per capita—a total of $554 million—more than any other Central or Eastern European country on a per capita basis.[17] Within the region, Poland received the largest FDI in 1998—a total of $5.1 million. On a per capita basis, Lithuania placed second, with $251 in foreign investment; Czechoslovakia was third with $247. In 1997 the top three were Latvia, Hungary, and Estonia.[18] Nordic countries such as Sweden and Finland, however, attracted much larger FDI than the economies of any states formerly in the Soviet sphere.[19]

The reborn Baltic republics offered investors cheap, skilled labor, with immediate export potential to Northern and Eastern Europe, Germany, and Russia. They became magnets for FDI, expanded financial and banking services, and bolt-on links joining Nordic and Western European producers with Baltic firms. Hansa Investments in 1999 predicted that 80 percent of the leading companies in the Baltics would soon be owned by Western corporations or have a Western corporation as a strategic partner.[20]

Unlike the EU, the three Baltic republics charged no import taxes on new cars. Some BMW models cost one-fourth less in Latvia than in Germany. The Russian Lada and German Volkswagen sold the most cars in the Baltics in 1999, but Asian brands—Honda, Toyota, Hyundai, and others—took one-third of the Baltic market, compared to only 14 percent in Western Europe. The only indigenous auto manufacturer in the Baltics, RAF of Latvia, shut down in 1997. But Scania buses were assembled in Tartu from parts made in Sweden and Switzerland. And Estonian parts manufacturer Norma supplied General Motors Opel in Europe as well as Russian auto makers.

Baltic proximity to Russia could encourage or deter foreign investment in the Baltic republics. Foreigners might see the Baltic lands as providing safe passages for the turbulent economies of Russia, Belarus, and Ukraine. But if chaos prevailed in the East, foreign investors might shy away from the Baltic region as well.

Crime and corruption in the Baltic lands could also scare off foreigners and give some Russians levers of influence. Politicians and public officials in Latvia were perceived in the late 1990s as the most corrupt in Europe except for Russia. The Corruption Perceptions Index of Transparency International in 2000 rated Finnish and Danish officials the most honest in the world. Estonia ranked as 27th most honest in the world; Lithuania placed 43d, tied with Malawi and Poland; Latvia ranked 52d, tied with Belarus, China, Ghana, Senegal, and Slovakia, though well ahead of Russia, which was 82d. But each Baltic country was rated a few notches higher (cleaner) than in previous years, while Russia was lower (more corrupt).[21]

Technology

Finally, table 9.6 helps us compare Baltic strengths in technology with those of distant Singapore, nearby Sweden, and three large centers of research and development—Russia, Japan, and the United States. Estonia and Lithuania had nearly as many scientists and engineers per capita as Singapore, though they had far less than Sweden. Latvia, however, had only half as many as Estonia or Lithuania. The high-tech component of Baltic exports was comparatively low. Trying to protect their future interests, however, nonresidents applied for nearly as many patents in each Baltic country as nonresidents in Singapore.

Table 9.6
Science and Technology Indicators

Economy	Scientists and engineers in R&D per million people 1987–1997	High technology exports as % of manufacturing exports in 1998	Number of patent applications filed by residents 1997	Number of patent applications filed by nonresidents 1997
Estonia	2,017	9	18	26,626
Latvia	1,049	4	163	26,860
Lithuania	2,028	3	125	26,673
Singapore	2,318	59	8,188	29,467
Sweden	3,826	20	7,893	107,107
Russia	3,587	12	15,277	32,943
Japan	4,909	26	351,487	66,487
USA	3,676	33	125,808	110,884

SOURCE: World Bank, *World Development Report, 2000/2001* (New York: Oxford University Press, 2000, table 19.

Peripheral Adjuncts, Ferrymen, or Participants in the Grand Game?

What roles would the Baltic states play in Europe's economic future? First, they could be peripheral adjuncts to the strong economies of Western and Northern Europe—production sites using cheap labor and forest products to serve Europe's core economies. Second, they could serve as "ferrymen" for trade between Europe and Russia. Third, they could be participants in the Grand Game of globally networked creation of wealth and knowledge. This third role would require them to harness brain power and other human resources to geographical assets.

Fifty years of Soviet domination did not prepare the Baltic economies for an information-based, interlinked global economy. Even Estonia, the fastest-moving Baltic economy, faced major obstacles to joining the Grand Game. Soviet secrecy kept even the Baltic ports and shipping industries from interacting freely with global markets. The Soviets built few large-scale enterprises in Estonia except in the energy sector and fishing. With independence, however, Estonians moved quickly to fill poorly developed sectors such as banking, commerce, services, seaports, transit, and tourism.

By the end of the 1990s Estonia was a leading candidate for EU membership, but the country's economy and exports did not yet tap its intellectual strengths. And the low level of research funding did not prepare it well for the future. Estonia's government did not foster the kinds of industrial policies that benefited Japan, the Asian Tigers, and the United States (government support for innovations from hybrid corn to jumbo jets and the Internet).[22] Aggravating these problems, Estonian firms were loath to cooperate with each other in technology or marketing.

Foreign enterprises used Estonia to produce—not to develop new goods. Still, an echo of the Asian Tigers could be seen in Estonia as Elcoteq, a leading Finnish-based provider of electronics manufacturing services (for example, for mobile telephone makers Nokia and Ericsson), set up plants there. Concerned to obtain more college graduates among its workers, Elcoteq signed cooperation agreements in 2000 with the Tallinn Technological University and with Tartu University. Elcoteq employees would explain industry standards to both professors and students. Estonia offered outside ventures not just low wages but diligent workers and well-trained engineers and researchers.[23]

Latvia and Lithuania were less prepared than Estonia for the Grand Game. The large size of enterprises erected by Soviet planners in Latvia added to the country's difficulties in making the transition to market-based enterprises. Still, by 1998 two-thirds of all jobs in Latvia were in the private sector. There were fourteen thousand sole proprietorships. Strikes were rare. The dominant political parties shared a liberal, market orientation. But except for IT workers, scientists, and some business people, few Latvians plugged into and benefited from cross-border economic ties. Well-educated young people looked forward to taking part in the world economy, but most Latvians did not.[24]

In 2000 Lithuania hoped soon to join Estonia and Latvia in the World Trade Organization, but sought to protect the country's large agricultural sector. By September 2000 Vilnius had negotiated understandings with the large food exporters—the United States, Australia, and New Zealand—but still faced Canadian demands to lower tariffs on pork imports.

The government played a bigger role in Lithuania's economy than in Estonia or

Latvia. The Lithuanian government's expansionist fiscal policy promoted wage increases at a rate three times higher than GDP growth.[25] Still, when asked in 1998 what factors contributed most to productivity, Lithuanian entrepreneurs replied that information about markets and new technology were more important than state commissions or capital investment. The *Lithuanian HDR 1999* concluded that government should reform economic incentives so that firms invested more in human than in physical capital.

THE OUTLOOK

To sum up this discussion, box 9.3 compares Tiger assets and liabilities in the 1970s and 1980s with Baltic conditions at the turn of the century. A plus sign means the Balts were better off; a minus sign means they were worse; an equal sign about the same as the Tigers. In many domains, we must place a question mark where the answer is inconclusive.

The Tigers showed that self-reliance combined with a favorable international climate could help small nations to achieve a prosperous independence. Like the Tigers, the Baltic republics faced a large and sometimes threatening neighbor; like the Tigers, they possessed valuable ports and looked out to the sea and the world at large. Baltic acceptance in the United Nations and in regional institutions gave them a surer global footing than the Tigers enjoyed before their takeoff.

The overall picture is that Baltic prospects in 2000 looked no worse—and were probably better—than the Tigers' just before their rapid climb to prosperity. Balts' tangible assets in 2000 appeared superior to those of the Tigers three decades before. If Balts used their potential as well as the East Asians, they too could prosper.

The big questions concerned intangible qualities. Balts—especially Latvians and Estonians—were once noted for their Protestant work ethic. But fifty years of Soviet rule probably weakened the know-how, work habits, and institutions needed for development. Could Balts put aside the distrust and assumptions of zero-sum struggle learned in Soviet times to make development an enterprise of mutual gain? Would Balts—like East Asians—have sufficient determination to hold fast, labor, create, save, and invest for the long haul? Would they think in optimistic terms ("If Finland can do it, so can we!") or pessimistically ("We'll never catch up")?

Neither East Asia nor Scandinavia presented Balts with a simple formula for success. There were few clear-cut "lessons." In Singapore government played a large role in development; in Hong Kong it contributed very little, while Taiwan and South Korea ranged between these poles.

If Balts perceived useful lessons abroad, those lessons would have to be adapted to the circumstances of each Baltic country. Moving away from Soviet central planning, each republic would have to find its golden mean between rugged individualism and state direction.

If Balts tried to learn from others' experiences, negative lessons were more evident than positive. Could Balts avoid the behaviors that kept other societies from becoming prosperous democracies: The oligarchy and corruption of Russia? The ethnic, clan, and border wars of Georgia, Armenia, and Azerbaijan (often aggravated by Russian interventions)? The crony capitalism of Indonesia and Thailand? Authoritarian rule as

Box 9.3. Comparing Tiger and Baltic Assets and Liabilities

The 1970s–1980s

Tiger Liabilities
- Poor resource base
- Vulnerability to weather
- Dense population
- Small domestic markets
- External threats

- Little democracy
- Heavy defense burdens

Tiger Tangible Assets
- Location/ports
- Foreign aid
- Inducements to foreign capital
- Investment from outside
- Financing by bank loans

Tiger Intangibles
- Fresh start
- Strong work ethic
- High saving and investment
- Cheap labor
- Much autonomy for the economic sphere from politics
- Entrepreneurial spirit
- Ability to meet demands of world markets
- Support for education
- Family-owned enterprises
- A pliant and willing labor force
- Ethnic homogeneity
- Land reform
- Strong government
- Industrial/strategic trade policy

- External political-military support
- Japanese model to emulate

- Global free trade environment

The 1990s

Baltic Pluses and Minuses
- + Better but badly polluted resources
- + More stable weather
- + Population not so dense
- − Even smaller markets
- − External threats and a potential Fifth Column
- + More democracy
- + Light burden but almost no defense capacity

Baltic Pluses and Minuses
- = Equally good location/ports
- − Less
- − Less, laws in flux
- − Less
- − Little

Baltic Pluses and Minuses
- = Similar
- ? Time will tell
- − Less
- = Cheap relative to EU
- = Estonian free market model leading the way
- ? Time will tell
- ? Time will tell
- = Similar
- − Not strong
- − Not pliant
- − Deep divisions
- − In flux
- − Weaker with deep factions
- − Weaker but this is a plus if neomercantilism is harmful
- − Weaker
- − No comparable model in Eastern Europe
- − Balts faced myriad EU restrictions and economic warfare waged by Russia

in Malaysia and Singapore? The public health failures sweeping not just Africa but Russia?

Could Balts avoid the lingering problems of developed First World countries: The paralyzing taxes of Sweden and other welfare states? The racial intolerance of many Germans? The sometimes "irrational exuberance" of the U.S. stock market? The widening income gaps in many countries (China and Russia as well as the United States)? Drug addiction and sedentary lifestyles of people too depressed or too comfortable to enjoy a walk in the park? The smog of places more devoted to production and today's profits than conservation?

Differences of time and place make comparisons of other parts of the world with the Baltic precarious. Serendipity and synergy could upset all predictions. Still, planet earth at the onset of another century seemed to be a place where mice could roar if not intimidated by dragons or bears.

Caption for Chapter 9 Photo: Shifting toward market economics in the 1990s, Baltic societies acquired ATM machines and modems that helped many people become "wired" to the world. In Riga's Central Market, housed in former Zeppelin hangers, farmers still sold goods in the late 1990s much as they did in Soviet times.

NOTES

1. One would think that surface areas would be well known and relatively stable, but the *World Development Report* published in 2000 shows much larger surface areas for many countries than did the report issued in 1999. For example, Germany appears to have increased from 349,000 to 367,000 square kilometers and Estonia from 42,000 to 45,000 square kilometers.

2. See Transparency International, "The 2000 Corruption Perceptions Index," at <http://www.transparency.org/documents/cpi/2000/cpi2000.html>

3. In 1991 Russia's average labor productivity was 30 percent of U.S. levels; by 1997 this figure dropped to 19 percent. On the deleterious effects of subsidies, tax breaks, and favoritism, see "Survival of the Fattest," *Financial Times,* October 19, 1999.

4. The survey placed Italian media giant L'Espresso as best performing. Two French firms and one UK firm placed in the top ten. One Norwegian and one Belgian firm did well in 1999. No German company placed high. See "European Performance League," *Financial Times,* June 23, 2000.

5. Survey of Finland, *Financial Times,* July 10, 2000.

6. *Handbook of Economic Statistics, 1991: A Reference Aid* (Washington: Central Intelligence Agency, 1991), p. 144.

7. Daniel Cohen, *The Wealth of the World and the Poverty of Nations* (Cambridge, Mass.: MIT Press, 1998), p. 24; World Bank, *World Development Report 1998/99* (New York: Oxford University Press, 1998), table 13; report by Jung Chuen-wen summarized in "Savings Drop Worries Economist," *Free China Journal,* November 29, 1991, p. 8.

8. Cohen, *Wealth of the World,* p. 23.

9. Korea under Japanese rule bore a greater resemblance to the Baltic. The Japanese forced many Koreans to take Japanese names. Japanese rule in Taiwan was less harsh and was remembered as having positive as well as negative features. In the 1990s some professors at Taiwan universities—age 60 and up—still told jokes among themselves in Japanese. Balts might curse but seldom joke in Russian.

10. See the special issue, "Baltic Economies in Transition," *Journal of Baltic Studies* 31 (summer 2000).

11. Estonia benefited initially from the receipt of gold stocks held by Western governments since 1940 and then by the transshipment of base metals and metal products from Russia to Scandinavia. But these initial advantages lapsed and Estonia gradually developed its own assets for economic takeoff and steady growth. Base metals made up 8 percent of Estonian exports in 1994 and 6.8 percent in 1995. See Arvo Kuddo, "Macroeconomic Policy and Finan-

cial Stability in Estonia" (Washington, D.C.: World Bank, unpublished paper, 1996), appendix 8.

12. Lithuanian prime minister Gediminas Vagnorius told journalists on August 26, 1998, that his government had begun to prepare for possible upheavals in the Russian financial market many months before. He claimed on August 1—before the Russian financial crisis broke— that Lithuania's gold and foreign-currency reserves exceeded its total foreign indebtedness— $1.6 billion versus $1 billion.

13. From January to April 1998 trade with Russia accounted for 22 percent of Lithuanian exports and 24.4 percent of Lithuanian imports; 17.4 percent of Latvian exports and 13.6 percent of Latvian imports; and 8.3 percent of Estonian exports and 8.5 percent of Estonian imports. Michael Wyzan, "Lithuania Finds Maintaining Fixed Exchange Rate Increasingly Difficult," *RFE/RL Newsline 169,* September 2, 1998.

Lithuania's transport industry—rail, road, air, and port traffic—accounted for 7 percent of the country's GDP and 4–5 percent of employment before August 1998. The industry profited from shipping Western goods to Russia. After the August crisis, Lithuanian railroads and ports relied on exporting Russian raw materials—against strong competition from the other two Baltic countries. Lithuania's main port, Klaipeda, loaded 7 percent fewer goods in 1998 than in 1997. Indexes for rail transport and air cargo were down by one-fifth or more in 1999 compared to 1998.

14. When Russian naval commanders in Kaliningrad warned in August 1998 that their forces had food for only forty days, however, Seimas chairman Landsbergis called for humanitarian relief for the Russian navy, coordinated with Poland and the EU. Estonia, however, could not help because heavy rains ruined crops that year.

15. Economic growth rates varied: Estonia's GDP advanced at 4 percent in 1996, 11 percent in 1997, and 4 percent in 1998. For Latvia, the rates were 3, 9, and 4 percent and for Lithuania they were 5, 7, and 5 percent. Poland was a steady performer, with 6, 7, and 5 percent growth. Bulgaria did worse, with years of minus growth.

16. <http://www.heritage.org/index/>

17. Estonians also invested heavily abroad. See statistics in *Baltic Times,* May 28–June 3, 1998, p. 12.

18. Kairi Kurm, "U.N.: Estonia most attractive to investors," *Baltic Times,* October 7–13, 1999, pp. 9–10.

19. The largest investments in Estonia in 1998 came from Finland and Sweden and went to Hansapank, Uhispank, and the telecommunications sector. Privatization of the Estonian Railways; the power company Eesti Energia; and Tallinna Vesi, the water utility, were expected to attract large investments in the early twenty-first century.

20. "Baltic Sea Region," special section, *Financial Times,* June 11, 1999; see also "Central and Eastern Europe," *Financial Times,* October 24, 2000.

21. <http://www.transparency.org/documents/cpi/2000/cpi2000.html>

22. Estonia's urban intellectuals favored individual family farms more than did most farmers. Unlike many in EU governments, the liberals governing post-Communist Estonia did not subsidize agriculture. While white-collar types in Tallinn and Tartu dreamed of networking, Estonia's post-Communist agrarian reforms and restitution of property to pre-Communist owners foundered. In the late 1990s only ten thousand Estonians worked on profit-making farms, while most farmers depended on subsistence farming or welfare. Skilled labor, capital, and a strong work ethic were in short supply. With production and incomes down, many farmers moved to cities.

23. In August 2000 the United States eased controls on computer exports to Estonia. As regards such controls, Estonia became the only former Soviet republic to advance from tier

three to tier two—a domain that included most of Latin America and Africa plus South Korea and Slovenia. The change would make it easier for large firms such as Hansapank and other Estonian banks to acquire advanced IT infrastructure.

24. Contradictions abounded. As the *Latvia Human Development Report 1999* noted, many Latvians still displayed collectivist behavior. Many expected government to take care of them; many lacked enterprise and showed a poor work ethic. Two-thirds of the population approved of a market economy free from state intervention, but more than half thought the emerging system was developing too slowly and was too unfair and too corrupt. More than half thought the government should intervene to decrease income disparities. Many farmers wanted protectionist measures. Despite economic growth in the late 1990s, half the Latvian population deemed their financial position bad or very bad. Per capita incomes in Latvia and Lithuania were among the lowest of countries being considered for EU membership—not one-third the EU average. Income inequality increased in the late 1990s. Latvia's region of Latgale, bordering Russia and Belarus, was one of the poorest in Europe. Latvians, like other Europeans, did not welcome immigrants. Nearly half of all Latvians wanted sharp limits on immigration. Many did not want to live near immigrants and guest-workers.

25. Household consumption accounted for 65 percent of overall expenditures in Lithuania, 64 percent in Latvia, 60 percent in Estonia, and just 51 percent in Slovakia.

10

Russia: Threat or Partner?

Walter C. Clemens Jr.

The most pressing threats to Baltic security in the 1990s arose from social and economic problems *within* each republic. Quite unlike earlier times, Balts faced no military threat from the west or the south. The only perceptible danger came from the east—from Russia.

WHO OR WHAT IS "RUSSIA"? COMPLEXITY IN RUSSIAN POLITICS

The post-Soviet Russian Federation (RF) was no monolith. There was no unified Russian policy rationally calculated by "Moscow" to maximize Russian interests in the Baltic region or anywhere else. The end of one-party hegemony meant that Russian behavior, at home and abroad, was shaped by many individuals and groups. Three main foreign policy lines were championed by different coalitions:

Atlanticist-internationalism: Accommodate the West and join the world of democratic, market economies. This orientation was favored, at least for a time, by Westernizing democrats in the Foreign Ministry, in some think tanks, and in some business circles. There were even Westernizing nationalists.[1]

Great powerism: Restore Russia as a strong state. This approach was backed by statists (known in Russian as *derzhavniki,* from *derzhava,* "state"), by nativists upholding the superiority of Russian ways, and by some past or present Communists.

Some statists focused on internal reconstruction of Russian power; others sought a strong influence for Russia in the former Soviet republics bordering the RF; still others wanted to recover Russia's former role on the world scene.

Derzhavniki differed on how much force to use in achieving their goals. Vladimir Putin might begin his presidency as a moderate statist focused on reconstruction but become more expansive and more aggressive if the correlation of forces tilted toward Russia. Thus, reconstruction could lead to expansionism. Stalin, we recall, rebuilt the economy and prepared the country for war in the 1920s–1930s and expanded its domain when circumstances permitted.

Neoimperialism: Reintegrate the lost empire, using economic, political, and other means. This line won support from some realists, Eurasianists, and Communists stressing Russia's place in Asia as well as Europe. Great powerism could become imperialism.

No single orientation dominated RF policy in the 1990s. There was often more cacophony than rational harmony. Russia could follow an Atlanticist course toward the United States *and* a great power or neoimperialist policy toward the *pribaltika*. As in U.S. policy toward Castro's Cuba, factions pushed and pulled, petulance and other emotions swelled, misinformation and bias distorted analysis, and some fumed that a former colony had gone over to the other side.

Consider the number and diversity of actors shaping Russian policy toward the Baltic:

The Kremlin. Many of the younger technocrats who served as ministers or advisers to President Boris Yeltsin felt no nostalgia for the Russian empire and wanted to focus on the country's domestic problems. Thus, Foreign Minister Andrei Kozyrev sought ways for Russia to join the West. By 1993, however, he began to compromise with hard-liners. From that time on, he and other Russian foreign ministers, such as Evgenii Primakov, gave priority to helping Russia recover its role as a great power.

Yeltsin was the only lasting fixture in the Kremlin in the 1990s. Prime ministers came and went at the whim of an ailing, mercurial president—five PMs served in just seventeen months in 1998–1999. Yeltsin's hand-picked successor, V. V. Putin, elected president in 2000, called for rebuilding Russia's power, but he also sought better ties with the West, beginning with trade and investment. Having worked in East Germany and then in St. Petersburg, Putin could be expected to have active concerns in the *pribaltika*. Indeed, Putin walked out of an EU seminar held in Hamburg in March 1994 when Estonian President Meri, with whom Putin was well acquainted, spoke of Russian troops as "occupiers"—an act that elicited a commendation by the RF Foreign Ministry.[2]

Russia did not keep its word even with a superpower: On November 3, 2000, the RF Foreign Minister informed the U.S. secretary of state that Moscow would not comply with the 1995 Gore-Chernomyrdin accord by which the RF pledged not to supply Iran with sophisticated weapons after 1999. If the Kremlin casually shredded a commitment to Washington, how long would it honor promises to lesser powers?

Parliament. The Russian parliament includes the lower house, the State Duma, and the upper house, the Federation Council. The Communist Party of the Russian Federation and the ultranationalist Liberal Democratic Party of Russia, led by Vladimir Zhirinovskii, finished first and second in the 1995 Duma elections. Both groups opposed President Yeltsin and the system he represented, but their rhetoric and agitation pushed Yeltsin, whatever his personal preferences, away from Atlanticism toward a blend of great powerism and some neoimperialism.

In the December 1999 Duma elections the Communists again won a plurality, while the Zhirinovskii bloc did poorly but cleared the 5 percent threshold needed for representation.

The newly rich commercial oligarchs. While most of this group focused more on *biznes* than empire, Oligarch Boris Berezovskii benefited from close ties with the

Yeltsin family, which in turn benefited from Berezovskii's economic ties and influence on the media. Elected to the Duma in 1999, he gained immunity from prosecution for alleged crimes.

The energy industrial complex. The many privatized, vertically integrated companies shipping oil and gas to the Baltic and other foreign countries depended on the Kremlin for favors, and had to observe quotas and prices set by the center. Viktor Chernomyrdin, the longest-serving PM under Yeltsin, had headed the Soviet oil and gas ministry under Soviet president Mikhail Gorbachev and then the RF fuel and energy industry under Yeltsin. A reputed billionaire, Chernomyrdin had a personal financial stake in the energy industry. If Yeltsin or Chernomyrdin told LUKoil to close the spigot or use a Finnish port, it could hardly say *nyet*. And yet, as we saw in chapter 8, when LUKoil threatened to leave Lithuania without crude, its rival Yukos stepped in.

Military elites. All top military officers in the 1990s were holdovers from Soviet times, sensitive to the Baltic region's strategic importance and Kaliningrad's vulnerability. In the early 1990s, however, their immediate problem was housing for officers and troops withdrawn from East Germany and the Baltic. Embarrassed by their poor showing in the first Chechen war, 1994–1996, and by other developments, many Russian officers joined the great power if not the neoimperialist camp in the late 1990s.

Criminal gangs. Members of organized crime were often aligned with or protected by Russian politicians. What they pillaged in Russia could be shipped through the Baltic states to the world beyond. The RF Ministry of Internal Affairs acknowledged in 1993 that four hundred banks in Russia were then controlled by organized crime.

Secret service agents. Russian operatives, including some still in the Baltics, may have had a role in the collapse of several Baltic banks and in smuggling. Their influence might increase in the early twenty-first century as President Putin brought many former associates from the Soviet and post-Soviet security services into his administration. (Reflecting on his work in divided Germany, Putin shed light on how the Soviets did or did not develop technology. KGB operatives might pay several million dollars for information about an important scientific discovery that would cost the USSR billions of dollars to develop on its own. Presented with this information, the "Center" would send the operatives "kisses" and recommend them for medals. "But then they wouldn't use the intelligence. They would not even try. The technical level of our industry simply didn't allow for it.")[3]

The liberal intelligentsia. In many places—think tanks, business, ministries, even the Duma—were moderate politicians and analysts who understood Baltic anxieties and believed that the best interests of Russia and the Balts required cooperation, not dictates.[4] Some of these people changed their opinions or muted their voices as tensions mounted between an expanding NATO and Russia. All but a few liberals were silent when Russia decimated Chechnya in 1999.

The Russian public. Most Russians in the 1990s focused on relieving their material problems, but their sense of political identity was fractured by the demise of the USSR. Who or what were Russians without their empire? In the 1999 Duma elections fewer than one in ten Russians voted for Iablako, the only party clearly committed to democracy, a free market not dominated by oligarchs, and peace in Chechnya. Injured pride and frustration led many Russians to scapegoat outsiders. Anti-Americanism nourished neoimperialism. Two-thirds of Russians polled in late 1999 said that Stalin's rule did more good than ill for the country or had equally good and bad consequences. Many children in Moscow secondary schools surveyed in 2000 opined that the tsarist or Soviet borders needed to be restored.

RUSSIAN PRESSURES ON THE BALTIC REPUBLICS

The Russian Federation in the 1990s had problems far more pressing than any challenge from the *pribaltika*. Order gave way to chaos. The economy sank. Tuberculosis and other public health problems became acute. Male life expectancy fell by years. RF troops struggled against insurgents in Central Asia and the Caucasus. Criminal gangs sucked blood from the economy and society. Corruption bounced from Moscow to Geneva to the Bank of New York and ricocheted back to Moscow.

If only to concentrate on larger issues, post-Soviet Russia might have sought to normalize relations with the Baltic republics. But it did not. Beginning in 1992, as we saw in chapter 8, Russians manipulated the oil spigot to shape Baltic behavior, and tried to limit Russian use of Baltic ports. Economic warfare was part of a larger syndrome: the Kremlin and the Duma pursued a great power or a neoimperialist line on four sets of issues:

- Russia's claims in the Baltic countries
- Former Soviet forces still stationed in the region
- Definition of borders
- Baltic efforts to join NATO

Russian Claims in the "Near Abroad"

The Soviet State Council recognized the independence of Estonia, Latvia, and Lithuania on September 6, 1991. In December 1991 the USSR disappeared. But the new Russian Federation did not renounce its imperial heritage.

Even before the breakup of the USSR, some Russians lamented the fate of "children of Russia"—kinspeople living in non-Russian republics. A conservative literary critic published a book in 1990 entitled *We Are All Children of Russia*. In 1991 a literary periodical introduced a series on "the children of Russia" by affirming: "We are all your children, Russia, both those of us living on the land of our ancestors, and those living beyond her borders. We have the same roots. We have had the same fate. And now there is pain, desperation, anxiety." If, as numerous observers hold, many Russians partake in a moral culture of masochism, some Russians might even enjoy dwelling on the suffering—real or imagined—of those living detached from the motherland.

Boris Yeltsin's Kremlin maintained that the Federation was the legal successor to the USSR. Thus, the RF took the USSR's seat at the United Nations and accepted most of the arms control and other treaty obligations of the former Soviet regime.

Yeltsin's Kremlin and the RF parliament agreed that the RF has special interests, rights, and duties in the "near abroad"—the erstwhile border republics of the USSR. This posture permitted the RF to play the card of human rights and the rights of "compatriots" (*sootechestvenniki*) living in the former border republics, including the *pribaltika*. This "Karaganov doctrine" (named for Sergei Karaganov, an early adviser to Yeltsin) could justify Russian intervention in the internal affairs of other countries. The Karaganov thesis looked like a descendant of the 1968 Brezhnev doctrine, which claimed that the interests of the "socialist commonwealth" outweighed those of national sovereignty, thereby entitling the USSR and its allies to invade Czechoslovakia.

RF authorities estimated that there were nearly 45 to 50 million compatriots abroad—with 25 to 27 million living in the CIS and the Baltic states. Discrimination against Russians in the CIS and the Baltic states made the "Russian nation aware of its partitioned situation." RF officials and MPs alleged severe discrimination against the one or two million Russian speakers in the Baltic republics—many of whom refused to study the local language, apply for citizenship, or even to ask for a residence permit! Seeming to implement the Karaganov doctrine, the RF mounted diplomatic protests and economic pressures on behalf of "compatriots" in the Baltic republics. Some Duma deputies also complained that half million Russians were "squeezed out" of Kazakstan in the 1990s, but none lamented continuing Russian abuse of dark-skinned RF citizens, visitors, and foreign students. Nor did RF officials apologize for the 50 to 90 million people killed by their predecessors in Russia, Ukraine, Kazakstan, the Baltic states, and other parts of the ex-Soviet realm.

The Russian Federation claimed to be the legal successor to the USSR. It took the USSR's seat at the United Nations and accepted most of the arms control and other treaty obligations of the former Soviet regime. The RF parliament asserted that RF citizenship "is correlated with the principle of succession (continuity) of Russia's statehood." Deputies noted that the RF Constitution (Articles 80, 84, 90, 103) protects the rights of compatriots wherever they happen to be. Deputies claimed that these articles harmonize with the rules of the European Court of Human Rights, the Council of Europe, and the CIS. They averred that the former Soviet republics share a common past with the Russian Federation—the historic rights, titles, and customs that protected Russian interests in the near abroad.[5] Duma deputies declared false the perception of the RF as "merely one of the many successors of the USSR." The RF parliament portrayed the RF as the successor state not just to the USSR but also to the Russian empire, the 1917 Russian republic, and the Soviet Russian Republic— "the same continuous subject of international law that never ceased to exist." The RF "is the bearer of the continuity of Russia's statehood . . . [and is] entitled to implement the rights and obligations stipulated in more than sixteen thousand international agreements concluded by the Russian empire and the USSR." Parliament implied that the successor republics were not truly or fully sovereign—that the boundaries of the Russian empire and USSR remained intact.[6]

Russia's claims to protect "compatriots" could foster irredentist demands to retake former Soviet borderlands. Hitler made similar claims when he annexed Austria and the Sudetenland, taking their Germans *heim ins Reich*—home in the Third Reich.[7] A similar irredentism rationalized Belgrade's support in the 1990s for Serbs in Bosnia, Croatia, and Kosovo.

Who or what is a "compatriot"? Articles 2 and 8 of the 1999 Federal Law on State

Policy of the Russian Federation concerning Compatriots Abroad defined a "compatriot abroad" as

- an RF citizen resident in or passing through a foreign country;
- a citizen of the former USSR living in a state that had belonged to the USSR—whether as a citizen of that state or as a stateless person;
- "emigrants" (whether from tsarist Russia, the 1917 Russian Republic, the Soviet Russian Republic, the USSR, or the RF) who became citizens of other countries, had dual citizenship, had residence permits abroad, or were stateless;
- descendants of such persons.[8]

If applied to Latvia, for example, the 1999 law would relate not only to Russian speakers but to all citizens there who had once been Soviet citizens—not just to those with RF passports or stateless documents but to all persons who had *become* Latvian citizens. The law applied even to compatriots' offspring born after the demise of the USSR! And it applied to their ancestors who emigrated to Latvia from tsarist Russia before 1917.

Indeed, the Legal Department of the State Duma's Secretariat warned that the law's definition of compatriot included all residents of Finland, Poland, and Alaska who might be "direct descendants of nationals of the former Russian empire."

Both the Legal Department and the Yeltsin government warned that the concept of compatriot had no basis in international law or the laws of other countries. Other countries with large diasporas—China, France, Germany, Hungary, and Israel—did not try to define "compatriots" or attempt with their internal laws to create international obligations. The Yeltsin government warned that the law could be construed as intervention in the internal affairs of other states. If the RF issued documents or gave privileges to so-called compatriots abroad, this "would most probably impair the security of this country, as well as its economy and budget."[9]

Article 7 of the 1999 law guarantees RF protection and support for RF citizens abroad. They enjoy the same rights and duties as RF citizens on RF territory, unless otherwise specified by RF treaties or laws. Article 8 adds that the RF government has the right and duty to protect not just RF citizens abroad but all former Soviet citizens living in states once part of the USSR! Such persons may claim RF backing even if they become citizens of the newly formed [or reborn] states or are stateless. Relations with such persons—citizens of the USSR—"have priority significance" for the RF.

Article 14 warns that "discrimination against RF citizens" can trigger a review of RF policy toward that state. Nonobservance by foreign states of the generally recognized principles and norms of international law regarding compatriots' human rights and citizenship will justify the RF's defense of the interests of compatriots.

Article 15 requires equal rights for compatriots before the law of whatever state where they live—equal with the rights of citizens of those states. By implication, the host state could not limit property ownership or voting rights to its own citizens. Article 15 forbids not only discrimination by reason of race, religion, or language but also by reason of political viewpoints or associations.

Article 25 requires government *monitoring* (now a Russian word *analiz*) and evaluation of conditions facing compatriots.

The 1999 law provided that compatriots could (*mogut*) form councils (*sovety*) or commissions within the organs of the RF government to provide oversight of compatriot issues. The 1999 law dropped the requirement set out in the September 1998 draft law to establish a Council of Compatriots within the Russian parliament. Neither the 1998 nor 1999 version explained whether compatriot representation would be by elected MPs or outsiders.

President Yeltsin in a letter dated March 31, 1999 (Pr-428) rejected the Law on Compatriots, saying that the term "compatriots" had no legal basis and that the bill violated the international legal principle of noninterference in the internal affairs of other countries. But the State Duma (April 16) and Federation Council (May 17) approved the law over Yeltsin's objections, in accordance with Article 107 of the RF Constitution, and he promulgated the law on May 24, 1999.

The practical impact of the law was uncertain. Like economic sanctions authorized by the U.S. Congress on countries trading with Cuba and Iran, much would depend on implementation by the executive branch. The law called on the RF government to give economic, cultural, and informational assistance, as well as tax and tariff privileges, to compatriots. Despite its broad aspirations, however, the law does not say what organs of the RF government should carry out its mandates. Nor does it specify new departments to handle compatriot issues.

Still, the RF ambassador to Tallinn probably implemented the compatriot law when, in April 2000, he summoned representatives of NGOs for Russian speakers in Estonia and offered to help coordinate their activities. Ambassador Aleksei Glukhov told the NGOs that he did not wish to interfere in their internal affairs, but he said nothing about Estonia's!

Citing amendments to the 1999 law, RF authorities actively intervened in criminal trials against former Communist activists in Latvia in 2000.[10] Later in the year reports circulated in Moscow that the State Duma had set aside 200 million *roubles* (more than $7 million) in a secret chapter of the RF budget for 2001 to back publications in the CIS and Baltic countries orienting public opinion in ways favorable to Russia.[11]

If a Goethe Institute offered German language classes, chamber music, or film festivals in 2000, these programs would not subvert the host country. In more troubled times, however, such activities could incubate a Fifth Column. The same could be said of Russian embassies and cultural programs in the near or far abroad.

Russian Forces in the Near Abroad

Despite Moscow's formal recognition of Baltic independence, the Kremlin kept substantial numbers of Russian forces in the Baltic republics until 1993–1994. Moscow explained that it pulled its forces from Lithuania earlier than from Estonia and Latvia because Vilnius immediately granted citizenship to all residents of Lithuania. But Russia withdrew from the *pribaltika* less because of Baltic words or deeds than in response to U.S. and German financial inducements. Also, some Russian leaders still hoped in 1993–1994 for a new era in their relations with the West.

Russian forces remained for a few more years at the naval training base in Paldiski, Estonia, and even longer at a radar station at Skrunda, Latvia. When Russian forces closed down the Skrunda station in October 1999, dozens of foreign ambassadors observed the ceremony, but the Russian ambassador did not attend. His absence came at a time when Moscow protested Latvia's prosecution for crimes against humanity of several Latvian men (now in their 80s) charged with helping the Red Army to arrest and deport to Siberia thousands of Latvians in the 1940s. It was a "witch hunt," said a Duma deputy.

Borders

The Baltic republics argued in the 1990s that they that were the successor states to the interwar republics. Tallinn and Riga maintained that their 1920 treaties with Russia were still valid and that their 1920 borders—altered to Russia's benefit in the 1940s— should be restored. Russian negotiators, however, argued that the previous treaties were voided when their signatories joined the USSR.[12] To be sure, the USSR Congress of People's Deputies on December 24, 1989, condemned the secret protocols of the 1939 Molotov-Ribbentrop pact as "legally untenable and invalid from the moment they were signed."[13] But Kremlin spokesmen nonetheless argued that incorporation of the Baltic republics in 1940 was legal and did not hinge on any deals with Hitler.

For the sake of an overall settlement, both Tallinn and Riga renounced their border-lands that had been incorporated into Russia. Thus, Estonia entered an agreement with the RF in November 1996 that did not mention the 1920 treaty and accepted the borders established in Soviet times. Even when Tallinn and Riga abandoned what had been theirs between the wars, however, some Russians preferred to keep things unsettled. The Duma refused in the 1990s to ratify the new treaties and raised additional issues.

Duma deputies put off ratification for various reasons. They objected to treatment of Russians in Estonia and Latvia. At a deeper level, many deputies seemed reluctant to accept that Russia had lost a vital part of its former empire. Moscow gained bargaining muscle from the fact that, so long as the Baltic states had border disputes with their neighbors, they were unlikely to gain admittance to the EU or NATO.

Lithuania did not call for restoration of its 1920 frontiers, because it took Klaipeda in 1923–1924 and because Stalin later transferred the Vilnius region from Poland to Lithuania. In the 1990s Lithuania faced Russia only in the west, at Kaliningrad, while confronting Belarus in the east. Vilnius and Moscow in the 1990s staked out conflicting claims to the Baltic Sea shelf adjacent to their territories.[14] As we see from box 10.1, Kaliningrad was an increasingly sensitive issue for all parties.

On October 2, 1997, Lithuanian and Russian negotiators signed an agreement regulating the Kaliningrad border and offshore resources. But Communists and nationalists in the Duma termed the accords capitulation and "cowardice." The Duma appealed to Yeltsin not to approve them.

A few weeks after the border accords were signed, Yeltsin on October 24 offered some unilateral security guarantees to the Baltic states, anticipating—he said—that legally based mutual agreements would follow. Yeltsin expressed the hope that these guarantees would make Baltic participation in NATO unnecessary. But the Baltic governments in late October and early November rejected Yeltsin's offer and reiterated their determination to join NATO.

Worries about NATO expansion spilled over into debates within the Duma about ratifying the START II arms control treaty. An attitude gained momentum that,

Box 10.1. Kaliningrad

Having taken East Prussia in 1945, Stalin made its northern part the Kaliningrad Oblast' (region) of the USSR's Russian Republic, and gave the southern part to Poland. Most Germans left and nearly one million Russian speakers settled there. With its ice-free ports, Kaliningrad (at 21,000 square kilometers) became a forward bastion of the Soviet Armed Forces.

When the USSR collapsed, Kaliningrad represented a geopolitical anomaly—a Russian exclave supplied by land across two sovereign countries (Lithuania and Belarus) or by sea. Vytautas Landsbergis denounced the continued Russian military presence in Kaliningrad as unnatural, serving no defensive purpose, and useful only to pressure neighboring countries—restocked in 2000–2001 by a cache of tactical nuclear weapons.

Some Kaliningrad residents hoped that Germany would somehow reestablish control. The main town had been Königsberg, a Hanseatic port and later home to Immanuel Kant. An easier pill for Moscow to swallow would be for Kaliningrad to become a demilitarized, free-trade emporium. Lithuanian prime minister Rolandas Paksas and Russian prime minister Sergei Stepashin on June 29, 1999, pledged to cooperate on Kaliningrad. A month later, however, Sergei Baburin, deputy chairman of the Duma, declared: "It is time to stop speculating about demilitarization of the Kaliningrad region and instead to set up a serious defense system that guarantees security in the whole northwest region of Russia."

When I crossed the bridge from Lithuania into the Kaliningrad border town of Sovetsk in 1998, I was besieged by scrawny children begging for food. A police woman explained that many came from homes with one parent or where both were employed or on drugs. Kaliningraders looked as poor and unhappy as any people I had seen in Russia. In the 1990s the region became a center for drugs, filling the local jails with HIV-positive youths.

whatever the West favored, Russia should oppose it. The Duma's Anti-NATO Commission denounced Norwegian intrigues in the north as well as Riga's decision to permit Latvian veterans who fought with Germany to celebrate the 55th anniversary of their enlistment.

In 1999 Sergei Baburin, deputy chairman of the Duma, called the agreements with Lithuania "rash and politically inexpedient" and promised to block their ratification. He objected to "obscurities in the sea section" and unresolved transit issues between Kaliningrad and the rest of Russia. But his main concern was NATO. "Only a madman, a fool or a traitor can attempt to remove the obstacle to open Lithuania's way into that military bloc."

Before Lithuania denounced the Molotov-Ribbentrop Pact, Baburin said, its government should think about returning the territories it received according to the pact—a reference to the Vilnius region and to Klaipeda. There were no legal grounds, he said, to make Klaipeda part of Lithuania.[15]

After the Seimas ratified the border accords in October 1999, however, former Russian prime minister Primakov paid a private visit to Vilnius in November. As noted in chapter 8, Primakov promised President Adamkus that the Duma would also ratify them.

While each Baltic state waited for the Duma to ratify its border accords with Russia, the borders in many places were poorly monitored and porous, permitting smuggling. Here too was an obstacle to Baltic membership in the EU, for each EU member was expected to master its own borders and keep out illegal migrants and goods.

IMPERIAL LUSTS VERSUS CAPABILITIES

Ambitions and Threats

While the Duma argued legalities, some Russian strategists called for reassertion of Russia's geopolitical interests in the long rivalry with the West over the Baltic.[16] Thus, the Russian Defense Research Institute (a "private" think tank supported by the Ministry of Defense) produced a study in 1996 warning that Russia might need to fight in the Baltic in the near future. Anton Surikov, a researcher at the institute, explained to an Estonian reporter that Russia would reoccupy the *pribaltika* if the Baltic states joined NATO or tried to exterminate or expel Russian speakers. He ranked Estonia's defensive capability as very low—nothing like that of the Chechens or Armenians. "Your problem is that, when the Russian troops come in, instantly your society will divide between the two larger ethnic groups. Russians simply do not have anywhere to go other than to pick up a weapon and to fight against you." If a larger country such as Poland joined NATO, Surikov predicted in 1996, Russia would not invade but Moscow might increase military cooperation with Iran or provoke anti-American conflicts in Asia or the Middle East.

Surikov expected a weak world response if Russia invaded the Baltic. Washington would do no more than cancel airplane flights or boycott a sports event. Germany would never give up the oil and gas it gets from Russia. Neither China nor India nor even Turkey would join in sanctions. If sanctioned, however, Russia might retaliate by sending missile technology all over the world. The West would do nothing for fear of triggering a nuclear war. If Russia itself were invaded, Moscow would respond in less than an hour with nuclear weapons.[17]

Even stronger words came from the Russian nationalist Vladimir Zhirinovskii, leader of the misnamed Russian Liberal Democratic Party. Zhirinovskii did not speak for the Kremlin or even for a majority of Russian voters. His party never won any seats in individual constituencies. Some authorities suspected that Zhirinovskii's presence in the Duma was abetted by the Kremlin, to which he sold his votes on key issues. By the late 1990s his bombastic statements had alienated many supporters. Balts, nonetheless, wondered whether, behind so much smoke, there was not a real fire.

Zhirinovskii declared in 1996: "I am doing everything to liquidate the Baltic states." He predicted that Russian speakers in Estonia would "begin to eliminate [Estonia] as a subject of international relations. You feel that you are independent, but this will end for you with your own blood."[18]

To defuse alarm about such talk, Russian diplomats coyly observed that such views were just private opinions to be expected in a democracy and were not shared by the Yeltsin government. But Yeltsin never disavowed them.

Two Russian defense experts in 1998 listed sixteen cases of armed intervention within the USSR and the post-Soviet space—from the crushing of demonstrations in Kazakstan in December 1986 through the Chechnya war of 1994–1996. They opined that most of these interventions were fully or partially successful; only three failed outright—Tbilisi in April 1989; Vilnius in January 1991; and Chechnya in 1994–1996. To decide whether an intervention was "justified" the authors evaluated its success in stopping riots, lowering tensions, resolving a problem, or localizing a conflict.[19] The end justified the means, with the implication that Russia should consider armed intervention in the Baltic if this could "resolve a problem."

These, too, were not official views. But Balts could not ignore them. Where there was smoke (threats), there might be embers (imperialist dreams) if not fire (active plans). Still, when the governor of Russia's Pskov region, Evgeny Mikhailov, declared on November 14, 2000, that Russian military units in his region could overrun Estonia in forty-eight hours, Estonian Foreign Ministry official Taavi Toom denied that Estonia faced any direct threat from abroad. Unless Mikhailov took charge of the paratroopers in Pskov, his words would remain empty rhetoric, said Toom. The real threats facing Estonia, he averred, were nonmilitary risks such as those from Soviet-era nuclear power plants in the Leningrad region.

National Strategic Concepts of 1997 and 1999

If some Russians yearned to retake the imperial patrimony, did they have the means? The Russian armed forces were underpaid, badly supplied, unhappy, and disillusioned. Russian troops were hungry; officers were not paid for months; even the rocket forces had trouble paying their electricity bills.[20]

Post-Soviet Russia had no official security doctrine for six years. In 1997, however, President Yeltsin signed into law a National Strategic Concept positing that the main threats to Russian security came from within—not from without. It stressed that Russia's foreign economic interests called for building economic ties, while at home Russia needed to cultivate "civil peace, national harmony, territorial integrity, a unified legal space, the stabilization of state power . . . [and] the neutralization of the reasons and conditions contributing to the eruption of social and interethnic conflicts, national and regional separatism." Kremlin planners argued that rebuilding the economy should take priority over improving military strength.[21]

Faced with similar though not identical problems in 1922, the Soviet government cut back the Red Army to a cadre of less than 600,000 troops while training a large territorial militia. When Party leader Nikita Khrushchev confronted an economic squeeze in 1960, he also sought to trim regular forces and rely more on missiles.[22] As some Western wags put it, Khrushchev wanted "more rubble for the rouble."

Borrowing from 1922 and 1960, the strategic concept adopted in 1997 called for a smaller professional army and, if necessary, the first-use of nuclear weapons. Tight budgets meant that the Russian government in the 1990s did not have the means to support its military in their present configuration nor to fund properly their transformation into the smaller, all-professional force it planned for 2005. Still, expenditures for new weapons under the State Defense Order (*oboronnyi zakaz*) increased by at least four times from 1994 through 1997.[23]

But finances remained tight. A Russian general said in 1999 that the state could not afford to spend even 3.5 percent of GDP on defense—the goal set by President Yeltsin.[24] A Western source said that Russian defense spending decreased from 11 or 12 percent of Russian GDP in 1992 to 5.2 percent in 1998. In dollar terms, the Russian defense budget in 1997–1998 approached $64 billion—compared to a U.S. Pentagon budget more than four times that size.[25] Outlays of $64 billion would surpass those of any European country, Japan, or China, but not approach the combined spending of U.S. allies.[26]

Despite tight budgets and pressing needs elsewhere, Russia continued to deploy a vast array of nuclear and conventional weapons in the 1990s. Russia's total armed forces in 1998 numbered nearly 2 million. More than a million served under the Ministry of Defense in 2000 (down by 155,000 from 1997). A half million or more other troops served under the Federal Board Guard Service, the Ministry of Internal Affairs, the Forces for the Protection of the Russian Federation, the Federal Security Service, and the Federal Communications and Information Agency. This last agency alone had 54,000 troops—a mere footnote to the Russian armorarium—but more than twice the total of active duty military personnel in the Baltic republics in the late 1990s!

Russia's early warning systems in the late 1990s suffered from old age, poor upkeep, electricity shortfalls, and the shutdown of the radar station in Latvia. Russians talked about completing a mothballed radar in Belarus, but worried about the cost.[27] Washington considered ways to improve Russia's eyes in the sky to guard against false signals.

Just east of Estonia, Russian forces near Pskov were strengthened in the mid-1990s—probably in violation of the flank limits set by the 1990 Conventional Forces in Europe Treaty, even after the West agreed to raise these limits to accommodate a Russia bereft of allies.

The Kremlin could still project power. Russian forces in 1999 conducted their most extensive maneuvers since the mid-1980s—large combined exercises that impressed Westerners with their coordination. The exercises were supposed to simulate a response to a cruise missile attack on Kaliningrad and Belarus. They posited that Russia could make the first use of nuclear weapons.[28]

The summer 1999 maneuvers took place on land and sea near to Latvia and Estonia. Russia's Baltic fleet announced in early August that five minesweepers had been deployed and that this action would be followed on August 16 by a mass outflow of Russian ships into the Baltic. Neighboring countries would not be notified about the details or dates of the training exercises, since they would take place in Russia's territorial and economic waters.[29]

Landsbergis called the 1999 maneuvers "a gesture of psychological cold war against the Baltic states." Estonian parliamentarian Mart Nutt said the exercises showed that the Russians recognized they were "not able to hinder the Baltic states from joining NATO."

Still, the bear that growled at the mice that roared was itself puny next to NATO. Germany alone had fifteen surface combatants—three destroyers and twelve frigates, plus thirty patrol and coastal combatants, while Russia's Baltic Fleet possessed only six surface combatants—two destroyers and four frigates—plus thirty patrol and coastal combatants. To be sure, Russia's Baltic Fleet also had two nuclear missile submarines, but they were useless except for deterrence or nuclear war. Having lost most of the *pribaltika,* Russia's Baltic Fleet had a base at Kronstadt near St. Petersburg and was headquartered at Baltiisk in Kaliningrad. Russia's Northern Fleet (Arctic and Atlantic), however, was much stronger than its Baltic navy.

Russia could probably not hold its own against NATO using conventional forces.

The huge Soviet tank armies that for decades seemed poised for a dash to Hamburg were gone. So, after the 1987 INF Treaty, were the Kremlin's vaunted SS-20 and other intermediate-range nuclear missiles. So were thousands of tactical nuclear weapons withdrawn from front-line Russian and U.S. units since late 1991.

When Russia reinvaded Chechnya in October 1999, it still lacked a professional army with modern equipment. It had new ICBMs—SS-25s and SS-27s—but no night-capable attack planes or helicopters. More than 90 percent of all privates and sergeants were conscripts—badly trained and poorly commanded teenagers. Despite a decade of promises, the Defense Ministry had still not created a corps of noncommissioned officers—the backbone of a professional army. Even Interior Ministry troops fell back when told to advance, leaving their general, Mikhail Malofeev, to perish.

This was the situation in September 1999 when Russia's Security Council reviewed a New Strategic Concept proposed by the Ministry of Defense. The new concept was signed into law by Acting President Putin in January 2000. It reiterated that the most serious threats to Russian security came from within the country, but it also listed a series of external threats:

- the weakening of the Organization for Security and Cooperation in Europe and the United Nations
- reduced Russian influence on the world stage
- eastward expansion of NATO and the possibility of foreign military forces being located on Russian borders
- proliferation of weapons of mass destruction
- weakening of the CIS plus escalation of conflicts on CIS members' borders
- territorial claims against Russia

The 1999 doctrine called on Russia to resist U.S. unilateralism and NATO actions not approved by the United Nations. It called not for partnership but for cooperation with the West. The concept reflected anger that NATO had taken in three new members in 1999 and waged a war against Serbia without UN or Russian approval, and that Washington was threatening to scrap the antiballistic missile treaty unless Russia agreed to weaken its terms.

The revised concept embodied a contradiction. It said the best way to improve Russian security in the long run would be to improve Russia's economy and technology and open world markets to Russian exports. But it also insisted that Russia maintain the potential to mobilize millions of reservists and a massive industrial potential to multiply defense production in times of crisis.[30]

The revised strategic concept neither added to nor diminished the dangers facing the Baltic. The 1999 doctrine repeated that Russia might resort to the first use of nuclear weapons even for coping with a nonnuclear threat. But unless some outside actors planned to attack Russia, this threat lacked plausibility and credibility. If Russia wished to retake the *pribaltika,* nuclear arms would be unnecessary. Russian troops and tanks could probably reconquer the Baltic republics very quickly—perhaps overnight. Such an attack, however, could end Russia's economic ties with the West, risk a military riposte by NATO, and expose Russian vulnerabilities elsewhere.

Implications of Putin at Russia's Helm

Political culture shapes foreign policy. The liberal peace requires that each party perceives the other as sharing in democratic values. Dealing with President Putin, Balts had to presume that his KGB background stamped his political culture forever. Balts did not wish this assumption to become a self-fulfilling prophecy, but they had to presume, with Laertes, that "best safety lies in fear."

Baltic governments worried that the presidency of Vladimir V. Putin portended an increased threat to their security. The new president seemed to relish the role of tough but enlightened despot. The former KGB officer was more ruthless and efficient than his hapless predecessor. Putin promised Russia a dictatorship of law—good news for Russians wanting a strong fist to restore order.

In winter 1999–2000 Putin intensified Russian military actions against Chechyna, boosting his popularity among the many Russians glad to scapegoat non-Russians. Putin said the intervention dispensed with "ephemeral ideas" and reflected "the realities of life."[31]

But Putin's outlook was multifaceted. In 2000 the RF president strove to restore Russian power and demanded that Russia be treated seriously by NATO. Putin claimed that Russia was part of European culture but not NATO culture.[32] He opined that Soviet military interventions in East Germany (1953), Hungary (1956), and Czechoslovakia (1968) had been "major mistakes" leading to "Russophobia in Eastern Europe."[33] Working in East Germany in the 1980s, Putin concluded that a system based on walls and dividers could not last. But he wanted something different to take its place. "We would have avoided a lot of problems if the Soviets had not made such a hasty exit from Eastern Europe."[34]

President Putin placed former KGB associates in key jobs and assigned military officers to supervise Russia's many regions. He turned his police loose on journalists and business oligarchs whom he wished to dominate. In August 2000 he showed a Soviet-like indifference to the lives of more than one hundred seamen in the *Kursk,* a disabled RF submarine lying at the bottom of the Baltic Sea. Putin was at the helm in September 2000 when Estonia expelled two Russian diplomats for "activity incompatible with their status" (spying), a move then reciprocated in Moscow, where two Estonian diplomats were ousted.

Baltic security gained from Russia's parlous economy—so taut that RF naval exercises in the Baltic Sea in the summer 1999 consumed the northern fleet's entire fuel allowance for the year. Putin seemed to be pragmatic regarding Russia's economic and social problems. At Russian Naval Day celebrations in Kaliningrad on July 31, 2000, President Putin told representatives of other Baltic Sea states that Russia sought to maintain stability in the region. A Russian commander offered to assist the three Baltic states in clearing unexploded mines. He said Russia might provide information on the location of mines laid by Soviet ships during the war and about blank and live ammunition lost during subsequent maneuvers. In August 2000 a Russian TV reporter begged officials in Murmansk to send more cigarettes and fuel to the ships attempting to rescue the *Kursk.* In September 2000 Vice Admiral Vladimir Valuev, acting commander of the Baltic Sea Fleet, called for a $2.5 billion international project to render harmless corroded shells likely to leak within a few years, contaminating Baltic waters and harming fish and humans. At the same time RF authorities asked U.S. officials for money to cope with the nuclear-powered Soviet-era ships rusting and rotting near Russia's Pacific Ocean and northern ports. In autumn 2000 Putin called for a one-third reduction in Russia's military forces over the next few years. The prospect that an enlightened despotism could make Russia more fit, however, was low. Balts had to assume they would continue to face a large and malcontent neighbor.

WHY SOME RUSSIANS WORRIED ABOUT THE WEST

Who or what sapped the euphoria of the East-West honeymoon that followed the collapse of the USSR? Did Russia revert to great powerism and neoimperialism because the West proved hostile or vice versa? Or did one or both sides hearken mainly to their internal drummers?

The chronology is clear. RF claims to special rights and duties in the near abroad emerged in 1992–1993. Russia used its oil and gas spigots and its armed forces in the Baltic states to reward or punish the Baltic states for their behavior. Having shelled and prorogued a defiant parliament, Yeltsin in 1993 pushed through a new constitution that vastly enlarged the president's powers. In 1994 Yeltsin inaugurated the first Chechen war. Meanwhile, Russia's oligarchs were robbing the country's wealth for their Swiss bank accounts.

These developments took place while the West labored to bolster Russia's incipient market economy and democracy. Russia's pressures on Balts began two or three years *before* U.S. and German officials began to push for enlargement of NATO's functions and membership. Western aid to Russia may have been too little; some Western advice may have been ill considered; but no Western elites tried to keep Russia down—just the opposite.

By the mid-1990s, however, both the West and Russia began to pursue divergent paths regardless of the damage to mutual relations. Western leaders called for enlarging NATO to consolidate democracy in East Central Europe. Also, they wanted to expand NATO's tasks to include stability and peacekeeping in the Balkans.

Critics argued that NATO expansion eastward could undermine rather than bolster security in Eastern Europe and the Baltic region. First, for the foreseeable future there was no credible threat to Russian's western neighbors. If Russia again menaced its western neighbors, there would be time to take countermeasures. For the present, however, NATO expansion could become a self-fulfilling prophecy—a fillip to Russian nationalism and militarism.

Second, if Eastern Europeans or Balts wished to join NATO, they would have to modernize their armed forces, siphoning funds needed for urgent economic and social needs.

Finally, if a Russian threat emerged, NATO guarantees might not be effective. The original NATO partners might not be ready to risk London, Brussels, or Chicago for Warsaw—much less Tartu—especially if local armies were weak and no Western forces were based in the region. The absence of a "trip wire" (such as protected West Berlin) risked another 1938-type appeasement (Sudetenland to Hitler for "peace in our time").

Some Westerners hoped that Russians would see that NATO's continued vitality served not only to "keep the Russians out" of Europe but to keep the "Americans in" and the "Germans down." The U.S. presence as well as NATO's eastward expansion would reinforce Germany's determination to be a model member and bulwark of the new Europe. But such views amounted to wishful thinking.

Ordered by the White House to conciliate Moscow, Pentagon officials tried to deepen their working relationships with Russian generals and embellish the Partnership for Peace (PfP).[35] The partnership was launched in 1994 to bring nonmember states into closer cooperation with NATO. Soon, more than forty countries were taking part in the PfP, including neutral Switzerland and all former Soviet union-republics and Warsaw Pact allies. The PfP helped bring together twelve non-NATO countries, including Russia, with NATO countries in Bosnian peacekeeping operations. It brought non-NATO members into planning for crisis prevention and management of combined joint task forces. It also sponsored regional exercises requiring bilateral and multilateral coordination. The PfP operated under the authority of the North Atlantic Council—not the Euro-Atlantic Cooperation Council established by NATO to dialogue with the former Warsaw Pact countries.

The West encouraged Russian participation in PfP activities even when these exercises hinted at NATO's ability to support non-NATO members in what Moscow claimed as its near abroad. NATO invited Russian forces as well as former Soviet allies to conduct maneuvers on Russia's doorstep—on the Baltic coast, in the Black Sea, and even in Central Asia. Russia's Baltic Fleet joined a search-and-rescue maneuver with NATO and Baltic navies in June 1997, but declined to take part in the Baltic Challenge exercise a month later.

The Western allies sought to win Russia's acquiescence in a limited expansion of NATO by giving Russia in 1997 a consultative voice (not a veto) in NATO.[36] Also, Secretary of State Madeleine Albright said that the West did not intend to deploy tactical nuclear weapons in the new member states.

Russian representatives talked as though they hoped this consultative relationship would move all parties to develop a strengthened OSCE or some other form of pan-European security organization. But this was not what NATO had in mind.

An Anti-NATO Commission was formed in the Duma in 1997 and soon claimed some 300 members from 450 deputies. The Kremlin and Duma began to indicate that they could live with Polish, Hungarian, and Czech membership in NATO. The Baltic republics, however, were in another category. President Yeltsin threatened to pull out of the 1997 consultative arrangements if the Baltic republics were also admitted. In 1998 the Russian Foreign Ministry asserted that there was a red line that NATO could not cross—it surrounded the territory of the former USSR, including the Baltic region.[37]

THE BALTIC LIMBO

NATO in 1999 admitted Poland, Hungary, and the Czech Republic as members—keeping Balts and others waiting until a possible second round of enlargement. The West hoped to have its cake and eat it too—strengthen NATO without provoking the

Kremlin; buttress Baltic security while keeping Balts out of the Western alliance; promote democracy and capitalism in Russia while drawing a line between potential NATO members and Russia. But the net result of NATO enlargement was to leave Balts and Russians feeling less secure.

Balts believed they were now in a no-man's land. When Poland joined NATO, the Western alliance advanced to Russia's border at Kaliningrad. Lithuania was squeezed on three sides. In the west they faced Russian bases in Kaliningrad; in the east, Belarus, whose dictator sometimes hinted at the need to revise the Belarusian-Lithuanian border and who sought to unite Belarus with Russia; to the south, Lithuania faced Poland, a country with which Lithuania had minority issues and memories of border disputes. As we see in box 10.2, other states were also left in limbo.

Estonia and Latvia faced Russia directly only on the east but could also be attacked from the sea. As noted earlier, the Russian Duma in the 1990s did not ratify border accords with Estonia, Latvia, or Lithuania. In October 1999, however, a senior Russian commander suggested that Russian troops might be pulled back from the Baltic frontier if the Baltic countries did not join NATO.

NATO's war against Serbia and Russia's against Chechnya in 1999 exposed many inconsistencies in East-West security arrangements:

- Russia's voice in Brussels counted for little. NATO attacked Serbia over strong Russian objections.
- But NATO welcomed the aid of former RF prime minister Viktor S. Chernomyrdin in mediating a deal whereby Serbian forces withdrew and international forces sought to establish order in Kosovo. Even more important, Chernomyrdin warned Belgrade that Russia would do no more to assist Serbia, even if NATO invaded with ground forces.[38]
- Before NATO forces could enter Kosovo, however, Russian units dashed in and preempted control of the Pristina airport. Later, however, when Serbs killing Al-

---

Box 10.2. Other States in Limbo

Squeezed between NATO Poland and a volatile Russia, Ukraine in the late 1990s shifted from its earlier avowed neutrality toward alignment with the West. If Ukraine entered NATO, however, Moscow would likely respond more vigorously than when Poland, an historic foe, allied with the West. Kyiv, Russians remembered, was the capital of ancient Rus'—and Ukraine was a potential great power. Pressured by Washington, however, Ukraine had surrendered its nuclear weapons in the mid-1990s. By the end of the decade, with Ukraine's economy in convulsions, Kyiv could not pay for a large conventional military establishment. Ukraine was far more dependent on Russian oil and gas than were Balts.

Slovakia, Romania, Slovenia, and even Albania sought to join NATO, but they experienced no direct Russian pressures. Bulgaria and Moldova were also in limbo, but neither bordered directly on Russia. NATO appreciated that all these countries (except Moldova, which was too remote to help) had facilitated the West's 1999 campaign against Serbia on behalf of Kosovars.

banians shot at Russian peacekeepers, Russians shot back—winning praise from NATO secretary-general Javier Solana for their even-handed behavior.

- Russia's campaign against Chechnya resumed in late 1999 and helped Putin win the presidency in March 2000. But human rights violations in Chechnya cost Russia its voting rights at the Council of Europe in 2000 and elicited condemnation by the UN Human Rights Commission for "disproportionate and indiscriminate use of Russian military force, including attacks against civilians." Still, UK prime minister Tony Blair and other Western leaders lined up to shake the hand of an alleged war criminal—or, as Latvian PM Skele saw it, a genocidist—with whom they hoped to do business.

- U.S. satellite photos showed that Russia in 2000 had moved short-range nuclear weapons from St. Petersburg to a storage facility in Kaliningrad—weapons that had been removed in the early 1990s in tandem with the withdrawal of most U.S. nuclear weapons from Europe. Putin called the U.S. assertions "rubbish" and RF officials claimed that Russia was unconditionally fulfilling its earlier pledges to keep the Baltics as a nuclear-free zone.[39]

All these factors framed the security dilemma facing Balts: the very actions they took to improve their own security could provoke hard-line responses in Moscow dangerous to Baltic security.[40] The ways in which they could deal with this dilemma are explored in chapter 11.

Caption for Chapter 10 Photo: Is Russia a threat or a trading partner to the Baltics? In 1492 Ivan III of Russia built a fortress (in photo) opposite the Hermann fortress across the Narva River in what is now Estonia. Russians hoped Ivangorod, despite its shallow harbor, would rival Narva as a trading center. Russians based in Ivangorod fought for centuries with Livonian, Swedish, Estonian, and Nazi forces based in Narva. If Estonia joined NATO, Russians would face the Western alliance here. Post-Soviet Balts worried that Russia might again seek to dominate the pribaltika. Meanwhile, trade flourished across the narrow bridge linking the Russian Federation and Estonia.

NOTES

1. Contending strains of nationalism in post-Soviet Russia included Westernizing nationalism, nativism, moderate statism, aggressive statism, and national patriotism. See Astrid S. Tuminez, *Russian Nationalism since 1856: Ideology and the Making of Foreign Policy* (Lanham Md.: Rowman & Littlefield, 2000), table 5.1.

2. Recollection by Vladimir Churov in Vladimir Putin, *First Person: An Astonishingly Frank Self-Portrait* (New York: Public Affairs, 2000), p. 103.

3. Putin, *First Person*, p. 86.

4. See the long report by Aleksei Arbatov and other members of the Council on Foreign and Defense Policy, "Rossiia i Pribaltika," *Nezavisimaia gazeta,* October 28, 1997, pp. 4–5. Council members included leaders of the State Duma and its relevant committees, the Russian Union of Industrialists and Entrepreneurs, the Association of Russian Bankers, the Federation of Independent Trade Unions, foundations, and many other such institutions.

5. See Presidential Decree No. 1681, On the Principles of State Policy of the Russian Federation concerning Compatriots Abroad, August 11, 1994, and resolutions no. 1064 of August 31, 1994; 636-II of April 5, 1995, On the Council of Compatriots at the State Duma; 763-II GD25 of October 25, 1996; and 1476-I GD of December 8, 1995, On the Declaration of Support to the Russian Diaspora.

6. Resolution of the State Duma, On the Draft of the Federal Law on the State Policy of the Russian Federation concerning Compatriots Abroad, submitted by N. G. Bindiukov and seven other deputies to the session of the State Duma no. 32, Secretariat of the State Duma Documentation Department, September 29, 1998. The draft federal law had been approved by the State Duma on July 2, 1998 by a vote of 336 to 13, with 2 abstentions; 99 did not vote.

7. Hitler also summoned "home" people of German language, culture, and ancestry—the so-called *Volkdeutsche*. Some seven hundred thousand Germans (and some non-Germans) were moved from the Baltic states, Bukovina, South Tyrol, and elsewhere, but most were resettled in western Poland. Andrew Bell-Fialkoff, *Ethnic Cleansing* (New York: St. Martin's, 1999), p. 37.

8. O gosudarstvennoi politike Rossiiskoi Federatsii v otnoshenii sootechestvennikov za rabuzhem, *Sobranie Zakonadatel'stva Rossiiskoi Federatsii*, no. 22 (May 31, 1999), item 2670, pp. 4937–49. For some previous actions by the State Duma and Federation Council, see *SZ RF* (1998), items 5734, 5735, and 5986, and *SZ RF* (1999), items 1273, 1511, 2093, and 2542.

9. Legal Department of the Secretariat of the State Duma to the Committee of the State Duma on the Affairs of the CIS and Relations with Compatriots, September 23, 1998, no. 22–15/2173, ref. no. 3.17–1144 of 07.09.98 (September 7, 1998). Similar points were made by the RF vice prime minister in a July 2, 1998, letter to G. N. Seleznev, chairman of the State Duma, regarding the draft compatriot law dated July 20, 1998. For both legal opinions and the text of the law adopted by the State Duma in September 1998, see <http://www.mailbase.ac.uk/lists/civil-society/1998–11/0028.html>.

10. To develop provisions in the law the RF government on November 12, 1999, issued regulation no. 1241, on the Federal Target Program "Humanitarian Cooperation of the Russian Federation with the CIS and Baltic States for 1999–2000" (*SZ RF*, no. 47 [1999], item 5701). Government activities regarding implementation of the law were discussed by the Federation Council on October 13, 1999, and a nonbinding resolution (*SZ RF*, no. 43 [1999], item 5151), was issued. In July 2000 the State Duma amended the Statute on the Council of Compatriots at the RF State Duma (*SZ RF*, no. 29 [2000], item 3037) and extended its authority. The Procedure for Resolution of Citizenship Related Issues was amended by decree of the Russian president no. 865 (*SZ RF*, no. 21 [2000], item 2167).

11. The stories inspired much "harsh criticism in the Russian press" according to the Baltic News Service on October 24, 2000.

12. V. Svirin, interview in *Baltic Independent,* March 15–21, 1996, p. 5; also comments of Russian ambassador to Lithuania Konstantin Mozel in *Baltic Times,* January 29-February 4, 1998, p. 2.

13. *Vestnik Ministerstva inostrannykh del SSSR* 60 (January 31, 1990), pp. 9–16.

14. Vilnius objected to a 1995 agreement between Russian and German oil companies to exploit the offshore resources near Lithuania, contending that no mining agreement should be signed until borders were settled. Vilnius also protested live-fire military exercises by Russian forces in March 1996 in a disputed area of the Baltic Sea, maneuvers carried out without consulting or even informing Lithuania beforehand.

15. "Tough Talk from Russian Duma," *Baltic Times,* July 29-August 4, 1999, p. 3.

16. Aleksandr Dugin, *Osnovy geopolitiki: Geopoliticheskoe budushchee Rossii* (Moscow: Arktoreia, 1997). This work is purportedly a handbook for Russia's policy makers.

17. Anton Surikov, interview by Marko Mihkelson in *Postimees,* April 27, 1996.

18. Zhirinovskii said that Russia would not attack Estonia directly but would unleash prisoners from Russian jails. "I'll tell them: You'll get your freedom if you make some moves in Tallinn." He predicted that Estonia, Latvia, and Lithuania would "disappear completely and finally from the world political map" when the inevitable war broke out between Russia and the West between 2001 and 2011. He forecast that the Soviet-era Estonian president Arnold Rüütel or an Estonian Communist sent from Moscow would then rule Estonia. "You small nations," he concluded, "are like small change" in the struggle for power by big nations. See Vladimir Zhirinovskii, interview by Marko Mihkelson in *Postimees,* April 26, 1996.

Zhirinovskii spoke again in this vein on August 20, 1999 (anniversary of the 1968 intervention in Czechoslovakia). He said that Russia should take "radical measures" against all three Baltic countries. He charged that "the Balts are laundering illegal money in the North Caucasus" and "supporting terrorists" there.

19. Oleg Belosludstev and Vladimir Suvorov, "Ustav dlia brandmeisterov 'goriachikh tochek,'" *Nezavisimoe voennoe obozrenie* 5 (February 6–12, 1998), p. 2, summarized in Richard F. Staar, "Russia's New Blueprint for National Security," *Strategic Review* (spring 1998), pp. 31–42 at 38–39.

20. Thus, the Russian Defense Ministry said in April 1996 that its outlays for food were slashed in 1995 from 3.5 trillion to 1.7 trillion roubles (about $350 million at current rates), forcing the Russian Army to use emergency food reserves to feed its troops. Some commanders turned their troops into farmers or foragers.

21. Presidential decree on December 17, 1997, "On the Establishment of a Concept of National Security of the Russian Federation," *Diplomaticheskii vestnik* 2 (February 1998), pp. 3–18.

22. See Walter C. Clemens Jr., "Soviet Disarmament Proposals and the Cadre-Territorial Army," *Orbis* 7 (winter 1964), pp. 778–99; "The Soviet Militia in the Missile Age," *Orbis* 8 (spring 1964), pp. 81–105; "Militias in the Missile Age," *Military Review* 52 (August 1972), pp. 28–47.

23. Staar, "Russia's New Blueprint," p. 35.

24. V. Yesin, interviewed by *Krasnaia Zvezda* and reported by Itar-Tass, August 5, 1999. Colonel-General Yesin, an official on the Russian Security Council, said that real outlays for 2000 would equal those for 1999, adjusted for inflation.

25. International Institute for Strategic Studies, *Military Balance, 1999/2000* (London: Oxford University Press, 1999), p. 110. Other sources give higher and lower percentages and dollar estimates.

26. In 1998 France spent $31.3 billion and Japan about $41 billion on defense; China spent $12.6 billion (up from $11 billion the previous year). Ibid., pp. 52, 186, 191.

27. Iuri Golotiuk, "Moscow Will Keep an Eye on American Missiles After All," *Izvestiia,* August 4, 1999.

28. The operation Air Bridge–99 in March exercised more than one hundred aircraft and twelve thousand personnel from the Moscow and Leningrad military districts along with elements from the Baltic Operational Strategic Group. A much larger operation, West–99, took place in June, July, and August. It involved Russia's Northern, Baltic, and Black Sea Fleets plus land forces drawn from the Leningrad military district, the North Caucasus, and the Urals. West–99 included—for the first time—a unified Russian-Belarusian group. This information comes from the *Military Balance 1999/2000,* p. 105, and various radio and periodical sources.

29. If Russia chose to use its two-hundred-mile exclusive economic zone, however, its operations could extend into waters claimed by Finland, Estonia, and Lithuania. Russian spokes-

men added that the Baltic Fleet would not announce the number of participants involved, because they would not exceed those permitted by international agreements.

West–99 included the dispatch of several long-range bombers to probe NATO defenses around Iceland and Norway. In September 1999 two Tu-95M bombers approached Alaska, the first time such an action had been taken in six years, until the aircraft were turned back by U.S. interceptors.

30. Celeste A. Wallander, "Russian National Security Policy in 2000," Policy Memo Series No. 102, Program on New Approaches to Russian Security, January 2000; Pavel Felgenhauer, "Russia's Forces Unreconstructed," *Perspective* 10 (March-April 2000), pp. 1, 8–10.

31. Putin, *First Person,* p. 193; see also Putin's comments on reporting from Chechnya, pp. 165–74.

32. Putin, *First Person,* p. 169. On some points, the student of international law is completely confused. He claims that the USSR wanted to join NATO but was rejected and that, in response, Moscow created the Warsaw Pact. Ibid., p. 177. But NATO was formed in 1949 and the Pact in 1955, after West Germany's entry. In 1947, Stalin's regime turned down even participation in the European Recovery Program.

33. Putin, *First Person,* pp. 174-78.

34. Putin, *First Person,* pp. 80–81, where he attributes similar views to Henry Kissinger.

35. Ashton B. Carter and William J. Perry, *Preventive Defense: A New Security Strategy for America* (Washington, D.C.: Brookings Institution Press, 1999), chapters 1 and 2.

36. *The Founding Act on Mutual Relations, Cooperation and Security between NATO and the Russian Federation,* May 27, 1997. For the text of this agreement and comments by presidents Bill Clinton and Boris Yeltsin, see the *New York Times,* May 28, 1997.

37. J. R. Black, "Russia and NATO Expansion Eastward: Red-Lining the Baltic States," *International Journal* 54 (spring 1999), pp. 249–266 at 264.

38. Russia's main contribution had been to supply Serbia with radar information on incoming NATO planes. Steven Erlanger, "NATO was closer to ground war in Kosovo than is widely realized," *New York Times,* November 7, 1999, p. A4.

39. *Washington Times,* January 3 and February 15, 2001.

40. When RF Ambassador Aleksei Glukhov was replaced in November 2000, after serving three years in Estonia, he became the first foreign ambassador to leave the country after restoration of independence without a state order. Glukhov turned down an offer by the Estonian Foreign Ministry to award him the Cross of the Terra Mariana.

11

Martin Avameri

Enhancing Baltic Security: NATO and Other Options, 2000–2010

THE PERSISTENT SECURITY DILEMMA

Russia's frailties reduced dangers to Baltic security early in the twenty-first century. But Balts still had cause to worry, for Russia could rise like an angry phoenix.

For small countries the coherence of state and society are the ultimate bulwark against internal and external foes. But external fitness is also a condition for domestic fitness. Fitness in the world requires both coercive and persuasive powers, both of which depend on and contribute to security and influence.

Thus, security for the Baltic states would depend on their own efforts, alone and with each other; on the West; and on the East—Russia and Belarus. But distrust permeated each domain. Balts did not fully trust one another, yet tried to show their solidarity. Balts wanted Russian oil and markets, yet doubted Russia's dependability in trade or security. The West distrusted Russia, yet wished to keep it as a partner. Russians distrusted the West, yet needed its financial support.

The security dilemma remained: whatever Balts did to shore up their defenses could be interpreted in Moscow as hostile. Balts alone could never threaten Russia. But if they linked arms with major Western powers, the Kremlin might respond in ways that endangered Baltic security, turning a remote threat from Russia into a proximate one.

Ten basic ways were open to Balts seeking to enhance their security. Some were complementary, some quite divergent. But each approach embodied contradictions and posed hard choices.

I.   Improve relations with Russia
II. Cultivate a strong home front and defenses
III. Strengthen Baltic and East Central European cooperation
IV. Downgrade NATO and upgrade the OSCE
V.   Neutralize the Baltic republics and adjoining countries

VI.   Join the West but not NATO
VII.   Join NATO
VIII. Broaden NATO to include Russia
IX.   Abolish NATO and upgrade the United Nations
X.   Self-organize for global governance

Let us consider each option and, if implemented, its likely consequences. In each case the biggest question was: How would Russia respond?

I. IMPROVE RELATIONS WITH RUSSIA

The best hope for peace in Europe was probably to strengthen democracy in Russia and other former Communist states, and give their peoples reason to trust in democracy and markets. Movement in this direction depended mainly on factors within each country. But external factors could encourage or retard such evolution.

In an ideal world Balts and Russians would put aside their past, like French and Germans after 1945, and search for mutual gain. In the 1990s, however, Balts and Russians seemed trapped in a past blocking the road to a better future. Given their history, Balts erred on the side of caution.

When weak, Moscow might offer Balts freedom and then renege when it could. Thus, Soviet foreign commissar Chicherin in 1920 extolled Moscow's relations with Estonia as "the touchstone of peaceful coexistence." But such hopes soon gave way to mutual recrimination. When the USSR became stronger, Stalin annexed the Baltics.

Balts perceived a rapid reversal in Russian policies after Boris Yeltsin became

---

Box 11.1. How Peaceful Coexistence Can Go Wrong

Though Soviet foreign commissar G. V. Chicherin expressed his hope in 1920 that the Tartu Treaty would prove a model of "peaceful coexistence," neither side was happy with its implementation. On July 10, 1920, Chicherin complained to his Estonian counterpart that Polish agents, Russian Whites, and anti-Soviet Ukrainians had established recruiting bureaus in several Estonian cities in violation of the Tartu Treaty.

Equally or more serious in the 1920s, Estonian Communist leaders in exile, supported by the Communist International, backed an attempted coup d'etat against Estonia's "bourgeois" government. The Red Army partially mobilized along the Estonian border during the coup, but then returned to its normal status.[1]

On February 26, 1921, Chicherin complained that Latvia's representative in Moscow was abusing his diplomatic privileges by feeding false information to the Latvian Telegraphic Agency, which reported on an "armed uprising" in Moscow on February 25 and, a few days earlier, on allegedly inhumane conditions in Soviet prisons. Very similar charges were directed against the Latvian embassy in Russia and Latvian journalists as Russia stepped up its assault on Chechnya in late 1999.

---

[1]See Walter C. Clemens Jr., *Baltic Independence and Russian Empire* (New York: St. Martin's, 1991), pp. 40–44.

master of the Kremlin. Before that time, in 1990 and for much of 1991, Russian president Yeltsin had supported Balts and adapted parts of their program in his campaign to undermine the Soviet Union. Once Yeltsin displaced Gorbachev, his regime usually tried to intimidate—not conciliate—the Baltic states.

Responding more to Western carrots and sticks than to local demands, most Russian troops withdrew from the Baltic in 1993–1994. As we saw in chapters 8 and 10, Russia continued to wage economic, psychological, and political warfare on the Balts.

Baltic diplomacy in dealing with post-Soviet Russia was less than optimal. First, Tallinn, Riga, and Vilnius did not form a united front. As in 1920, they dealt with Moscow bilaterally. Second, they did not link the many outstanding issues with Russia into one package that could produce a definitive, overall settlement. Neither did the three republics take a joint stance on the compensation due to them for damage caused by Soviet occupation nor did they not link this issue to others on the table. Latvian officials did raise some of these issues bilaterally in September-October 1991, but conditions in Moscow were too fluid then to negotiate seriously on such matters.[1] Russia, of course, admitted no wrongdoing and had limited means to make restitution, but this issue could have given Balts bargaining leverage on other issues. In the late 1990s each Baltic country began again to calculate its human and material losses under Soviet rule, but they did not use the same methodology or otherwise present a united front.[2]

Perhaps Balts should have sent observers, as Georgia did, to meetings of the CIS, formed by the presidents of Russia, Belarus, and Ukraine in late 1991 and soon joined by most other former union-republics. Balts could have supported the Georgians and others opposed to Russian dictation.

To break vicious cycles of distrust, psychologist Charles Osgood outlined a strategy of "GRIT" (graduated and reciprocated initiatives in tension-reduction). Osgood recommended that one side announce its determination to conciliate and initiate modest steps which, if the other side reciprocates, would graduate to larger steps.[3] Beginning in 1955, Soviet and U.S. leaders often followed the logic of GRIT to reverse Cold War conflict.[4]

Which side should take the first step in GRIT? The stronger party, Russia, could more readily afford risks for better relations than the small Baltic republics. Russian diplomats such as Andrei Kozyrev probably understood the logic of GRIT, but Moscow rarely applied it to Baltic affairs. If Balts made concessions to show their good will, Moscow could pocket these offerings and exploit them to undermine the frail foundations of Baltic security.[5]

Balts had few sticks. Did they have carrots? Lithuania was small compared to Russia but rich next to Kaliningrad. Lithuania initiated cooperation with Kaliningrad on issues of transport, energy, environmental protection, health care, trade and investment, and combating crime. Lithuania provided medical supplies and food to Kaliningrad after Russia's August 1998 financial meltdown.

Multilateralizing cooperation might help Balts and Russians transcend their own tensions. Balts and Russians joined the Nordic countries, Poland, and Germany in activities of the Council of Baltic Sea States.

Western countries could reduce Kaliningrad's isolation by promoting investment there and helping to convert military to civilian activities, dispose of chemical weapons, and develop a civil emergency response plan. Kaliningrad could be a test of how to create an integrated Europe without new lines of division.[6]

In the 1990s the EU sponsored more than a dozen projects to assist Kaliningrad. One endeavor spent 1 million euros to modernize the Kaliningrad port; another invested 2 million euros to improve health care in the RF's Kaliningrad, Murmansk, and Arkhangelsk regions. In the 1990s the Nordic Investment Bank and the European Bank for Reconstruction and Development funded wastewater and water purification projects in Kaliningrad. The Kaunas University of Technology worked with the U.S. Democracy Support Fund to train municipal administrators in the Kaliningrad region.

In the late 1990s, at Finland's initiative, the EU embraced a "Northern Dimension" aimed at the Baltic Sea countries and the North West region of Russia including Kaliningrad.[7] The Northern Dimension was to become part of other EU programs such as TACIS (Technical Assistance to the CIS) and PHARE. The Northern Dimension sought, for example, to secure and to liberalize energy flows from the two main exporters, Norway and Russia, to importing states.[8]

Under the aegis of the EU's Northern Dimension Action Plan, the RF and Lithuania jointly proposed a number of projects later approved at the EU Feira summit in June 2000. These included:

- modernization of the transport corridor connecting the Baltic states, Kaliningrad, and the European transport system;
- construction of a gas pipeline across Lithuania to Kaliningrad;
- management of the Nemanas River Basin and delta, deepening of the Skirvyte River, and restoration of the eel population in the Curonian Lagoon;
- establishment of a Eurofaculty at Kaliningrad State University in cooperation with Vilnius University;
- fighting AIDs with special centers at Klaipeda and Kaliningrad;
- tightening controls to fight crime at the Panemune-Sovetsk and other border crossings.

But there were limits on all sides. Most EU projects in the 1990s had a pilot rather than a long-term character, and did not mesh smoothly with one another. The EU had no plans to invest in modernizing Kaliningrad's industry or its agriculture. Moscow held back from bold initiatives lest the West encourage Kaliningrad to split from the RF.[9]

There was no agreement on how to apply EU border control regimes to Poland— not to speak of Kaliningrad or Lithuania. If Warsaw and Vilnius became part of the EU "Schengen Convention," they might have to abolish their visa-free regimes with Kaliningrad. This would obstruct tourism, shuttle-trading, and functioning of the Special Economic Zone being fostered in Kaliningrad. But if all borders were open, this could increase soft security risks from crime, disease, and pollution.[10] Still, the number of migrants from the former Soviet realm likely to enter the EU if border controls were liberalized would add little to the existing migrant population—even in Austria and Germany. Experts agreed that improved police cooperation between countries was more efficient than investing in border guards and surveillance technology.[11]

Looking east, Balts perceived challenges and opportunities in other cities and regions of Russia. All of Latvia's western border and most of Estonia's face the RF region of Pskov. Based on their 1920 treaties with Soviet Russia, both Latvia and Estonia claimed territory transferred to Pskov by Stalin in the 1940s. Hoping to qualify for NATO membership, Riga and Tallinn gave up these claims in 1996. But if Latvia and Estonia joined NATO, the Western alliance would then abut Pskov. Some politicians in Pskov called for strengthening RF military forces in the region to stem the Western tide. They recalled how Alexander Nevsky checked the Livonian Knights on nearby Lake Peipsi (*Chudskoe* in Russian) in 1242.

But Pskov abounded in contradictions. Would it be a bulwark of Fortress Russia or Russia's gateway to the West?[12] More than half a millennium before, Pskov had been an outpost of Hanseatic commerce. But Pskov was harder for Hanseatic merchants to reach than Novgorod, one of four major Hanseatic trading centers. In the twentieth century, however, Pskov became far better positioned for east-west trade than Novgorod. To be sure, Novgorod straddled the rail and road routes from Moscow to St. Petersburg. But Pskov became the main rail and highway corridor between Russia and Europe. Also, major oil and gas pipelines from Russia ran through Pskov to Belarus and to the Baltic countries. Pskov was equidistant from St. Petersburg, Tallinn, and Riga. (When I first visited Riga in 1959, I took the night train from Leningrad, but was ordered not to disembark in Pskov for security reasons. When the train jolted to a halt in Pskov early in the morning, two KGB agents stood in the corridor to monitor my behavior.)

Pskov was the only RF region where a member of Vladimir Zhirinovskii's ultra-nationalist party was elected governor in 1996. Evgenii Mikhailov, elected Pskov's governor in 1996, was also a study in contradiction. While Zhirinovskii denounced the West, Mikhailov campaigned on the need to expand trade links with Europe because the region could not expect financial support from the federal government. After customs controls were tightened along the border with Latvia and Estonia in the mid-1990s, Pskov earned more from tolls than from any one industry.

Mikhailov also sought and obtained large subsidies from the center. How much aid and when it would arrive, however, was a guessing game. The center claimed it wished to help the region, but Moscow's anti-Baltic stance often trumped Pskov's development needs. President Yeltsin spoke of a possible free trade zone in Pskov but only in hypothetical terms. His government talked more often of building new ports and promoting trade with Europe through St. Petersburg or Murmansk. It imposed double tariffs on goods coming from the Baltic, thereby driving up the price of imported goods for Pskovians and limiting what they could earn from traffic.

Despite Alexander Nevsky's rhetorical flourishes in Pskov, the region's politicians and business leaders sought closer ties with firms, towns, counties, and the national governments of Estonia, Latvia, and Lithuania—from nearby Tartu to distant Ventspils and Klaipeda.

Culture conditioned both commerce and politics. Whereas Kaliningrad's heritage as Hanseatic Königsberg had been eradicated, the post-Soviet leaders of Novgorod stressed the city's earlier place in Hanseatic commerce and its self-rule by a merchant oligarchy.[13] Post-Soviet Novgorod attracted substantial foreign investments for small and medium-sized manufactures (from bricks to optics to electronics), paid wages on time, and fostered trust and civil society.[14]

Novgorod probably gained from its historic ties with the West. But if this factor suf-ficed to build a good life, why did Kaliningrad, Pskov, and even St. Petersburg languish? Western influences could assist but not guarantee development. Like the three Baltic republics, Novgorod utilized positive influences from the past and jettisoned others.

Despite chaos in Russia, Baltic leaders such as Estonian president Meri and Seimas chairman Landsbergis urged the West in 1999 not to give up on Russia. They argued that the democratization of Russia was inevitable, but would take time. Meanwhile, Balts looked for other ways to shore up their security.

II. CULTIVATE A STRONG HOME FRONT AND DEFENSES

At home, as we have seen in previous chapters, each Baltic republic struggled to build or rebuild a healthy polity; to raise living standards for most people while promoting economic growth; to forge a national identity while coping with settlers who did not speak the official language.

Civilian Defense

Balts used a nonviolent Singing Revolution to *regain* their independence in 1991. In the early 1990s some Baltic leaders wanted to combine civilian defense with military force to *protect* their independence against foreign invasion and internal coups. Civil-ian defense would use nonviolent resistance to make a country ungovernable. Nonvio-lent methods could include symbolic actions, walkouts, civil disobedience, strikes, pro-viding sanctuary, sit-ins, exposure of who did what to whom. Balts received advice from specialists on nonviolent techniques to prevent a putsch.[15] To be effective, how-ever, such actions would require wide-scale training and discipline. As patriotism waned and hedonism gained in the 1990s, Baltic leaders shifted their hopes to conven-tional means of defense—soldiers, modern weapons, and alliances.[16]

If Moscow chose to intervene in the *pribaltika,* it could call on former Soviet mil-itary personnel and KGB agents still residing in the Baltic republics.[17] Perhaps they could sabotage Baltic defenses and mobilize disgruntled Russian speakers.

Since lustration was limited, former Communist politicians were free to take part in Baltic politics.[18] Many did so, and they often won at the polls.[19] But no former Communists openly acted to subvert the Baltic governments. Rather, most wrapped themselves in a nationalist cloak.[20] One former Soviet police officer wanted for crimes in Latvia in August 1991, however, ran for a seat in the Russian Duma in 1999 as a Liberal Democrat in the Zhirinovskii bloc.

Baltic governments also learned from CIA instructors how to infiltrate, control, and weaken organizations bent on weakening the existing government. Whatever the rea-son—cooption, resignation, infiltration—neither mass nor conspiratorial movements seriously challenged Baltic democracy after 1991.

Baltic Military Forces

If Russian forces again attacked, could Balts put up a fight? In the 1990s many Balts recalled with pride how they repulsed the Red Army in 1918–1920.[21] They were determined to avoid another supine surrender as took place in 1940. Some pointed out that "forest brethren" guerrillas fought the Soviet occupation forces from 1944 until 1956.[22] As box 11.2 reminds us small can be tough.

Balts' military preparedness at the onset of another century was hampered by deficiencies in many areas—funds, hardware, tradition, leadership, experience, and fighting spirit. Not only was there a shortage of equipment but existing weapons derived from three different standards. Some arms were hand-me-down Soviet, some were NATO-standard, some Israeli. Given the many shortfalls, many Balts thought it futile to try to organize their own military defense.

Estonia's military commander Colonel Johannes Kert in 1996 envisioned a nation in arms—regular army, the paramilitary Defense League (*Kaitseliit*), border guards, reserves—backed by a patriotic citizenry. Kert said that Chechens showed that a small people could resist the erstwhile superpower. "It's possible to beat an army," said Kert, "but not an entire nation."[23]

For better or worse, however, a Swiss-style militia was probably not in the cards so long as the Baltic countries remained ethnically divided. To arm all residents could invite a civil war, while discrimination against one group could heighten divisions.

Hoping to meet NATO standards, Balts pledged in the late 1990s to spend 2 percent of GDP on defense. Faced with mounting economic problems and a budget squeeze in 1999, each put off fulfilling this commitment. If a country were genuinely intent on saving itself from a powerful neighbor, it would tighten its belt and spend a much larger share of GDP on defense.

Box 11.2. The Role of Spirit

The militia of Hanseatic Tallinn, utilizing the town's powerful fortifications, helped turn back Russian invasions in 1560 and the 1570s. A century later, however, the town was governed by Sweden. The German bourgeoisie retained many privileges, but their spirit of self-reliance had evaporated. A much weakened militia did little but peer out from watchtowers. The Swedish overlord, King Charles XI, and the mayor of Tallinn decided to reconstitute a more serious militia. But, the mayor said, the *Undeutsche* (Estonians) were undependable. From a population of some 13,000, the town's German elite formed a militia of 732 men. The highest-placed Estonians had the rank only of foreman, *Rottmeister*.[1]

Some Estonians were recruited by the Red Army in 1941, but were suspected of disloyalty. In 1944, however, the self-styled German *Herrenvolk* was happy to let Estonians resist the advancing Red Army. Some 38,000 Estonian men appeared and joined others already conscripted, to form a force of 50,000 to 60,000. They stalled the Red Army for six months at the Narva River and near Pskov.[2]

Skeptical that nonviolent tactics could win, some Estonians in the late 1980s collected arms to wage guerrilla war against Soviet occupiers, Mart Laar told me on June 11, 1998. But other Estonians said this was the mere bravado of a few students.

---

[1]Heinz von zur Mühlen, comp., *Die Revaler Münster-Rolle Anno 1688: Ein Verzeichnis der Bürger und Einwohner* (Lüneburg, Germany: Verlag Nordostdeutsches Kulturwerk, 1992), pp. 1–11.
[2]Toivo U. Raun, *Estonia and the Estonians,* 2d ed. (Stanford, Calif.: Hoover Institution, 1991), pp. 159–60.

Estonia's defense outlays were 1.3 percent of GDP in 1998 and 1.5 percent in 1999.[24] Of the three Baltic republics, Latvia had the most serious problems with Russia, but spent the least on defense—less than 1 percent of GDP in the late 1990s. Lithuania had the best relations with Russia, but spent over 2 percent of GDP in 1997, though this share declined to 1.3 percent in 1998 and to 1 percent in 1999.[25]

Some small states, including Israel and three of the Asian Tigers, paid out 10 to 25 percent of GDP for defense for many years to build up their forces against external threats. But the three Baltic republics in the 1990s spent a much lower share of their GDP on defense than most other NATO partners, even though the Balts were building on much weaker foundations.

How minuscule was the Baltic defense effort can be seen also by how much each country spent per capita on defense in 1999: Latvia $24, Lithuania $28, Estonia $48. Among their neighbors, Belarus spent $48, Russia $380, and Sweden nearly $600. The United States spent more than $1,000, Israel spent about $1,500, and Qatar spent more than $2,000 (highest in the world).

Vilnius sought in the late 1990s to pick up Soviet-designed arms on the cheap from Eastern Europe or Russia. Latvia and Estonia, on the other hand, looked to the West for new or hand-me-down arms. In the late 1990s Lithuania had no combat aircraft, while Estonia and Latvia had a few fixed-wing aircraft (mainly the Ukrainian-made An-2 "Colt") and some aging Russian-made helicopters.

Many young Balts felt little motivation to do military service. Military morale was low throughout the Baltics. There was much drinking and hazing in each Baltic military establishment. Discipline within the Latvian Army was criticized by President Guntis Ulmanis on March 22, 1996. Official Latvian statistics showed that nearly every officer breached discipline in 1995. In June 1999 an Estonian lieutenant was sentenced to prison for negligence in the deaths of fourteen soldiers in a training exercise. In March 2000 Lithuanian authorities reported that only 20 percent of young Lithuanian men qualified for military service. One-third failed health requirements, one-fourth had student deferments, and one-twentieth had a previous criminal record.

Baltic forces were much smaller in the late 1990s than in 1922—as we see in table 11.1.[26] Polish and Finnish forces, however, were comparable for both periods. Soviet Russia reduced Red Army regulars to less than 600,000 in 1923, but they were still far more numerous than the forces of all three Baltic states plus Finland. Russian forces in the late 1990s—even without counting the heavily armed units of the Interior Ministry—were much larger relative to Baltic forces than they had been in 1922.

Just how small was the per capita strength of Baltic forces in the late 1990s is suggested by comparison with two other states: Macedonia, a country with a population about the size of Latvia's, fielded 16,000 troops in 1999 compared to 22,550 for all three Baltic republics combined; Denmark, with a population the size of Estonia and Lithuania fielded nearly 22,000 actives.[27]

In the 1990s half the regular troops in each Baltic army were conscripts serving for just twelve months. Lithuania called up just 6,000 a year from a pool of 97,000 men aged 19 to 25. Baltic leaders hoped that today's conscripts would contribute to larger reservoirs of trained reservists, but they did little to maintain martial skills among those who had put in their twelve months as regulars. Estonia's reserves, however,

Table 11.1
Baltic, Russian, and Other Armed Forces: 1922 and 1999

State	Size of armed forces in 1922	Size of armed forces, active duty paramilitary, and reserves in 1999
Estonia	21,000 (Soviet estimate, 14,000)	4,800 + 2,800 + 14,000
Latvia	25,000 (Soviet estimate, 19,500)	5,050 + 3,500 + 14,500
Lithuania	more than 27,000 (Soviet and Polish estimates)	12,700 + 3,900 + 27,700
Soviet Russia/RF	850,000 in 1922; 562,000 in 1923 (Soviet sources)	1,004,100 + 478,000 + 2,400,000
Poland	294,000 (Soviet estimate, 320,000 to 370,000)	240,650 + 23,400
Finland	33,000 (Soviet estimate, 28,000) + 97,000 reserve	31,700 + 3,400 + 540,000

SOURCES: *Conférence de Moscou pour la limitation des armaments* (Moscow: Commissariat du Peuple aux Affaires Étrangerès, 1923); *Izvestiia* and other Soviet newspapers in 1922; International Institute for Strategic Studies, *The Military Balance 2000/2001* (London: Oxford University Press, 2000).

included a Defense League (*Kaitseliit*) of 8,200 volunteers trained for both combat and noncombat missions.

International Assistance

An International Defense Advisory Board for the Baltic States, founded by General Sir Garry Johnson, former Commander, Allied Forces North Europe, consisted of retired NATO officers who helped Baltic leaders to analyze their security options.

The Nordic countries provided wide-ranging training for Baltic officers and incorporated Baltic troops in some of their peacekeeping missions. In 1994 the three Baltic states put together a combined Baltic Peacekeeping Battalion (BALTBAT) with headquarters in Adazi, Latvia. BALTBAT in the mid-1990s was a 721-person force with equal numbers from each Baltic country and a rotating command. In 1997 more than 220 Baltic troops served in Bosnia; Estonia had 18 political officers in Croatia, while Lithuania had 8. Lithuania and Poland were creating their own combined peacekeeping battalion. In 1998–1999, however, Lithuania cut back its force in Bosnia from 140 to 41, but placed 30 in KFOR (the NATO-led force in Kosovo). Latvia and Estonia maintained 40 to 45 troops with the NATO-led SFOR (Stability Force) in Bosnia; Latvia also had some troops with KFOR. One or two Estonian observers served with Norwegians in the UN Truce Supervision Organization in Lebanon. Overshadowing Baltic contributions, however, the RF in 1999 deployed some 1,300 troops with SFOR II and 3,600 in KFOR; it had more than 34,000 troops in other CIS countries, on UN missions, and on bilateral arrangements with countries such as Syria and Vietnam. This total declined to about 22,000 in 2000.[28]

The three Baltic navies, aided by Western partners, set up a Baltic Naval Squadron

(BALTRON) based in the former Soviet base at Paldiski, Estonia. In 1998 I observed German minesweepers working out of Riga, searching the Baltic Sea for World War II mines.

Denmark transferred a twenty-five-year old frigate to Estonia in November 2000. Renamed "Admiral Pitka," after the founder of the Estonian navy in 1918, the frigate became the flagship of the Estonian navy. It had a helicopter pad, equipment to refuel at sea, and a hospital.

The Whole Baltic Airspace Surveillance Network (BALTNET) was established in Karmélava, Lithuania, in 2000 as a comprehensive radar network compatible with NATO systems. There were also national surveillance centers in Estonia and Latvia.

One goal of the U.S. Defense Department was "environment shaping." To this end the U.S. Military Liaison Team in Estonia planned fifty familiarization events in 2001 to promote military professionalism in Estonia and NATO interoperability. Each event would last three to five days and be held either in the United States or in Estonia. U.S. planners had organized nearly five hundred such events between 1993 and 2000.

The U.S. Congress authorized $20 million in fiscal year 2001 for military assistance to Estonia, Latvia, and Lithuania. Earlier U.S. financing helped Balts to purchase radios, naval radar, air-traffic equipment, and navigational systems. The Pentagon also donated used equipment to the Baltic countries—millions of dollars worth of rifles, small ships, clothing, mobile field hospitals, camouflage systems, tents, and trucks. In 2000 the offices for "Security Assistance" in U.S. embassies in the Baltic countries became offices for "Defense Cooperation."

It was difficult for Balts to find qualified military leaders. Older personnel had imbibed Soviet methods, but to train an officer corps in NATO ways of thinking and acting could take more than a decade. Former U.S. officers took leading roles in the Baltic forces.[29] Thus, Colonel Jonas Kronkaitis, after twenty-seven years in the U.S. Army, became commander of Lithuanian forces in 1999.

President Meri sacked Lt. Gen. Johannes Kert as commander of Estonia's defense forces in June 2000 without consulting the Riigikogu. Two months later, however, a narrow majority in parliament approved the move and endorsed Meri's recommendation to replace Kert with Rear Admiral Tarmo Kouts, who had performed well as director general of Estonia's Border Guard. Some observers said that Kert had been a good soldier but a poor manager.

Baltic military officers and some civilians attended military schools in NATO countries in the 1990s. They participated in training and education programs ranging from eight weeks to four years in duration.[30] Baltic officers polished their English. Baltic forces took part in annual NATO-sponsored PfP exercises—Baltic Challenge, Cooperative Endeavor, Baltops, and Cooperative Nugget.

The 28th annual maritime exercise Baltic Operations (Baltops) took place in the Baltic Sea for two weeks in June 2000. The Estonian, Latvian, and Lithuanian navies joined with seven other navies in the largest Baltops exercise to date. Baltops 2000 was initiated by the United States but hosted by neutral Sweden. Some fifty ships and submarines and twenty aircraft trained together to improve interoperability in gunnery, undersea warfare, radar tracking, and mine countermeasures in potential real-world crisis scenarios.[31] A Baltic Challenge exercise in 1997 involving eight navies demonstrated a capability to ship military supplies from Sweden to Estonia. On a much smaller scale, U.S. marines from Quantico, Virginia, in October 1997 trained Estonian *Kaitseliit* troops in a nature preserve near Tartu that had once served as a bombing range for Soviet planes flying all the way from the Kuril Islands!

The Baltic Defense College (BALTDEFCOL) was established in Tartu in 1999 with Western instructors and financing to train top-level officers from each Baltic country. The initial course in 1999–2000 had thirty-two students from eight countries: ten from Estonia, eight from Lithuania, eight from Latvia, two from Denmark, and one each from Germany, Hungary, Sweden, and the United States. A Swedish officer chaired the college board, and the teaching staff came from twelve countries. Some forty students for the 2000–2001 course were expected from more than ten countries. The college commandant, Danish brigadier general Michael H. Clemmesen, predicted that the Baltic armies would soon have a higher average level of NATO interoperability than any other force in East Central Europe—indeed, higher than the average for longtime NATO members. There was talk of founding a similar institution to train noncommissioned officers.

A Swedish-Baltic project created a database, known as BALTPERS, to help mobilize military personnel and civilians. The Baltic Security Assistance Group (BALTSEA) coordinated Western military assistance with the foreign and defense ministries of each Baltic country.

But could the three Baltic republics ever form a force capable of deterring or slowing a Russian advance? Could a combined population of 7 or 8 million (some of whom might join the enemy) resist the force of 148 million? History gave some encouragement. Baltic armies, cooperating with Finnish and Western forces, drove back the Red Army in 1919–1920. Finland, operating with no help from others, imposed great losses on Stalin's forces in 1939–1940. Switzerland's territorial militia helped deter an invasion by Hitler or Mussolini.[32]

The balance of power was more complicated than 8 million versus 148 million people. Russia could not attack the Baltic republics without worrying about threats from other quarters. If Balts improved regional military cooperation, they might generate a force that would make the Kremlin think long and hard before deciding to invade. The more resistance Balts could mount on their own, the more time and reason Western governments would have to assist them. The stronger Balts became militarily, the more NATO could view their admission as something other than a strategic liability.

III. STRENGTHEN BALTIC AND EAST CENTRAL EUROPEAN COOPERATION

Could the Baltic republics integrate their military and other strengths so as to buttress their common security interests? Could they—should they—cooperate with neighbors in East Central Europe?

In the 1920s and 1930s the three Baltic states cooperated very little with one another, with their Nordic neighbors, or with Poland. Each Baltic state assumed its own position was more secure than the others' and feared that association with them could undermine its own vital interests. Thus, Estonia and Latvia eschewed entanglement in

Lithuania's dispute with Poland over Vilnius. Even so, Lithuania's strident stance on this issue at the League of Nations undermined the prestige of all three Baltic states. And while Kaunas looked to Moscow for help against Warsaw, Tallinn and Riga hoped London and Paris would back them against the USSR. Each Baltic state misread both Germany and Great Britain. Apart from the Vilnius question, the Baltic states espoused no large causes at the League of Nations. They maintained a neutral diplomatic position and tended to go along with the great power-led majority. The Baltic Entente of the 1930s was more facade than reality.[33]

Breaking away from the interwar pattern, elites and common people of the three Baltic republics collaborated in many ways in the 1980s run-up to independence. After 1991, however, cooperation among Balts languished. Mart Laar told an interviewer in 1998 (before he again became prime minister), "We used to be friends; now we are rivals." The Baltic countries often competed for trade, investment, and transit utilization. Nearly a decade after independence, there was no intra-Baltic customs union.

Balts looked west. They saw their salvation in ties with Western Europe—not with one another. Some Balts feared that if they created effective subregional institutions, Western Europeans would say there was no need to integrate the formerly Communist states with the EU and NATO. The Baltic republics were more concerned to show how different they were from the Russian sphere than to link arms with each other or with Poland, Hungary, or the Czech Republic.

The main support for Baltic unity in the 1990s came from Western Europe—not from Balts. Subregional institutions could best elicit local support if they promised involvement of member countries with pan-European organizations.

Some Russians noted—gloated—that the Baltic republics in the 1990s had border disputes with one another—more serious, said the Russians, than with Russia.[34] Lithuania had unresolved borders at sea not just with Russian Kaliningrad but with Latvia. Estonia and Latvia had serious differences over fishing rights in the Gulf of Riga.[35] In 1998 the Estonian and Latvian foreign ministers debated the border where an Estonian minority lived in a town with a Latvian majority.

Concurrent with rivalry, however, were movements toward regional cooperation. Thus, Estonia invested far more per capita in Eastern and Central Europe than any other country—with half of this investment in Latvia and Lithuania.[36]

Representatives of all three states in the Baltic Council and Baltic Assembly sought common positions. In 1998 Lithuania and Estonia stood faithfully by Latvia when the latter suffered an upsurge in Russian pressures.

Impressed by Estonia's radical economic reforms, the EU in 1997 included Estonia among the next countries to be considered for admission. Some Western officials regarded Estonia as a stronger candidate for admission to NATO than the other two Baltic countries. The U.S. Defense Department gave more training grants to Estonians on a per capita basis than to any other Baltic or East Central European country.

In 1998–1999, however, President Meri often called for the three Baltic countries to be considered together for EU and NATO membership. On June 28, 1999, the three Baltic presidents and Poland's President Aleksander Kwasniewski met in Riga and called for Latvia and Lithuania to join Estonia and Poland in the "fast-track" group for EU enlargement so as to "consolidate the power of the northern wing of the European Union."

As in the interwar years, attitudes of "each-for-himself" facing external pressure diminished Baltic solidarity. Estonia, Latvia, and Lithuania in 1999 asked the EU for permission to keep in place the Baltic States Free Trade Agreement on agricultural goods for a transitional period in case just one or two of them were accepted into the EU. In 2000, however, Estonia in August, Lithuania in September, and then Latvia in November bowed to EU demands and abandoned this request. Latvia's chief negotiator asserted, or hoped, that "the EU market would fully compensate the possible losses." Farmers would have time to adjust to EU trade rules, he said, since EU membership was more than a year away.

IV. DOWNGRADE NATO AND UPGRADE THE OSCE

During the Cold War the Kremlin struggled to supplant if not eliminate NATO with an all-European security pact. In the 1990s Moscow called for replacing NATO with an upgraded Organization for Security and Cooperation in Europe.

The OSCE fostered stability and human rights during the Cold War. In the 1990s the OSCE facilitated political consultation. It sent diplomatic missions to Estonia, Latvia, Georgia, Moldova, Macedonia, Nagorno-Karabakh, Bosnia, and Kosovo.[37] At the November 1999 OSCE summit in Istanbul, Russia agreed to permit an OSCE team to look at the Chechnya situation. The Kremlin also accepted that OSCE members had a right to concern themselves with each other's compliance with individual and minority rights. And Moscow agreed to new force ceilings under the Conventional Forces in Europe Treaty, but insisted Russia must temporarily exceed (violate) them in Chechyna. Moscow even promised to pull back some Russian forces from Moldova and Georgia, whose governments did not want them.

But the OSCE was unwieldy. In 2000 the OSCE had fifty-four members—each with a veto. They included all NATO members; Russia and all former Warsaw Pact members plus the fourteen other former union-republics of the USSR; plus virtually all other European countries—from Finland to the Vatican. The territory of many members, such as Kyrgyzstan, was remote from Europe.

To make the organization more flexible, Russia in September 1994 proposed creating a ten-member Security Council for the OSCE (then called the CSCE), but was rebuffed.

There was no chance that the West would give up a successful alliance for an upgraded OSCE. The OSCE was no substitute for NATO, and it was weaker than the UN. The OSCE had no armed forces, had a limited budget, and found little consensus. The West and Russia were often at cross purposes. When the OSCE sent representatives to Georgia, Kosovo, or the North Caucasus, their mandate was uncertain.

V. NEUTRALIZE THE BALTIC REPUBLICS
AND ADJOINING COUNTRIES

Another alternative would be to declare the entire region between NATO and Russia a neutral zone—its neutrality formally recognized by Russia as well as the West.[38] The neutral countries would commit not to permit foreign troops or bases on their soil. Guarantors would pledge not to violate the integrity or sovereignty of the neutral states. As we see in boxes 11.3 and 11.4, some precedents can be found in the 1920 Tartu Treaty, but a fuller model was elaborated in the 1955 Austrian State Treaty and in separate statements issued by the era's Big Four.

Neutralization need not mean demilitarization. If states adjacent to Russia opted for neutrality, Balts might choose the 1955 Austrian model of lightly armed neutrality; Ukraine might prefer a heavily armed neutrality as practiced by Sweden and Switzerland. Absent any special restrictions, neutral countries could take part in PfP exercises.

Neutrality and neutralization can be a snare and a delusion. Germany violated Belgium's neutral status in 1914 and again in 1940. Friendship treaties and nonaggression pacts were abused by the USSR and other states both before and after World War II. But neutrality served some countries well—Switzerland, Sweden, Finland, Ireland. Austrian neutrality enhanced its interests and those of its guarantors, though the Kremlin later objected that Austria's entry into the European Community could breach its neutrality.[39] Yugoslavia, India, and other Third World countries probably gained more than they lost from their nonaligned status. Turkmenistan did not suffer from its self-proclaimed neutrality in the 1990s.

There was little discussion of an Austrian model for the Baltic and other Eastern European countries in the late 1980s to early 1990s. Atlanticist hopes still high, Russians did not then want to formalize their distance from the West in this manner, while Balts did not wish to stake their security on promises.[40] A decade later, governments moved toward alignment rather than nonalignment. In 1999 Poland, Hungary, and the

---

Box 11.3. The 1920 Tartu Treaty Precedents

The February 2, 1920, Tartu Treaty between Soviet Russia and Estonia stipulated that, if Estonia's neutrality were recognized internationally, Russia would recognize and guarantee it. Both Estonia and Russia agreed to take part in and observe an international accord neutralizing the Gulf of Finland, but neither of these measures was ever implemented.

In the treaty, Estonia also pledged to demilitarize a belt of territory and waters from Narva to Lake Peipsi (Chudskoe, Peipus) and extending southwest from Lake Pihkva (Pskov). Russia agreed to demilitarize an area east of that line up to the Velikaia River west of Pskov. These commitments bound the parties only until January 1, 1922. On lakes Peipsi and Pihkva, however, both sides pledged not to deploy warships, and no time limit was indicated.

Each side agreed not to permit its territory to serve as a base for armed aggression against the other. Each would disband guerrilla bands, prohibit recruitment on its territory for armies hostile to the other side, and prohibit transit by such armies. A rapid demobilization of irregular forces was required, and was to be inspected by mixed commissions with access to a telegraphic hot line linking them with the Estonian and Russian capitals.

Unlike the Tartu Treaty, the peace treaty between Soviet Russia and Latvia on August 11, 1920, had no provisions for demilitarization. Indeed, it permitted the Red Army to retain a unit known as the Latvia Rifles.

Box 11.4. The 1955 Austrian Model

Austria was divided and occupied by France, Great Britain, the Soviet Union, and the United States in 1945. Ten years later, Austria proclaimed its "perpetual neutrality" and its determination to "maintain and defend this with all means" at its disposal; Austria declared it would join no alliance and permit no foreign military bases on its territory. Each of the Big Four in a separate note declared it would respect Austria's neutrality. The four guarantors recognized Austria's independence but stipulated that Austria could not possess weapons of mass destruction, guided missiles or torpedoes, poisonous gases or biological materials for military use, or even "guns with a range exceeding 30 kilometers." The Big Four reserved the right to ban future weapons "evolved as a result of scientific development." But they placed no legal limit on the size of Austria's armed forces. For the individual declarations and the Austrian State Treaty, see Richard Dean Burns, ed., *Encyclopedia of Arms Control and Disarmament,* 3 vols. (New York: Scribner's, 1993) 3: pp. 1338 and 1402–1403. For neutralization arrangements starting in 440 B.C., see ibid., 3: pp. 1319–1364.

Czech Republic joined NATO. Sweden, Finland, and Austria debated whether to take the same step. Belarus, on the other hand, drew closer to Russia.[41]

As the twenty-first century began, a belt of neutral states could still be formed extending from the northern shores of the Baltic Sea to the northern shores of the Black Sea. It could include Finland, Sweden, Estonia, Latvia, Lithuania, Belarus, Ukraine, Austria, Slovakia, Moldova, Romania, and Bulgaria. If any of the last four demurred, the belt would nonetheless stretch from the Baltic to the Black Sea. Austria could join the belt only at its border with Slovakia. The former Yugoslav republics could also be part of the large neutral zone.

Insecurities would remain, but might be compensated for by a less hostile confrontation between Russia and Europe. Were Moscow assured that Ukraine and the Balts could not join NATO, the Kremlin could reciprocate by thinning its forces in European Russia. With Belarus part of the neutral zone, an alliance between Minsk and Moscow would also be excluded. If Kaliningrad were demilitarized, the region and its ports could hope to flourish in a zone of free trade unburdened by a heavy military presence. An East-West understanding on such matters could help Russia become a partner in security rather than a menacing pariah.

VI. JOIN THE WEST BUT NOT NATO

Balts could enhance their security by increasing ties with the West short of joining NATO. Even without joining a military alliance, Baltic security would improve from expanded cooperation with the EU, other all-European insititutions, and the PfP. Reasonable Russians, two Rand analysts proposed, would not object to such arrangements.[42]

Each Baltic republic campaigned effectively for acceptance into Western institutions. Baltic negotiators also argued that all of Europe would benefit from rapid growth in the Baltic economies. They urged Western firms to tap the skilled but low-wage labor force available in the Baltics.

Estonia blazed a path to the EU, as we see in box 11.5, with Latvia and Lithuania not far behind. The Baltic governments gradually made their laws converge with EU codes. All three Baltic republics achieved associate status in the EU in 1995 and hoped for full membership early in the twenty-first century. Indeed, in October 1999 the European Commission announced that Latvia and Lithuania would be included in the next set of candidate countries considered for EU accession—the others being Bulgaria, Malta, Romania, and Slovakia.

Each Baltic government hoped that EU membership would open trade opportunities not just with Europe but with the world; encourage both domestic and foreign investment in the Baltic countries; constrain arbitrary trade and tax changes; lock in well-defined property rights; and bolster competitive practices and legal norms.

But many EU members preferred to shut out any East Central Europeans or Balts. They may have agreed to expand NATO as a substitute for enlarging the EU. But some feared competition from low-wage farmers and producers of light industry; some did not wish to relax EU voting procedures to accommodate a much larger membership; some doubted that the Eastern states would soon meet Western standards of democracy; some worried about papered-over ethnic and border conflicts (for example, between Hungary and Romania); some doubted the easterners could

---

Box 11.5. Estonia's Path to the West

August 27, 1991—The European Commission recognizes Estonian independence and establishes diplomatic relations

January 1992—The Estonian ambassador is accredited to the European Commission in Brussels

November 1994—Estonia becomes an associated partner of the Western European Union

January 1995—The Free Trade Agreement between the EU and Estonia becomes operational with no transition period

June 1995—Estonia signs the Association Agreement with the EU, institutionalizing relations on many levels; the agreement enters force in February 1998 after ratification by all EU members

November 1995—Estonia applies for EU membership

July 1996—The European Commission recommends the EU begin accession negotiations with Estonia

December 1997—The Luxembourg Summit of the European Council decides to begin EU accession negotiations with six "first round candidate countries"—the Czech Republic, Cyprus, Estonia, Hungary, Poland, and Slovenia

March 1998—The EU Accession Conference begins reviewing the laws of the six candidates for compliance with EU standards on thirty-one topics such as industrial policy, health protection, and statistics.

Estonia's prime minister was responsible for European integration issues, the foreign minister for accession negotiations. The Riigikogu Committee on European Affairs monitored Estonia's government and pursued ties with the European Parliament.

defend their frontiers from illegal immigrants and goods; and some feared food contaminated by Chernobyl. Some also worried that ethnic or other issues in the Baltic countries could trigger complications with Russia. A former French president and German chancellor warned that the EU could collapse and turn into a mere free-trade zone if it took in many new members with diverse political traditions and economic conditions. If the EU must expand, they said, its original members and a few other candidates should form a core of "Euro-Europeans" that would create a single political entity like the United States in North America.[43]

Apart from the EU, the reborn Baltic republics quickly obtained full membership in the Council of Europe in Strasbourg. Estonia's foreign minister in May 1996 took over the rotating six-month chairmanship of the Committee of Ministers of the Council of Europe. Mice could roar. Estonian delegates set out standards for Russian membership in the Council and, after Russia joined in 1996, underscored the gaps between Moscow's commitments to the Council and its performance.[44] One Estonian parliamentarian complained that the quality of Council work suffered from Russia's participation.[45] Balts urged all governments to oppose any signs that Russia intended to reassert a heavy hand in its former borderlands. Denouncing Russia's wars in Chechyna, the Council of Europe suspended the RF delegation's voting rights in April 2000 and did not reinstitute them until early 2001, despite some blandishments from the Putin Kremlin.

Balts' security also benefited from Western investment and joint ventures in the Baltic region. Giving a U.S. firm such as Williams International a major stake in Baltic enterprises meant that, if Russia threatened a Baltic state, Western investments were also at risk. Balts hoped Moscow would perceive that its ties with the West could suffer seriously if Russia attacked any of its European neighbors.

VII. JOIN NATO

Balts saw full membership in NATO as the best guarantee against dangers from the East. They did not wish to reside in a "gray zone" or security vacuum. Balts were not content with any half-way security arrangements. Balts wanted to belong with the "united democracies," as Landsbergis called the Western alliance. If the lines were clear, Moscow would lose any temptation to reimpose Russian dominion over the *pribaltika*. Neither Finlandization nor satellization would be feasible.

Membership in EU and NATO would contribute to Baltic wealth and defense. EU membership would foster "soft" security as well as economic development. Admission to NATO would bolster soft as well as hard security. The alliance would help insure investments. Foreign investments in Poland and the Czech Republic doubled or trebled in the year after they joined NATO.

A survey by the Emor agency in June 2000 found that more than 60 percent of Estonian residents favored Estonia's entry into NATO—up 6 percent since January—while those wanting the country to join the EU made up only 40 percent—down by 7 percent since January. Ethnic Estonians tended to favor joining NATO while non-Estonians tilted toward the EU. NATO membership was favored by 68 percent of ethnic Estonians but by only 23 percent of non-Estonian ethnics. Thus, 58 percent of non-Estonian ethnics favored EU entry, compared to just 43 percent of ethnic Estonians.

While ethnic Estonians seemed to see NATO as a guarantor of their security and independence, many perceived the EU as a threat to their national identity. This possibility did not worry Russian speakers, who saw the EU as a defender of their rights.[46]

How could Balts enter NATO? A "Study on NATO Enlargement" released in Brussels on September 1, 1995, argued that the PfP could help candidate states gradually identify themselves as ready for NATO membership. The necessary conditions included transparency and accountability in defense planning and budgeting, democratic control of military forces, ability and willingness to contribute to international peacekeeping, participation in joint planning and training exercises with NATO forces, interoperability with NATO, and absence of border or other disputes with neighbors. Balts endeavored to meet these requirements.

Western and Baltic governments strove to improve Baltic interoperability with NATO. Indeed, NATO laid out a "pre-accession strategy"—a kind of super PfP—to cultivate for Balts a virtual associate membership in NATO. The gap between partner and NATO member would become paper thin, so that the transition from one to the other could be conducted smoothly and easily.[47] The United States and other NATO members strengthened their bilateral ties with the Baltic states. Also, Western arms sellers hyped their wares, even though it remained unclear who would foot the bill for additional weapons.

On January 16, 1998, the three Baltic republics and the United States signed a Charter of Partnership pledging to "consult together, as well as with other countries, in the event that a Partner perceives that its territorial integrity, independence, or security is threatened or at risk." These were not empty promises. Washington transferred military equipment to the Baltic republics and supported a bevy of Baltic military cooperation institutions, from BALTBAT to BALTNET and BALTSEA.

But NATO left the Balts on the doorstep when it admitted three new members in 1999. Balts' most active backer among NATO allies was a country with no armed forces, Iceland—also the first state to recognize Baltic independence in 1991.[48]

Was the PfP a step toward joining NATO or a substitute for membership? Balts feared that without formal admission to NATO the West might consign them to Russian domination. There were hints that some NATO governments would accept the Baltic republics in the West's economic and cultural realm while relegating them to Russia's security sphere. Indeed, one Rand Corporation study recommended letting Russia reassert its leadership in its border regions—in the south and southeast if not the west.[49] Balts were allergic to suggestions in 1999 by Condoleeza Rice, an adviser to George W. Bush, that the United States should intervene abroad mainly to uphold its vital interests—not to support ethnic minorities. Balts remembered that, when Dr. Rice worked for Mr. Bush's father, she resisted Baltic Americans' requests for U.S. pressure against Soviet intervention. In 2001 she became National Security Assistant to the new president.

Balts lobbied for admission in a next round of NATO enlargement. PfP activities were useful but provided no formal guarantee—even Russia took part in these exercises. If Chechnya revealed Russia's weaknesses, Kosovo underscored Europe's. Without the United States, Europe lacked long-range punch. Neither the PfP nor the WEU nor an EU rapid replacement force could take the place of an Atlantic alliance backed by a staunch U.S. presence in Europe.

The WEU promised much but did little—so little that it was laid to rest in November 2000. Within weeks, the fifteen EU members pledged to create within three years a sixty-thousand-strong rapid reaction force able to go anywhere in the world at sixty days notice and to be sustained for a year. A decision to use the force would require a unanimous vote by the fifteen-member Council of Ministers, but no country would have to take part. Non-EU members such as the Baltic countries and Turkey could also contribute to the force. If the EU force eroded the U.S. commitment to Europe, however, Western solidarity would decline. The project could give Moscow another lever for dismantling NATO. Russia, meanwhile, continued to field the largest military forces in Europe.

One, two, three, or more? Each Baltic government sought admission to NATO either alone or in tandem with the other Baltic states. In 2000 Lithuania and Slovenia sponsored a conference in Vilnius calling for simultaneous admission of all nine applicant countries into NATO. Still, if NATO accepted only one or two Baltic states in the next tranche, their admission could open the door for the others.

As the century began, however, NATO as well as the EU kept the Baltic republics at arm's length even as Western actions in Kosovo and elsewhere seemed to make Russia more bellicose. Some Balts complained that they were treated like high-risk applicants for insurance—suspected of having a preexisting condition or being in remission. As a result, those who most needed insurance were denied coverage![50]

VIII. BROADEN NATO TO INCLUDE RUSSIA

Another way to reduce dangers from the East would be to admit Russia into NATO, along with the Baltic republics and more East Central European states. Proponents said that if Russia were admitted into the Atlantic community, the forces of militarism and imperialism in Russia would be diminished; democracy and openness in Russia would be enhanced; and Moscow might halt economic and other pressures on the Baltic republics and cooperate more fully with the West on arms control and peacekeeping.

In the era of good feeling following the breakup of the USSR, some Russian leaders hinted that NATO, if not abolished, should include Russia. But much happened in the 1990s to revive mutual distrust.

As President Putin succeeded President Yeltsin, Russia was still ruled from the top down by elites seeking to dominate their borderlands. To admit Russia into NATO would be to remove the alliance's raison d'être. Should NATO open its doors to the very country the alliance was meant to contain? Political realism said no. The risk was simply too great. The security dilemma remained: whatever either side did to buttress its security could be seen as a threat by the other.

IX. ABOLISH NATO AND UPGRADE THE UNITED NATIONS

President Franklin Roosevelt hoped the great powers could work through the United Nations to maintain world peace. But Washington persuaded Western Europeans in 1949 to form the North Atlantic Treaty Organization to contain Soviet expansion and skirt Moscow's veto power in the UN Security Council.[51] At the onset of a new millennium, however, Russia no longer posed an active threat to its European neighbors.

NATO's role in Kosovo-type operations mocked the United Nations and antagonized not just Russia but China. Was it time to abolish NATO and transform the United Nations into a limited world government?

A stronger United Nations could enhance Baltic interests if it bolstered the rights of all states—even the smallest—to be treated as sovereign equals. It could provide forums and resources for solving regional and international problems.

Still, the United Nations at the onset of the twenty-first century was a weak reed. For Balts it seemed a fragile barrier to aggression compared to NATO. It was often paralyzed by the inclination of its members to put their own narrow interests above the common good. The U.S. Congress wanted to contribute only to those UN programs it approved. Russia, China, and any other permanent member could still veto Security Council decisions. Even when no great power blocked action, the United Nations moved very slowly—if at all. The Secretary-General had no rapid reaction force. Would the UN act if Balts were again under siege?

Both the United Nations and NATO played constructive roles on the world stage. Both needed to be strengthened. It would be foolhardy to do away with either unless better alternatives existed.

X. SELF-ORGANIZE FOR GLOBAL GOVERNANCE

A transnational civil society was evolving in the early twentieth century. It developed in tandem with complex interdependence across many countries and regions. The Baltic countries were quick to join this movement. Russia could do so too, if its leaders and people wished.

In medieval times the Hanseatic city-states showed how, with minimal formal structures, cooperation could enhance shared objectives. The Internet made the same point for the twenty-first century. Existing structures and procedures were bypassed as humanity self-organized for mutual gain. Not just security but human development could gain from the collaboration of governments, firms, international organizations, NGOs, and transnational movements. Self-organization could generate "order for free."

World governance was not world government. States retained sovereignty, but every state was permeable. States shared power with a medley of business and labor groups as well as NGOs. Together they formed an expanding network of institutions designed to meet a wide range of human needs. Both territoriality and culture weakened as principles of organization. More and more individuals, NGOs, and even states seemed to act on convictions of human solidarity—as if they were the keepers not only of their brothers and sisters but of distant cousins and absolute strangers.

If state power is not the last word, intangible power can also count. In the late summer 2000 a conference of the Unrepresented Nations and People's Organization met in Tallinn and condemned China's repressive occupation of Tibet. Estonian parliamentarians announced that the Dalai Lama would visit the Baltic states in June 2001. Some Estonian MPs again voiced support for Chechnya and for Taiwan—even as China's parliamentary chairman Li Peng paid an official visit to Estonia.

PRC leader Li Peng, blamed by many for the bloodshed at Tiananmen Square in 1989, arrived in Vilnius in September 2000 when "Nuremberg 2"—the International

Congress on the Evaluation of Crimes of Communism—was meeting in the Lithuanian parliament. Some Lithuanian parliamentarians took part in this forum convened by former political prisoners and by human rights groups in the Baltic and elsewhere in Europe. Though Li Peng had planned to spend two days in Lithuania, he chose to stay at the Vilnius airport for just three hours and then depart. At the airport VIP lounge, he talked with Landsbergis, still the chair of Lithuania's parliament. Outside, protestors waved "Free Tibet" signs and carried portraits of the Dalai Lama.[52]

In September 2000 Prime Minister Laar, President Vike-Freiberga, and President Adamkus all addressed the UN summit of world leaders. Laar reminded delegates that the United Nations in 1972 had ignored the appeals of Estonian freedom fighters then being dragged off to Soviet prisons. He called on the UN to do more for human rights in the new millennium. And Prime Minister Laar told the United Nations summit in September 2000 that Estonia favored a strengthened role for UN peacekeeping. Estonia, he said, would renounce the 80 percent discount it had enjoyed and pay its full share for UN peacekeeping missions. Estonia planned to enlarge and extend its twenty-one–soldier force serving in Kosovo. Laar also signed an accord promising to help Macedonia bring IT into schools and to promote private enterprise.

World governance was global public policy responding to the dangers and opportunities inherent in globalization. National governments conferred among themselves and with responsible specialists from national, international, and transnational agencies. This was functionalism writ large—decision making informed and managed by experts (an "epistemic community"), mediated and supervised by representatives of elected governments.

POLICY GUIDELINES FOR THE EARLY TWENTY-FIRST CENTURY

Each approach to Baltic security outlined in this chapter contained nuggets of good sense combined with lurking pitfalls:

I. Balts needed to continue efforts to improve relations with Russia, but without wishful thinking or impatient self-righteousness.

II. Balts needed to strengthen their home fronts—widening social safety nets and integrating Russian speakers—and buttress their defense forces.

III. Balts needed to cooperate more with one another and neighbors in East Central Europe. Done properly, such policies could facilitate links with the rest of Europe.

IV. The security of each Baltic state, as well as all-European security, could benefit from strengthening OSCE functions such as monitoring elections and treatment of refugees. A stronger OSCE did not require a weaker NATO.

V. Balts might still gain from a neutral belt stretching from the Baltic to the Black Sea. An "Austrian" model writ large could liberate Baltic and Russian energies to raise rather than raze human development.

VI. Whether or not Balts joined NATO, they needed to intensify cooperation with the EU and other Western institutions.

VII. If Balts joined NATO, however, they could not rest on paper assurances. And they would need to give meaning to the principle "one for all, all for one."

VIII. Western countries needed to restore constructive partnerships with Russia, but too many clouds hung over the country for it to join NATO in the early twenty-first century.

   IX. The United Nations needed upgrading but it would be premature to eliminate NATO.

   X. Balts and other Western countries could do more to strengthen systems of global governance and include Russia in them.

Let us now examine how the concept of self-organization, derived from complexity theory, harmonized with Immanuel Kant's vision of a democratic peace, the model of complex interdependence, and the theory of mutual gain to shape European security and international relations.

Caption for Chapter 11 Photo: Balts contemplated many paths to security in the twenty-first century—one of them, self-defense. Here, officers training at the Baltic Defense College conduct maneuvers at Klaipeda, Lithuania. Established at Tartu in the late 1990s, the college's staff and students were international—from the United States, Denmark, and other NATO countries; from neutral countries such as Sweden; and, of course, from the three Baltic republics, determined to meet standards for admission to NATO.

NOTES

1. On September 6, 1991, Latvian officials stated that Latvia would not pay compensation for Soviet assets on Latvian soil, because the republic suffered 63 billion roubles in losses when the USSR invaded in 1940. On October 1, 1991, Latvia agreed to pay a share of the USSR foreign debt, provided it received its share of Soviet gold reserves and credits owed to the USSR. Latvia demanded and began to receive payments by the USSR for use of the oil terminal in Latvia. In May 1992 a Lithuanian delegation to Moscow demanded $150 billion for the damage done during fifty-two years of Soviet occupation.

2. Estonians estimated in 1998 that the bill for cleaning up Soviet-caused environmental damage, especially at the submarine base on the Pakri peninsula, could total $5 billion. A Lithuanian study completed in 1997 concluded that the USSR, from 1940 to 1991, had inflicted $668 billion in damage on Lithuania. Damages included the wrongful death or forced emigration of a large fraction of the population, the bill for slave labor performed in concentration camps, and damage to churches and art treasures. *Baltic Times*, April 15-21, 1999, p. 3.

3. Charles E. Osgood, *An Alternative to War and Surrender* (Urbana: University of Illinois Press, 1962).

4. Walter C. Clemens Jr., *Dynamics of International Relations: Conflict and Mutual Gain in an Era of Global Interdependence* (Lanham, Md.: Rowman & Littlefield, 1998), chapter 7.

5. Despite asymmetries of power, Beijing and Taipei entered a GRIT-like interaction in the late 1980s. See Jun Zhan, *Ending the Chinese Civil War: Power, Commerce and Conciliation between Beijing and Taipei* (New York: St. Martin's, 1993).

6. Vygaudas Usackas, "Linking Russia with New Europe," *Washington Times,* January 12, 2000.

7 See Chris Patten, "A Northern Dimension for the Policies of the Union: Current and

Future Activities," speech to the Foreign Ministers' Conference on the Northern Dimension, Helsinki, November 12, 1999, available at the EU website under "programs."

8. An Energy Charter Treaty (not initially signed by energy-rich Norway, Russia, Poland, or Iceland) provides for the rules of the World Trade Organization to be applied to energy trade with and among non-WTO members parties to the treaty. See "Strengthening the Northern Dimension of European Energy Policy," European Commission communication of November 8, 1999.

9. For an incisive analysis by a professor at Nizhny Novgorod Linguistic University, see Alexander A. Sergounin, "Russia and the European Union: The Case of Kaliningrad," Policy Memo Series no. 172, Program on New Approaches to Russian Security (Washington, D.C.: Council of Foreign Relations, 2000).

10. Arkady Moshes, "EU Enlargement in the Baltic Sea Region and Russia: Obvious Problems, Unclear Solutions," Policy Memo Series no. 171, Program on New Approaches to Russian Security (Washington, D.C.: Council of Foreign Relations, 2000).

11. "Expanding the EU: The Debate over Border Management," *Strategic Comments* 6 (London: International Institute for Strategic Studies, 2000).

12. Mikhail A. Alexseev and Vladimir Vagin, "Fortress Russia or Gateway to Europe?" in *Center-Periphery Conflict in Post-Soviet Russia: A Federation Imperiled,* ed. Mikhail A. Alexseev (New York: St. Martin's, 1999), pp. 167–203.

13. Even a Soviet-era history acknowledged this role: V. N. Vernadskii, *Novgorod i novgorodskaia zemlia v XV veke* (Moscow, Leningrad: Izdatel'stvo Akademii Nauk SSSR, 1961). Vernadskii also wrote about Novgorod in the twelfth to fifteenth centuries.

14. Nicolai Petro, "The Novgorod Region: A Russian Success Story," *Post-Soviet Affairs* 15, no. 3 (1999), pp. 235–61.

15. Gene Sharp's writings on this topic were translated into Baltic languages and given serious consideration by some Baltic leaders. See Gene Sharp et al., *Human Rights and Coups d'Etat* (New York: International League for Human Rights, 1994).

16. The cause of civilian defense was not helped when one of its leading exponents, Dr. Audrius Butkevicius, Lithuania's minister of defense in the early 1990s, was accused of taking bribes and jailed for several years. Released in 2000, he maintained his innocence.

17. Responding to charges by Duma deputies in 1999 that Estonian authorities were discriminating against former Soviet servicemen, the OSCE criticized ex-Soviet servicemen who failed to leave Estonia and utilize housing in Russia built with foreign assistance, despite their earlier agreement to do so. Uwe Mahrenholtz, a representative of the OSCE mission in Estonia, said these persons "should not receive Estonian resident permits." Baltic News Service, November 3, 1999.

18. Dominated by the anti-Communist Home Union Party, the Lithuanian parliament passed a tough lustration law in July 1998 but President Valdas Adamkus vetoed it. He, along with the opposition Democratic Labor Party, proposed that parliament obtain a ruling on the law's constitutionality from the Constitutional Court.

19. In Latvia, however, the Center for Documentation of the Consequences of Totalitarianism had files on than four thousand KGB informers that could be checked against candidates running for office. Social Democrat leader Juris Bojars warned against opening the files. A former three-star lieutenant in the KGB, he himself was barred from running for elective office, and probably knew something about the contents of the files. Benjamin Smith, "Secret KGB files in spotlight again," *Baltic Times,* October 21–27, 1999, p. 8.

20. In 1999, however, a former KGB agent changed his name from Vladimir Tomilov to Valter Lants and won a seat on the Narva City Council, in violation of laws requiring that candidates for election avow they had not collaborated with the security bodies of countries that occu-

pied Estonia. Tomilov-Lants ran on the Center Party's ticket, though the party expelled him after the KGB connection came to light. Baltic News Service Daily Report, 1000 GMT, 21 Oct 99.

21. Landsbergis told me in 1996 that his family often talked about how his father took part in Lithuania's battles against Soviet Russian troops.

22. British turncoat Kim Philby and several Baltic comrades helped Soviet agents to ambush infiltrators dispatched to the Baltic by British and U.S. operatives.

23. Burton Frierson, "New Defence Commander Takes over a Tough Position," *Baltic Independent,* March 15–21, 1996, p. 7.

24. For defense expenditures, force levels, and aircraft inventories, see International Institute for Strategic Studies, *The Military Balance, 2000–2001* (London: Oxford University Press, 2000), pp. 93–99, and table 38.

25. Asked about this decline, Landsbergis (interviewed on November 14, 2000) attributed it to the economic squeeze caused by the collapse of trade with Russia in 1998. For background, see A. M. Zaccor, "The Lithuanian Army: A Tool for Re-Joining Europe," *European Security* 6 (spring 1997), pp. 100–113.

26. In 1999 Estonia's army numbered 4,320, its navy 250, and its air force 140; it had 2,800 paramilitary border guards and a reserve of 14,000. Latvia's army numbered 2,400, its national guard 1,600, its navy 840, and its air force 210; it had 3,500 border and coast guards and a reserve of 14,500. Lithuania's army numbered 9,340, its territorial defense regiments 2,000, its navy 560, and its air force 800; it had 3,900 border guards and a reserve of 355,650, of which 27,700 were first-line, ready to fight in seventy-two hours.

27. International Institute for Strategic Studies, *The Military Balance 1999/2000* (London: Oxford University Press, 1999), pp. 51, 87–93.

28. *Military Balance 1999/2000,* p. 117; *Military Balance 2000–2001,* pp. 125–126.

29 The top Estonian military commander in the mid-1990s was a retired U.S. officer, Alexander Einseln. Interviewed in Chicago on May 3, 1996, Einseln blamed his recent ouster on Russian blackmail threats against Estonian president Lennart Meri. Einseln was replaced by Colonel Johannes Kert, a 36-year-old former wrestling coach who had served in 1983–1985 as a Soviet officer based in Kaliningrad. Kert helped organize the Estonian Defense League in 1990 and became its operational commander in 1992. Though Kert graduated in 1994 from the U.S.-run Marshall Center for Security Studies in Germany, some Estonians wondered about his military competence. Meri fired Kert in 2000, without explaining why.

30. The U.S. Department of Defense International Military and Training programs brought some dozens of Estonians to the United States for courses ranging from English-language training to general-staff planning to air-traffic control. Estonian students studied at West Point (eight cadets in 1997) and other U.S. military academies. Balts also studied at the Marshall Center for Security Studies in Bavaria, funded by the German and U.S. governments. For reports from the U.S. Defense Attache's Office in Estonia, see http://www.usislib.ee/dod.html.

31. See Baltops web homepage at <www.cnsl.navy.mil/ccg8/index.htm>.

32. Switzerland, like the Baltic countries, was at a strategic crossroads. Its population was about the size of the three Baltic countries combined. Switzerland suffered no invasions after Napoleon. Universal military training (for men only) generated a large reserve meant to slow if not halt an invasion by larger countries. If Hitler's or Mussolini's armies had stalled in Switzerland, their vulnerabilities elsewhere would have increased.

To fuse units from twenty-six Swiss cantons speaking four different languages could not be much easier than coordinating forces of three Baltic nations. On the other hand, Swiss forces could retreat to Alpine redoubts, while Balts had to survive in flat lands. And a neutral Switzerland proved useful to Germany and other countries. As the twenty-first century began, the Swiss debated whether they, like most Western countries, should not rely on an elite professional force instead of a citizens' militia.

33. Rita Putins Peters, "The Baltic States and the League of Nations: A Study of Opportunities and Limitations," *Journal of Baltic Studies* 10 (1979), pp. 107–14, and "Problems of Baltic Diplomacy in the League of Nations," ibid., 14 (summer 1983), pp. 128–49.

34. Sergei Karaganov et al., "Russia and the Baltic States," for the Council on Foreign and Defense Policy, reported by Baltic News Service, August 2, 1999. This was a continuation of the 1997 analysis cited in chapter 10. The 1999 report was less sober and more given to wishful thinking. It said that Estonians regarded Latvia and Lithuania as their chief enemies after Russia, and reported that Lithuanian television criticized Estonians as "arrogant and ambitious."

35. On March 1, 1996, the Estonian and Latvian prime ministers expressed optimism about prospects for a border settlement. A few days later, however, an Estonian coast guard ship boarded a Latvian fishing vessel in what the Estonians thought was their economic zone. Soon they recognized a mistake and the Estonian foreign minister apologized.

36. Toomas Hendrik Ilves, "Estonia's Membership in the EU: Effects in Estonia and in Finland" (address to a seminar in Helsinki, May 26, 1998).

37. To avoid a veto when the OSCE took up Yugoslav issues, it set up a Committee of Senior Officials that excluded participants in a conflict. This committee agreed to impose an arms embargo on Yugoslavia in 1991—a move then endorsed by the UN Security Council. As Balkan issues became more complicated, the U.S. persuaded other OSCE members to suspend Belgrade's participation.

38. Walter C. Clemens Jr., "An Alternative to NATO Expansion," *International Journal* 52, 2 (Spring 1997), pp. 342–65, and "An Austrian Solution for Eastern Europe," *New York Times,* July 10, 1989, translated and critiqued in *Der Standard* (Vienna), July 12, 1989, and *Sovetskaia Estoniia* (Tallin), November 22, 1989. For other proposals, see Stephen Blank, "Russia and the Baltic: Is There a Threat to European Security?" Strategic Studies Institute, U.S. Army War College, March 31, 1993; Heinz Gärtner, "Models of European Security and Options for the New 'Neutral' Members of the European Union—the Austrian Example," *European Security* 5 (winter 1996), pp. 604–13.

39. In the 1990s Austrian leaders debated whether to join NATO as if the 1955 restraints had evaporated, even though Russia claimed to inherit the rights and duties of the USSR after the Union dissolved in 1991. The other three guarantor states still existed, but belonged to NATO. As NATO members, each could block Austria's admission if it applied. In 1931 France blocked Austria's joining Germany in a free-trade zone.

40. But neutrality was recommended by Viktor Andreev, chairman of one of two parties in the Estonian parliament representing Russian speakers. See *Baltic Times,* April 23–29, 1998, p. 4.

41. In 1999 the pro-Russian organization in Minsk, Belaia Rus, predicted the imminent creation of a Union of Sovereign Republics (SSR) federating Russia and Belarus. But many Belarusians opposed a government that had debased the mother tongue, closing six hundred Belarusian-language schools since 1994 and leaving only 11 percent of the country's children instructed in Belarusian.

42. Ronald D. Asmus and Robert C. Nurick, "NATO Enlargement and the Baltic States," *Survival* 38 (summer 1996), pp. 121–42.

43. Valéry Giscard d'Estaing and Helmut Schmidt, "Time to Slow Down and Consolidate around 'Euro-Europe,' " *International Herald Tribune,* April 11, 2000.

44. See Parliamentary Assembly of the Council of Europe, Opinion No. 193 (1996) on Russia's request for membership in the Council of Europe. Conditions included bringing to justice

those responsible for human rights violations in Chechyna and elsewhere; assistance to Balts deported to Russia and wishing to return to their homelands; and improvement in Russia's predetention and other jail facilities.

45. Russia, he said, failed to carry out all its reform commitments. The Council had permitted Russian ultranationalists such as Vladimir Zhirinovskii to address it. Tunne Kelam, interview by author in Tallinn, June 12, 1998. Kelam had warned of such developments in an article, "The End of Europe As We Know It?" *Baltic Independent,* January 26–February 1, 1996.

46. "Estonian Citizens Favor NATO over EU—Survey," *Baltic Times,* August 10-16, 2000, p. 4.

47. A. Thomas Lane, "The Baltic States, the Enlargement of NATO and Russia," *Journal of Baltic Studies* 28 (winter 1997), pp. 295–308 at 305.

48. When President of Iceland Olafur Ragnar Grimsson visited the Baltic republics in June 1998, he expressed interest in the evidence of a case when forces from the East decisively helped the West. I pointed out to him in a Vilnius church a Turkish drum taken by a Lithuanian-Polish force that helped break the Ottoman siege of Vienna in 1683.

49. Richard Kugler, *Enlarging NATO: The Russian Factor* (Santa Monica, Calif.: RAND Corporation, May 1996).

50. Some Balts said they felt as though they were living next to a big, unruly family—the Russians. Some family members (Zhirinovskii and others) leaned out their windows and yelled to Balts, "We'll burn your house down!" Other family members (such as the former Russian foreign minister Primakov) told Balts not to worry—even as other members burned down houses further afield, as in Chechnya or Georgia.

51. The UN Charter's articles 53 and 51 allowed for "regional" organizations and for self-defense pending Security Council action to uphold peace and security.

52. It was not clear whether these events would harm Lithuanian–PRC relations. Li Peng was reported to have said that Beijing respected Lithuania's wish to join the EU and NATO. Li Peng had earlier met Lithuanian President Adamkus in Reykjavik as they traveled to and from meetings at the United Nations.

12

Baltic Fitness, European Security, and International Relations: What Does Complexity Theory Explain?

Milda B. Richardson

How can we conceptualize security and development issues facing the recently reemerged Baltic states and their large, long-established neighbors? The Baltic and all of Europe are parts of larger wholes—microcosms within macrocosms. Studying the trees should help us to understand the forests—and vice versa. This chapter reviews the ways that complexity theory does—and does not—illuminate Baltic fitness, European security, and international relations (IR).

The chapter argues that complexity theory enhances our ability to describe and understand the past and present. The theory has less utility for projecting alternative futures or prescribing policy. Still, complexity theory can enlarge our vision and complement other approaches to knowledge. Our understanding of Baltic, European, and world security can gain from linking complexity theory to insights gained from Immanuel Kant's prognosis for a liberal peace, from the model of complex interdependence, and from mutual gain theory. These insights converge with the basic thesis of complexity theory: that a capacity for self-organization is a weighty factor in survival and prosperity.

SECURITY AND DEVELOPMENT IN THE BALTIC REGION

Let us review how complexity theory helps us to analyze security and development, first, in the Baltic region, then in Europe as a whole, and finally, in the broad arena of international relations.

Complexity Theory's Power to Analyze

Complexity theory helps our understanding by pressing us to think of Baltic and European security as parts of a complex adaptive system. The theory demands that we analyze the system's agents, the material elements, and the strategies they employ as they seek greater fitness. How do agents measure their own fitness? How do agents become more or less fit? What makes the system endure or change?

We can analyze and compare Baltic and European security networks by posing basic questions used to study any complex adaptive system. What are the rules of thumb and routines that agents rely on as they act and interact? What tools or resources do they employ? What are the populations of agents in the system? How do inputs such as new information shape behavior and outcomes? Who can copy strategies from whom? What processes of copying and recombining attributes create and destroy the variety of types in a system? What interventions create or destroy variety? How do errors occur in current processes? Is selection acting upon agents or upon strategies? How should the selection of agents or strategies be used to promote adaptation?[1]

Fitness and the Baltic Region

For most of the second millennium, as we saw in chapter 2, Estonians, Latvians, and Lithuanians seldom coped well with complexity. Balts wasted their limited assets by feuding among themselves and failing to utilize opportunities for mutual gain.

Fitness, of course, has to be measured against local conditions. The cards were usually stacked against Balts—small peoples surrounded and often pressured by larger ones. However, Balts were not alone in these respects. Swiss cantons were small and backward relative to the Hapsburg empire. Still, adept at self-organization, the Swiss achieved independence at roughly the same time that Balts lost theirs. Balts also fared worse than other small peoples—for example, the Danes and the Dutch—who maintained their cultures and independence for centuries in the face of powerful and sometimes aggressive neighbors.

Despite everything, Estonians, Latvians, and Lithuanians survived—aware and proud of their national identities. Survival was a major achievement, for many other peoples and cultures along the Baltic coast disappeared.

Emergence and Agent-Based Systems

The best example of an emergent property in the Baltic was the self-organization of the Hanseatic city-states. The Hansa merchants cooperated to form a whole—a "flock," as they were called—far stronger than its constituent elements. Their cooperation emerged from the actions of independent agents. The Hansas behaved like the "boids" in an experiment illustrating how birds form a flock. Each independent agent follows three rules of behavior:

1. Try to maintain a certain minimum distance from other boids.
2. Try to match velocities with other boids in the neighborhood.
3. Try to move toward the perceived center of the boid mass in the neighborhood.

None of these rules says "Form a flock." Instead, the rules are entirely local. When the boids formed a flock, it was from the bottom up—an emergent phenomenon. In similar fashion, other economies took shape before and after the Hanseatic mode. Many moved from barter to stock companies and trade unions. Independent actors, the merchants did not follow a set of differential equations but learned from experience.[2]

Hanseatic vigor wilted as larger, stronger forms of political organization formed in much of Europe. The governments, armed forces, and consular services of sovereign, territorial states could foster long-range commerce more efficiently than a loose confederation of city-states.

Imperial hegemony imposes order from above—the antithesis of cooperation by independent agents. Domination of the amber coast by non-Balts rested not on consensus or persuasion but on command and coercion. To be sure, some Balts "bandwagoned"—allied with powerful outsiders rather than resisting them. Latvian tribes, for example, aligned with the Sword Brothers for protection against Lithuanians.

Hanseatic fitness also suffered because the German bosses of towns and manors were an upper class of exploiters who did little to integrate native Balts in value-creating enterprise for mutual gain. Some Balts became part of the ruling apparatus set up by German lords, Swedish kings, Russians tsars, Soviet commissars, and Nazis. But when imperial rule faltered, there was little native support to sustain it.

When the USSR weakened, the three Baltic peoples regained their independence. Each began to master the transition from Soviet colony to political democracy, to a market economy, and to constructive participation in the international community. The time was ripe and Balts took advantage of it. Russia spun from a malaise of rigid order into a malaise of chaos. Balts, however, emerged from long periods of repression with an ability to deal effectively with extremely complex challenges at home and internationally.

There is no simple and persuasive explanation why Balts made the transition to freedom better than Russians. A variety of explanations were outlined in chapter 1. But the answer seems to lie in the Balts' proximity to the West and acceptance of Western values of individual dignity, self-reliance, and freedom—combined with confidence that virtue and hard work should and will be rewarded.

Coevolution

Fitness is not an absolute quality. It emerges from coevolution of one actor with others in the context of a changing environment. Balts coevolved along with the rest of Europe, Russia, and the world.

Balts, Russians, and other peoples living along the Baltic Sea have long shared vulnerabilities—economic, military, environmental. Increasingly, interdependence is a fact of life. *If* post-Soviet Russia were friendly *and* a good trading partner for the Baltic republics, the fitness of each actor could improve. But in the 1990s Balts became richer in spite of Russia—not thanks to it.

Environmental pollution reduced the fitness of Balts, Russians, and others sharing the Baltic littoral. The residues of Soviet-style industrialization and militarization remained in the Baltic lands and waters as well as those of Russia, and would cost billions to clean up. Some shared environmental problems such as pollution of the Narva River became more acute in the late 1990s.

Landscapes of Coevolving Fitness

The coevolving fitness of fruit flies and their predators can be effectively summarized in graphic form. But measures of sheer size and material assets do not reveal the intangibles that help people convert their assets into influence and fitness.

Complexity theory represents fitness as a peak that can rise or fall. The greater an actor's fitness, the higher its peak. As a country loses its fitness, its peak declines; its people may wander in the valley, looking for ways to rebuild their country's fitness. The security peak of each Baltic state rose in the 1990s due to many factors in the process of coevolution. Balts began to build their own defense forces, participate in the Partnership for Peace, and join a uniting Europe. But the main reason was that the peak of Russian military-imperial capacity had declined.

Since fitness in human affairs is multidimensional, it is difficult to portray the fitness of any actor—much less two or more—in a single landscape. It would be difficult if not impossible to represent even the economic-social performance of a single Baltic republic by just one set of peaks and valleys. Gains in GDP per capita, for example, did not extend to the oldest and weakest elements of society. Nor did they convert in linear fashion to improved environmental quality.

One could plot the growth of GDP and social indexes such as infant mortality and life expectancy, and compare their rise and fall in several countries. In the 1990s we would see that life expectancy in Russia fell more sharply than in the Baltic countries and was slower to bounce back.

Changes in relative Baltic and Russian fitness would be imperceptible in a graphic landscape of evolving fitness, because the scale of these actors defied comparison. Whatever happened, Russia would bulk over the Baltic republics in most measures of gross material power. A graph of power would show Russia as mighty and Balts as tiny.

Another version of landscape theory depicts the valley floor as a place of peace rather than a realm of impotence. Peaks, in this version, do not indicate fitness but "frustration," defined as actors' distance from their preferred coalition. "Energy" is the sum of every actor's "frustration" weighted by size. Looking back to Europe before World War II, this approach predicted that the Baltic countries, Finland, Poland, and Portugal would align with Germany. A binary model required each actor to join one of just two configurations. Actors could not remain nonaligned. The model did not anticipate Hitler's attack on Poland or Portugal's tightrope neutrality.[3] This application shows the dangers of trying to compress historical nuance into formal models. Ironically, this happens in a book meant to show that social life is not stationary and often defies linear models.[4]

A useful way to graph multiple attributes has been devised by INSEAD researchers in Paris. Instead of drawing peaks and valleys, INSEAD plots actors' attributes on spokes extending from a central hub. If a firm ranks high in customer relations, its grade for this attribute is marked far from the hub; if it does poorly in innovation, its grade on that spoke is close to the hub. Using this approach, INSEAD compared average grades for the electronics industry with average scores for the world's largest companies. INSEAD found that the electronics industry scores differed little from those of other major industries, such as automobiles. However Nokia, the Finnish manufacturer of cell phones, scored higher on many dimensions than the average for electronics firms.[5]

Complexity Theory's Power to Predict

Were the Baltic republics becoming less or more fit as a new millennium began? How did their prospects compare with those of other European countries? Russia? Singapore? Taiwan? The growth of overall fitness in the Baltic region could rival the economic and political wonders of post-1945 Germany and the East Asian Tigers. It rested on strong foundations, but could be derailed.

Self-Organized Criticality

The continued growth of self-organized fitness in the Baltic republics was not assured. The Baltic democracies faced nested tangles of exacting challenges: the scowls and growls of a powerful neighbor; recurrent economic warfare by that neighbor, including intermittent suspension of energy flows; the disaffection of many Russian speakers settled in the Baltic lands; bitter infighting among Baltic politicians, including Communists and anti-Communists; bank failures; corruption and naiveté among the new political and economic elites; mafia networks, both local and transnationally linked to Russia; an unsure and sometimes dispirited populace; pressures from the West as well as Russia to change citizenship and other laws.

Had ethnic or other problems been more intense, had more of them gone critical at the same time, or had they been aggravated by natural catastrophes, the fragile equilibrium underlying the Baltic transformation could have collapsed. Of course a fit society can cope with multiple challenges. But the resilience of Balts was uncertain as the new century began. Could some extra grains of sand collapse the emergent structures of self-rule?

Punctuated Equilibrium

The theory of punctuated equilibrium reminds us that neither progress nor regress is likely to continue indefinitely. Political and economic development in the Baltic will not occur in a straight line. Relapses and long plateaus are likely and may set the stage for another advance, or a dramatic retreat. Progress is possible—perhaps even likely—but not foreordained. A glance to the West recalls that movement toward European unity has occurred in jumps and starts for more than half a century, along with occasional backsliding.

Many challenges also confronted Russia after 1991, their variety and intensity eroding the very foundations of the country's fitness. If challenges intensified, the Russian Federation could splinter. Chaos could beget chaos, destroying hopes for self-organization in Russia and threatening its neighbors as well.

No one could know how long Russia would decline. An earlier "Time of Troubles" lasted fifteen years—from 1598 to 1613. When Russia again stabilizes, the country might not recover quickly. Russians could face a long walk in the valley before they succeed in raising its peak upward.

Complexity Theory's Power to Prescribe

Complexity theory gives few suggestions on how to achieve fitness—the ability to cope with complexity—but it is clear on what to eschew. A fit society should avoid both the rigid hierarchy and the outbursts of anarchy that characterized Russia for much of the second millennium, including its final decade.[6] The policy implications sketched in this chapter are logical inferences from the concept of fitness as a point poised between rigid order and chaos. But they gain specificity from the historical experiences and other theories reviewed here.

The Wealth of Nations

A global perspective—an outlook that asks how best to compete and cooperate with buyers and suppliers around the world—is needed to prosper in an interdependent world. In economics as in politics it is wiser to search for strategies for mutual gain over the long haul rather than for short-term profits. Both the Tigers and the Nordic countries demonstrated the utility of cooperative value-creating over exploitative value-claiming. Both the Tigers and the Nordics cultivated strong ties between suppliers and the marketplace—loyalty to and by consumers, and loyalty by and toward the work force. Such practices and attitudes were rare in the former Soviet realm, but many Baltic businesses internalized them after 1991.

The implications for policy makers from complexity theory are extremely general: Here are a few guidelines:[7]

- Utilize what has worked in the past but also explore new ways to deal with emerging challenges and opportunities. Arrange organizational routines to balance time-tested solutions and innovation.
- Harness the benefits of uniformity with extreme variation. (Thus, the agents developing the Linux operating system maintain the integrity of the basic system but collaborate to improve performance characteristics such as execution speed.)
- Do not sow large failures while reaping small efficiencies. Ask if there is a risk of disaster from attempting a bold strategy.
- Look for shorter-term, finer-grained measures of success that can promote longer-run, broader goals.
- Assess strategies in light of how their consequences can spread, for example, closer ties with the EU for Baltic societies.
- Building on social capital, cultivate networks of reciprocal interaction that foster trust and cooperation. Use social activity to support the growth and spread of valued criteria.
- Promote effective neighborhoods. Tag cooperators so that they can recognize and support each other (but beware of defectors, as in Prisoner's Dilemma, discussed in chapter 5).

Politics

The optimum role for government in development is not clear. Surely government must maintain order, collect taxes, build a modern infrastructure, support education, and create a climate hospitable to domestic and foreign investors. It is still not clear whether industrial and strategic trade policies are useful or necessary. Laissez-faire may have served Hong Kong better than neomercantilism did the other Tigers.

In East Asia, prosperity preceded democracy, but this may not be the ideal sequence—especially for Europeans smarting from long alien rule. In Scandinavia, democracy and wealth advanced side by side—both preceded by devotion to literacy. Balts in the 1990s seemed to want all good things simultaneously.

The examples of the Tigers and the Nordic countries illustrate the importance of social peace to development. Civil war can quickly undermine many decades of human development—witness Sri Lanka. Balts would be wise to conciliate rather than alienate the settlers in their midst.

Integration

Complexity theory says little about the value of maintaining or mixing cultures. Cultural homogeneity probably helped Japan's fitness while heterogeneity probably benefited the United States. For the world at large, cultural diversity—like genetic diversity—is a plus, so long as it coexists peacefully with others. Each Baltic people was right to maintain and enhance its language and culture. The cultures of small societies need more protection than those of large ones.

Social and cultural integration, like peace, can be positive or negative. Positive integration signifies creative harmony, negative integration merely a lack of violence. Positive integration is dynamic; negative, static. Less than a decade after regaining independence, each Baltic society was moving from negative toward positive integration.

Security

The perspective of coevolution should lead rivals to understand and act on their shared vulnerabilities. But, for Balts, it did not change their security dilemma. Mutual gain was still thwarted by mutual fear. Since Russia posed less of a military threat in the 1990s, the external fitness of the Baltic republics improved. But Balts feared Russia's ambitions, while Russian strategists feared NATO expansion.

IS COMPLEXITY THEORY RELEVANT TO EUROPEAN SECURITY?

Complexity Theory's Power to Analyze

Complexity theory integrates many concepts that help us to describe key issues of European security, identify its strengths, and diagnose its problems.

The concept of *fitness tied to coevolution* reminds us that European security must be evaluated in tandem with the security of other actors, including Russia, along with trends in their shared environment. Western leaders in the 1990s ignored how Russians might perceive and respond to the expansion of a sometimes hostile alliance on their doorstep. They slighted what they once esteemed—Mikhail Gorbachev's insight that for security to be genuine, it must be mutual.

The idea that *optimal fitness is found between rigid order and chaos* illuminates Europe's deep assets. In the last half of the twentieth century Europe shed much of the rigid order that undermined its fitness in previous times, while reducing or transcending chaos. Late-twentieth-century Europe showed that it could cope with many complex challenges, though not all. Thus, Europeans continued to search for better ways to cut joblessness, assist refugees, and organize effective military forces able to function "out of area."

The concept of *emergence* gives insight into European integration. In the second half of the twentieth century an emergent property of European unity took shape—

laws, customs, and institutions plus an expectation that Europeans would cooperate to address their problems. This emergent phenomenon was cultivated by functionalist and neofunctionalist leaders who saw opportunity as well as challenge in the dynamics of technology and economics.

The notion of *punctuated equilibrium* prepares us for surges toward European unity, long intervals of stability, and possible regressions.

The concept of *coevolution* reminds us that societies adapt. They do not necessarily "advance." Social groups and political actors are reluctant to experiment with new institutions unless serious shocks challenge internal familiar ways and alignments. One might have expected the bloodletting of 1914–1921 to shock Europe into a new, more cooperative way of life, but the opposite happened. The shocks of World War II plus gifted European and U.S. leadership—abetted by Stalinism—pushed Europe in a new direction. Without such shocks, the status quo tends to prevail with only marginal institutional change. Transaction costs, set beliefs, and standard operating procedures mitigate against frequent overhaul.

Defining *fitness* as the *ability to cope with complexity* helps us to compare the EU with other international organizations striving to tap the energies of still sovereign states. Despite many growing pains, the EU became far more fit than the CIS or the OSCE. Most CIS members feared a return of Russian hegemony and focused on creating values mainly for themselves. As a result, the CIS experienced more chaos than order in the 1990s.

The OSCE suffered from a large membership and little central power. As the EU membership becomes larger and more diverse, it could acquire problems similar to those of the OSCE. The EU could lose as well as gain fitness.

Complexity theory stimulates us to think about *landscapes of fitness*. The fitness peaks of individual European states rise and fall relative to one another. The internal fitness of Europe gained relative to Russia in the 1990s, but probably declined relative to the United States. Balts' fitness, however, increased in the 1990s compared to major European powers as well as in relation to Russia. While Germany faced the burdens of unification, Balts' energies were liberated from alien rule.

Complexity Theory's Power to Predict

Some complexity theorists assert that evolution generates "order for free." If this is so, why are large hunks of humanity entombed in rigid order while others suffer from virtual anarchy? Can we know when the unfree and the ungoverned will self-organize?

History shows that certain regions lost fitness while others gained. Beginning around 1500, Chinese, Islamic, Aztec, Incan, and other civilizations declined relative to the West, which was joined later by Japan and, intermittently, by Russia. Chinese and Islamic civilizations suffered from too much order or too much chaos. Since most humans start with similar genes, differential fitness must be partly explained by culture and luck. Geography is important but rarely decisive. Thus, affluent Japan is resource-poor while impoverished Russia has vast resources. The key to the riddle is culture—the matrix. Western and Japanese cultures, each in its own way, permitted and encouraged autonomous economic and other activity. In the West they also encouraged democracy—self-organization.

Looking back we divine that freedom to innovate helped Westerners become more fit. But in 1500 the content of an optimal fitness policy was not clear. The Ottomans, for example, took Constantinople in 1453 and besieged the disorganized Europeans for more than two centuries before being driven back from Vienna in 1683; the undemocratic Russian empire was a major actor in nineteenth-century politics; the totalitarian dictatorships of Mussolini, Stalin, Hitler, and Japan looked quite formidable for many years. Only in retrospect do we know that authoritarians started and lost most major wars of the twentieth century.

Complexity theory implies that freedom to innovate is a vital ingredient in fitness. But complexity theory cannot anticipate whether a unified Europe will nurture or throttle innovation. The theory cannot reveal whether Europeans—individuals, countries, regional organizations—will try to claim values or create them with others.

Complexity theory expects punctuated equilibrium but cannot predict whether Europe will surge toward greater unity or remain at a given level for a long period. The concept of punctuated equilibrium does not tell us how long any period will last or in what direction change will proceed.

A time of equilibrium, of course, need not be followed by closer integration; fragmentation is also possible, as happened to the Association of Southeast Asian Nations when buffeted by economic chaos starting in 1997. The EU could unravel as it accepts more and more members.

Complexity Theory's Power to Prescribe

While complexity theory helps us to comprehend recent trends, it offers little guidance on how to enhance Europe's fitness. The theory holds that self-organization, like the "invisible hand" of Adam Smith, arises spontaneously from nature. If this is so, proactive policy guidance and rules are unnecessary. They could even be counterproductive.

"Fitness for whom?" is a pervasive issue. Which should have priority—the European whole or its parts? If the latter, *which* parts—business interests or labor? Germany or Portugal? Young or old? Traditionalists or innovators?

Complexity theory cannot say which security issues have priority. Do the most pressing threats come from within or from outside Europe? If the greatest menace is internal, should Europeans worry more about environmental degradation, social disorder, unemployment, lagging competitiveness, unwanted immigration, or falling birth rates? Both internal and external threats exist, but their salience varies across Europe. Germany, for example, is more attuned to threats from Russia than is Portugal. Also, some threats are latent but can quickly become actual.

Military Security

If Europe's greatest threats are external, do they come from renewed Russian military pressures, from Balkan-type conflicts on the periphery, from U.S. bullying, or from rogue states and movements in the South?

If a resurgent Russia should again menace Europe, complexity theory's devotion to emergent properties might imply that Europeans should strengthen their collective military prowess. But this recommendation *could* be wrong, for a unified Europe might be weaker than the sum of its parts. Perhaps Europe could better resist external threats if it consisted of many distinct fatherlands—each heavily armed like Sweden or Switzerland. A unified Europe might suffer from hubris or from free-riding. The parasitic logic of collective action might tempt a "unified" Europe to invest fewer resources in defense than would a single state relying on its own resources. An ultimatum from a reborn Russian leviathan might conceivably bring a unified Europe to its knees. A Europe of strong individual states might be more difficult to subdue.

If Europeans worry about the spread of Balkan-type wars, should they unite to extinguish those fires without depending on the United States? The answer could depend on many factors. By 2000–2001 the EU states had demonstrated very little ability to deal with military threats. Europe might be better off without its own rapid reaction force than with one that occasions false hopes. The EU states might prefer to let U.S. diplomacy and arms do most of the work. This would economize European resources but reinforce European dependence on the one superpower and undermine European pride.

Should Europeans pool their strengths to become a superpower? Complexity theory doesn't give an answer, but neither do traditional IR theories. One can argue whether stability is best served by unipolarity, bipolarity, or multipolarity. But the dynamics of time and place are more important than our speculative logic. For example, if a resurgent Russia challenged a European superpower and the United States, the West's combined strengths would be daunting. But the European and American giants might pass the buck to one another—doing nothing until it was too late, as in the 1930s, when France and Britain faced a revisionist Germany.[8]

Economic Security

What if the main threat to Europe is thought to be economic stagnation? Complexity theory cannot tell Europeans whether they should continue to give high priority to social welfare or do more to enhance industrial competitiveness. The needs of each locality may differ. Some may need more welfare, while others need to be more competitive. Complexity theory cannot advise how to balance these competing demands. Nor can it say whether policy objectives can best be furthered by local or more centralized efforts.

If some Europeans want to strengthen their industry, complexity theory cannot say whether more or less integration is optimal. Some planners will say that a more integrated Europe could better tap disparate strengths, bolster critical industries, and promote exports. But the merits of a Japanese-style industrial and trade policy are unclear. Honda succeeded in making world-class autos against the advice of Japan's central policy planners. The United States, with far less industrial or trade policy than Japan or Europe, set the pace in high-technology research and development in the 1990s.

Whose economic fitness should have priority? Should the EU subsidize farmers? Switzerland subsidizes its farmers to keep them in the fields and uphold the country's self-reliance. But these subventions increase the cost of food for most Swiss. Subsidies also distort trade within Europe and globally, overriding complementary strengths. What is good for some Swiss may be bad for Europe as a whole; it may also be bad for most Swiss—unless a global crisis limits food imports.

Cultural Security

What if the most salient threat to Europe is thought to be cultural—the homogenizing forces of McDonald's and MTV? Cultural diversity may hold some inherent advantage akin to biodiversity or genetic diversity in humans.[9] Surely there are special forms of wisdom, beauty, and other values in the many cultures at risk from homogenization.

The pressures for "McWorld" expediency may push Europeans to march in lockstep toward American- or Euro-English, eroding other languages. But many Catalans, Scots, and other minorities believe that their cultural autonomy will be better served by pan-European institutions than by the nation-state in which they are a minority.

Still, if Europeans are more closely wedded to their local cultures than to Europeanism, if most prefer a local language that few others know (such as Catalan, Danish, or Estonian), European unity may be a distant dream. Many analysts see the common tongue and shared cultural aspirations of most Americans as a source of U.S. fitness. If a growing percentage of U.S. residents regard English as their second language, U.S. fitness will probably suffer.

On these topics, complexity theory can articulate neither an appropriate strategy nor tactics. Complexity theory cannot say whether fitness will be better served by promoting cultural diversity or by cultivating a common tongue and culture.

Multiple and Conflicting Priorities

What if we could just ignore minority interests and assert that the basic criterion for policy should be the well-being of the largest number of Europeans. Even then, complexity theory cannot say what policy is appropriate except to avoid the poles of rigid order and chaos. Because complexity theory does not say *whose* fitness should be promoted or *how,* it cannot answer basic questions such as:

- Is overall fitness best promoted at the local, regional, pan-European, trans-Atlantic, or global level?
- Should Western Europeans—for their own good or the good of "Europe"—admit Eastern Europeans and Balts to the EU? If so, should they admit all or just some? If some, which?
- For policy guidance, should Europeans look to the governments of their distinct fatherlands, to bureaucrats in Brussels, or to bankers in Frankfurt?
- For defense, should Europeans cultivate an EU force, or NATO, or the OSCE? Should they integrate national aerospace companies to compete with American giants or try to maintain national vitality? For example, should British Aerospace align closer with Airbus Industrie, with Lockheed, or go it alone?
- For environmental fitness, should Europeans follow the lead of their governments, international organizations, or transnational Green movements?
- Should Europeans try to perfect the EU, a transatlantic union, or the United Nations?

Some tasks can probably be done more effectively at one level than another. We can speculate that an integrated Europe will be better able to cope with terrorism and environmental threats than will a continent of self-centered fatherlands. Europe's industrial competitiveness, for example, in defense and aerospace, probably requires large markets and limits on the number of producers.

But more unity is not necessarily better for all forms of fitness. When the Baltic states were Soviet Republics, their ability to clean up their own and the regional environment was constrained by Moscow's relative disinterest in such projects. When the Baltic republics regained their independence, they could and did devote more resources to environmental quality at home and in the neighborhood.

When state sovereignty is kept strong, border controls are likely to be stricter. If common borders prevail, incentives for vigilance decrease because the costs from lax controls are shared like a collective good.

On other issues it is difficult even to speculate: would Germany and Greece be better able to generate jobs by unilateral actions or by cooperation in an integrating Europe? Time frames are important: long-term gains might require short- and medium-term sacrifices. Social scientists may think of long-term horizons, but politicians focus on the next elections and CEOs on quarterly balance sheets.

Complexity theory reminds us that the ability to cope with complexity is crucial to European security. Our planet and its denizens coevolve, their landscapes sometimes changing rapidly. Opportunities and challenges arise, taxing our imaginations and other resources. Balts and other Europeans have great assets—intellectual and moral as well as material—but have often squandered them in the past and could do so again. At either wing of Europe, Americans and Russians also shape and are shaped by the condition of European security. Our shared vulnerabilities offer a vast expanse in which we can help or hurt one another.

Political realists can offer no better guidance on how to juggle multiple priorities. They tell us to "maximize power" and to "balance" or "bandwagon." They do not say how to balance the quest for power against welfare, cultural, environmental, and other goals, for their concept of fitness is one dimensional. They focus on the nation-state as the basic actor in IR but cannot say when it should be supplanted or superseded by an alliance, a transnational corporation, or a European superstate. They lack any transcendent standard by which to justify individual sacrifice for the good of the whole.[10] A study of greedy economic and political interests in one Danish city offers little further guidance. It suggests only that reformers must be prepared for narrow self-seeking by the wealthy and powerful—a lesson familiar to the authors of the *Federalist Papers* from their reading of world history.[11]

COMPLEXITY THEORY AND INTERNATIONAL RELATIONS

Complexity theory is another step in the long quest for a general systems theory. It should help us understand the place of IR in the great chain of being. From ancient Greeks to today's long-cycle theorists, scholars have searched for systemic patterns within political and economic networks. Systems thinking steps past linear thinking and instructs us to look at how parts interact to shape a whole. It alerts us to the prospect of nonlinear behavior, multiplier and threshold effects, positive and negative feedback, unforeseen and unintended consequences. It warns that actions meant to advance a certain goal may unleash system effects making the goal less attainable.

Certainly students of world affairs need to see the forest, but they must also know the trees, the bushes, and other parts of the whole. They must trace not only structure but actual behavior. Systems theorists in IR often minimize subjective elements such as culture and self-identity. They make such elementary errors as comparing states with firms. Traditionalist IR, with its emphasis on the particulars of time, place, culture, and individual personalities—all contingent and shaped by *fortuna*—offers a corrective to the sweeping generalizations of systems theories.

The main value of complexity theory for IR and comparative politics may be its way of looking at and classifying reality. Let us survey how the basic concepts of complexity theory sharpen our tools for understanding IR.

Fitness and IR

Fitness is a more comprehensive and deeper concept than power or influence, the foci of IR realists and neorealists. Realists tend to define power by material assets—"How many divisions has the pope?" What is the GDP of the Vatican? Fitness comes closer to the true purpose of politics, as understood by many political theorists, than do power or influence.

Fitness signifies societal well-being—the ability to cope with challenges and expand choices. This view denies that the purpose of foreign policy is to dominate other societies; to gratify the psychic needs of power-hungry individuals; to benefit a ruling class; to divert the masses from other issues; to amass rockets and tanks; or to possess more autos per capita than any other country. To possess military power, material wealth, or influence is not tantamount to fitness; their pursuit can even undermine fitness.

Fitness implies a utilitarian morality: the goal of politics should be the greatest well-being for the greatest number of people. A similar perspective underlies the UN Human Development Index. While the IR realist focuses on a state's material power and influence, the HDI targets the ability of states to expand their members' choices by improving their health, education, and purchasing power and by decreasing gender and other inequalities.

Domestic fitness and HDI scores, however, can be destroyed by external agents. To be fit, every society needs a capacity to neutralize or repulse threats from outside. Complexity theory cannot assess comparative risks, for they depend on time and place. But the logic of complexity theory warns against imperialist ventures likely to sap domestic strength or devoting more resources to external defense than required by present and foreseeable dangers.

Emergence and Self-Organization in IR

Strong on generalities, complexity theory is weak on specifics. It gives little instruction on how to achieve fitness. The most detailed advice offered by complexity theory is to cultivate many communication nodules with vibrant links (not too many, not too few) between and among them. This, of course, is precisely what dictatorships wish to avoid![12]

Complexity theory cannot advise whether international security will benefit more from unipolar, bipolar, or multipolar politics. It merely counsels: "Not too chaotic—not too rigid." But this advice does not enlighten policy makers who wonder whether the only superpower should serve as world policeman or retreat to Mount Olympus.

Some grand theories attempt to answer such questions, but they spur more debate than consensus.

Agent-Based Systems and IR

Complexity theory reminds us that vast systems can be built from the bottom up by independent actors. Unlike insects and fishes, humans may utilize reason to promote their objectives. They may also choose ethical criteria that go beyond promoting their genes.

But complexity theory does not say what is the optimum scale or hierarchy of organization. Should North, Central, and South Americans go it alone, cooperate regionally, or devote their efforts to a universal international organization? If they decide to cooperate beyond their borders, how should they reach decisions? By majority rule? Plutocracy? Hegemonic power? Complexity theory cannot answer these questions because it is too general; also, it has no way of prioritizing the values of individual actors relative to collective interests. It cannot answer "for whom?" or "how?"

If presented with the motto *e pluribus unum,* complexity theory cannot say what is the many from which one is to be formed. The theory contains no standard by which to decide whether Scots should remain within the United Kingdom or become independent, or whether Narva or Ivangorod should secede or each stay where it is. Nor can it say whether minority cultures such as Basques can flourish better within national structures (Spain, France) or in larger entities (the EU). Of course all manner of realists and idealists will also disagree on these points.

Complexity theory cannot answer fundamental questions about how to cultivate a competitive economy: What is the tradeoff between large-scale efficiency and unfettered competition? Should the U.S. government bar Microsoft from packaging all kinds of software with its computer operating system? Is America fit because of its individualism or its welfare provisions? If both, is there an optimal balance? For a society to be fit, should women go out or stay at home? Complexity theory has no answers for these questions, but neither do other grand theories of IR or development—at least no answers that elicit wide consensus.

Coevolution and IR

The very word "coevolution" reminds us that world affairs are in flux. No society, no state, no organism evolves alone. Each society interdepends with some other societies and with their shared environment. If one society gains or loses fitness, this will impact its neighbors' fitness. The idea of dynamic, relative power is central to both realism and neorealism. But many realists and neorealists downplay the dependency of states on their shared environment. Because the environment shapes and is shaped by IR, the biosphere should probably be treated as a distinct level of IR analysis.

Fitness Landscapes and IR

This concept is evocative but problematic. As we saw when discussing the Baltic-Russian landscape, fitness among humans is multidimensional. To show fitness properly, one would need to display a separate landscape for each element of fitness. A fitness peak would have to represent not just domestic but also external fitness — relative to threats from within and without. Domestic fitness could be reduced to a separate number, such as an HDI score, but this would oversimplify. There can be huge variations in HDI within countries — by region, gender, race, age, and other divisions.

As we also saw in the Baltic case, differences in scale make it difficult to portray the changing security relationship between a large and a small country. No matter what happens within or between Taiwan and mainland China, the former will be a speck next to the latter. A nuclear arsenal in Taiwan might achieve deterrence, but would not remove China's other assets.

Self-Organized Criticality and IR

This concept warns us that societies are often more fragile than they appear. The domestic order and international position of any country can resemble a sandpile which, if one more grain of sand is added, collapses in an avalanche. To use another metaphor, even the apparently strong may buckle from some "last straw."

Punctuated Equilibrium and IR

We know that societal change often occurs at intervals of varying lengths. Change sometimes comes at a fast and furious pace, stabilizes for many years, and then resumes again for a short time. But punctuated equilibrium is a concept based on geologic time. No one can say how long are the ups and downs of human life. We dare not impose some preconceived categories upon the cycles of human history, as did Arnold Toynbee. Contrary to what his theory forecast, Europe early in the twenty-first century did not look as though it had been "routed."[13]

Complexity theory, like other forms of systems analysis, can be highly deterministic, ignoring the differences between individual units in the system. Systems theorists sometimes exaggerate their ability to map the whole. Such hubris can also harm IR theory.

The inability of complexity theory to deal adequately with the whole-parts problem could be ameliorated, at least partially, by the constructivist insight that each entity's interests are a product of its identity — its self-portrait. Both identities and interests, constructivists say, are generated by social practices.[14] Giving priority to these variables could help to overcome the excessive determinism of complexity theory. Attention to these variables reminds us of the fundamental questions: fitness for what — for what values and for whom?

Complexity Plus Other Theories: Complementarity and Convergence

Complexity theory and several other IR perspectives relevant to Baltic and European security are summarized in table 12.1. Each contributes to the total picture but no one perspective is complete.[15]

Realism/Neorealism

Hard power is still basic to security, but realism and neorealism risk overstating the weight of material factors in IR. They cannot explain, for example, how a "Singing Revolution" could help subvert a superpower. On the other hand, Grotian legalism

Table 12.1
IR Perspectives on Baltic and European Security

Approach to IR	Description of Cold War	Analysis of 1990s	Expected problems, 2000–2025	Policy descriptions for the west
Complexity theory	Contest between a top-down empire and a self-organized coalition. The fitter system wins.	Balts raised their fitness while Russia and most other former Soviet republics "wandered in the valley" between fitness peaks.	Baltic fitness may plateau or regress. Self-organized fitness is weaker in Russia than authoritarianism and anarchy.	Promote self-organization and value-creation in the Baltic countries and in Russia. Support liberal forces—not Russian oligarchs or statists demanding a "dictatorship by law."
Realism	Great powers struggled to dominate a strategic vacuum, but the West accepted the Baltic as part of Soviet sphere because the Red Army got there first.	The USSR lost control of its periphery due to imperial overreach and internal weaknesses. Yeltsin's Russia wanted to regain control of the Baltic but Moscow's policies were dominated by other priorities.	Balts want to balance against Russia by joining the West, but NATO and the EU place the Baltic low next to other priorities. The West concentrates on absorbing the "heartland" (Polish, Czech, Slovak, Hungarian republics), leaving Balts on the periphery between East and West.	Conciliate Russia but keep NATO positioned against a revived Russian threat. Cultivate close ties between NATO/the EU and the Baltic states.

Nuclear security and arms control perspective	The terror of nuclear war kept the West from challenging Soviet rule over captive nations. The Soviets valued Baltic lands for their forward bases and as a defensive buffer with antiaircraft and anti-missile defenses.	Nuclear weapons promised deterrence but endangered survival. NATO expanded to Russian borders while the U.S. pursued a national missile defense. The West invested little to promote Russian disarmament. U.S. Senate rejected the comprehensive test ban.	Russia strives to rebuild its military might and dominate former border republics. Moscow pledges to modernize its conventional forces, but is constrained by a weak economy and declining numbers of healthy young men. It brandishes nuclear arms and pledges a "first-use-if-necessary" policy.	The West should do more to promote arms limitations efforts such as START II and III; reaffirm restraints on tactical nuclear weapons; deal with missile defenses in ways not conducive to another arms race; collaborate with Russia to control "loose nukes" and curb horizontal nuclear spread to other states.
Clash of civilizations	Balts yearned to rejoin Western civilization but were repressed by Soviet power.	Estonia and Latvia were torn by a domestic split between Western-ized titulars and settlers from the East. Russia sided with "compatriots" from the East.	Balts deepen ties with the West, generating conflict with Russian speakers in the Baltic and with Moscow.	Promote the integration of Russian speakers in the Baltic countries. Build bridges spanning the cultural divide between East and West.
Kantian liberalism	There was conflict between Moscow's totalitarian dictatorship and the West. Refusing to recognize Soviet annexation of Baltic republics by force, the West used the Helsinki process to bolster	"Democratic peace" and harmony were more feasible as Russia edged toward the Kantian model. International law and EU norms shaped the policy of the Baltic states and established	International law and human rights norms become stronger worldwide, but face obstacles in Russia, where the Kantian model is still distant. Russia's political culture does not	Recognize that democracy in Russia depends mainly on Russians, but try to promote foundations of a democratic political culture there. Avoid words and deeds that bolster authoritarian

(continued)

Table 12.1
IR Perspectives on Baltic and European Security (Continued)

Approach to IR	Description of Cold War	Analysis of 1990s	Expected problems 2000–2025	Policy descriptions
	human rights in the Soviet empire.	standards that Russia also endorsed, if only to secure Western aid.	conduce to a stable, deep-rooted democracy. Hence the democratic peace lacks a dependable partner in the East.	and xenophobic strains in Russia.
Interdependence and mutual gain	The "Iron Curtain" divided an organic whole.	The logic of interdependence helped reduce political distrust and promote "value-creating" among all actors, but the security dilemma reemerged. Russia turned inward and blamed its economic and political failures on the West.	Slavophilism and imperialism compete with modernizing liberalism in Russia. Nationalism obstructs cooperation among the Baltic republics, and between them and Russia. Europeans fear competition from low-cost Baltic products.	Cultivate the common interests of Balts, all Europeans, and Russians—insistent upon reciprocity and safeguards. Enhance fitness by mutual gain.

exaggerates the role of legal norms. The West's principled refusal to honor Soviet annexation of the Baltic republics did not save the Balts from a half century of repression.

Nuclear Security/Arms Control

Nuclear weapons shape the context but are not very relevant to Baltic security. Whether or not Russia relies more on nuclear arms to counter NATO expansion, RF conventional forces and nuclear power plants pose greater risks to Baltic security.

The Clash of Civilizations

This thesis seems to fit the East-West divide southward from Narva. But it exaggerates the weight of culture and understates the role of national interests and power in alignments. Contradicting the thesis, Russian tsars permitted the German lords to maintain their hegemony in the Baltic region. Stalin and Hitler, too, found ways to cooperate. Also confounding the thesis, the Orthodox Christians of Bulgaria, Romania, and Montenegro in 1999 sided with Western Christians in support of Kosovo's Muslims. Besides power interests, the appeals of liberty and prosperity also undermine the civilizational divide.

Kantian Liberalism

The basic insight from complexity theory parallels Kant's vision of peace: that a capacity to meet complex challenges arises from creative self-organization, liberated from destructive anarchy and from the dead weight of rigid hierarchy. Kant portrayed peace as an emergent property—the synergized product of representative government, commerce, law, and international organization. Kant's prognosis has inspired a liberal peace theory with great descriptive, prescriptive, and predictive power. This theory suggests that the best guarantee for Baltic security would be a world in which each Baltic state and its neighbors shared a republican political culture of mutual respect and tolerance.[16]

Oligarchic republics such as Novgorod and the Hanseatic city-states lived in peace for centuries. Allied and Finnish forces caused each other no combat casualties in World War II.[17] But stable republican rule can be elusive. States in transition from one political system to another are often war prone. And liberal peace theory does not tell status quo countries how to cope with aggressive revisionists except to push them toward democracy—not an option in a time of crisis.

Post-Communist Russia was not stable. It veered from chaos toward authoritarian order. The more that Russia was ruled from the top down, the less the prospect it could become fit; the less fit, the more likely that it might seek relief in aggression against weak neighbors.

The security dilemma became more acute: the more authoritarian Russia became, the more Balts feared for their security and sought protection within NATO. The more that NATO expanded eastward, however, the greater the prospects that Russia would become not just authoritarian but autocratic.

Complex Interdependence

This model, developed by Robert O. Keohane and Joseph S. Nye, overlaps both with complexity theory and Kantian synergy. Interdependence, these authors say, amounts to mutual vulnerability. But when states are linked by *complex* interdependence, the threat of force is almost excluded from their interactions. Such states have many issues on their shared agenda, but none so important that it could justify a resort to arms. These states do not just have summit meetings; their societies interact on many levels.

Complex interdependence is a model toward which states may move or from which they may withdraw. A form of emergence, complex interdependence can make the participants stronger than the sum of their parts. Underscoring the many dimensions of fitness, complexity theory adds to our understanding of shared vulnerabilities.

Complexity theory and the model of complex interdependence took shape nearly at the same time, but complexity theory is cast as a general theory, while the Keohane-Nye model focuses on IR. Like Kant's vision, complex interdependence spells out conditions that, if realized, conduce to peace. Neither complexity theory nor the model of complex interdependence advises how to save and enhance local values while promoting broader ones. Neither says how to balance the needs of internal fitness against the demands of external security.

Mutual Gain Theory

This approach to IR integrates key assumptions from theories of complexity, liberal peace, and interdependence. It also builds upon case studies that illustrate the greater utility of value-creating relative to value-claiming as an orientation in policy and negotiation.

Mutual gain theory accepts that many actors are interdependent. The theory expects that political actors are more likely to enhance their objectives if they can frame and implement strategies aimed at mutual gain than if they attempt exploitation for one-sided gain. Policies oriented to conditional cooperation are more likely to enhance an actor's interests than zero-sum competition. The success of cooperation, however, is conditional—it requires reciprocity backed by self-interest, sanctions, safeguards, and—if available—shared values.

Cooperation for mutual gain is both a cause and a result of complex interdependence. Prodded by the Marshall Plan, most European countries moved then toward complex interdependence in the second half of the twentieth century. This movement may continue toward a closer union, stall, or even switch directions. Russia and the United States tried to move closer in the early 1990s but withdrew from each other later in the decade.

COMPLEXITY, INTERDEPENDENCE, CONSILIENCE

The insights of complexity theory, liberal peace theory, interdependence, and mutual gain may help IR scholars to transcend the limits of political realism and idealism. The synergy of these insights presses for a new paradigm rooted in the interdependence of states and other IR actors—their shared vulnerability and capacity to hurt or help one another.[18]

The more that scientists from different fields communicate, the greater the prospects of "consilience"—that their insights will spring forward together.[19] Thus, in the 1990s geologists, meteorologists, and public health experts found themselves agreeing that extreme events—from severe earthquakes to storms to epidemics— occur more frequently than predicted by bell-curve statistics. Similarly, the study of politics and IR will probably gain from more positive linkage with other streams of knowledge. Of course it is dangerous to draw inferences about humans from other life forms. Still, students of security and world affairs should consider the efforts of complexity theorists to refine our understanding of fitness and coevolution.

Caption for Chapter 12 Photo: Complex ties link each Baltic country with its neighbors. The Cathedral of Saints Stanislavas and Vladislavas in the center of Vilnius was built, rebuilt, expanded, and decorated by Polish, Lithuanian, and Italian masters in Gothic, Baroque, and Classical Doric styles. The first cathedral here was built in the thirteenth century on the site of a temple to the pagan god Perkunas. In later centuries the cathedral suffered from Swedish and Tsarist Russian invasions and from Soviet rule. Soviet authorities banned the saying of Mass in the cathedral; removed exterior statues, reliefs, and crosses; and made the building into a museum, concert hall, tourist office, bar, and coffee shop. Twenty-eight other churches in Vilnius were secularized in the 1960s. In 1990 the cathedral was returned to the Roman Catholic Church and renovation begun.

NOTES

1. See Robert Axelrod and Michael D. Cohen, *Harnessing Complexity: Organizational Implications of a Scientific Frontier* (New York: Free Press, 2000), pp. 154–55.

2. M. Mitchell Waldrop, *Complexity: The Emerging Science at the Edge of Order and Chaos* (New York: Touchstone, Simon & Schuster, 1992), p. 241.

3. The author is alert to the difficulties of his enterprise and hopes to add options to future versions. D. Scott Bennett, "Landscapes as Analogues of Political Phenomena," in *Political Complexity: Nonlinear Models of Politics,* ed. Diana Richards (Ann Arbor: University of Michigan Press, 2000), pp. 46–82 at 48–54.

4. Diana Richards, "Nonlinear Modeling: All Things Suffer Change," *Political Complexity,* pp. 1–23.

5. Regina Fazio Maruca, "Competitive Fitness," *Harvard Business Review* 78 (July– August 2000), p. 24.

6. Russia's *Primary Chronicle,* a hoary document written by monks in the early Middle Ages, relates that, late in the first millennium, the Slavs invited in Varangians to bring order.

7. Adapted to the Baltic context from Axelrod and Cohen, *Harnessing Complexity,* pp. 155–57.

8. Thomas J. Christensen and Jack Snyder, "Chain Gangs and Passed Bucks: Predicting Alliance Patterns in Multipolarity," *International Organization* 44 (spring 1990), pp. 137–68; also Randall L. Schweller, "Tripolarity and the Second World War," *International Studies Quarterly* 37 (March 1993), pp. 73–104.

9. A heterogeneous population with great diversity of genes is probably more disease-resistant than a relatively homogeneous population. See J. C. Stephens et al., "Dating the Origin of the CCR5-Delta 32 AIDS-resistance Allele by the Coalescence of Haplotypes," *American Journal of Human Genetics,* 62, 6 (June 1998), pp. 1505 ff.

10. Thomas Hobbes argued that rational individuals will seek their security by bowing to a common sovereign, but he conceded that in battle they may go over to the other side if it seems likely to win; similarly, a prisoner condemned to die will (should?) try to escape.

11. Bent Flyvbjerg, *Rationality and Power: Democracy in Practice* (Chicago: University of Chicago Press, 1988).

12. The Internet poses a major problem for leaders in countries such as Syria and China wanting to promote commerce and science but striving to retain control over communications and information.

13. Toynbee argued that the typical rhythm by which civilizations die is three and one-half beats: rout-rally, relapse-rally, relapse-rally, relapse (Arnold J. Toynbee, *A Study of History,* 2 vols., abridged [New York: Oxford University Press, 1947–1957], 1: pp. 548–54; 2: pp. 270–74). But how do we identify and measure a major "rout" or "rally"? Some scholars think that Western civilization died during World War I or—if not then—surely during World War II. But did the twentieth century experience two destructive world wars or just one? Toynbee escapes by saying there was not yet a universal civilization to rout (ibid., 1: p. 552). Toynbee also allows that some civilizations may seem to follow a two-, four-, or even five-beat rhythm (ibid., 1: p. 549). He says that the world experienced a "general war" from 1914 to 1945 (ibid., 2: p. 272). By that reasoning, Europe should have been "routed."

14. Henry L. Hamman, "Remodeling International Relations: New Tools from New Science," in *International Relations in a Constructed World,* ed. Vendulka Kubalkova (Armonk, N.Y.: Sharpe, 1998), pp. 173–92.

15. For more on these and other approaches, see *Stability and Security in the Baltic Sea Region,* ed. Olav F. Knudsen (London: Cass, 1999).

16. Spencer R. Waert, *Never at War: Why Democracies Will Not Fight One Another* (New Haven: Yale University Press, 1968).

17. Attacked by the USSR, a semidemocratic Finland aligned with Nazi Germany. Western democracies then declared war against Finland, but the two sides did not fight.

18. Evolutionary success depends not just on individual strength and luck but on a capacity for cooperation. This insight from complexity theory was expressed at the beginning of the twentieth century in Petr Kropotkin's book, *Mutual Aid.* Challenging social Darwinism, Kropotkin drew his conclusions from his analysis of the evolution of all life forms—from insects and Siberian moose to medieval guilds and modern cooperatives.

19. Edward O. Wilson called for "consilience" ("jumping together") of natural and social science, ethics, and the arts. See his *Consilience: The Unity of Knowledge* (New York: Knopf, 1998). This kind of quest engaged many Russian thinkers—Petr Kropotkin, Vladimir Vernadsky, Andrei D. Sakharov, and others. See, for example, Kendall E. Bailes, *Science and Russian Culture in an Age of Revolutions: V. I. Vernadsky and His Scientific School, 1863–1945* (Bloomington: Indiana University Press, 1990).

Selected References

References are listed under headings related to but somewhat broader than this book's chapter headings: 1. Political Science/International Relations Theory; 2. Baltic History; 3. The End of Empire; 4. Baltic Politics; 5. Political Culture; 6. Human Development; 7. Integration; 8. Energy; 9. Economic Models; 10. Russia; 11. Security; and 12. Complexity Theory. Where readings relate to more than one topic, they are usually listed in the first relevant section. An exception is items on complexity theory, which are all in section 12.

1. POLITICAL SCIENCE/INTERNATIONAL RELATIONS THEORY

For current essays on many political science topics covered in the present book—comparative political parties, citizens, gender issues, political communications, legislatures, global political economy, international conflict—see Ada W. Finifter, ed., *Political Science: The State of the Discipline* (Washington, D.C.: American Political Science Association, 1993).

For trends in international relations theory, see Peter J. Katzenstein et al., eds., *Exploration and Contestation in the Study of World Politics* (Cambridge, Mass.: MIT Press, 1999).

For political realism, see Hans J. Morgenthau, *Politics among Nations: The Struggle for Power and Peace* (New York: Knopf, 1948 and later editions); for neorealism, see Kenneth N. Waltz, *Theory of International Politics* (New York: McGraw-Hill, 1979); on power transitions, see Ronald L. Tammen et al., *Power Transitions: Strategies for the 21st Century* (New York: Chatham House, 2000). For critiques of realism/neorealism, see Jack Snyder and Robert Jervis, eds., *Coping with Complexity in the International System* (Boulder, Colo.: Westview, 1993), and Graham Allison and Philip Zelikov, *Essence of Decision: Explaining the Cuban Missile Crisis,* 2d ed. (New York: Longman, 1999), esp. pp. 26–33.

For examples of political idealism, see Richard A. Falk, *A Study of Future Worlds* (New York: Free Press, 1975), and Falk, *Explorations at the Edge of Time: The Prospects for World Order* (Philadelphia: Temple University Press, 1992).

On interdependence, see Robert O. Keohane and Joseph S. Nye, *Power and Independence,* 2d ed. (New York: HarperCollins, 1989), and Walter C. Clemens Jr., *Dynamics of International Relations: Conflict and Mutual Gain in an Era of Global Interdependence* (Lanham, Md.: Rowman & Littlefield, 1998).

On constructivism, see Vendulka Kubalkova et al., eds., *International Relations in a Constructed World* (Armonk, N.Y.: Sharpe, 1998), pp. 173–92, and Ted Hopf, "The Promise of Constructivism in International Relations Theory," *International Security* 23 (summer 1998), pp. 171–200.

On negotiating for mutual gain, see David A. Lax and James K. Sebenius, *The Manager as Negotiator: Bargaining for Cooperation and Competitive Gain* (New York: Free Press, 1986), and Howard Raiffa, *The Art and Science of Negotiation* (Cambridge, Mass.: Harvard University Press, 1982).

Relevant journals for the above topics are *American Political Science Review, Comparative Politics, International Journal, International Organization, International Security, International Studies Quarterly, Negotiation Journal, Political Science Quarterly,* and *World Politics.*

On nationalism, see Louis L. Snyder, ed., *The Dynamics of Nationalism: Readings in Its Meaning and Development* (Princeton, N.J.: D. Van Nostrand, 1964); Liah Greenfeld, *Nationalism: Five Roads to Modernity* (Cambridge, Mass.: Harvard University Press, 1992); and Rogers Brubaker, *Nationalism Reframed: Nationhood and the National Question in the New Europe* (New York: Cambridge University Press, 1996); Heinz Gärtner, "States without Nations: State, Nation and Security in Central Europe," *International Politics* 34 (March 1997), pp. 7–32.

Journals relevant to nationalism include *Nationalities Papers, Nationalism and Ethnic Politics,* and *Nations and Nationalism.*

For liberal peace theory, see Michael W. Doyle, *Ways of War and Peace: Realism, Liberalism, and Socialism* (New York; Norton, 1997); Michael E. Brown et al., *Debating the Democratic Peace: An International Security Reader* (Cambridge, Mass.: MIT Press, 1996); Jack Snyder, *From Voting to Violence: Democratization and Nationalist Conflict* (New York: Norton, 2000); and Bruce Russett, John Oneal, and David R. Davis, "The Third Leg of the Kantian Tripod for Peace: International Organizations and Militarized Disputes, 1950–1985," *International Organization* 52 (summer 1998), pp. 441–67; Miriam Fendius Elman, ed., *Paths to Peace: Is Democracy the Answer?* (Cambridge, Mass.: MIT Press).

Critics point out that the sample on which liberal peace theory rests and its relatively brief historical basis may be too narrow to form solid inferences. The theory may omit other variables that could explain the same outcome, such as simple satisfaction with the status quo. See David L. Rousseau, Christopher Gelpi, and Dan Reiter, "Assessing the Dyadic Nature of the Democratic Peace, 1918–1988," *American Political Science Review* 90 (September 1996). Surveying history since ancient Greece, however, Spencer R. Waert finds no cases when republics—oligarchies such as Hanseatic cities or democracies such as Swiss Forest cantons—fought states with similar political cultures. See his *Never at War: Why Democracies Will Not Fight One Another* (New Haven: Yale University Press, 1998). But even Waert may have missed at least one relevant case—the belligerent oligarchies of Rome and Carthage, as noted by Stephen M. Walt, "Never Say Never," *Foreign Affairs* 78 (January–February 1999), pp. 146–51. See also John A. Vasquez, ed., *What Do We Know about War?* (Lanham, Md.: Rowman & Littlefield, 2000).

Journals relevant to peace theory include *Journal of Conflict Resolution, Journal of Democracy,* and *Journal of Peace Research.*

On the role of culture in international politics, see Samuel P. Huntington, *The Clash of Civilizations and the Remaking of World Order* (New York: Simon & Schuster, 1996), and Michael C. Desch, "Cultural Clash: Assessing the Importance of Ideas in Security Studies," *International Security,* 23 (summer 1998), pp. 141–70.

2. BALTIC HISTORY

For bibliographies and surveys, see *A Reader's Guide to Estonia, Latvia, Lithuania* (Washington, D.C.: School of Area Studies, Foreign Service Institute, U.S. Department of State, 1991); William Urban, "Victims of the Baltic Crusade," *Journal of Baltic Studies* 29 (fall 1998), pp. 195–212; Inese A. Smith and Marita V. Grunts, comps., *The Baltic States: Estonia, Latvia, Lithuania* (Santa Barbara, Calif.: ABC-CLIO, 1997); John Hiden and Patrick Salmon, *The Baltic Nations and Europe: Estonia, Latvia, and Lithuania in the Twentieth Century* (London: Longmans, 1990); Laurence Kitching, comp., *Baltic Studies Indexes: Journal of Baltic Studies, Bulletin of Baltic Studies, 1970–1997* (Hackettstown, N.J.: Association for the Advancement of Baltic Studies, 1998); and *Baltische Bibliographie: Schriftum über Estland, Lettland, Litauen* (Marburg: Verlag Herder-Institut, 1994).

For 515 pages on politics, law, economics, ecology, sociology, and culture in Estonia, Latvia, and Lithuania, see Heike Graf, ed., *Handbuch Baltikum heute* (Berlin: Berlin Verlag, 1998). The twenty-five-page bibliography lists materials in English and German.

For naval history, see Archibald R. Lewis and Timothy J. Runyan, *European Naval and Maritime History, 300–1500* (Bloomington: Indiana University Press, 1985).

The notes in chapter 2 cite many excellent studies of the Hansas, but these are mostly written from a Western European or Nordic standpoint, with little attention to the indigenous peoples.

For monographs on many aspects of Baltic history, see the series sponsored by the Department for Baltic Studies, Stockholm University, Studia Baltica Stockholmiensia, for example, Erik Tiberg, *Moscow, Livonia and the Hanseatic League, 1487–1550* (Stockholm: Almqvist & Wiksell International, 1995).

On Swedish rule, see Aleksander Loit and Helmut Piirimäe, eds., *Die schwedischen Ostseeprovinzen Estland und Livland im 16.–18. Jahrhundert* (Stockholm: Almqvist & Wiksell International, 1993); for bibliography, see Stig Appelgren, comp., *Estlands Svenskar och Svenskbygd: Bibliografi Sammanställd* (Stockholm: Almqvist & Wiksell International, 1997).

On the German Order and other Baltic polities across time, see S. E. Finer, *The History of Government from the Earliest Times,* 3 vols. (New York: Oxford University Press, 1997).

On the Baltic in world affairs, see Stewart P. Oakley, *War and Peace in the Baltic, 1560–1790* (New York: Routledge, 1992), and David Kirby, *The Baltic World, 1772–1993: Europe's Northern Periphery in An Age of Change* (New York: Longmans, 1995).

On the first period of Baltic independence, see Georg von Rauch, *The Baltic States: The Years of Independence, 1917–1940* (New York: St. Martin's, 1995); also see Royal Institute of International Affairs, *The Baltic States: A Survey of the Political and Economic Structure and the Foreign Relations of Estonia, Latvia, and Lithuania*

(London: Oxford University Press, 1938). On the Soviet period, see Romuald Misiunas and Rein Taagepera, *The Baltic States: Years of Dependence, 1940–1990,* rev. ed. (Berkeley: University of California Press, 1993).

On Estonia, see Toivo U. Raun, *Estonia and the Estonians,* 2d ed. (Stanford, Calif.: Hoover Institution, 1991).

On Latvia, see Andrejs Plakans, *Historical Dictionary of Latvia* (Lanham, Md.: Scarecrow Press); also see Andrejs Plakans, *The Latvians: A Short History* (Stanford, Calif.: Hoover Institution, 1995); Alfred Bilmanis, *A History of Latvia* (Princeton, N.J.: Princeton University Press, 1947); and Bilmanis, *Latvian-Russian Relations: Documents* (Washington, D.C.: Latvian Legation, 1944).

On Lithuania, see Saulius Suziedelis, *Historical Dictionary of Lithuania* (Lanham, Md.: Scarecrow Press, 1997); Alexandra Ashbourne, *Lithuania: The Rebirth of a Nation, 1991–1994* (Lanham, Md.: Lexington Books, 1999); Alfred Erich Senn, *Lithuania Awakening* (Berkeley: University of California Press, 1990); V. Stanley Vardys and Judith B. Sedaitis, *Lithuania: The Rebel Nation* (Boulder, Colo.: Westview, 1997); Alfonsas Eidintas et al., *Lithuania in European Politics: The Years of the First Republic, 1918–1940* (New York: St. Martin's, 1998).

On other countries in the region, see George Maude, *Historical Dictionary of Finland* (Metuchen, N.J.: Scarecrow Press, 1995); Jan Zaprudnik, *Historical Dictionary of Belarus* (Lanham, Md.: Scarecrow Press, 1998); George Sanford and Adriana Gozdecka-Sanford, *Historical Dictionary of Poland* (Metuchen, N.J.: Scarecrow Press, 1994); Boris Raymond and Paul Duffy, *Historical Dictionary of Russia* (Lanham, Md.: Scarecrow Press, 1998); Irene Scobbie, *Historical Dictionary of Sweden* (Metuchen, N.J.: Scarecrow Press, 1995); Eino Jutikkala with Kauko Pirienen, *A History of Finland,* rev. ed. (New York: Dorset, 1988).

For illuminating comparisons, see Eberhard Demm, Robert Noël, and William Urban, eds., *The Independence of the Baltic States: Origins, Causes, and Consequences: A Comparison of the Crucial Years 1918–1919 and 1990–1991* (Chicago: Lithuanian Research and Studies Center, 1996).

For the history of a family uprooted from Latvia and later settled in Canada, see Modris Eksteins, *Walking Since Daybreak: A Story of Eastern Europe, World War II, and the Heart of Our Century* (Boston: Houghton Mifflin, 1999). On the psychological stresses and fatalism induced by foreign occupation, see the writings and conversations analyzed by Vieda Skultans, *The Testimony of Lives: Narrative and Memory in Post-Soviet Latvia* (London: Routledge, 1998). For documentation and statistics in two languages on arrests and incarcerations in Estonia, see Hilda Sabbo, comp., *Voimatu Vaikida; Nevozmozhno Molchat',* 2 vols. (Tallinn: Cultural Foundation of Estonia, 1996).

For historical legacies, national identities, the politics of religion, and many other dimensions of the Baltic and "new states of Eurasia," see Karen Dawisha and Bruce Parrott, eds., *The International Politics of Eurasia,* 10 vols. (Armonk, N.Y.: Sharpe, 1994–1997).

Relevant journals are *Europe-Asia Studies, Journal of Baltic Studies, Lituanus, Nations and Nationalism, Nationalities Papers, Nationalism and Ethnic Politics, Post-Soviet Affairs, Problems of Communism,* and *Problems of Post-Communism.*

3. THE END OF EMPIRE

For comparisons of empire, see Edward Gibbon, *History of the Decline and Fall of the Roman Empire,* 6 vols. (1776–1788); Michael W. Doyle, *Empires* (Ithaca, N.Y.: Cornell University Press, 1986); Richard R. Rudolph and David E. Good, eds., *Nationalism and Empire: The Habsburg Empire and the Soviet Union* (New York: St. Martin's, 1992); Karen Dawisha and Bruce Parrott, eds., *The End of Empire: The Transformation of the USSR in Comparative Perspective* (Armonk N.Y.: Sharpe, 1997), the ninth of ten volumes in the series *International Politics of Eurasia,* edited by Dawisha and Parrott; Kristen Gerner and Stefan Hedlund, *The Baltic States and the End of the Soviet Empire* (New York: Routledge, 1993). For a review and prognosis, see Rein Taagepera, "Expansion and Contraction Patterns of Large Polities: Context for Russia," *International Studies Quarterly* 41 (1997), pp. 475–504.

On the collapse of the USSR, see Murray Feshbach and Alfred Friendly Jr., *Ecocide in the USSR: Health and Nature under Siege* (New York: Basic Books, 1992); John B. Dunlop, *The Rise of Russia and the Fall of the Soviet Empire* (Princeton, N.J.: Princeton University Press, 1994); Jack F. Matlock, *Autopsy of an Empire: The American Ambassador's Account of the Collapse of the Soviet Union* (New York: Random House, 1996); and Mark Kramer, ed., *The Collapse of the Soviet Union* (forthcoming).

For Baltic resistance movements, see Walter C. Clemens Jr., *Baltic Independence and Russian Empire* (New York: St. Martin's, 1991); Anatol Lieven, *The Baltic Revolution: Estonia, Latvia, and Lithuania and the Path to Independence* (New Haven, Conn.: Yale University Press, 1993); Nils R. Muiznieks, "The Influence of the Baltic Popular Movements on the Process of Soviet Disintegration," *Europe-Asia Studies* 47, no. 1 (1995), pp. 3–25. The potential importance of Baltic resistance was stressed in Clemens, "Estonia, A Place to Watch," *The National Interest* 13 (fall 1988), pp. 85–92 and Clemens "Foreign Policy Implications of National Unrest," *Nationalities Papers* 18 (spring 1990), pp. 20–23.

On Estonia, see Rein Taagepera, *Estonia: Return to Independence* (Boulder, Colo.: Westview, 1993). On Latvia, see Juris Dreifelds, *Latvia in Transition* (New York: Cambridge University Press, 1996), and Rasma Karklins, *Ethnopolitics and the Transition to Democracy: The Collapse of the USSR and Latvia* (Washington, D.C.: Woodrow Wilson Center Press, 1994). On Lithuania, see Alfred Erich Senn, *Gorbachev's Failure in Lithuania* (New York: St. Martin's, 1995).

For a comparison of Estonia with Moldova, Croatia, and Czechoslovakia, see Soren Rinder Bollerup and Christian Dons Christensen, *Nationalism in Eastern Europe: Causes and Consequences of the National Revivals and Conflicts in Late-Twentieth-Century Eastern Europe* (New York: St. Martin's, 1997).

For fuller documentation on chapter 3, see Clemens, "Who or What Killed the Soviet Union? How Three Davids Undermined Goliath," *Nationalism and Ethnic Politics* 3 (spring 1997), pp. 136–58.

4. BALTIC POLITICS

For analytical surveys, see U.S. Department of State, *Country Reports on Human Rights Practices* (Washington, D.C.: U.S. Government Printing Office, annual);

Freedom in the World (New York: Freedom House, annual); Economist Intelligence Unit, *Country Profiles* and *Quarterly Reports,* for each Baltic republic.

On post-Communist politics, see Ian Bremmer and Ray Taras, eds., *New States, New Politics: Building the Post-Soviet Nations* (Cambridge: Cambridge University Press, 1997); Mary Ellen Fischer, ed., *Establishing Democracies* (Boulder, Colo.: Westview, 1996); Anton Steen, *Between Past and Future: Elites, Democracy, and the State in Post-Communist Countries. A Comparison of Estonia, Latvia and Lithuania* (Aldershot, England: Ashgate, 1997); Dzintra Bungs, *The Baltic States: Problems and Prospects of Membership in the European Union* (Baden-Baden: Nomos Verlagsgesellschaft, 1998); and *Aus Politik und Zeitgeschichte* B 37/98 (September 4, 1998), special issue on Baltic affairs.

For electronic updates on Baltic and regional affairs, see "RFE/RL Baltic States Report," available from <listmanager@list.rferl.org> and "The NIS Observed: An Analytical Review," available from <mlanskoy@bu.edu>.

5. POLITICAL CULTURE

General works relating to this topic are Lucian W. Pye, "Political Culture," in *Oxford Companion to Politics of the World,* ed. Joel Krieger (New York: Oxford University Press, 1993), pp. 712–13; related articles on "Political Development" and "Political Participation" in the same volume; Gabriel A. Almond and Sidney Verba, *The Civic Culture: Attitudes and Democracy in Five Nations* (Boston: Little, Brown, 1965); Edward C. Banfield, *The Moral Basis of a Backward Society* (Glencoe, Ill.: Free Press, 1958); Robert D. Putnam, *Making Democracy Work: Civil Traditions in Modern Italy* (Princeton, N.J.: Princeton University Press, 1993); and Francis Fukuyama, *Trust: The Social Virtues and the Creation of Prosperity* (New York: Free Press, 1995).

For comparative works on transitions, see Juan J. Linz and Alfred C. Stepan, *Problems of Democratic Transition and Consolidation: Southern Europe, South America, and Post-Communist Europe* (Baltimore: Johns Hopkins University Press, 1996); Stephen White, Judy Batt, and Paul G. Lewis, eds., *Developments in Central and East European Politics* (Durham, N.C.: Duke University Press, 1998), especially Sarah Birch, "In the Shadow of Moscow: Ukraine, Moldova, and the Baltic Republics," pp. 59–80; Adrian Karatnycky et al., eds., *Nations in Transit, 1998: Civil Society, Democracy, and Markets in East Central Europe and the Newly Independent States* (New Brunswick, N.J.: Transaction, 1999); and Vladimir Tismaneanu, ed., *Political Culture and Civil Society in Russia and the New States of Eurasia* (Armonk N.Y.: Sharpe, 1995).

For two views of Estonia, see Brian D. Silver and Mikk Titma, "Support for New Political Institutions in Estonia: The Effects of Nationality, Citizenship, and Material Well-Being," *Problems of Post-Communism* 45 (September-October 1998), pp. 37–47; Cynthia Kaplan, "Estonia: A Plural Society on the Road to Independence," in *Nations & Politics in the Soviet Successor States,* ed. Ian Bremmer and Ray Taras (New York: Cambridge University Press, 1993), pp. 206–21. For all three republics, see Walter C. Clemens Jr., "The Baltic Reborn: Challenges of Transition," *Demokratizatsiya* 6 (fall 1998), pp. 710–33.

The major sources used in chapters 5 and 6 are United Nations Development Programme, *Human Development Report* (New York: Oxford University Press, annual) and the studies conducted in each country, for example, United Nations Development Programme, *Estonian Human Development Report* (Tallinn, annual). The broadest listing of UNDP global and country reports can be found on the worldwide web under "United Nations Development Programme."

For public opinion on many issues, see Richard Rose, *The New Baltic Barometer III: A Survey Study* (Glasgow, Scotland: Centre for the Study of Public Policy, University of Strathclyde, 1997).

6. HUMAN DEVELOPMENT

For UNDP reports used in chapter 6, see the foregoing paragraph; on methodological issues, see the appendix to chapter 6. For a regional overview, see United Nations Development Programme, *Transition 99: Human Development Report for Central and Eastern Europe and the CIS* (New York: UNDP, 1999). This regional overview, however, appears quite uneven and less reliable than the global and national reports.

Human development is included in the analysis and data provided in World Bank, *World Development Report* (New York: Oxford University Press, annual); for detailed background, see the ongoing studies by Arvo Kuddo, for example, his *Social Transition: Social and Unemployment Policies in the Former Soviet Union States* (Washington, D.C.: World Bank, unpublished manuscript, 1998).

Gender issues are analyzed in the UNDP and World Bank reports. See also Suzanne LaFont, ed., *Women in Transition: Voices from Lithuania* (Albany: State University of New York Press, 1998); Nijole White, "Women in Changing Societies: Latvia and Lithuania," in *Post-Soviet Women: from the Baltic to Central Asia,* ed. Mary Buckley (New York: Cambridge University Press, 1997), pp. 203–18.

Environmental issues underlie human development and other issues. Feshbach's *Ecocide in the USSR,* cited in section III, gives the background. For one case, see Matthew R. Auer, "Environmental Restoration, Economic Transition and Nationalism in Estonia," *Journal of Baltic Studies* 23 (winter 1992), pp. 377–86.

On Poland and other countries, see Ethan B. Kapstein and Michael Mandelbaum, eds., *Sustaining the Transition: The Social Safety Net in Postcommunist Europe* (New York: Council on Foreign Relations, 1997), and *Making Transition Work for Everyone: Poverty and Inequality in Europe and Central Asia* (Washington, D.C.: The World Bank, 2000).

7. INTEGRATION

On nationality issues within the USSR and post-Soviet Eurasia, see Walker Connor, *The National Question in Marxist-Leninist Theory and Strategy* (Princeton, N.J.: Princeton University Press, 1984); Bohdan Nahaylo and Victor Swoboda, *Soviet Disunion: A History of the Nationalities Problem in the USSR* (New York: Free Press, 1989); Lubomyr Jajda and Mark Beissinger, eds., *The Nationalities Factor in Soviet Politics and Society* (Boulder, Colo.: Westview, 1990); and Ronald Grigor Suny, *The Soviet Experiment: Russia, the USSR, and the Successor States* (New York: Oxford

University Press, 1998). For analysis by a leading Russian ethnographer, see Valerii Tishkov, *Ethnicity, Nationalism and Conflict in and after the Soviet Union: The Mind Aflame* (Thousand Oaks, Calif.: SAGE, 1997).

On methodology, see John A. Armstrong, "Toward a Framework for Considering Nationalism in East Europe," East European Program Occasional Paper no. 8 (Washington, D.C.: Wilson Center, 1987). Also see Alexander Motyl, *Sovietology, Rationality, Nationality: Coming to Grips with Nationalism in the USSR* (New York: Columbia University Press, 1990).

On Estonia on the eve of independence, see Mikk Titma et al., eds., *Estonia's Transition from State Socialism: Nationalities and Society on the Eve of Independence* (Armonk, N.Y.: Sharpe, 1997).

On the post-Soviet era, see Michael Mandelbaum, ed., *The New European Diasporas: National Minorities and Conflict in Eastern Europe* (New York: Council on Foreign Relations Press, 2000). For Estonia, Latvia, Ukraine, and Kazakstan in this era, see David D. Laitin, *Identity in Formation: The Russian-Speaking Populations in the Near Abroad* (Ithaca, N.Y.: Cornell University Press, 1998). For a study of Russian speakers in Estonia, see Valerii Tishkov, *Russkie kak men'shinstva: primer Estonii* (Moscow: Institute of Ethnology and Anthropology, 1993). Also see Rasma Karklins, "Ethnic Integration and School Policies in Latvia," *Nationalities Papers* 26, no. 2 (1998), pp. 283–302, and *Economic and Social Change: A Question of Balance. Selected Conference Papers* (Tallinn: Tru Kirjastus, 1997).

For reports on each Baltic country, see U.S. Department of State, *Country Reports on Human Rights Practices* (Washington, D.C.: Government Printing Office, annual), also at http://www.state.gov/; *Country Reports: Inside the Newly Independent States of the Former Soviet Union* (Washington, D.C.: National Conference on Soviet Jewry, 1994–); the International Helsinki Federation for Human Rights report "Protection of Ethnic Minorities," submitted to the UN Commission on Human Rights in 1998 and available at http://www.ihf-hr.org/reports/9804prot.htm; and *Freedom in the World* (New York: Freedom House, annual). For a nongovernmental web site on crimes against humanity, see <http://vip.latnet/LPRA>.

For integration and other social issues, see the UNDP reports listed above in section 5.

8. ENERGY

For the historical context, see Daniel Yergin, *The Prize: The Epic Quest for Oil, Money, and Power* (New York: Simon & Schuster, 1991). On the ways that oil and other factors could shape Russia's future, see Daniel Yergin and Thane Gustavson, *Russia 2010—and What It Means for the World: The CERA Report* (New York: Random House, 1993).

For statistical information, see *Energy Statistics and Balances of Non-OECD Countries 1994–1995* (Paris: Organization for Economic Co-operation and Development, 1997); energy statistics are also compiled and published by the World Bank, the International Energy Agency (Paris), the U.S. Department of Energy, and the U.S. Central Intelligence Agency. For specialized reporting, see *Oil and Gas Journal.*

On energy and the environment, see Jes Fenger et al., eds., *Environment, Energy and Natural Resource Management in the Baltic Region: 3rd International Conference on Systems Analysis* (Copenhagen: Nordic Council of Ministers, 1991); Hans Aage, *Environmental Transition in Nordic and Baltic Countries* (Northhampton, Mass.: E. Elgar, 1998); Jorg Kohn and Ulrich Schiewer, eds., *The Future of the Baltic Sea: Ecology, Economics, Administration, and Teaching* (Marburg, Germany: Metropolis Verlag, 1995); *Energy Market Study in the Baltic Sea Region* (Copenhagen: Nordic Council of Ministers, 1999); Ing-Marie Gren et al., *Managing a Sea: The Ecological Economics of the Baltic* (London: Earthscan, 1999).

For additional references to materials in chapter 8 above, see Clemens, "The Baltic Republics, Russia, and Energy: From Dependency to Interdependence?" *SAIS Review* 19 (winter-spring 1999), pp. 190–208. See also additional articles in this issue of *SAIS Review* and "Fueling the 21st Century: The New Political Economy of Energy," *Journal of International Affairs* 53 (fall 1999).

9. ECONOMIC MODELS

For historical approaches, see Nathan Rosenberg and I. E. Birdzell Jr., *How the West Became Rich: The Economic Transformation of the Industrial World* (New York: Basic Books, 1986); Daniel Cohen, *The Wealth of the World and the Poverty of Nations* (Cambridge, Mass.: MIT Press, 1998); and Michael E. Porter, *The Competitive Advantage of Nations* (New York: Free Press, 1990). Opposed to the views of these works is the world-system approach in Immanuel Wallerstein, *Capitalist World-Economy* (Cambridge: Cambridge University Press, 1979), and Wallerstein, *Geopolitics and Geoculture* (Cambridge: Cambridge University Press, 1991).

On economic versus military power, see Richard Rosecrance, *The Rise of the Trading State: Commerce and Conquest in the Modern World* (New York: Basic Books, 1986), and Rosecrance, *The Rise of the Virtual State: Wealth and Power in the Coming Century* (New York: Basic Books, 1999).

For comparative works, see Wing Thye Woo et al., eds., *Economies in Transition: Comparing Asia and Eastern Europe* (Cambridge, Mass.: MIT Press, 1997); World Bank, *The East Asian Miracle: Economic Growth and Public Policy* (New York: Oxford University Press, 1993); Horst Brezinski and Michael Fritsch, eds., *The Economic Impact of New Firms in Post-Socialist Countries: Bottom-up Transformation in Eastern Europe* (Cheltenham, England: E. Elgar, 1996).

On small states, see Peter J. Katzenstein, *Small States in World Markets: Industrial Policy in Europe* (Ithaca, N.Y.: Cornell University Press, 1985).

On Russia and its neighbors, see Oleh Havrylyshyn and John Williamson, *From Soviet disUnion to Eastern Economic Community?* (Washington, D.C.: Institute for International Economics, 1991); Roman Frydman et al., *The Privatization Process in Russia, Ukraine and the Baltic States* (Budapest: Central European University Press, 1993); Anders Äslund, *How Russia Became a Market Economy* (Washington, D.C.: Brookings Institution, 1995); Jeffrey D. Sachs, "Russia's Struggle with Stabilization: Conceptual Issues and Evidence," *World Bank Research Observer, Annual Conference Supplement* (1994), pp. 57–80; Jeffrey D. Sachs and Katharina Pistor, eds., *The Rule of Law and Economic Reform in Russia* (Boulder, Colo.: Westview, 1997); and

David M. Woodruff, *Money Unmade: Barter and the Fate of Russian Capitalism* (Ithaca, N.Y.: Cornell University Press, 1999).

On transitions to the market economy, see World Bank, *Latvia: The Transition to a Market Economy* (Washington, D.C.: World Bank, 1993); *Estonia: The Transition to a Market Economy* (1993); and *Lithuania: The Transition to a Market Economy* (1993). Also see Raphael Shen, *Restructuring the Baltic Economies: Disengaging from Fifty Years of Integration with the USSR* (Westport, Conn.: Praeger, 1994; *The Baltic Economies in Transition: A Study of the Transforming Economies of Estonia, Latvia and Lithuania* (Edinburgh: Scottish Financial Enterprise, 1995); Christian von Hirschhausen, ed., *New Neighbors in Eastern Europe: Economic and Industrial Reform in Lithuania, Latvia, and Estonia* (Paris: Presse de l'Ecole des mines, 1998); and Antanas Buracas, *Lithuanian Economic Reforms: Practice & Perspectives* (Vilnius: Margi Rastai, 1997).

For economic and financial prospects, see OECD Economic Surveys. *The Baltic States: A Regional Economic Assessment* (Paris: OECD Centre for Co-operation with Non-Members, 2000); Julian Berengaut, *The Baltic Countries: From Economic Stabilization to EU Accession* (Washington, D.C.: International Monetary Fund, 1998).

For a sample treaty, see *Treaty between the Government of the United States of America and the Government of the Republic of Estonia concerning the Encouragement and Reciprocal Protection of Investment, with Annex* (Washington, D.C.: Government Printing Office, 1996).

Each Baltic government publishes economic and other statistics in English, for example, *Survey of the Lithuanian Economy* (Vilnius: Department of Statistics, Government of the Republic of Lithuania, 1995). The United Nations publishes regional and country studies on the Baltic area, for example, *Environmental Performance Reviews: Lithuania,* no. 4 (New York: United Nations, 1999). The World Bank publishes country studies, for example, *Lithuania: An Opportunity for Economic Success,* 2 vols. (Washington, D.C.: World Bank, 1999).

Each Baltic government has an official web site. On Latvian demographic statistics, for example, see <http://www.pid.gov.lv/statist/iedznac.htm>.

Data on the Baltic countries is included in World Bank, *World Development Report* (New York: Oxford University Press, annual). Country studies are also published by the Organisation for Economic Co-operation and Development, for example, *Investment Guide for Lithuania* (Paris: OECD, 1998).

For economic news, financial statistics, and stock quotations, see *Baltic Times* (Riga); also see the *Country Profiles* and *Quarterly Reports* by the Economist Intelligence Unit and occasional surveys of the Baltic countries in *Financial Times* (London).

10. RUSSIA

On struggles in Soviet policy between hard-line and globalist thinking, see Walter C. Clemens Jr., *The U.S.S.R. and Global Interdependence: Alternative Futures* (Washington: American Enterprise Institute, 1978), and Clemens, *Can Russia Change? The USSR Confronts Global Interdependence* (Boston: Unwin Hyman, 1990).

On the post-Soviet period, see Mette Skak, *From Empire to Anarchy: Postcom-

munist Foreign Policy and International Relations (New York: St. Martin's, 1996); Celeste Wallander, ed., *The Sources of Russian Foreign Policy after the Cold War* (Boulder, Colo.: Westview, 1996); Timothy J. Colton and Robert Legvold, eds., *After the Soviet Union: From Empires to Nations* (New York: Norton, 1992); Eduard Ponarin, "Security Implications of the Russian Identity Crisis," Policy Memo Series no. 64 (Cambridge, Mass.: Program on New Approaches to Russian Security, Davis Center for Russian Studies, Harvard University, June 1999).

On Baltic-Russian relations, see Walter C. Clemens Jr., "Negotiating a New Life: Burdens of Empire and Independence," *Nationalities Papers* 20 (fall 1992), pp. 67–78; Wayne C. Thompson, "Citizenship and Borders: Legacies of Soviet Empire in Estonia," *Journal of Baltic Studies* 24 (summer 1998), pp. 109–34 at 127; J. R. Black, "Russia and NATO Expansion Eastward: Red-Lining the Baltic States," *International Journal* 54 (spring 1999), pp. 249–66.

For essays on trade and other aspects of Kaliningrad, see Pertti Joenniemi and Jan Prawitz, eds., *Kaliningrad: The European Amber Region* (Aldershot, England: Ashgate, 1998).

11. SECURITY

For alternative approaches, see Helga Haftendorn et al., eds., *Imperfect Unions: Security Institutions over Time and Space* (New York: Oxford University Press, 1999); Olav F. Knudsen, ed., *Stability and Security in the Baltic Sea Region: Russian, Nordic and European Aspects* (London: Frank Cass, 1999); Birthe Hansen and Bertel Heurlin, eds., *The Baltic States in World Politics* (New York: St. Martin's, 1998); and Bo Huldt and Ulrika Johannessen, eds., *1st Annual Stockholm Conference on Baltic Sea Security and Cooperation* (Stockholm: Swedish Institute of International Affairs, 1997).

On regional cooperation, see Daina Bleiere, "Cooperation between the Baltic States and the Central European Countries: Problems and Prospects," in *The Baltic States at Historical Crossroads: A Collection of Scholarly Articles* (Riga: Academy of Sciences of Latvia, 1998), pp. 128–50. For background, see Peter van Ham, *The European Community, Eastern Europe, and European Unity: Discord, Collaboration and Integration since 1947* (London: Pinter, 1995).

On nonviolent defense, see Roger S. Powers and William B. Vogele, eds., *Protest, Power, and Change: An Encyclopedia of Nonviolent Action* (New York: Garland, 1997).

On NATO, see Philip H. Gordon, ed., *NATO's Transformation: The Changing Shape of the Atlantic Alliance* (Lanham, Md.: Rowman & Littlefield, 1997); Hans Binnendijk and Jeffrey Simon, "Baltic Security and NATO Enlargement" (Washington, D.C.: Institute for National Strategic Studies, National Defense University, 1995); and Stephen Blank, *NATO Enlargement and the Baltic States: What Can the Great Powers Do?* (Carlisle Barracks, Pa.: Strategic Studies Institute, U.S. Army War College, 1997). Also see the Rand Corporation studies cited in chapter 11.

12. COMPLEXITY THEORY

For early work at the Santa Fe Institute, see Roger Lewin, *Complexity: Life at the Edge of Chaos* (New York: Macmillan, 1992). Major books by Stuart Kauffman are

The Origins of Order: Self-Organization and Selection in Evolution (New York: Oxford University Press, 1993); *At Home in the Universe: The Search for the Laws of Self-Organization and Complexity* (New York: Oxford University Press, 1995); and *Investigations* (New York: Oxford University Press, 2000). On coevolution, see also Charles J. Lumsden and Edward O. Wilson, *Genes, Mind, and Culture: The Coevolutionary Process* (Cambridge Mass.: Harvard University Press, 1981); Martin A. Nowak et al., "The Arithmetics of Mutual Help," *Scientific American* 272 (June 1995), pp. 76–81; and Edward O. Wilson, *Consilience: The Unity of Knowledge* (New York: Knopf, 1998).

The Santa Fe Institute publishes the journal *Complexity* and Institute working papers such as "Game Theory, Complexity, and Simplicity, Part I: A Tutorial" (98-04-027) and "Arborscapes: A Swarm-Based Multi-Agent Ecological Disturbance Model" (98-06-056).

On complexity in the universe, as suggested by Navajo myths and by astronomical findings at Tartu Observatory in Estonia, see George Johnson, "The Real Star Wars: Between Order and Chaos," *New York Times,* January 19, 1997, p. E4.

For agent-based systems in social science and an extensive bibliography, see Joshua M. Epstein and Robert Axtell, *Growing Artificial Societies: Social Science from the Bottom Up* (Cambridge, Mass.: MIT Press, 1996); also see the special issue "Evolutionary Paradigms in the Social Sciences," *International Studies Quarterly* 40 (September 1996).

Complexity theory has stimulated much work by Robert M. Axelrod, though he has focused on solving complex problems by a variety of methods, rather than on applying complexity theory as developed by Kauffman et al. See Robert M. Axelrod, *The Complexity of Cooperation: Agent-Based Models of Competition and Cooperation* (Princeton, N.J.: Princeton University Press, 1997). Also see Axelrod, "Advancing the Art of Simulation in the Social Sciences," paper presented at the International Conference on Computer Simulation and the Social Sciences, Cortona, Italy, September 22–25, 1997; Robert Axelrod and Michael D. Cohen, *Harnessing Complexity: Organizational Implications of a Scientific Frontier* (New York: Free Press, 2000).

For an application of complexity theory by a former student of Axelrod, see Lars-Erik Cederman, *Emergent Actors in World Politics: How States and Nations Develop and Dissolve* (Princeton, N.J.: Princeton University Press, 1997). For a book that blends historical analysis, international relations theory, and systems analysis, see Hendrik Spruyt, *The Sovereign State and Its Competitors: An Analysis of Systems Change* (Princeton, N.J.: Princeton University Press, 1994). In the same vein, Robert Jervis, *System Effects: Complexity in Political and Social Life* (Princeton, N.J.: Princeton University Press, 1997) examines the complex interactions of social units, but says little about self-organization. Compare this with James N. Rosenau, *Turbulence in World Politics: A Theory of Change and Continuity* (Princeton, N.J.: Princeton University Press, 1990).

For related work by IR specialists, see Michael Lipson, "Nonlinearity, Constructivism, and International Relations: Or, Changing the Rules by Playing the Game," paper presented at the annual meeting of the American Political Science Association, Chicago, August 31–September 3, 1996; Matthew J. Hoffmann, "Constructivism and

Complexity Science: Theoretical Links and Empirical Justification," paper presented at the annual meeting of the International Studies Association, Washington, D.C., February 16–21, 1999.

For applications of nonlinear models to analysis of federalism, alliance formation, epochs in political economy, environmental regimes, and outbreaks of war, see Diana Richards, ed., *Political Complexity: Nonlinear Models of Politics* (Ann Arbor: University of Michigan Press, 2000). The utility of complexity theory is assessed by Hayward R. Alker and Simon Fraser, "On Historical Complexity: 'Naturalistic' Modeling Approaches from the Santa Fe Institute," paper presented at the American Political Science Association annual meeting, San Francisco, August 31, 1996. See also Hayward R. Alker, *Rediscoveries and Reformulations: Humanistic Methodologies for International Studies* (Cambridge: Cambridge University Press, 1996). For a skeptical view, see John Horgan, *The End of Science: Facing the Limits of Knowledge in the Twilight of the Scientific Age* (Reading, Mass.: Addison-Wesley, 1996), chapters 5–9. For a more balanced appraisal, see the "Edge of Chaos" and many relevant entries in Ian Marshall and Danah Zohar, *Who's Afraid of Schrödinger's Cat: All the Science Ideas You Need to Keep Up with the New Thinking* (New York: Morrow, 1997). For applications to management, see Roger Lewin and Birute Regine, *The Soul at Work: Listen, Respond, Let Go: Embracing Complexity Science for Business Success* (New York: Simon & Schuster, 2000).

Complexity theory builds on the work of systems theorists such as Ludwig von Bertalanffy, Ervin Laszlo, and Jay W. Forrester. See Forrester, *World Dynamics* (Cambridge, Mass.: Wright-Allen Press, 1971), adapted in several Club of Rome studies of the global problematique and evaluated in Walter C. Clemens Jr., "Ecology and International Relations," *International Journal* 28 (winter 1972–3), pp. 1–27. See also Nazli Choucri and Robert C. North, *Nations in Conflict* (San Francisco: Freeman, 1975).

Index

Page numbers in italic indicate tables or figures.

About the Author

Walter C. Clemens Jr. is professor of political science, Boston University, and an associate at Harvard University's Davis Center for Russian Studies and Belfer Center for Science and International Affairs. His books include *Dynamics of International Relations, Baltic Independence and Russian Empire, America and the World,* and *Can Russia Change?* His columns have appeared in the *New York Times, Christian Science Monitor,* and *Wall Street Journal.* Clemens has been a consultant to the U.S. Department of State and has lectured in Europe, Asia, and Latin America on Baltic and Russian affairs. He studied at Columbia University, Moscow University, the University of Vienna, and Notre Dame University.